Readings in
Applied Microeconomics

SECOND EDITION

edited by
LESLIE WAGNER

OXFORD UNIVERSITY PRESS
IN ASSOCIATION WITH
THE OPEN UNIVERSITY PRESS
1981

Oxford University Press, Walton Street, Oxford OX2 6DP
London & Glasgow New York Toronto
Delhi Bombay Calcutta Madras Karachi
Kuala Lumpur Singapore Hong Kong Tokyo
Nairobi Dar Es Salaam Cape Town
Melbourne Wellington

and associate companies in
Beirut Berlin Ibadan Mexico City

Published in the United States
by Oxford University Press, New York

Selection and editorial material
© The Open University 1973, 1981

First published 1973
Second edition 1981

British Library Cataloguing in Publication Data
Readings in applied microeconomics.
1. Microeconomics — Addresses, essays, lectures
I. Wagner, Leslie
338.5'08   HB171.5   80-41207
ISBN 0-19-877163-0
ISBN 0-19-877162-2 Pbk

Set by Hope Services, Abingdon
and printed in Great Britain by
Richard Clay & Co. Ltd., Bungay

Preface

It would be remiss of me to allow this Reader to appear without a word of thanks to the members of the Open University Micro-economics Course Team for their help and co-operation. Neil Costello first raised the idea of a revised edition and had an important in-fluence on the early thinking before his duties took him away from the Course. Alan Gillie, Catherine Price, and Sonja Ruehl responded constructively to the proposals as they were developed, and com-mented on the editorial matter. The prize for devotion to duty must go, however, to the Course Team Chairman, Don Cooper, who not only encouraged the enterprise through all its stages but provided a systematic and comprehensive critique of the editorial material which has served to improve both its style and its content. I am grateful to a most congenial group of colleagues. As always the final responsibility both for the selection of readings and the accompany-ing commentary remains mine alone.

Leslie Wagner

Contents

Introduction

The first edition of this reader was devised as part of the Open University second-level course on Microeconomics. The distance learning method which characterizes the Open University's approach makes the production of a Reader particularly appropriate. Students are scattered over the length and breadth of the United Kingdom which makes their access to specialized libraries difficult. Open University courses are carefully structured, thus making it easier to identify readings relevant to particular areas of the course.

However, these were not the prime reasons for the production of the original Reader. Relevant articles could, after all, be off-printed and sent to the students. The decision to embark on a general commercial publication implied that such a reader would be of interest and value to other students besides those at the Open University. More particularly it was felt that a gap existed in the material available to undergraduate students. There were publications which covered the classical papers in the development of microeconomic theory. Others concentrated on particular elements of the subject, such as the theory of the firm or demand theory. Some concentrated on applied or policy-oriented work but often in the context of the USA. There seemed to be a need for a reader that would cover contemporary studies in the applied area related largely to the British economy. The Course Team considered that no existing publication covered this ground at the appropriate level of sophistication.

The reception accorded to the reader that eventually appeared seems to have backed this judgement. It appears on a number of basic microeconomics course reading lists, and from comments received it seems to have filled a need. (As this is an economics text, it might. appropriately be added that the sales figures indicate that it has filled a want as well.) It is now seven years since the original compilation. The Open University course itself has changed, and in the nature of applied studies more up-to-date readings with new material are now available. Hence the impetus for a second revised edition.

Whilst the structure to a large extent follows the pattern of the first edition, the changes are not without significance. In the first edition the first part compared different systems, planning and market, and studied how they allocated a particular commodity, namely housing. Now the approach is via the mechanisms of resource allocation rather than the systems, and the studies chosen show how different goods and services are allocated within the same economy. In addition the inclusion of an article on the economic effects of North Sea oil on the local economy allows the idea of economic interdependence to be introduced and a wider perspective to be taken.

The two middle sections on demand and the theory of the firm cover much the same ground as before. In the demand section, the readings from the first edition covering methodology, and the demand for tobacco, herring, and cars have been retained, largely because they now form an integral part of the Open University course but also because each offers a different insight into the nature of empirical demand studies. The readings in production and the theory of the firm are all new. The evidence on economies of scale is now more comprehensive, while the other studies illustrate or provide evidence relating to important postulates or predictions of the theory of the firm. In particular, evidence on the assumptions and predictions of the 'managerial' theories is presented together with an evaluation of oligopoly behaviour.

The last section moves away from the catch-all title 'Contemporary Problems' to a clearer focus on the divergence between social and private criteria for resource allocation. Cost–benefit analysis as an important tool in attempting a reconciliation of social and private criteria is well represented. The Mishan guide to cost–benefit analysis is retained from the first edition, but the three studies are all new. Two cover the transport area, while the third evaluates a public investment in a new market. One reports on a possible effect of the potential withdrawal of a facility, the second evaluates the possible effects of the provision of a serivice, while the third studies the results of an investment that has already occurred. The externalities which are at the heart of a divergence between social and private criteria are often given practical expression through the effects of pollution on the environment. Two new readings evaluate appropriate methods of pollution control and the income distribution effects of such control. The final reading retains the study by Douty on the effects of sudden external changes on resource-allocating behaviour. In all some two-thirds of the readings in this second edition are new.

One of the difficulties facing an editor is to find readings which not only fit into the guidelines established for the orientation of his volume but are also compatible with the expected level of theoretical and statistical knowledge of his potential readership. There is no shortage of applied work in microeconomics, but most of the papers are not suitable for a second-year undergraduate publication. In some cases they relate to theory not introduced until either final-year or postgraduate study. Alternatively, they employ statistical and econometric techniques beyond the expertise of the typical second-year student.

The assumption behind this particular selection is that the student has followed or is following a course of microeconomic principles similar in level and approach to the Open University course, i.e. the material covered by the wide range of intermediate texts now available. In addition the student is expected to have had little or no experience in manipulating estimating equations or deriving least squares coefficients.

The resulting selection indicates a wide definition of the term 'applied'. The bulk of the readings provide empirical evidence to test particular theoretical assumptions, relationships, and predictions. The contributions by Baumol and Mishan, however, are concerned with the methodologies and techniques of applied work which are then illustrated as in the demand and cost–benefit studies. There are case studies such as those on the petrol market and the impact of North Sea oil, while the papers on pollution are concerned with the evaluation and prediction of particular policy effects. Finally there are the more general papers by Richardson and Douty which begin and end the book.

This diversity is reflected in the range of sources. Half the studies come from journal articles and a further significant element from texts or specialized books. In addition, however, there are extracts from government reports and studies, together with independent research and consultancy studies.

It is clear from this survey that a great deal of applied work is being undertaken in a variety of places. The difficulties of such work are also evident. Part of the problem arises from disagreements about the nature and purpose of microeconomic theory. For example, are the marginalist principles of the traditional theory of the firm concerned with the derivation of the industry supply curve or with the actual behaviour of the individual firm?

The lack of systematic data is another problem. It is here that the applied macroeconomist is at an advantage. Macroeconomic statistics have been refined, developed, and extended over the years on both a national and an international basis. The needs of governments ensure a regular and comprehensive flow of national income statistics. And as new theories such as monetarism develop or come into fashion, the statistics are similarly developed. The applied microeconomist is not so fortunate. While his macroeconomic colleague is largely concerned with analysing data collected by others, the microeconomist is often concerned with both collecting and analysing his own data. Even where data are available through government reports or company accounts, they have often been collected with other purposes in mind and require manipulation and refinement before they are of practical use. Often the most interesting questions of pricing, demand, and firms' behaviour involve questions of confidentiality with firms being understandably reluctant to provide information which may be of value to a rival.

The studies included here not only reflect the technical economic skills of their authors, they are also testimony to their perseverance, powers of detection, ingenuity, and capacity for sheer hard work. It is hoped that after studying the contributions readers will share the editor's view that progress in understanding the application of microeconomic principles to the UK economy is being achieved.

PART I
ALLOCATION AND INTERDEPENDENCE

Introduction to Part I

The choice of readings for this first part may seem at first glance a little quixotic. Only the papers by Richardson and the Monopolies Commission report appear to have any connection, through their titles at least, with the traditional concerns of microeconomics. However, if these traditional concerns are accurately reflected in the concepts of allocation and interdependence which form the title of this opening section, a wider and more varied illustration of their meaning is required than is usual in introductory texts.

A conventional introduction to microeconomics would begin with an explanation of its major concern as a study of the principles of the allocation of scarce resources between competing wants. Often this explanation might be broken down into a series of questions such as what to produce, how much to produce, and for whom to produce, which all forms of economic organization have to answer and which microeconomic principles can illuminate. These central questions would then be investigated by providing two contrasting forms of economic organization, the competitive market and the planning system, whose characteristic features are outlined and whose advantages and disadvantages are highlighted.

There is much to be said for this approach. Besides the intrinsic utility of making students aware of alternative systems and approaches to resource allocation, it enables the detailed study of the workings of a price system and a market economy, on which most courses concentrate, to be placed in context. In the midst of the detailed complexities of demand or oligopoly theory it is right for the student to be reminded of the broader picture to which it all relates.

However, the competition versus planning approach can oversimplify and mislead. Sometimes the distinction is insufficiently drawn between forms of property ownership, capitalist and socialist, and forms of resource allocation, market and planning. Whilst market systems do operate more fully in economies where private ownership of capital predominates, and planning systems operate more fully in economies where public or state ownership is the norm, the separation is not all that clear. On the one hand there has been sufficient theoretical and empirical investigation (e.g. Meade 1974, Vanek 1970) to justify the view that market systems of allocation can operate successfully under non-capitalist modes of production. On the other hand, and perhaps more important, there is the view that all forms of economic organization require some element of planning. It is not the planning *requirement* which distinguishes different systems but its nature.

The key to this need for planning is the need for information. In the perfectly competitive model the information which the firm requires to enable it to know how much to produce in order to maximize profits is given by the market. With price fixed and the firm assumed to know the price of its inputs, it can relate costs to revenues to find the profit maximizing output. If consumer preferences change, so that, for example, more is demanded, market price will rise and firms will produce more.

As part of his discussion of conditions which favour competition and planning systems, Richardson in the first reading points out that even this simplified perfectly competitive model does not solve the information problem for the individual firm. For in deciding its future output a firm requires knowledge of future prices of both inputs and outputs and not past or present prices. Even if future prices were known Richardson argues that the existence of an unlimited number of firms all able to respond to a profit opportunity makes the outcome for the individual firm uncertain. The characteristic of most market economies, however, is imperfect competition and the existence of large firms. Here, Richardson argues, there will be a mixture of planning and market systems, with the latter being particularly appropriate in markets with heterogeneous products and constant product development.

However, planning is a particular characteristic of the large-firm economy brought about, as Galbraith has argued, by the need for the large firm to master the unpredictability of its economic environment. With high levels of capital investment and employment at stake, changes in consumer preferences can have large repercussions on individual firms. In part, firms rely on what Richardson terms the law of large numbers to smooth out individual demand fluctuations. But planning is also a necessary element of the firm's operations. There is the link between the large firm and its suppliers, which Richardson terms piecemeal planning, as well as the link between the large firm and the national economy characterized by indicative planning. Richardson is certainly more favourably disposed to the former than to the latter, influenced no doubt by the disastrous experience of indicative planning in the UK in the latter part of the 1960s, the years immediately before his paper was published. Certainly the attitudes of governments during the 1970s towards indicative planning followed closely his own prescription that 'government should not attempt to set detailed output targets in the manner of the French and British plans, but there is good reason why it should endeavour to estimate the growth of total output and to influence the way in which it divides between investment, exports, government expenditure, and the like'.

Richardson's paper therefore is a useful reminder that all economic systems contain both market and planning characteristics and in particular that the modern market-oriented economic system requires important planning elements to enable it to function efficiently.

An important aspect of the UK economy as in most market-orientated systems is the large and growing proportion of output not allocated through the market mechanism. These goods and services are usually provided by governments. However, not all government output is provided through non-market mechanisms, so that taking government expenditure as an indicator of non-market output may be misleading. Thus the Open University Microeconomics Course Unit 3 basing itself on OECD data estimates the proportion of total final consumption expenditure spent by all levels of government in the UK to have risen from 22.2 per cent in 1970 to 26.7 per cent in 1975. Bacon & Eltis (1978) on the other hand divide output into marketed and non-marketed, the former being distinguished by the fact that it is sold to someone. They calculate that in 1975 non-marketed output took up some 38 per cent of total output, having grown from below 30 per cent in 1961.

In neoclassical economics the justification for non-market allocation has been found in the existence of 'market failure'. The presence of public goods, merit goods, externalities, and economies of scale leads to situations where exchange between individual buyers and sellers may not produce the optimum social welfare. Thus external defence and internal law and order can be classified as public goods, and education and health services as merit goods. Various transport services may create externalities whilst monopoly power may result from economies of scale.

The policy followed in some of these cases has been to allow market allocation to continue but to regulate or condition the parameters of exchange by legal restraints or taxation. In other cases, however, the provision of goods and services has been transferred to government, financed by taxation and allocated by political or bureaucratic decision rather than through the market. Prime examples in the UK are education, health and social services, together with such activities as road construction and refuse collection.

But how are decisions on the 'correct' level of such activities to be made? And what does 'correct' mean in this context? Writers such as Buchanan & Tullock have explored these and many other aspects of public choice in the system of representative democracy which obtains in market-oriented economies (see for example Buchanan & Tullock 1962).

Glennerster in the extract from his book on the way social service budgets are allocated evaluates two alternative models. The first, which he characterizes as rational comprehensive, is based on the work of Simon and others and seeks to provide some form of analogue for the market process. Glennerster characterizes the elements of such a process as 'the clarification of objectives . . . ; the presentation of alternative means of achieving these objectives, the costing of each alternative approach; the creation of input–output models which show how much resources had to be expended in order to achieve given outcomes; the choice of some criterion with which to judge between alternatives'.

What Glennerster calls 'the idealised model for allocating resources' is severely criticized by Lindblom, amongst others, who advocates a political pluralist model as an explanation of how resources are allocated. Lindblom sees a constant interaction between ends and means as competing interest groups seek to influence policy. There is no simple external objective for policy but different objectives for different groups and the task of policy makers in making allocation decisions is to achieve agreement. 'The *only* test of a good policy is agreement—not that it is consistent with some abstract objective.'

The political pluralist model is as open to criticism as is the rational comprehensive model in Glennerster's view. In particular, its political market approach to decision-making suffers from many of the handicaps of the economic approach—notably in the way in which power is ignored. Just as in the market model decisions reflect economic power—the values of the rich are more highly regarded than those of the poor, so in the political market model the values of the more politically powerful are likely to carry the greater weight. As a result 'there is no reason to suppose that competition between existing interest groups will of itself produce an outcome that takes account of the full range of community interests.'

Glennerster himself inclines more to an economic model in that he sees the rationing concept as the most helpful in understanding resource allocation in the social services. Resources, be they money, manpower, or time, are scarce and decision-makers at all levels seek to cope with the demands made on them. If market methods are not used then administrative mechanisms such as deterrence, eligibility rules, delay, and so on come into play.

The third reading takes us back to the market. The simple two-dimensional partial equilibrium analysis of supply and demand with its *ceteris paribus* assumptions offers powerful insights into the working of markets. The effects of changes to the independent variables on equilibrium price can be shown even in the limited form of comparative static analysis.

Whilst the analysis is a powerful one, for the beginning student it is difficult to find empirical examples of market behaviour that conform to the stated assumptions in a simple enough way to illustrate the basic analytical lessons. The behaviour of the wholesale petrol market in the UK as explained by the Monopolies Commission seems, however, to meet the criteria in terms of a homogeneous product, competitive suppliers (including new firms), and changes to price and non-price variables in the period after 1974 whose effects can reasonably easily be traced. The Monopolies Commission points out that the oil price rise in 1974 had both price and income effects. In terms of simple supply and demand analysis the initial rise caused by a shift in the supply curve to the left was balanced by a subsequent shift in the demand curve to the left as income effects took a hold. An important prediction of the competitive model, namely that the entry of new firms will reduce the prices and the excess profitability of existing firms, is also well recorded.

The concept of interdependence is an important feature of both micro- and macroeconomics. In microeconomics the idea can be traced back to Adam Smith's division of labour and the view that man would be better off economically by allowing some of his wants to be met by his neighbours. In macroeconomics the multiplier concept developed by Kahn & Keynes emphasized the interdependence of national as well as individual prosperity both between and within countries.

Input–output analysis straddles the concerns of both micro- and macroeconomics in illustrating the nature of economic interdependence. More specifically it deals with industrial interdependence, enabling the effects of changes in one sector of the economy to be traced through to other sectors. Both micro and macro effects can be studied. A fall in demand in one industry will affect both specific industries as well as demand as a whole.

The importance of interdependence both in its micro and its macro effects can best be seen when something disturbs the balance of relationships in the national and, indeed, international economy. An example of such a disturbance was the sharp increase in oil prices from 1974 onwards which produced both macro income and price effects in oil-consuming countries and particular micro effects in specific industries.

In the UK the discovery of oil in the North Sea has had both micro and macro effects, particularly in the north of Scotland, the mainland closest to the area of oil discovery. The final reading of this section concentrates on the micro effects analysed by two separate studies. They provide some useful examples of interdependence and of how a development can sometimes have unintended results as its effects work through the economy.

Lewis & McNicoll look at the effect of North Sea oil development on particular industries, sectors, and regions of the Scottish economy. The authors show how the decision to allocate resources to oil exploration in turn required additional resources being allocated to housing, transport, education, and particular professional services. The authors indicate also that in certain areas rapid expansion of demand has inevitably outstripped supply in the short run. These bottlenecks have resulted, as market theory would predict, in price increases and 'queueing'. Moreover, shortages and high prices in particular key infrastructure sectors such as housing have resulted in labour shortages.

It is these employment effects which are studied in the extract from the report by Gaskin & Mackay. They note that the extra employment in production platform construction was recruited largely from the construction industry. Not surprisingly this has had an effect on the relative wages of workers in the construction industry. In the period under study, 1974–6, the fierce competition for construction workers saw their over-all earnings rise sharply. Whilst this might be largely short-run effects through the use of high levels of overtime,

Gaskin & Mackay point out that in the longer run the male standard weekly earnings excluding overtime increased by 10 per cent more for construction workers than for workers as a whole. They point out, however, that construction workers are highly mobile and this produces a quicker response to market signals. For all indigenous industries in the Grampian region, earnings over the period did not rise relatively to Scottish or British averages. The oil developments did not seem to affect relative wages in many sectors because the labour force was largely immobile in terms of location, skills, and aptitudes. Interdependence and indeed efficient resource allocation require an ability and a willingness to respond to market signals.

References

R. Bacon & W. Eltis (1978), *Britain's Economic Problem: Too Few Producers* London: Macmillan).

J. M. Buchanan & G. Tullock (1962), *The Calculus of Consent* (Ann Arbor: University of Michigan Press).

J. E. Meade (1974), 'Labour-Managed Firms in Conditions of Imperfect Competition', *Economic Journal*, Dec.

J. Vanek (1970), *The General Theory of Labour-Managed Market Economies* (Cornell University Press, 1970).

1

Planning Versus Competition

by G. B. Richardson

Scope and Method

What are the proper roles, in economic organization, of planning and of competition? In what circumstances should economic activities be fitted together deliberately through a coherent set of instructions given by a central authority? And when should this co-ordination be left to the spontaneous interaction of independent, decentralized decisions? Is planning essentially an alternative to competition or can it be employed, in an indicative form, not to replace but somehow to illuminate, guide and thereby improve the operation of market forces? These questions, it need hardly be said admit of no definite answer, objectively valid irrespective of time and place. Nevertheless, they are real questions of obvious practical importance, so that it is worth while trying to find some answers to them, however partial and provisional these may be.

I wish to make only two preliminary observations, one about scope, the other about method. The scope of this paper is very wide. But its subject is competition versus planning, not capitalism versus socialism; the questions which I raised at the outset pose themselves in countries which have no private property in the means of production but seek to decentralize decision-taking. In so far as method is concerned, I seek justification in terms of what Sir Roy Harrod has called, rather grandly, the need for Continuing Conceptual Refurbishment. I try to take a fresh look at the first principles. Progress in economics does not depend only upon rigorous analysis, observation and measurement; it requires also that effort of imagination that enables us partially to escape from conventional categories of thought. Being realistic is not merely a question of testing hypotheses, important though this is; it also requires sustained and strenuous effort to consider whether our inherited stock of theoretical constructions do not distort our vision of the plain facts of economic life.

The task of economic organization

Let us begin at the beginning and ask what it is that we want competition or planning to accomplish. The answer might be that their

From *Soviet Studies*, vol. xxii, No. 3 (Jan. 1971), pp. 433–47. Reprinted by permission of the author and the editor of *Soviet Studies*.

function is to secure an efficient allocation of resources. To say
this, however, although obviously correct, may be misleading.
For we normally concentrate, in economic theory, on the
pure logic of resource allocation and, in order to exhibit this
logic, early, we assume that both ends and means are given. Thus
we assume, in the so-called theory of consumers' behaviour,
that income, prices and tastes are given and concern ourselves
exclusively with the logic of choice. And when we turn to the
economy as a whole and seek to establish conditions for efficient
allocation in Pareto's sense, we follow the same procedure; we
adopt the vantage point of someone standing outside the system
with full knowledge of all the relevant preferences, resources and
productive techniques. This approach is justified in that it enables
us to focus our attention on the pure principles of economizing;
but it is important, when we turn to consider the working of
economic organization, to keep well in mind the obvious fact that
in reality no one is provided with a bird's-eye view. Allocative
decisions are in fact taken, and in the nature of things have to
be taken, on the basis of individual beliefs and opinions, usually
uncertain and sometimes contradictory. It is not merely that our
knowledge is probabilistic in character; the point is that it is
fragmented, in the form of imperfectly consistent estimates held
by different people. The function of economic organization is
therefore to make the best use of this knowledge, and in
appraising the relative effectiveness of different systems, we have
to think in terms not only of allocative logic but of search and
discovery.

Let us suppose that a body of men land on a desert island on
which, in a variety of places, buried treasure is to be found.
If the men have with them a map showing the location of
treasure throughout the island, then a plan of campaign can
readily be drawn up. The appropriate organization is that of central
planning, each man being given a particular job to do. Of course
there will be problems of incentives, of distribution and so on,
but the propriety of centralized decision-taking can scarcely be
in doubt. But let us now suppose that there is no map, or at
least no map in existence that can be presumed accurate. Each
man may have bits and pieces of information that he considers
relative to the location of the treasure, but no more. There is
now room for choice between alternative forms of organization.
The centralized solution would be to invite the men to pool their
information and opinions and endeavour therefrom to construct
a map of the most likely location of the treasure; a plan of campaign could then be drawn up and jobs allocated. The purely decentralized solution would be to allow each man to go forth and
dig where he liked. Now these alternative approaches differ in
two ways. Under central planning, the activities of different men
will be co-ordinated by means of a set of integrated instructions

which, ideally, will produce an optimum pattern of search—or allocation of resources—with respect to the evidence and opinion embodied in the map. Under *laissez-faire*, on the other hand, such co-ordination as does take place will be the unintended result of each man taking account of what the others are doing; if, for example, men start to crowd in one corner of the island, then some will no doubt be induced to seek their fortunes in other areas where, if the evidence of treasure is less strong, the competition is weaker. Clearly, therefore, planning and competition represent alternative techniques of co-ordination; less obvious, perhaps, is that they differ also in the way in which they make use of knowledge. Under central planning, evidence and opinion will be consolidated in order to construct the map on which the programme of search is to be based. Under *laissez-faire*, however, each and every opinion will affect the pattern of search provided that whoever holds it is in possession of a pick and shovel. Now it does not seem to me possible, unless the circumstances are further specified, to say whether the consolidation of knowledge will improve the pattern of search; it is easy to see that something will be gained, as bits of the jigsaw are fitted together, but easy to see also that something may be lost if heterodox opinions are sacrificed in the name of consistency, and new findings, if they appear to threaten the presumptions of the plan, are quietly put aside. All that one can say at this stage is that the relative merits of planning and competition are not solely a matter of the way in which they co-ordinate interrelated activities; they depend also on whether, in a particular set of curcumstances, it is desirable to endeavour to weld a variety of estimates and opinions into some kind of coherent whole.

I hope that the relevance of this naive analogy is reasonably clear. In normative economics, when considering how best to adapt means to ends, we assume that we have knowledge of the available resources, opportunities and objectives in order to concentrate on the logic of the problem. In positive economics, on the other hand, when we come to consider how particular systems would work, this assumption has to be abandoned. Maps are not provided; economic organization has to find some way of constructing maps or of doing without them. In a centrally planned system, the authorities take steps to prepare a map; after discussions with the subordinate bodies in the hierarchy, with the various industrial commissions or their equivalents, they specify a feasible and desired future composition of output and then proceed to give appropriate instructions designed to ensure that it is produced. Consistency is thereby produced not necessarily, of course, with resources, technical possibilities and needs as they objectively exist, but with one central agreed or imposed conception of what these are. In practice, of course, planning systems will differ as to the detail in which the future pattern of output is set down, but the essence of the matter is that resources are allocated according to some central view of objectives and opportunities built up through some organized consolidation of the information in the hands of the central and subordinate bodies.

In competitive systems, firms do what they like in pursuit of profit and a large part of economic analysis is devoted to discussing whether this will cause the right things to be produced in the right amounts. The price mechanism is supposed to do the trick if too much of a good is produced, the price will sink below costs; if too little, it will remain above them; in either event the profit motive, combined with free mobility and competition, should bring the required adjustment. For the flawless operation of this mechanism—subject to qualifications about externalities, etc.—most economists put forward an institutional blue-print, perfect competition, while acknowledging with regret that scale economics may make it impossible to secure its full realization in practice. Now I have maintained elsewhere that perfect competition, even if realizable, could never do what is claimed of it.[1] The essence of the matter can be put quite briefly, but there is no room here for the full supporting argument. Under perfect competition, it would be quite impossible for any firm to know how much of a good to produce. According to the usual story, entrepreneurs are guided by prices; each of them sets an output that equates the price of the good he sells to its marginal cost. Now it is clear that current prices cannot be the appropriate signals; they reflect the appropriateness of past output decisions but are not directly relevant to decisions about what to produce for the future. Presumably, therefore, firms are supposed to equate marginal costs to future prices. But how then is a producer able to predict future prices, depending as they do both on the demands of consumers and on the supply plans of all his competitors? This the textbooks do not tell us; the most we are likely to be told is that producers are assumed to know what the relevant future prices are. But a little reflection suffices to show that even this is not enough to ensure that firms know what to do and that, as a result of their actions, the equilibrium configuration of output is obtained. For let us imagine that the system is out of equilibrium but that the true equilibrium prices are somehow announced to all producers as from on high. How would the possession of this information enable the individual firm to know which goods to produce, or cease producing, and in what quantities? If the future

---

[1] See my *Information and Investment* (London, 1960), chs. 1 and 2. The same matter is dealt with, though less fully, in my article 'Equilibrium, Expectations and Information', *Economic Journal*, vol. lxix (1959), pp. 223–37.

price of a good were known to be greater than the current cost of making it, then a profit opportunity may be said to exist; but if there is an unlimited number of firms equally able and ready to respond to the opportunity no individual firm will know whether to do so. A profit opportunity which is available equally for everyone is in fact available to no one at all.

My own view, therefore, is that there would be no tendency under conditions of perfect competition for the equilibrium associated with it ever to be attained. My fear is that the brief argument just provided will not persuade anyone who has not already accepted this view now to accept it. In any case a large number of economists—perhaps even an increasing number —continue to maintain (even although unable to prove) that perfect competition would produce the outputs and prices associated with its so-called equilibrium position. But it is particularly interesting to note that the founding fathers of the doctrine—or at least Walras and Edgeworth—had their doubts; they were aware of the informational deficiencies of perfect competition and sought to offer some remedy. Both suggested hypothetical systems of recontracting designed to ensure that the plans of producers and consumers were welded into a consistent set. Offers to supply a particular good were made, it will be recalled, first on a provisional basis, and did not become firm commitments until, after repeated revisions, plans to buy were seen to be consistent with plans to produce and sell. We shall consider later the way in which these proposals prefigure the organized dialogues of indicative planning. The question now before us is whether such a network of forward contracts, quite apart from administrative cost and complexity, does in fact provide a theoretical answer to the problem of co-ordination that the price mechanism, in perfect competition, cannot by itself resolve. I maintain that it does not. The obstacle to creating a complete and consistent network of contracts, in the last analysis, is simply the imperfection of our knowledge. Consumers do not wish to contract for their future purchases because they cannot foretell what their future needs and opportunities will be; and producers do not generally wish to commit themselves to forward purchases of inputs because they cannot predict the productive possibilities that will be open to them. By supposing that the network of contracts could ever be complete and closed, we assume away that essential imperfection of knowledge with which economic organization has somehow to cope.

How competitive systems work

But where do we go from here? I have rejected the traditional model of the working of a decentralized economic system, perfect competition; the introduction of a complementary apparatus of forward contracts, I have further argued, merely evades the problems created by the imperfection of knowledge. But free enterprise systems, as even their keenest critics would admit, do in fact work, at least imperfectly; central planning might work better, but one could not maintain that we have chaos without it. Let us therefore endeavour to set out how the market system does work, for until this is clear we are not likely to be able to judge how far, and in what ways, central planning can usefully supplement or replace it.

If we are to explain how the economic world goes round—at least, the capitalist world—we have, I believe, to attend to three circumstances. First, there takes place within it a great deal of what, for want of a better term, I shall call piecemeal planning. Secondly, much reliance is put on the fact that aggregates are often more predictable than are, on average, their several components. And thirdly there have evolved market structures and codes of business behaviour which facilitate foresight and thereby permit enterprise planning. We shall now deal with each of these circumstances in turn.

(a) *Piecemeal Planning*

Walras taught us, in his general equilibrium analysis, that all economic activities are interdependent; but although this interdependence is universal, some activities are more interdependent than others. Consider the relationship between intermediate and final output. General-purpose inputs, such as steel and fork-lift trucks, will normally be bought on a market; the individual user will not choose to place contracts much in advance of his future requirements, and the individual seller will hope to secure some stability and predictability in the demand for his output by having a number of different accounts on his books. But in the case of specific-purpose inputs bought by only one firm or very few firms, other arrangements will generally prevail. Piecemeal planning will generally be the best means of dealing with close complementarity, both quantitative and qualitative, between output plans. It has to secure quantitative co-ordination, in the sense of making the rate of output of a final good appropriate to the rate of output of the required inputs; thus refining capacity has to be in balance with crude oil supplies. It has also to secure qualitative co-ordination where, for example, the development of a nylon polymer has to be hand in hand with the development of the processes used to spin it. Joint production planning and joint product development can be secured by a variety of techniques ranging from loose inter-company understanding to full vertical integration. A highly informal but highly effective form of piecemeal planning is conducted by Marks and Spencers. Although it concerns itself with the product development, the output and even the investment decisions of its suppliers, yet its relationship with them is based merely on mutual trust and goodwill. The operations of a major international oil company provide an example of extensive and highly developed piecemeal planning through vertical integration. The plain fact is that so-called market economies do not rely entirely on market mechanisms; their structure permits, and has in fact been adapted to permit, a great deal of piecemeal planning. It is in terms of the need for such planning, rather than in terms of conventional scale economies, that much industrial morphology has to be interpreted.

(b) *The Law of Large Numbers*

But, if planning is all around us, it is far from complete. A great bulk of output, final and intermediate, is, as we say, for the market. Producers of intermediate goods commonly deal with a large number of buyers and the producers of consumer goods almost always do. In such cases, refuge from uncertainty is sought not in planning but in what has been called the unstrict law of large numbers. Brick manufacturers do not try to forecast the demand for bricks by adding up the several demands that the many builders and contractors with which they deal say are likely to put upon them. They study the trends in aggregates. They rely on the cancelling out of random elements to which the demands of individual customers are subject. Of course, we should not rush to the conclusion that for a firm of a given size the larger the number of its independent accounts the better. In the first place, the gain from grouping does not rise in proportion to the number of accounts grouped but—if sampling theory can be followed in this context —to the square root of their number. And, secondly, the firm's forecasts will generally be part synthetic, part analytical; they will supplement the projection of aggregate trends with particular information about the likely demands of particular customers or groups of customers and the larger the number of accounts the greater the cost of acquiring this information is likely to be.

In her critique of French planning Mrs Lutz[2] puts great stress on this unstrict law of large numbers and refers to a German school of writers who make it the corner-stone of their account of how foresight and co-ordination is made possible in market economies. Certainly the principle seems to me important, but I do not think that it can bear the full weight of explanation. It is certainly true that the aggregation of the component demands for a particular product makes for predictability, but if this is to result in predictability in the demand for the output of particular firms, then the structure of the markets in which they are operating

[2] Vera Lutz, *Central Planning for the Market Economy* (London, 1969).

has to be appropriate. Here, it seems to me, is the third essential requirement for the working of decentralized systems; market structure and business behaviour must be such as permit firms to plan current output and investment decisions; they must facilitate enterprise planning. Perhaps this too, like much else I have said, may seem obvious and certainly ought to be. In fact, however, the point is almost completely ignored in almost all the literature, and I have had very little success in drawing attention to it.

(c) *Market Structures*

Let us suppose that we are asked not to explain how markets work but to design them. We may imagine that we have been invited to advise the government of an East European economy, currently organized by detailed central direction, on how best to introduce some decentralized decision-taking. Let us suppose that we are concerned with an industry (producing a homogeneous commodity), in which enterprises are to be given freedom of decision with respect both to current output and to investment. We are asked to design an appropriate market structure and prescribe the rules to which the enterprises are to be made subject. Those who really believed in this theory of perfect competition might recommend along these lines; set up as many independent enterprises as the relevant scale economies permit, give them equal access to finance, instruct them to seek maximum profits and forbid them to limit the competition in any way. If this recipe were adopted, its proponents would urge, we would get as close as possible to the ideal self-regulating system with prices constantly varying to ensure the optimal adjustment of supply to demand. Were these recommendations to be accepted, then the enterprise managers would, I fear, be in despair. Even if they could form a capable estimate of the likely total demand for the product, they would have no idea how much they each and individually ought to plan to produce. We must hope, therefore, that these recommendations would be rejected.

But what then ought we to recommend? We could of course suggest that the authorities divide up the market between the several enterprises according to geographical area or some stated percentage share. This, at any rate, unlike the previous recommendation, could give to each enterprise something they could usefully try to predict; and the success or failure of their individual predictions would be made manifest. But most of the merits of decentralization would be lost; neither costs nor profits would be subject to competitive pressures, and it would be absurd not to arrange for the accidental surpluses that might develop in some part of the market to be used to offset scarcities in others. Let us then consider a further set of recommendations which, for ease of exposition, I shall put in somewhat simple-minded form. Let the price of the homogeneous commodity be fixed on the basis of some estimate of normal unit costs. Allot customers between the several enterprises in such a way that each of them has a regular supplier from whom he is normally obliged to buy. But lay it down that, should a buyer find his regular supplier unable to meet his full demands, then he will be transferred, in some pre-arranged fashion, to an enterprise with additional supply available.

How would these arrangements work? First we note that each supplier has now something he can aim at. His first job is to predict the demand from his regular clientele and plan to meet it. He can do this without the fear that, if other suppliers over-produce, he will no longer have a profitable outlet for his goods. Secondly, we should note that each supplier has a strong incentive not to underestimate his regular demand, for, if he does so, he will lose custom on a quasi-permanent basis to those who have the capacity to meet demands in excess of those from their regular customers. Thirdly, suppliers have an incentive not to overestimate demand, for, if they do so, they themselves will bear the losses occasioned by excess capacity. And finally, suppliers have an incentive to consider whether their rivals are likely to have underestimated demand, for, if this is so, there is an opportunity to wrest custom from them.

A market of this type, it seems to me, would have clear advantages over the perfectly competitive, flexible-price type of market that often represents the textbook ideal. Not only does it facilitate foresight; it ensures that errors of forecasting are borne by those who make them. In a flexible-price system, the sins of the few may be borne by the many; for over-investment, by causing a collapse of prices, will penalize all suppliers.

It is not difficult to discern the strong family resemblance between these recommended arrangements and competitive markets that actually exist in the manufacturing sector of free enterprise economies. These markets, to use the Hicksian terminology, are normally of the fix-price rather than the flexible-price variety; they are so usually because of oligopoly, sometimes because of inter-firm agreements, sometimes because of governmental controls. Firms do generally have regular clienteles, either because of transport costs, or product differentiation, or goodwill or for some other reason. If they cannot meet the demand of the regular customers, they lose them. If they install too much capacity, they suffer loss, but prices do not normally fall to the level of marginal costs. Of course, there is the danger, which engages the exclusive and almost obsessional attention of many economists, that prices may be kept too high in relation to unit costs. Inter-firm rivalry or the threat of entry may, and I am inclined to believe usually do, prevent this; but, if they do not, the public authorities can intervene.

But let us return to our hypothetical East European economy. The task given to us was that of designing a framework for workable competition in the supply of a homogeneous product. But it is natural to ask whether, in this context, the gains from decentralized decision-taking are really worth while. It is true that we have introduced competition in forecasting, but it is arguable that a central bureau, by collating all the available evidence, might make a better forecast than could any individual enterprise. Might it not therefore be better to maintain centralized control, fix an industry output target and give to the enterprises individual output targets derived from it? After all, it would still be possible to stimulate competition in cost reduction simply by fixing a uniform price and rewarding enterprises with the highest profits.

It seems to me that, so long as we take the case of a homogeneous product, or near-homogeneous product, the argument for decentralization is not strong. I for one would not wish to denationalize the coal mines. It is when we turn to the general case of product differentiation and, more especially, of continuous product development, that the merits of competition of decentralized forecasting and investment decisions, come into their own. So long as there is uncertainty merely with regard to the future total demand for a homogeneous product then it seems not unreasonable to pool all the individual opinions and distil some kind of average view therefrom; central planning, in other words, may be appropriate. But, where there exists uncertainty in its more general form, I can see little merit and much danger in endeavouring to agree or impose some central view about what lines of development, in product or process, ought to be pursued or about what product varieties will best meet the needs of consumers. In considering how we might design a workable market structure, I took the case of a homogeneous product, for it is in that context that the forecasting problem, created by the interdependence of individual producers' plans, presents itself most sharply. I wished to show how it was possible to reconcile competition with the requirements for informed output planning even in this extreme case. But our imaginary East European reformers might have been better advised not to select homogeneous product markets as the first place in which to introduce decentralized decision-taking. For not only do product differentiation and development make it more important to have competition, they make it possible to dispense with the special hypothetical arrangements according to which customers were allotted among suppliers. Provided that we have short-run price stability as indeed we generally do in manufacturing business, then firms will generally be able to proceed from estimates of the total demand for their product class to estimates of the sales which they themselves will be able to make; but they will be obliged to recognize, in this general case, that they may lose custom not only if they are unable to supply but also if they cannot offer a price product combination as attractive as that offered by rivals.[3]

[3] How strange it is that economists have often set up, as a paradigm of decentralized decision-taking, the hypothetical system—perfect competition—in which not only the workability but also the advantages of decentralization would be most in doubt.

I set out, in this section of the paper, to say something about the way in which market economies cope with the problem of allocating resources under conditions of imperfect competition. Of course, this summary account is quite inadequate; nothing has been said, for example, about prices, but then their role in promoting efficient allocation is well known. My aim was to make these points; first, that critical interdependencies both quantitative and qualitative are dealt with by private, piecemeal planning; secondly, that in the absence of such deliberate co-ordination enterprise planning and prediction depends very largely on what has been called the unstrict law of large numbers; thirdly, that an essential condition for this prediction and planning is the existence of market structures and codes of business behaviour different from those to which economists usually give their warmest approval; and, fourthly, that the merits of competition are strongest where products are heterogeneous and subject to constant development.

Indicative Planning

It is perfectly apparent, from the preceding discussion, that planning and competition are in one sense compatible; they can and do co-exist peaceably, on the basis of a division of labour, within the same economy. But I maintained at the outset, nevertheless, that planning and competition were essentially alternative ways of organizing economic activity with different roles to play. For the remainder of this paper I wish to consider whether there is a kind of planning, indicative planning, which can be adopted in conjunction with competition to co-ordinate the same set of economic activities. Can indicative planning be used, not to replace decentralized decision-taking, but to make it better informed?

Indicative planning, as practised in France and Britain, is a procedure by which the government works out, after consultation with private industry, a set of more or less disaggregated output targets for the various commodity groups within the national product. These targets are said to be consistent and usually, in some sense or other, to be agreed; they do not correspond, however, to binding obligations imposed on individual firms. What can be said in the light of the analysis of this paper, about the logic and utility of these arrangements?

In terms of our analogy of the treasure hunt, indicative planning would correspond to an arrangement which brought the men together to compose a map but then left them free to seek their fortunes as they each saw fit. On the face of it, this would not appear to be a very effective procedure, for the searchers would have neither much incentive to disclose their true opinions about the location of the treasure nor any clear indication, once the map was constructed, of what they each and individually ought to do. Nevertheless, this combination of centralized forecasting and decentralized decision has sometimes been represented as the peculiar virtue of the system; the copious French literature on the subject abounds with references to the way in which indicative planning illuminates but does not dictate enterprise decisions, often moving on to references about the reconciliation of order with freedom, harmony with diversity, organization with initiative and so on and so forth, in a manner that seems to belie the reputation of the French language for clear and precise expression.

I recall reading that the origins of indicative planning might be sought in the work of Quesnay, whose Tableau Economique represents the earliest attempt in the field; be that as it may, it seems to me that, in so far as the logic of the process is concerned, Walras is the true forerunner. The process of consultation by which a set of consistent interrelated output plans is said to be built up under indicative planning reminds us forcibly of the hypothetical system of re-contracting, which both Walras and Edgeworth said could, theoretically, provide a direct route to equilibrium. If indicative planning is taken to be such a process, then the objections made against the Walrasian conception apply here also. Given that knowledge is imperfect, admitting of both uncertainty and difference of opinion, then individual expectations and plans cannot thus be knitted together into one single consistent set. It may indeed be that the remote origins of indicative planning, based as it is on a supposed concensus, ought to be sought not in Walras, nor even in Quesnay, but in Rousseau's influential if obscure notion of the General Will.

But perhaps the analogy with re-contracting should not be pushed thus far. In the first place, the output targets in the plan are not associated with contracts to buy or to deliver; they represent some agreed expectation about what future outputs are likely to be. Secondly, the disaggregation in the plan is not carried through right down to output targets for each individual firm's product lines; the figures relate to the outputs of branches or industries usually large and highly diversified. Given these qualifications, the logic of indicative planning is less easily assailed, if only, I fear, because it becomes more difficult to discover what it is.

The target output figures set out in the plan are normally obtained by a combination of two methods. One method is to estimate the future rate of growth of the national product and proceed from there to deduce the rate of growth of the component elements. Let us call this the analytical approach. The other method is to call for estimated output figures from industries; sometimes the firms or associations approached are asked to give two estimates, one corresponding to what they themselves expect to happen, the other to what they think would be appropriate to the particular rate of growth of output postulated in the plan. Let us call this the synthetic approach.

On the face of it, one might not wish to put much faith in industry output figures reached by the analytic method, if only for the reason that this method proceeds from what is more predictable, namely aggregates, to what is less predictable, namely components thereof. In so far as the larger sub-aggregates are concerned, such as consumption, investment, government expenditure and so on, the procedure makes some sense, if only because these totals are subject to governmental policy influence. But when we come to deduce industry outputs, far less the output of particular products, the approach becomes highly questionable. One reads not uncommonly that rates of output growth for individual products could be deduced from the rate of growth of national product, provided one could calculate the appropriate income elasticities of demand. If one conceives these in terms of the relationship between changes in aggregate output and particular outputs as manifested at the end of the planning period, *ex post*, then of course the statement is tautologous; but if income elasticities are taken to refer to the change in the demand for an individual product consequent on a certain change in national income other things being equal, then of course the statement is not true. Income changes represent only one of the many factors which influence the demand for particular products or product groups; they often appear more important than they are simply because we are working in terms of models which abstract from the elements of changing requirements, changing products, changing processes and costs and so on.

But let us wave aside these difficulties and suppose that industry output forecasts are produced and that, for the sake of argument, each and every firm becomes convinced that they are correct. What then? I cannot believe that an accurate forecast of the output of, say, the mechanical engineering industry, in the classification features in the British Plan of 1965, would have been of much use to an individual manufacturer of compressors, or diesel engines, or cranes, or pumps. No doubt forecasts would be somewhat more useful if they were further disaggregated, but even a forecast for cranes as such would not much help the individual manufacturer to estimate the demand for his particular type of dockyard crane, or steelworks crane, or moving overhead crane, diesel-powered crane, small electric crane and so on. And there is the further crucial point that, the more detailed the disaggregation, the less credible the analytic procedure becomes.

But forecasts, it may be said, are also synthetic. In general, moreover, they are agreed with the industries concerned. This latter claim, in my own experience, does not amount to much. The large firms or trade associations consulted are usually prepared to agree to a very wide range of industry output forecasts, not merely because they wish to please, but simply because the relationship between the likely size of the future output of their own product and the size of the so-called industry output figure is so very tenuous. The remedy then lies, it may be urged, in further and further disaggregation, down, if necessary, to the level of the outputs of each individual firm. But here we go out by the door through which we came. If indicative planning is taken to mean the knitting together of each and every output plan, then it does indeed come close to the Walrasian conception of a complete network of forward contracts. It presumes a consensus that simply does not exist, for no amount of organized dialogue, it seems to me, can hope to weld the expectations of each and every entrepreneur into a consistent plan.

If this analysis is correct, then there exists no coherent logical basis even in a closed economy for indicative planning; whether the process yields indirect benefits, such as creating confidence and inducing managements to look ahead, is a matter I do not propose to discuss. My own view is that the government should not attempt to set detailed output targets in the manner of the French and British plans, but there is good reason why it should endeavour to estimate the growth of total output and to influence the way in which it divides between investment, exports, government expenditure and the like. And I believe that the publication of its opinions and intentions on these matters will be of some use to some firms. It is evident, moreover, that governments will be much concerned with piecemeal planning; they will engage in it directly within the public sector or in partnership with the private sector and they may wish to supervise or even to stimulate the arrangements made by private firms. For many it seems natural that all the islands of piecemeal planning should gradually come together, that the sea of market relations should recede and that which was an archipelago become a continent. I believe that this is a mistaken view. My argument has been that there are sub-sets of economic activities so rigidly related that it is desirable to plan their co-ordination on the basis of some consensus of expectation and belief. Equally, there are wider areas within which the interdependence of individual activities is much looser; decentralized decision-taking, co-ordinated through the market, is here appropriate. Rather than endeavour to impose a consensus, it is better to let individual decisions be taken on the basis of a variety of opinions as to what an uncertain future may hold in store.

2

Social Service Budgets and Social Policy—Theories and Practice

by Howard Glennerster

As the public sector has grown, so have the efforts to improve the basis on which individual policy decisions are taken. Increasing attention has been directed to identifying the nature of the problem or need which calls for action; to specifying as precisely as possible the general aim of the policy and its particular objectives, in terms of standards to be attained or needs to be met; to analysing alternative ways in which these aims or objectives might be achieved; and to verifying after the event that the expected results were achieved, in time, and with the predicted level of expenditure . . . . Cost benefit analysis on a substantial scale is undertaken in relation to both minor and major policy decisions . . . . Studies of output budgeting methods and the introduction of systematic Programme Analysis and Review will help to ensure the regular re-appraisal of policies across the whole field of government.
(HM Treasury, *Public Expenditure White Papers Handbook on Methodology* (1972), pp. 1-2)

Economy in Government

In order to understand the development of the ideas that are reflected in this quotation it is necessary to go back thirty years or more to the works of Simon and other academic public administrators in America.[1] He had been concerned with decision making in general, and with what constituted rational behaviour by an organisation, but what he had to say was directly related to resource decisions. To operate efficiently, he argued, any organisation must be clear what its goals are and which goals are also means to more distant ends. It must choose from the alternative courses of action available to it the one which will lead to the greatest accomplishment of administrative objectives at the least cost. Later Simon came to stress more explicitly that administrators could only be expected to choose satisfactory alternatives rather than theoretically optimal ones, because of the limitations of time and knowledge at their disposal. He argued that once an organisation's objectives had been determined the structure of the agency should correspond to them. Nevertheless, it is by no means clear in Simon how or on what occasions goals are to be defined or alternative courses of action appraised.

The notable contribution which a group of RAND economists made in the late fifties and early sixties was to suggest that there were techniques that could be used to show which courses of action

From *Social Service Budgets and Social Policy* (George Allen & Unwin, 1975), pp. 17-40. Reprinted by permission.

were cost effective in a wide range of government activities. Moreover, they indicated that there was an appropriate vehicle to which to attach such regular reappraisals in government—namely the budget process.

Far from acting efficiently, they argued, public bodies had no incentives to make them use resources efficiently since there were no market incentives. Instead agencies tended to adopt concepts like 'need', or 'requirements' or 'priorities', which showed little awareness of the resource costs involved nor, in particular, was there any appreciation of the concept of opportunity cost. Budget discussions tended to be couched in terms like 'we need the best facilities available', ignoring the fact that the more resources that were made available to equip, say, a university physics laboratory, the less could be used for other purposes. Finally, they argued, there was no incentive for government agencies to concern themselves with the long term impact or cost of their activities. Politicians were only concerned with short term vote winning advantages. To achieve economy in government, public sector resource allocations should all be subject to 'sytematic analysis'.

The essence of this approach emerged most coherently in two publications—*The Economics of Defense in the Nuclear Age* by Hitch and McKean,[2] and *Efficiency in Government and the Use of Systems Analysis* by McKean.[3] The first was the byproduct of cost appraisal work done by RAND for the US Defense Department and the individual services. The second used cost benefit studies of water resource schemes as its starting point but both produced a generalised methodology relevant to all public sector resource decisions and McKean's book in particular argued that systems analysis was applicable to the greater part of the Federal Government's activities.

The essential elements of such systematic analysis were: the clarification of objectives, wthout this no analysis was feasible; the presentation of alternative means of achieving these objectives; the costing of each alternative approach; the creation of input–output models which would show how much resources had to be expended in order to achieve given outcomes; the choice of some criterion with which to judge between the alternatives.

Both Hitch and McKean were confident from their experience of costing defense contracts and water resource schemes that input–output relationships could be established if agency objectives were clearly specified. It was the last element that posed the most difficult problems, but their solution lay in an apparently common sense procedure they called 'sub-optimisation'. Issues or items for analysis had to be broken down into sufficiently discrete parts to allow acceptable cost comparisons to be made. The usual task of economic or quantitative analysis was to provide information for relatively low level decision making in, for example, the Military hierarchy. At that level it was necessary to take as given the larger questions of military strategy and advise on the cheapest way of achieving a limited goal.

'If the Air Force tries to decide between two gun sights for fighters, taking the general organisation, size and tactics of fighter defense as given, it is sub-optimising'.[4] But the same principle held higher up the decision chain.

The task of breaking down resource decisions into sufficiently discrete issues was an important one. If criteria were adopted at a lower level that were inconsistent with those applied at a higher

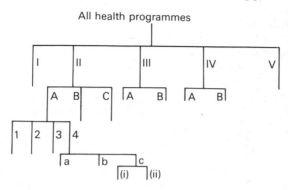

Figure 1

level the whole process was vitiated. It was at this point that the programme budget became conceptually important. Hitch and McKean argued that if resources were to be allocated according to specified objectives, the budget must be categorised in the same way. Subsequently the idea was elaborated into the notion of a hierarchical programme structure. The aim was to break down the budget into a logical hierarchy of programmes and sub-programmes[5] (see Figure 1). In such a structure activities (i) and (ii) ideally contribute to and only contribute to the goal of activity (c) which along with activities (a) and (b) contribute to and only contribute to the goal of activity 4 and so on right up to programmes I-V which might themselves be subsumed under one general purpose such as 'improved health'. When once this logical categorisation had been undertaken it would ensure that within it sub-optimising analyses between programmes or sub-programmes were consistent right the way through. It would then be possible to make 'trade offs' or adjustments between two sub-programmes that could be said to be fulfilling common objectives.

An example may help to make some of the implications clearer. Let us assume that the objective of activity (c) in Figure 1 is to extend the life expectancy of those suffering from kidney failure.[6] The size of the budget that can be devoted to this purpose is already fixed. No questions, at this stage, are being asked about whether such patients ought to be kept alive. There are basically two ways of achieving this end—hemodialysis (purifying the patients' blood with an artificial kidney), activity (i), or kidney transplants, activity (ii).

The first of these activities can be further subdivided into dialysis at home or in a hospital. It is not necessary to face difficult issues about the value of life since our aim is to maximise the length of life in both cases. The quality of life could pose difficulties since those who have transplants can lead a more active and varied life. (As it happened transplants in this particular study were deemed to be cheaper so the arbitrary measures introduced to account for the quality of life did not affect the result.) This gives us a situation in which a cost effectiveness study can help. With a transplant operation the high costs come early and in dialysis they are spread over a life time, but they can be compared by discounting the costs and giving each a present value. If the analyst has empirical evidence on the life expectancy of those who are on dialysis and those who have undergone a transplant it is possible to produce an estimate of the cost of each year of life gained for a given population following transplant, or dialysis at home or in hospital. From this it would be possible to shed some light on the appropriate size of (i) and (ii) given the constraints on the availability of kidneys for transplant purposes.

Another example might be that of the maternity service. This could constitute a major programme on its own, say III. The aim might be to reduce perinatal and maternal mortality to a minimum (in practice there would be other considerations). There are two kinds of provision—hospital (A) and domiciliary (B). Let us assume that costs associated with each hospital confinement are twice those associated with each home confinement at present levels of staffing and technology, but hospital confinements are also safer. With a given budget it would be economic to provide the maximum number of hospital confinements consistent with that constraint and ensure that those facing least complicated deliveries had their babies at home. Can the analyst take us further and advise on the size of the maternity care budget? An idealistic society might begin with the plea that it wanted to do the best for its mothers and provide 100 per cent hospital confinements at a cost of £100 million. It may then be established that to have 10 per cent home confinements would not in any way alter the mortality rates. Faced with the knowledge that he could reduce expenditure and still maintain the same 'output' from the programme the minister would be well advised to spend only £95 millions on maternity services—£90m on hospital and £5m on home confinements and spend the £5m he saved on other parts of the health budget. So long as such expenditure had any positive value it must increase the community's welfare. What happens if he reduces the hospital budget a further £5 millions and thus slightly increases the risk of maternal mortality? How are we to offset the value of, say, improved geriatric care, that £5 millions would buy against the increased risk of death suffered by the mothers. Some more optimistic exponents of systems analysis would argue a cost benefit analysis could do this. Various methods have been adopted to put monetary values on life expectancy, yet it is doubtful whether any of them satisfy the Pareto criterion that we ought to compensate each person who is to be worse off according to their valuation of the estimated change in risk.[7]

In practice all an economist can do, we would argue, is to show the consequences of spending different sums on maternity care of different kinds and leave the political process to decide. We can, however, say something about the political process. If 'the minister' takes the decision on the basis of his own judgement, or even worse if the medical profession does, with no reference to those affected any decision is less likely to conform to the Pareto criterion than if the decision is decentralised, the alternative consequences made known and discussed and in some way the expectant mothers' valuation assessed. But this is to stray from the original argument which laid considerable stress on what cost benefit and cost effectiveness analysis could achieve.

Next we reach the proposition that the Federal budget itself should be broken down into a hierarchy of expenditure categories each related to one discrete activity. Every activity that was delineated and separately costed ought to be aimed at achieving a measurable goal, for example, raising reading standards, reducing delinquency or speeding traffic flow. This would make cost effectiveness work possible.

When were these systematic analyses to be applied? The only regular assessment of resource priorities takes place within the annual budget cycle both in the preparation of the President's budget within government and in the discussion of it within Congress. Systematic analysis must therefore be applied as part of the budget round. However, the traditional process had major drawbacks. First, the President's budget was only concerned with expenditure covering the next financial year. This was far too short a period within which to seek to undertake strategic planning. New weapons systems had to be chosen far in advance of the period during which they would be operational. Small scale expenditure next year could entail vast sums five years hence. Within a constrained budget this would mean abandoning other projects in five years time or not completing the weapons system you had begun to install. It was necessary to foresee that eventuality. If this were true of military planning it applied equally to the rest of the Federal budget, not least to areas of social policy. Hence budgets should, in future, cover at least a five-year period.

Who was to ensure that this happened? The authors were quite explicit that these changes could only be undertaken if there were greater centralisation within each agency.

Indeed, as we shall see one of the aims of the Bureau of the Budget in extending programme budgeting was to strengthen Departmental heads' control over their agencies—many of which were seen to be virtually autonomous, and to tighten the Bureau's, and hence the President's control over Departments. The budget was the only instrument capable of doing this.

At the end of the day, then, what emerged was a proposal for a budget reform. It was by no means the first or the last of its kind.

The first stage of budget reform in the US had come with the Budget and Accounting Act of 1921. The aim was to create a reliable system of expenditure accounts, and to give the President control of the budget and of agencies' applications to Congress. The Bureau of the Budget was created and situated within the Treasury. The General Accounting Office was also set up. It was, in British terms a Gladstonian reform, concerned to ensure that money was not wasted or dishonestly used—the financial control function of a Budget.

In 1939 the Bureau of the Budget moved to the Executive Office of the President and became more concerned with management efficiency. Ten years later the Hoover Commission had recommended that the Federal Budget be presented in terms of functions, activities and projects, supported by information about accomplishments. They called this 'performance budgeting'. It could be seen as an attempt to give the budget a managerial function. The reformers saw these latest proposals as adding a strategic planning function to the budget.

At this stage it is worth examining the foregoing propositions as they stand before we begin discussing what happened to them in practice. What are we to make, first of all, of the assumptions with which the argument began, namely that government is necessarily inefficient?

So Inefficient?

This is not the place to enter into a discussion of whether what are now called social services ought to be provided by the private sector. We shall sub-optimise and assume that they are appropriately provided by some organ of government. Is it the case that they are not subject to any economising incentives? Those working for local authorities who are continually being bombarded by demands to economise both from the politicians, the local press and ratepayers organisations, as well as by central government, may wonder somewhat at this statement. It can indeed be countered by considering the political process by which budget allocations are made. Instead of a 'jungle of competing interests' the process can be seen as a political market place in which there is also an 'unseen hand' at work. While it is undoubtedly true that a wide range of interest groups, professional bodies, trade unions, client groups and cause groups are all at work bidding for extra funds, and while it is also true that spending departments and agencies have a vested interest in their own growth, there are also politicians with a vested interest in keeping taxation to an absolute minimum. There is, moreover, the Treasurer's department, the Treasury or the Office of Management and Budget whose role is to be the advocate of economy. Within a constrained budget, if one agency or department 'gets away with it' to an excessive degree other participants in the struggle get less. There is therefore an incentive for all spending ministers or agency heads to ensure that the rules of the game are kept. The more economy minded a department appears to be the better its relations may be with the finance ministry or Treasury. The more constrained the budget—the less growth there is from year to year—the more powerful such competition will be. Clearly the extent to which the Treasury or its equivalent win out will depend not only on the political climate but upon the economic situation and the buoyancy of tax revenue.

The same political market model provides us with another insight into the accusation that agencies or interest groups only talk in terms of absolute levels of need and requirements unaffected by the relative cost of their proposals. If any one such statement or calculation is viewed as the final word on the matter then the criticism is valid.[8] If, however, such a statement as 'we need half a million teachers to reduce class sizes to a maximum of 30' is taken as the opening bid in a competition for resources with other claimants, then it assumes different proportions.

So long as cost consequences are attached different measures and conceptions of need made by different groups of participants are essential if the political resource market is to work properly. Individuals and groups may want to make different 'trade offs' between one view of need and its relative importance compared to the 'need' for another policy. Bradshaw[9] has argued that although need is a normative concept and there are different approaches to measuring it, where these overlap or agree we can be sure there is something for administrators to fasten upon. This may be so, in the sense that if there is widespread agreement that view may carry political weight. But it could well be that agreement amongst numerous experts is not a good guide to political weight. Take 'family poverty' as an example. Numerous experts may agree about subsistence measures—an appropriate dietary and calorific intake that can be obtained from a given income, its historical antecedents, and its appropriateness in comparison with other countries. But another 'expert' may argue that all of these views are wrong and that the only morally justifiable measure to take is one related to average earnings. It will produce a quite different result but its political weight may be greater. So the absolute needs or requirements approach can be seen to be less naive than it seems if it is viewed as part of a political bargaining process.

Politics also help us to view differently the third criticism we mentioned—the view that governments rarely look or plan ahead. It would be more accurate to say that there are both political incentives and disincentives for government departments and local authorities to undertake long term planning. In pursuing the politics of planning a little further it may help to distinguish four different types of planning that will be useful as descriptive categories in later chapters.

Kinds of planning

As a starting point we shall take *planning* to mean 'an attempt to determine policies that relate to some future time period'.

It is certainly true that planning is time consuming and expensive. It has political costs too. It usually means that difficult choices have to be made earlier than otherwise would be necessary. It is natural for politicians to put off choices in the hope that they will resolve themselves in time. Moreover, plans and forecasts are frequently proved wrong. If the plans are published they may provide ammunition for an opposition party or rival agency. It is clear then that if planning is to take place there must be some political incentives in its favour. It would seem that there are in theory several that can be distinguished. The first two come about through a combination of technical necessity and political advantage—capital planning and manpower planning.

Capital planning first and foremost requires a whole train of decisions to be made well in advance of the time when buildings will actually be needed. If an urban authority like the Inner London Education Authority is to build any schools at all it must begin collecting together the plots of land which it will require to make up a site, seven to ten years in advance. Merely to buy plots and obtain planning permission on the off chance that they might be needed would not only be extremely costly. it would also be highly unpopular with other users—private and public. Land use and building plans in their turn require strategic planning. The authority has to have a fairly clear idea of the likely demand for school places area by area ten years hence, and if the authority also has a clear political intention to which it has publicly pledged itself, going comprehensive in this case, then that policy must be made to bite at the initial planning stage or it will never be attained at all. In exactly the same way if the central government has a clear political pledge to redeem— replacing Victorian primary schools—that too must be made effective at this point. Here we see political commitments and technical considerations combining to force fairly long term planning. Exactly the same kind of factors apply with hospital building, or the provision of old people's homes.

Closely linked to capital planning is *manpower planning*. It takes three years or more to train a teacher, seven or more to train a doctor and two or more to train a social worker. The period of training must be added to the time needed to increase the available building capacity before any impact at all is felt from a decision to expand the supply. Conversely a decision taken now to expand, say teacher supply, based on the existing position in schools could be wholly inappropriate in ten years time when new recruits are entering the schools. Population changes, up or down, prompt attempts at manpower planning. Professional organisations are particularly concerned to see that there will not be an 'over supply' in the future, by which they mean a tendency for their relative salary levels to fall.

On the other hand professional and other staff form the major resource input to the social services, so any policy a government may have for extending a service or changing its emphasis will affect demands for manpower.

The technical need to undertake capital planning or manpower planning may come to dominate other attempts by a social service agency to plan ahead but a third important incentive is the political pressure to contain the level of taxation. Just because policy decisions in the social services have such long term consequences on public expenditure, that part of government and those politicians who are anxious to contain or reduce tax levels will also be anxious to get spending departments to produce a statement of the long-term effect that any new proposal will have on expenditure and therefore on taxation. We can call the resultant activities *tax control planning* which is closely associated with *economic planning*.

Fourthly, impetus to planning can arise from outside government altogether. The external stimulus may be a crisis or an issue which assumes major political importance. For a government department *not* to be seen to be planning or producing a long-term policy carries political costs. The perceived shortage of places in higher education in the early sixties is an example. This might be called *responsive planning*. Kahn lists some of the factors which may initiate an attempt to plan.

'Planning begins with a problem, a widely felt need, major dissatisfaction, or crisis. Or it begins with a transfer of power and the decisions of new leadership to systematise their activities. Or it begins with urgent need to allocate scarce resources or personnel. Or it begins with a demand from a source of funds or of power that planning be done to qualify for continued subsidy. Or it begins with the access to considerable new resources (from unprecedented growth or the assignment of revenues from new sources, for example). Or, finally, it is undertaken because "everyone is doing it".'[10]

Each of these different kinds of planning are undertaken as part of an organisation's formal activities. It would be wrong to suppose that formal planning activities are the only ones in which government agencies indulge. Those working for an agency will often develop a consensus on which aspect of its activities needs attention next and where the service in question could be expanded or developed. We shall call this activity *promotional planning*. It is the least discussed but probably the most important. Organisations usually seek to expand their activities and powers. The phrase promotional planning is used here to mean the process by which agencies look ahead and make contingency plans for growth, plans which will enable them to take advantage of the political climate when it becomes favourable to that agency or department and the interests it serves. By no means all departments are as skilled at this as others.

We can see, therefore, that the political market offers, first of all, a competitive bargaining situation which does provide incentives for economy and some of the same conditions as a free market. Such a market also provides a forum in which different perceptions of need by different participants can be forced to stand the test of political debate, interdepartmental rivalry and Treasury scrutiny. Finally, there are political and technical incentives which force agencies to take long term perspectives despite pressures not to do so.

Objectives or Increments?

The proposals that had been made to increase efficiency in government, both by Simon, advocates of systematic analysis and later exponents of managerial methods, all begin, it will be recalled, with the proposition that government agencies must determine explicitly what their objectives are and distinguish these *ends* from the *means* of achieving them. Economists tend to say that inputs must be distinguished from outputs. This approach has had numerous critics but it has nowhere been more rigorously attacked than by the American author Lindblom, in his, by now, well-known advocacy of the 'science of muddling through'.[11]

The first characteristic injunction to the policy analyst or strategic planner is to clarify the values and objectives implicit in different policies or programmes before seeking to analyse them. Nonsense, says Lindblom, any programme, and it could be added any social service programme in particular, will be viewed differently by the various groups involved.

A housing redevelopment scheme will be seen differently by those on the council's waiting list, by those owner occupiers in the area, by tenants in the area, by tenants and owners in adjacent areas affected by the scheme, by amenity groups concerned with aesthetics, by the authority's architects who have their professional reputations to make and by local councillors who have their seats to save. Whose interests, whose objectives and which values is the administrator or analyst to take to be the most important? How are they to be measured one against another? If this proves difficult in the case of a simple housing development what price housing policy as a whole?[12] This is of fundamental importance because it means that even if some abstract ranking of objectives or 'needs' by some committee of 'experts' is invented, it has no general validity unless it commands widespread agreement amongst all these competing interests.[13]

Lindblom then turns the original position on its head and claims that you can only tell what a government's objectives are by examining in retrospect the policy choices it has actually made. 'I can only know what I believe by examining what I do'—to use the philosophical analogy.

'Except roughly and vaguely I know of no way to describe—or even to understand—what my relative evaluations are for, say freedom and security, speed and accuracy in governmental decisions or low taxes and better schools than to describe my preferences among specific policy choices that might be made between the alternatives in each of the pairs'.[14]

In order to ensure that all these contrasting values and objectives are taken into account and weighed, he argues, we can only rely on the normal pluralist political process. Every value stance neglected by one policy-making agency will be the concern of at least one other agency. Every important interest or value has its watch-dog or if it has not it should rapidly seek to train one.

'In the United States, for example, no part of government attempts a comprehensive overview of policy on income distribution. A policy nevertheless evolves, and one responding to a wide variety of interests. A process of mutual adjustment among farm groups, labor unions, municipalities and school boards, tax authorities, and government agencies with responsibilities in the fields of housing, health, highways, national parks, fire, and police accomplishes a distribution of income, in which particular income problems neglected at one point in the decision processes become central at another point.'[15]

In the same way Lindblom rejects the notion that analysts should seek to distinguish means from ends. Precisely because the ends of a particular policy may be in dispute, groups pressing for change do not seek to agree about ultimate objectives, which would destroy the political consensus on that issue, but to concentrate on the agreed *means* to different ends. This is frequently the situation where social policy is concerned. The recent campaign to extend nursery education is a good example. There were clearly a great many different motives behind that movement. There was the desire of a great many mothers for a bit of peace and quiet or the opportunity to go to work, the belief that education during this period was crucial to their children's intellectual and social development, the desire to give children from deprived homes a 'fairer start' in life, the pressure to employ more teachers in a slackening labour market for teachers and so on. In meetings concerned with pressing for an expansion of nursery provision there was no better way of bringing the whole activity to a halt than to ask what the objective was. The suggestion that pre-school provision should be designed to permit mothers to go out to work was enough to bring angry responses from the most ardent campaigners. Yet on the immediate aim a considerable degree of consensus was possible. *The 'means' was the only 'end' on which agreement was possible.*

Lindblom's conclusion is that the *only* test of a good policy is agreement—not that it is consistent with some abstract objective.

The second characteristic injunction which he challenges is 'be comprehensive', consider all the alternatives. He elaborates his objection to this in the book he wrote with Braybrooke *A Strategy for Decision*.[16] No one can comply with this injunction unless he postulates a single welfare function. What policy makers actually use, he claimed, was the practice he called 'disjointed incrementalism'.

That is to say they make small changes about which they have considerable understanding, ignoring most alternatives as impracticable. Even so they recognise there will be unanticipated consequences they would have avoided if they could have foreseen them and which if they monitor they can correct. As an example he cites the gradual liberalisation of the United States social security programme.

The idea is further developed in his later book where he argues that it is wrong to suppose that coordination is best achieved by some central body overseeing the actions of different agencies or ministries.[17] 'People can coordinate with each other without anyone's coordinating them, without a dominant common purpose, and without rules that fully prescribe their relations to each other,'[18]— a process he calls 'partisan mutual adjustment'.

When someone is crossing the road they do not have a clear plan of how they will avoid all the pedestrians coming the opposite way. What they do is to continually change course if they find someone is coming towards them. In the same way one agency may have different aims and values from another but it will still take account of other actions or proposals in making its own. The Appropriations Committee procedure in Congress is an example. One committee responds to what another has done and makes allowances for what another may do. This is equally, if not more, rational than some central agency trying to agree on some overriding strategy which corresponds to an interpretation of 'national interest' on which no one can agree. On the contrary the virtue of the American system lies in the multiplicity of agencies concerned. Where policy making is centralised those responsible for coordinating policy are inevitably found to *over* simplify just to be able to grapple at all with the issues they must decide. If decisions have to be made centrally planners will probably *not* use highly complex methods in order to take account of all the possible important consequences. The central administrator will instead be tempted to use arbitrary or indeed *no* method at all and not publish or give any account of the way he had reached his decisions.

What is more social cohesion is more likely to be promoted through a pluralist system than with central coordination. Where agreement has to be sought and attained before decisions can be made the pressures produce a degree of consensus and the public debate that is involved is a unifying force. If centralised decisions on resource allocation are imposed they merely breed resentment and dissension.

Taken together these arguments present a model for resource allocation very different from the preceding one. Though the model was designed to describe policy making in general it may be argued that it is particularly well suited to social policy where fact and value are so interwoven.

Who Carries Out the Orders?

So far we have been concerned with the difficulties social service organisations might encounter in seeking to formulate agreed goals or objectives. Other considerations may lead us to question whether even when such attempts succeed they can be made operative throughout the service delivery system. In the first place there are general arguments derived from organisation theory which suggest that in any organisation its formal goals are modified by informal procedures which are heavily influenced by the personal goals of officials. While this is a general proposition that may be said to hold for all organisations it is especially true of public bodies where there is no market discipline or easy criteria of success in the organisation's terms which will hold those lower down the bureaucratic hierarchy to the goals formulated at the top. Both Tullock and Downs have extended this argument. Tullock árgues that in any hierarchical system 'messages' are cumulatively distorted. The more vaguely defined the functions and the more difficult its outputs are to measure the greater the 'leakage'.[19] Downs emphasises that the particular perspectives and the self interest of bureau officials or civil servants will introduce biases into the transmission of information to their superiors or other parts of the agency—biases towards particular policies or practices or in the budget recommendations they make.[20] This is not to say that all public officials show equal concern for their own survival or advancement. Downs distinguishes five types: the 'climbers' who are primarily motivated by personal goals of advancement, the 'conservers' who are motivated by the desire to stay put and have a quiet life, the 'zealots' with a commitment to the narrow or immediate policies of the agency, the 'advocates' who are loyal to its broad goals and seek power in those terms, while there are, finally, a rare breed of 'statesmen' who concern themselves with societal goals. Nevertheless in public institutions 'a very significant proportion of all the activity being carried out is completely unrelated to the bureau's formal goals, or even to the goals of its topmost officials'.[21] In short, although a particular policy may be chosen because its declared objectives fit in well with a department's overall strategy its implementation may turn out to have quite different effects, which cannot then be altered because entrenched interests have been established and for usual reasons of administrative inertia.

These are general limitations which apply to the pursuit of formal goals within institutions, but in two particular respects the difficulties presented by the social services are even greater. The first lies in the importance of the professional worker who is the major 'factor of production' and whose very professional status provides him or her with a third set of goals or values distinct from both the bureaucratic and the narrow self interested ones. Even more crucial is the general consensus, perhaps more strongly held in the British public service than the American, that the professions, in their day to day dealings with clients, pupils or patients, ought to be the final arbiter of the values, purposes and priorities inherent in their activity. This view

lies behind the stress on clinical freedom and the teacher's right
to teach how and what he or she considers appropriate. Thus any
attempt to set goals or objectives which conflict with professional
norms, or an individual's appreciation of what those norms ought
to be, will be resisted. Moreover, they can be resisted not merely at
the level of the professional organisations, but also by the teacher in
her classroom or the general practitioner in his consulting room.
Tentative steps by the Ministry of Education in Britain over a decade
ago to merely study aspects of school curricula were stamped upon
by the teaching profession. An important safeguard to our individual
liberty may be seen to rest in the fact that relative valuations of the
worth of saving one kind of person's life as opposed to another are
not made by politicians or a central authority but by individual
doctors. An important safeguard to free personal expression may be
seen to rest in the liberty of the teaching profession to teach what it
thinks fit. There is certainly no universal agreement on either point
but in so far as these views are generally held the pursuit of wider
societal interests can be seen to favour maximising the discretion
exercised by the individual professional in the field.

The second and related difficulty is that often legal and political
responsibility is divided between two or more levels of government,
local and central or Federal, state and local. Again the prevailing
values inhibit detailed intervention by the centre in the way social
service resources are actually distributed at local level. There is therefore little point in central departments making detailed or systematic
analyses of the use to which funds are put even assuming they were
permitted to do so.

Both factors may be summed up by saying that prevailing values
often conflict with the notion that the level of government which
provides the funds ought to have any detailed say in the way they
are used.

So much, for the moment, for the initial premises on which the
systems analysts based their set of proposals. Even if we dismiss the
problems that have been raised so far there is still the concept of
sub-optimising to be considered.

Sub-optimising?

It will be recalled that the essence of this approach was to break
down major resource allocation decisions into a logical series of
smaller discrete problems each of which was susceptible to analysis.
An extension of the approach was to break down the budget into a
logical hierarchy of programmes, between which trade offs could be
made. It is crucial to the logic that such programmes represent
identifiable activities each of which contribute to and only contribute
to one other superior objective. The further real life departs from
that model the more complicated and unworkable it becomes. Let
us assume that sub-programmes (i) and (ii) in Figure 1 not only

contribute to (*c*) but also have different impacts on various programmes coming under the general headings of I, III and IV as well
as ultimately affecting II. This would involve not only seeking to
measure the impact (i) and (ii) had on these other programmes but
assessing the relative importance of such increments to the output
of I, III and IV. Yet the argument began with the assumption that
such comparisons were essentially political. Therefore, a lot turns
on how far social service activities can in fact be broken down into
discrete activities with single outputs and without large and un-
measurable 'spillovers' into the other programmes. This in turn
depends upon what Simon called their 'technology'.[. . .] Let us
for the moment asume that they can be overcome. The second
question is how do we know when the process of sub-optimising has
been well or badly done? To this there is, apparently, no theoretical
answer. It depends upon analysts' 'experience', 'intuition', 'inspira-
tion', 'judgement', 'common sense'. A set of qualities which sound
remarkably like those possessed by the gifted 'greats' scholar of old,
what Vickers called 'appreciation' of a problem.[22]

Finally, and quite apart from the technical problems to be encountered in any actual analysis, there is the objection which political
scientists have made that, so far from making political choices more
explicit, highly complicated cost benefit studies tend to hide within
them all kinds of implicit value judgements and give a spurious
objectivity to the course of action that is judged economically
preferable.[23] Economists criticise the use of the word 'need' as an
excuse for special pleading which hides value judgements, but exactly
the same can apply to cost benefit analysis. Both have a part to play
in an open political process where implicit value assumptions can be
forced into the open.

An Imperfect Political Market

Taken together these propositions present a formidable counter to
the idealised model for allocating resources advanced at the beginning
of this chapter. The first seeks to approximate public sector allocations to an economic market, the second relies on a political market.
Yet, those who would rely exclusively on a pluralist political process
do so very largely because of the virtues they see in the *process* without judging the outcomes of that process in policy terms. They are
primarily concerned with the achievement of consensus.

Just as the free market theorists have argued that competition
between the self interest of indviduals will produce an efficient distribution of resources, so pluralist theories assume that free competition between group interests will produce an efficient distribution of
public services. Yet, just as there are imperfections in the private
market, it can be argued, there are parallel imperfections in the
political market.

The political market is just as likely to ignore or at least not give full weight to certain social costs. A large mining corporation or property developers are well placed to mirror, in political power, the commercial power they wield in the economic market. Beside them small scattered voluntary amenity societies may not get very far. Or where they do amenity groups may themselves reflect only one group of interests in the community. Hence the importance of agencies whose role it is to work for other community interests, to analyse and quantify the impact of mining operations or redevelopment on all sections of the community. The potential supply of oil, the profitability of the scheme and much other information will be available to the oil company. At least as competent analytical resources are needed to identify the social costs.

Politically unacceptable degrees of income inequality that are seen to endanger the long term security of the society present difficulties for free market economists. So they do for the parallel political theorist. Poor people cannot work the interest group system as well as the better organised and wealthier sections of the population. The rationale behind, or at least the rhetoric that accompanies, the extension of social service provision is very often in terms of distributional justice. In practice extensions have often benefited the articulate and the rich —those who might be expected to benefit under the private market in any case. It may be that the rhetoric has, indeed, been no more than that. But it is also possible that politicians have often been misled by inadequate information about who was benefiting most from certain social programmes and tax arrangements. There is at least some indication that this has been the case in both Britain and America. If a government wishes to see redistribution of income take place in any direction, it must monitor the impact of its policies to this end.

In brief then, there is no reason to suppose that competition between existing interest groups will of itself produce an outcome that takes account of the full range of community interests.

Specifically this means:

(i) That there must be a substantial input of information and analysis into public debate and decision making which is not tied to particular interest groups. The analytical staffs in government can therefore act as efficiency advocates or 'public interest partisans' who can tackle what Self has called 'higher level problems'.[24]

(ii) That information brings power and should be seen as a way of strengthening weak interests and supporting those individuals, like heads of Departments, who have to make choices between the competing demands.

These might be said to constitute the beginnings of a pluralist planning model. It accepts that the planner cannot have a dominant or decisive a role, that the options he considers and the information system he seeks to create will reflect a variety of political values but unless the politician understands what is actually happening to the resources deployed in his name he cannot translate his values into a consistent set of decisions.

Participants in the decision process must have some knowledge of the social production functions that translate program specifications (inputs) into program consequences (outputs). Otherwise the advocacy and bargaining process cannot produce a meaningful translation of political values into specific decisions.[25]

Incremental change is as dependent on understanding the consequences of the previous increments of change unlike a more Utopian planning model. The objective is thus to sharpen and improve political debate not to stifle it in some managerial consensus.

The most frustrating part of public life is not the ability to convince others of the merits of a cherished project or policy. Rather it is the endless hours spent on policy discussions in which the irrelevant issues have separated from the relevant, in which ascertainable facts and relationships have not been investigated but are the subject of heated debate, in which the consideration of alternatives is impossible because only one proposal has been developed, and, above all, discussions in which nobility of aim is presumed to determine effectiveness of program. There are enough real value conflicts, institutional rigidities, and scarcities of information in the way of effective government action. Let us not add a massive additional obstacle by assuming that complex values can be effectively translated into necessarily complex programmes by nothing more than spirited debate.[26]

Schultze is here arguing for greater knowledge and greater explicitness but *within* an essentially pluralist system. He also argued later in his book for *decentralisation* in decision making. He was not optimistic about the capacity of centrally controlled management systems to produce results decreed by political heads of agencies. There were too many opportunities for slippage down the chain of command, especially in a country as large and diverse as the States. Instead he argued that relevant positive financial inducements were more effective. It was at least as important to avoid 'negative' financial inducements. (Grant structures or salary structures which may be detrimental to particular policies.) In this way detailed administrative controls from the centre could be relaxed, local officials or professionals could be left to make their own individual or local assessments of particular cases, in the knowledge that the overall outcome would tend to produce the kind of results the central government desires.

One example of the positive inducement principle in America is the health maintenance organisation. This is an organisation which agrees to provide a member with a comprehensive range of medical care in return for a fixed premium. It is argued that this is more efficient than a fee for services basis or the separate public funding of hospitals or family doctor services, which encourage excessive doctoring, rising fees and encourage patients to opt for more expensive forms of care. The HMOs are meant to reduce costs of medical care first because a patient goes on paying—or the State does—

through Medicare or Medicaid, whether he is ill or not. Hence the HMO has an incentive to utilise preventive medicine, and to attempt early diagnosis.

If this provides an example of positive financial inducements as a way of rationing resources, an example of a counterproductive inducement can be found in the finance of medical care in Great Britain. The division between central finance of institutional care and the local finance of community care discourages local authorities from expanding what is often supposed to be the cheapest as well as the more humane form of care for many mental patients and geriatric cases.

This, then, is the compromise position occupied by this particular prescriptive model. It accepts, from a realistic assessment of the American situation, that the political process has many centres of power and influence. It can, however, be improved by the injection of information and analysis at every point. The central decision makers in the allocation process should be particularly well equipped with information and analytical staffs. They are, however, only advocates along with all the other participants. Central management is likely to be ineffective unless supported by a system of financial inducements to local government which is consistent with the central department's view of resource priorities.

Once again this model gives little attention to the importance of the professional in the delivery of many public services especially those we normally call social services.

Rationing Processes

The concept which seems most helpful in seeking to understand the way social services are allocated is that which we briefly introduced in the last chapter—rationing. The word carries rather pejorative overtones. For some it raises memories of the second world war and austerity. Some economists see it as an authoritarian alternative to the perfections of a free market and some social administrators view it as a description of the way in which clients are denied their rights. Rationing is usually seen as a negative procedure. Yet it is more appropriately envisaged as a two-way process. Professional workers and other participants seek to regulate the demands made upon their limited resources in various ways, but they also seek to obtain more resources for the task in hand. For example, in 1960 the Ministry of Education imposed a ban on further provision of nursery school places. The ban was only partially raised in the mid-1960s for special categories of children. Thus local authorities were forced to adopt traditional rationing procedures. Waiting lists grew for nursery places, but for the most part headmistresses were given a free hand in operating these and quite frequently the criterion of first come first served was applied. The consequence was that competition for places often resulted in the most informed, active and educated mothers gaining places for their children while those children in greatest social and educational need failed to gain places. Social attitudes to the family and women's role began to change, economic and social pressures on married women and the increased professional attention devoted to the pre-school years combined to make both teachers' organisations and local authorities increasingly perturbed by the rationing process which they were called upon to administer. The pressures on the Department of Education and its pressure on the Treasury and the Cabinet finally broke this very explicit restriction. The fact that success was achieved largely because of the fortuitous decline in the birth rate after 1964 does not alter the basic point that one layer in the political or administrative hierarchy may be enforcing restraint on those layers below it while at the same time seeking to press its demands for resources on those above.

The participants are reacting upon one another in a continuous chain of events, but it is useful to categorise the locus and nature of resource allocation decisions using four distinguishing dimensions.

Central-peripheral.

Resource decisions which affect the social services extend from those taken in full Cabinet about the overall level of public expenditure all the way through interdepartmental bargaining in Whitehall and inter-committee bargaining in County Halls to decisions taken by a receptionist in an area office of a social service department. At each stage constraints are imposed on the level below.

Explicit-unrecognized.

It is important to seek to find out how far priorities are determined in an explicit way and how far they have emerged entirely unrecognised. An explicit resource allocation decision may be said to be one which is premeditated or planned, one in which an attempt is made to distinguish who is or has been receiving what resources, and one in which the outcome of the plans or policies are examined or evaluated in some way.

Open-closed.

The fact that resources are allocated in an explicit way does not necessarily mean that the knowledge on which decisions are taken are published or open to public debate. The more information on which decisions are based is published and the earlier in the decision process this happens the more open the allocation.

Technical-political.

It is also helpful to ask how far resource choices are made on technical or professional grounds and how far they are left to the inter-play of political pressures. This is a notably difficult thing to do but it is often possible to trace shifts along this dimension over a period of time. Take as an example the allocation of pupils between secondary schools in Inner London. At one time this was done on the basis of tests and head teachers' individual professional judgements. Later when the responsibility for choice was transferred to area offices criteria were drawn up in order of importance and were discussed by a subcommittee of councillors eventually becoming the subject of considerable public debate. They were altered in response to public pressure. This represents a shift towards the political end of the dimension.

While none of these dimensions are easy to measure or be precise about they do help to distinguish how the nature of allocation decisions may change over time or differ between countries.

Parker[27] has described some of the ways in which administrators and professionals at the periphery cope with demands on their time or resources. He categorised the following: deterrence, eligibility rules, deflection from one agency to another, delay, client ignorance, and dilution of professional 'standards'.

The practice of deterrence through 'less eligibility' is of course a classic example of a rationing device. As administered under the 1834 Poor Law Amendment Act it was a centrally promoted and explicit device for reducing the burden on ratepayers. It was interpreted with varying degrees of rigour at local level. The same device is still used in the administration of 'Part III' accommodation for the homeless. Until 'King Hill' and the publicity which surrounded it, central government showed no interest in the means by which welfare departments sought to keep demands on such accommodation within bounds.[28] The use of old workhouse accommodation, the separation of husband and wife and the harsh regulations within the hostels were all deterrent rationing devices operated at a local level, though probably not explicitly seen this way by elected representatives and only dimly perceived as such by many of those concerned.

As a rationing device it took place at the periphery, was unrecognised, closed and technical. It became somewhat more a matter of central concern, that was more clearly recognised, slightly more open in that a little more information has emerged about it, and more political.

The stigma which attaches to some services, notably in health and social work, is a common deterrent to their use. Attempts deliberately to stigmatise services may be rare in an explicit way today. Much more often professionals or administrators may tacitly avoid taking active steps to remove the stigma that surrounds that service in the knowledge that to do so would put an unmanageable strain upon it. The same considerations apply when it comes to advertising. 'The idea of a campaign to "sell" a particular service is not always welcome: understandably so, for it might prove impossible to cope with any sudden increase in demand without a simultaneous increase in resources. Such reluctance to advertise a service fully is often justified by the comfortable assumption that those *really* in need will find out about the service soon enough.'[29] This is a very apt description of the attitude adopted by the National Assistance Board in the 1950s and early sixties.

In the same way eligibility or entitlement to a service or benefit can be determined entirely at a professional level. A consultant may decide that priority use of a kidney machine will be given to young men with a family rather than elderly spinsters. Such resource allocation decisions may be largely unrecognised outside the profession and unchallenged politically because of conventions about clinical freedom.

At the other extreme eligibility rules may be determined entirely by central regulations laid down by Parliament as with National Insurance. Supplementary benefits are an example of combination of statutory regulations, a central code of practice which is unpublished and scope for officers' discretion in individual cases.

Again explicit rules of varying secrecy may be locally administered but subject to some central government pressure. The Cullingworth report on council house allocation procedures represents an excellent example of the delicate balance of responsibility in this field.[30] It also shows how one of the most common rationing devices—delay—has in the case of council housing excluded some of the groups in greatest housing need.

So it is possible to see most of the devices operating at any point between the professionals' contact with the client, right the way through to the central department.

It has been the task of academic social administrators to make explicit the unrecognised consequences of many of these practices but it is only relatively recently that government began to recognise the need for greater explicitness.

The apex of the system—the central government's control of public expenditure decisions—is a logical and natural place to begin to understand that rationing process. It is this point in the process which this study seeks to illuminate.

Often advocates of systematic analysis and managerial methods at least sound as if they are advocating more 'technical' and less 'political' choices, hence the hostile reaction of many political scientists. They also seem to favour more centralised decision-taking and indeed not to appreciate the importance of the periphery in the allocation process. They clearly favour explicit rather than unrecognised processes, while the muddling-through school of thought at times seems to make a virtue of the extent to which participants cannot recognise what they are doing. Finally, the managerial method, especially in the hands of the British civil service, appears to make a virtue of secrecy. The pluralist planning model stresses the virtues of open, political and explicit choices, with the periphery responding to appropriate incentives.

References

1. Simon, H. A., *Administrative Behaviour* (1st Edition 1945, Second Edition 1957) Collier Macmillan, Toronto (see Ch. IX).
2. Hitch, C. J., and McKean, R. M., *The Economics of Defense in the Nuclear Age*, Harvard University Press, Cambridge, Mass., 1961.
3. McKean, R. M., *Efficiency in Government and the Use of Systems Analysis*, John Wiley, New York, 1958.
4. Hitch and McKean, op. cit., p. 129 (1965 edition).
5. See the chapter on programme budgeting for health in Novick, D., *Program Budgeting*, Harvard University Press, Cambridge, Mass., 1965.
6. The example is taken from : Klarman, H. E., *et al.* 'Cost effectiveness analysis applied to the treatment of chronic renal disease', *Medical Care*, Vol. 6, 1968.
7. Mishan, E. J., *Cost Benefit Analysis*, George Allen & Unwin, London, 1972 (see chapters 22-3).
8. See the argument in Culyer, A. J., Lavers, R. J., and Williams, A., 'Health Indicators' in *Social Indicators and Social Policy*, ed. Shonfield, A., and Shaw, S., Heinemann, London, 1972.
9. Bradshaw, J., 'A Taxonomy of Need' in G. Maclaghlan, *Problems and Progress in Medical Care*, Oxford University Press, 1972.
10. Kahn, A. J., *Theory and Practice of Social Planning*, Russell Sage Foundation, New York, 1969, p. 12.
11. Lindblom, C. 'The Science of Muddling Through', *Public Adminsitration Review*, Spring, 1959.
12. Ferris, J., *Participation in Urban Planning: the Barnsbury Case*, Occasional Papers on Social Adminsitration, Bell, London, 1972.
13. See for example the proposed index of health needs in Culyer, A. J., Lavers, R. J., Williams, A., op. cit.
14. *Public Adminsitration Review*, Spring, 1959, p. 82.
15. Ibid., p. 85.
16. Braybrooke, D., Lindblom, C., *A Strategy for Decision*, Free Press, New York, 1963.
17. Lindblom, C., *The Intelligence of Democracy*, Free Press, New York, 1963.
18. Ibid., p. 3.
19. Tullock, G., *The Politics of Bureaucracy*. Public Affairs Press, Washington, D.C. 1965.
20. Downs, A., *Inside Bureaucracy*, Little, Brown and Co., Boston, 1967.
21. Ibid., p. 136.
22. Vickers, G., *The Art of Judgment: Policy making as a Mental Skill*, Chapman and Hall, London, 1965.
23. See for example, Self, P., *Administrative Theories and Politics*, George Allen & Unwin, London, 1972, p. 44.
24. Self, P., 'Is Comprehensive Planning Possible and Rational?', *Policy and Politics*, Vol. 2, No. 3, 1974.
25. Schultze, C. L., *The Politics and Economics of Public Spending*, Brookings Institution, Washington, 1968, p. 56.
26. Ibid., pp. 75-6.
27. Parker, R., 'Social Adminstration and Scarcity: the Problem of Rationing', *Social Work*, April, 1967.
28. Radford, J. 'From King Hill to the Squatting Association' in *Community Action*, ed. A. Lapping, Fabian Society, London, 1970. King Hill was the Kent County Council Hostel that was the subject of a protest movement 1965-6. Ministry of Health Circular 20/66, Home Office Circular 178/66, Ministry of Housing and Local Government Circular 58/66.
29. Parker, op. cit.
30. Ninth Report of the Housing Management subcommittee of the Central Housing Advisory Committee, 'Council Housing, Purposes, Procedures, and Priorities', Ministry of Housing and Local Government, London, 1969.

3

Competition in the Wholesale Supply of Petrol

by Monopolies Commission

---

1. Between 1953 (when Government price controls on petrol ended) and 1974 petrol prices in the United Kingdom, both at wholesale and retail levels, were more stable than in the years after 1974 and price competition was less vigorous. The 1965 Report noted the existence of a number of low-price wholesalers (such as Jet Petroleum and Isherwoods Petrol) whose policy was to set scheduled wholesale prices at a margin below those of their larger competitors. During the period up to 1974, however, the scheduled wholesale prices of most of the large suppliers moved broadly in parallel, with SMBP* most frequently being the initiator of price changes. Competition between the majors for the business of independent dealers was primarily in the level of solus rebate off scheduled wholesale price and in the offer of low interest loans and other financial assistance.

2. While price competition was much less evident before 1974 than after it, competition between wholesalers on matters other than price was probably more active before 1974 than afterwards. The major suppliers made considerable use of advertising to promote their brands of petrol and to emphasise the differences between their brands and those of competing suppliers. These efforts to associate brands of petrol with some aspect of technical superiority were greatly weakened in 1971 when it became mandatory to sell petrol by the 'star' octane grading (for which a British Standard had been introduced in 1967). Since then the petrol supplied, grade for grade, has for all practical purposes been an homogeneous product and has been so regarded by the majority of consumers.

3. The increase in price competition following 1974 reflected two sets of factors: the long-term developments in the petrol supply industry which were a source of increased competitive pressure throughout the 1960s and 1970s, and the particular factors which caused the sudden intensification of price competition after 1974.

*Shell Mex British Petroleum [Ed. note].
From *Report on Supply of Petrol in the U.K.* by Wholesale Monopolies Commission, (Cmnd 7433, 1979, HMSO), pp. 20–5. Reprinted by permission of the Controller of Her Majesty's Stationery Office.

Long-term changes in the petrol market which have increased price competition

4. The most significant change in the structure of the United Kingdom petrol wholesaling industry has been the fall in seller concentration since 1964 which was the result of the entry of new suppliers and the more rapid rate of growth of smaller suppliers than that of the largest suppliers. New entrants to the United Kingdom retail market since 1964 include the refining wholesalers Burmah, ICI, Elf and Chevron and a number of independent wholesalers without any refining facilities. The market share by gallonage of the largest suppliers (Shell, BP, Texaco (previously Regent), Esso and Mobil) was reduced from 89.4 per cent in 1964 to 78.1 per cent in 1970 and 69.7 per cent in 1977. [. . .] This loss in market share by the established majors was primarily to major oil companies which have entered the United Kingdom petrol market since 1960 (the 'new majors'). Prominent amongst these new majors in gaining market share were Total, Burmah, Conoco, Elf and Gulf.

5. The entry of new suppliers to the United Kingdom petrol market and their subsequent expansion were important in stimulating price competition. The nature of this stimulus varied with the different pricing policies adopted by the new entrants. The new majors adopted in the main scheduled prices similar to those of the established majors, but increased price competition mainly through the offer of larger solus rebates. Other wholesalers entering the United Kingdom petrol market competed in price principally by setting their scheduled wholesale prices below those of the major suppliers. Prominent among the low-priced wholesalers were ICI and some of the regionally-based independent wholesaling companies with no direct interest in refining. Many of the earlier of these independent wholesalers such as Curfew, Gainsborough, Isherwoods and Major were acquired by new majors seeking entry to the United Kingdom market and some went out of business during the 1973–74 oil crisis but other independent wholesalers have entered the petrol industry since 1970. The market share of the wholesalers without refining capacity in the United Kingdom or elsewhere [. . .], rose from 2.4 per cent to 4.3 per cent between 1970 and 1975, but declined to 3.9 per cent in 1977.

6. For two reasons many motorists tended to give increasingly more weight to the price of petrol than to other factors when selecting brand of petrol and retail outlet. The first was the introduction of the selling of petrol by star grading (see paragraph 2). The second was the rapid rise in petrol prices in relation to other prices during the 1970s (a rise which accelerated rapidly between 1973 and 1976, following the increased price of crude oil and increases in the tax and duty on petrol). Increased awareness of petrol prices at different outlets has recently been accentuated by the recent statutory requirement that retailers must prominently display pump prices. It may also have been increased by the marked decline in the offer of trading

stamps by filling stations, itself a consequence of the increased responsiveness of many motorists to offers of direct price reductions. The increased awareness of retail prices by many motorists and their increased responsiveness to differences in prices at different outlets had the effect of stimulating competition in price both by retailers and also by wholesalers of petrol.

7. Price cutting by retailers was encouraged by the desire of many retailers to increase the volume of their sales. The number of stations with sales of 500,000 gallons of petrol or more increased from 787 in 1970 to 1,886 in 1977 [. . .] while the total number of petrol stations fell from 33,772 to 28,640 over this period. The building of larger petrol stations encouraged price competition. The operators of these stations considered that they had to cut margins in order to build up throughput, and the operators of many smaller stations found themselves forced to follow. Retail price competition was also stimulated by the growth of chain retailers and the entry into petrol retailing of supermarket/hypermarket companies. By virtue of the volume of their purchases these large retailers have been attractive customers and have therefore been able to obtain favourable rebates from petrol wholesalers. At the same time some of these retailers adopted a low margin pricing policy.

Special factors leading to the 'price wars' of 1975–78

8. The process of gradual change in the structure of petrol supply in the United Kingdom which resulted in a steady increase in price competition during the latter 1960s and early 1970s at both wholesale and retail levels, was upset by the oil crisis which followed the 1973 Arab–Israeli war. Between June 1973 and the latter part of 1974 the shortage of petroleum products, Government allocation of petrol supplies and the fixing by Government of wholesale and retail prices for petrol had the effect of virtually ending price competition.

9. After 1973 the sharp increase in crude oil prices[1] together with the world-wide industrial recession caused a decline in the demand for petroleum products and consequent excess capacity in refineries. [. . .] A similar situation developed in other European countries. The increase in excess capacity at refineries stimulated competition in the supply of petroleum products. Price increases and the economic recession reduced United Kingdom consumption of petrol although by a smaller proportion than the reduction in the consumption of some other petroleum products. The sharp drop in the demand by the petrochemical industry for naphtha led to increased conversion of naphtha into petrol. This had the effect of further increasing competition in the supply of petrol.

[1] In £ sterling, the increase in the price of Arabian light crude FOB Persian Gulf between August 1973 and November 1974 was over 340 per cent.

10. At the retail level competitive price reductions and increased offers of trading stamps were made by retailers attempting to maintain sales volume by reducing retail margins. Retail price competition was further encouraged by the rise in the rate of VAT on petrol in November 1974 from 10 to 25 per cent which meant that an increased proportion of any price cut made by the retailer would be financed from a reduction in the amount of VAT payable. The Price Commission found that while petrol retailers' net margins increased between 1973 and 1974, between 1974 and 1975 there was a sharp fall.[2] Retail price cutting was often led by large retailers with multiple outlets and high-volume stations which received the larger rebates and were willing to operate on a low retail margin.

11. At the wholesale level, price cutting below the scheduled wholesale prices of the majors was encouraged by the surplus of petrol throughout Western Europe. Low prices on the Rotterdam market relative to the United Kingdom majors' scheduled prices encouraged established independent petrol wholesalers in the United Kingdom to import petrol from the Continent and to reduce the proportion of their requirements supplied by United Kingdom refiners on period contracts. New importing wholesalers were also attracted and the recession in organic chemicals also encouraged ICI to increase its output and sales of petrol.

12. Towards the end of 1974 increased prices for crude made it necessary for the oil companies to seek increased prices for petroleum products. Under pressure from HM Government, the companies agreed to load a disproportionate part of the cost increase on to petrol rather than spread the increased costs equally over all petroleum products. There was thus a sharp increase in United Kingdom petrol prices in December 1974 which increased the profitability of importing petrol from the Continent for wholesale distribution in the United Kingdom.

13. In response to these developments the refining wholesalers took steps to help their retailers to meet the keener competition. They increased rebates in new solus contracts and introduced rebates or rent reductions for many tenants and licensees of company owned stations. A greater disparity of scheduled wholesale prices also developed. In some market areas, however, the most important form of response was the introduction of temporary discounts and other forms of financial assistance to certain retailers, commonly known as 'selective price support'.

14. The decision of the refining wholesalers to respond to competition by giving temporary discounts of different amounts to certain retailers rather than by reducing scheduled prices reflected mainly the uneven geographic spread of the price competition and the uneven

---

[2] Between summer 1974 and February 1975 forecourt net profit margin as a percentage of turnover fell from 3.5 to 2.7 and a further sharp reduction was forecast between February and the summer of 1975 (Price Commission Motor Fuel Retailers' Margins Final Report 1975, page 13).

vulnerability of individual outlets to competition within the affected areas. Price competition was most intense in the marketing areas of low-price wholesalers and retailers. Therefore it would have been an excessively costly method of meeting competition for the major wholesalers to reduce net wholesale prices to all retailers throughout the country, or to reduce prices to all retailers within given areas. Selective support also had the advantage of greater flexibility than adjustments in scheduled wholesale prices. It could be changed to deal with shifts in the intensity and location of price competition. Moreover it could be withdrawn at the discretion of the companies whereas scheduled wholesale prices could be increased only with the approval of the Price Commission.

The development of the 'price wars' 1975–1978

15. Towards the end of 1974 and during the early part of 1975 the factors referred to in paragraphs 8–12 combined to increase price competition at wholesale and retail levels. The degree of price competition varied across the country, being most intense in the North of England which was the marketing area of ICI, several low-price independent wholesalers and a number of low-price retailers.[3]

16. Selective support schemes were introduced in February 1975 by some of the 'new majors', followed between March and July by most of the other refining wholesalers, SMBP and Esso were the last refining wholesalers to introduce selective support, but, having lost sales volume and under pressure from their retailers, Esso introduced special support in August 1975 and SMBP in September 1975 [. . .]. The various schemes were initially restricted to the most competitive areas, primarily in the North of England and the Midlands,

---

[3] To study in some detail price competition in particular localities, we sent questionnaires to petrol retailers in the Wakefield (West Yorkshire) and Sevenoaks (Kent) local authority areas requesting information on the buying and selling prices of petrol in February and June/July 1977 and whether or not the retailer was receiving selective support. Not all retailers replied to the questionnaire and in a number of cases the replies are believed to be inaccurate. Because of these deficiencies of the survey it was not possible to make detailed comparison of the results from the two areas, nor was it possible to draw any precise conclusions concerning the relationship between rebates and size of outlet or the differential treatment of different categories of outlet. However, we noted that wholesaler representation differed markedly between the two areas: the four largest suppliers supplied nearly two-thirds by number of the stations surveyed in Sevenoaks and only about one-third of the stations surveyed in the Wakefield area. Small low-price wholesalers were of much greater significance in the Wakefield area than in the Sevenoaks area. Company ownership was higher in the Wakefield area than in the Sevenoaks area. Both areas were within inner zones and both had easy access to coastal storage terminals. The difference in the intensity of competition between the two areas was reflected in the retail prices for petrol in the two areas (which were, on average, about 5 pence lower per gallon in Wakefield than in Sevenoaks in February 1977 and nearly 3 pence lower in Wakefield in June/July 1977) and in the more widespread selective support in the Wakefield than in the Sevenoaks area.

but during the summer price competition became more intense and more widespread. By October 1975 about half of aggregate petrol sales by all refining wholesalers was subject to some form of selective support. However, towards the end of 1975 most of the major suppliers withdrew selective support following increases in the price of crude oil and a depreciation of the £ sterling. SMBP, Esso and Texaco withdrew selective support on 31 October 1975 though some smaller wholealers continued to support price cutting by retailers.

17. Between November 1975 and January 1976 the market shares of the major suppliers which had withdrawn price support fell sharply. On 21 January Esso, followed by Shell, BP, Texaco and Mobil, reintroduced selective schemes to support price cutting by retailers. During this second period the level of selective support, both in the form of additional discounts per gallon and of assistance with increased offers of trading stamps, was higher and the area covered by the schemes was wider than in the first period. Seven major wholesalers informed us of the proportion of their gallonage sales to retailers which were subject to selective support during this period; this varied from 55 per cent to 80 per cent. By April 1976, however, sterling prices for spot cargoes on the Rotterdam market had risen (partly as a result of a fall in the exchange value of the £) and competitive pressures on the majors were reduced. Shell announced that it was ending its selective support scheme on 30 April. Esso, BP and Mobil quickly followed Shell and later in May they were followed by most of the other refining wholesalers.

18. Price competition, though less intense during the summer of 1976, was still strong. Some wholesalers did not withdraw support completely, while others reintroduced it during the summer. On 21 June Shell launched a new scheme of financial support for selected stations. Following increases in scheduled wholesale prices in July 1976, selective price support increased and was reintroduced during the following period by all the companies which had withdrawn it. The support schemes introduced during the summer of 1976 were more carefully adapted to individual circumstances than those which had operated earilier in the year. The Shell and Esso schemes in particular aimed at concentrating support on individual stations within the most highly competitive areas.

19. During 1977 the geographical coverage of price support increased. Major factors were the rise in the value of the £ sterling against the US dollar and the desire of some major suppliers to recoup lost market share. In July 1977 Shell cut its scheduled wholesale price for four star petrol (inner zone) from 16.08 pence per litre to 15.49 pence per litre. At the same time, Shell reduced the selective support given to outlets in the highly competitive areas, so that whilst net wholesale prices to those outlets were little changed, the net wholesale prices to all other Shell outlets were reduced by

the full amount of the cut. Only a few refining wholesalers followed Shell in reducing their published wholesale prices but in effect all refining wholesalers fell into line, since those wholesalers which maintained their scheduled prices gave an additional discount to all their customers approximately equal in amount to the price cut.

4

The Economic Impact of North Sea Oil

(i) Recruitment and the Labour Market

by M. Gaskin and D. I. Mackay

This chapter analyses the nature of the labour force recruited to oil and gas-related activities, a question on which there has been considerable speculation but so far little empirical evidence. The discussion relates to firms wholly engaged in North Sea oil and gas activities, for whom employment is heavily concentrated in the Grampian and the Highland Regions and the Islands.[1] The reason for this is that those concerns in which only a part of the labour force is engaged in oil-related work are largely in manufacturing industry and are heavily concentrated in Central Scotland, especially in the Strathclyde Region. The labour involved has seldom been specially recruited and its occupational characteristics and area of recruitment will not differ significantly from those of the total work force of these firms.

In contrast, recruitment by firms wholly engaged in oil-related activities has frequently created a demand for a quite new range of skills and, in view of the location of these activities outside the industrialised and urbanised Central Belt, has required a different geographical pattern of recruitment. Moreover, [. . .] the scale of employment in relation to the size of the labour market, is much greater in the Grampian and Highland Regions, and might therefore be expected to have an impact on the labour supply situation facing indigenous firms. These issues are considered in three sections: the first analyses the employment characteristics of firms in production platform construction; the second looks at this in relation to other oil-related activities; and the third examines wage movements in Grampian Region firms which are not engaged in oil-related activities.

Employment in production platform construction

We have singled out this sector of employment for particular examination for a number of reasons. First, production platform fabrication is the single most important source of employment among the activities

From *The Economic Impact of North Sea Oil on Scotland* (HMSO, 1978), pp. 35–42. Reprinted by permission of the Controller of Her Majesty's Stationery Office.
[1] At April 1976 these areas accounted for two-thirds of employment in companies 'wholly related to the offshore oil industries'. [. . .]

associated with North Sea oil and gas. Thus, in June 1976, employment in platform construction and other on-site activities in Scotland was 10,380 out of a total employment in wholly related companies estimated at 25,900. In addition, there is a substantial number of jobs in module construction which, operationally speaking, is directly related to platform fabrication. Second, production platform fabrication, which is a part of oilfield development, requires the concentration of very large labour forces, in contrast to the activities associated with the exploration and production phases of offshore oil and gas where employment is characterised by relatively small employing units, or in the case of larger companies, by a fragmented labour force working in different localities and with differing functions. In short, the production platform industry, at least superficially, most closely resembles the traditional, large-scale industrial plant, although as we shall see shortly it may come closer to some construction industry operations. Third, locational factors result in a situation in which platform yards dominate certain areas; this is particularly true of the sites in the Highland Region and it has important implications for the operation of labour markets and for the provision of necessary infrastructure. Fourth, employment in platform construction activity is particularly vulnerable to fluctuations and the long-run prospects for the industry look distinctly unfavourable. Factors three and four combine to present a major social and economic problem for the future—the dependence of some small and remote communities on one activity, which dominates the labour market and for which no replacement as a large employer may be available. [...]

At the present time there are five platform fabrication units in operation in Scotland. Taking them in the order in which they commenced production, they are: Highlands Fabricators (HF) at Nigg Bay, Cromarty Firth; McDermotts (McD), Ardersier, near Inverness; Redpath Dorman Long (RDL), Methil, Fife; McAlpines (McA) at Ardyne Point on Loch Striven, in the Strathclyde Region; and Howard Doris (HD), Loch Kishorn, in Wester Ross. In order to assess the implications of the labour employing activities of these units for the communities concerned we concentrate on analysing the nature of the labour force recruited—by sex distribution, marital and family status, area of origin, previous industry, and so on. Above all, we are concerned to establish the extent to which the labour force has been locally recruited, as this will help to establish the extent of social and economic impact on local communities both in the present and, should employment subsequently decline, in the future.

The data for the first three platform constructors were assembled in autumn 1974 by which time the labour force could be said to have 'stabilised': for example, the labour force employed at HF had fallen from its peak of 3,300 in June 1974, when it included a substantial number of employees recruited on a temporary basis, to a level of

2,500 at which it has remained over most of the subsequent period. Discussions with the companies involved confirmed that there has been no appreciable shift in the general characteristics of the labour forces over this subsequent period. Data for McA and HD relate to March 1976.

Males dominate the labour force for each yard accounting for the following percentages of total employment: HF, 92 per cent; McD, 97 per cent; RDL, 94 per cent; McA, 99.6 per cent; HD, 97.0 per cent. In view of this the following analysis relates to males only. When the labour force is recruited from a nearby urban area, as is the case with McA, or contains a high proportion of migrant labour, as is the case with HD, the sex composition of the labour force may have little impact on the local labour market. This is because the labour mobility involved does not carry with it a substantial permanent redistribution of population. The same is not true where the labour force is resident locally, in a region with a relatively restricted labour market. In the case of HF and McD, for example, the creation of large, male-dominated labour forces, resident locally, carries the risk of unbalancing the labour market by producing a relative shortage of female employment; this is especially likely if the labour force has a 'normal' composition in terms of marital and family status.

The information on these latter points suggests that the labour employed in platform fabrication is not notably distinctive, although there are some distinctions worth remarking. First, the age composition of the labour force varies as among the three yards in the Highland Region (HF, McD, HD), the yards in the more remote locations having a high proportion of the younger age groups. If we take those aged 39 years or less as a proportion of the total male labour force the position was as follows: HF, 62.5 per cent; McD, 64.8 per cent; HD, 62.8 per cent; and these compared with 52.2 per cent at McA and 48.0 per cent at RDL. The apparent explanation is that the three Highland Region yards have depended to a greater degree on long-distance in-migration, or long-distance commuting, to establish a labour force, whereas McA and RDL (particularly the latter) have drawn on an established labour force largely resident in a nearby urban area. Where the recruitment net has been cast more widely a higher proportion of the labour force has been drawn from the younger age groups; in consequence, in such areas the age structure of the labour force is likely to differ markedly from that of the local labour force. For example, in the former Easter Ross sub-region, males aged 15 to 39 accounted for only 33.1 per cent of the total male population aged 15 and over in 1971, whereas the proportion for HF (of males under 39, in 1974) was 62.5 per cent.

In view of the high proportion of younger men in the Highland Region yards, it might be expected that a relatively low proportion of the labour force would consist of married men. In fact the opposite holds true. Married men account for 60.3 per cent, 76.2 per cent and 61.4 per cent of the labour forces of HF, McD and HD respectively. In HF, for instance, the marital rate for each age group up to and including those aged 35–39 is substantially higher than that for Easter Ross males in the same age group. The contrast is even more marked for McD reflecting a recruitment policy which has always aimed at establishing a stable, long-service labour force. The establishment of these two large labour forces, with high proportions of young, married men, has significant implications for future population changes in the areas affected—for example, their school populations are likely to increase over the period immediately ahead. The same considerations do not apply to HD where much of the labour lives on site, away from their families, or where, as in the cases of RDL and McA, labour is recruited from established urban communities.

Table 1 shows the distribution of the labour force by place of birth and location of previous employment. Data on the former are only available for HF and McD.

The evidence suggests that each of the platform yards has a labour force dominated by native Scots and that recruitment has been heavily concentrated in labour markets within travelling distance of the yards. However, HD relies heavily on labour recruited over a wide area of the Highlands and Islands and has constructed a residential camp which houses the greater part of its workforce. Again, the apparent similarity between HF and McD is somewhat misleading. McD with a location close to Inverness, and able to draw on a fairly substantial labour market within reasonable commuting distance, has drawn three-quarters of its labour force from its immediate surrounding area. In contrast, HF has recruited more widely within the Highlands and Islands, drawing some 14 per cent of its employees from the Western Isles, Sutherland and Caithness, locations at a substantial distance from the employing unit. These more dispersed recruitment patterns of HF and HD reflect the more remote locations of their sites. Finally, RDL and McA have recruited, like McD, within a relatively localised area, the former drawing mainly from Fife and Edinburgh and the latter from its hinterland in Argyll and, most of all, from Glasgow and the Ayrshire coast.

These varying recruitment patterns can have important economic implications. Thus, the labour forces of McD, RDL and McA have been mainly recruited from narrow areas, and a fall in employment in these yards would have correspondingly concentrated effects. The same would be true of HF, since though it initially recruited more widely, permanent in-migration to the locality has produced an effective concentration of the workforce. The position of the fifth Scottish yard, HD, is different in that the adverse effects of a fall in employment would be spread through a wide number of Highland and Island communities.

In each of the yards, employees have been drawn from a wide range of industries, but it would be wrong to conclude that the industrial composition of the available labour supply is unimportant in determining recruitment. In fact, recruitment has drawn heavily from certain industries in which skills or working conditions produce

Table 1
Distribution by place of birth and location of previous employment

	Place of birth		Location of previous employment				
	HF	McD	HF	McD	RDL	McA	HD
Highlands and Islands	63.9	58.4	73.5	79.8	2.0	17.5	67.2
Rest of Scotland	23.5	26.7	17.3	12.3	85.4	74.1	19.0
England and Wales	10.1	12.2	8.6	6.6	10.3	8.0	13.0
Rest of World	2.5	2.7	0.5	1.3	2.2	0.4	0.7

Note: Percentages are of the total employees for whom the relevant data were
available. Place of previous employment is not known for a high proportion of those employed by McA and HD, but this is not believed to
impart any substantial bias to the results. As noted in the text, figures for
HF, RDL and McD relate to September 1974, those for McA and HD
to March 1976.

a labour force which transfers readily to platform construction. The
industrial composition of recruitment for each yard is shown in
Table 2, with details of the SIC Orders where these account for more
than 5 per cent of total recruitment in any of the yards.

Table 2
Industrial composition of recruitment

per cent

SIC Order		HF	McD	RDL	McA	HD
Primary Industry	1,2	7.4	6.4	0.4	1.9	2.8
Food, Drink and Tobacco	3	3.3	7.9	1.4	1.4	1.9
Metal Manufacture	6	4.1	1.3	8.8	3.6	0.3
Mechanical Engineering	7	3.8	10.5	40.1	4.5	1.0
Shipbuilding	10	1.1	0.5	8.1	1.7	1.0
Construction	20	44.8	34.5	12.7	73.4	76.0
Transport and Communications	22	3.8	5.7	2.7	4.1	3.9
Public Administration and Defence	27	7.4	11.8	3.8	1.7	0.2

Note: Figures are percentages of total workforces.

RDL has recruited a large proportion of its labour force from the
metal using industries and from shipbuilding—industries which would
appear to provide a range of skills appropriate to the construction of
steel platforms. However, the lack of such skills in a locality is clearly
not an insuperable handicap—witness the relative unimportance of
such recruitment for HF and McD, both steel platform yards. Both
these companies show a very dispersed pattern of recruitment,
industrially speaking, and indeed the distribution of recruitment by
industry is very similar to the industrial composition of employment
in the local labour markets. The exceptions are that McD drew a

relatively high proportion of its recruits from mechanical engineering, and both McD and HF drew heavily, absolutely and relatively, on labour from the construction industry. Predictably, this dependence on construction labour is even more marked in the case of McA and HD, both concrete platform yards, where three in four of all employees were previously employed in construction work. In the case of McA a substantial proportion of the labour force had been transferred direct to the yard from McA's construction labour force previously engaged in building the Inverkip power station.

We can sum up by drawing some tentative conclusions from these recruitment patterns. Thus, the experience of RDL suggests that where a steel platform fabricating firm can recruit labour with experience of the metal working and engineering trades it will show a strong preference for such labour. Where it is also drawing on labour in an established manufacturing area it may increase significantly the competition for labour within a narrow and important sector of the labour market. Indeed, in the case of RDL, and excluding employees transferred within the organisation, more than one in three of its workers were drawn from only nine outside firms. The experience of the other yards suggests that where a unit fabricates platforms, concrete or steel, in an area with little employment in metal using trades, it will draw heavily on the construction industry, particularly so in the case of concrete. This is hardly surprising in the case of the concrete yards, but in the steel yards some explanation is required. It could be that the site conditions of the yards—the nature of the work, the conditions in which it is performed (largely in the open air) and the variability of the work load—closely resemble those prevailing in the construction industry, and that the latter industry contains a high proportion of younger men who transfer readily to such employment. In any event, the establishment of platform yards in these circumstances carries the risk that its pattern of recruitment will impede the provision of infrastructure within the region affected, unless measures are taken to increase the supply of construction labour.

Employment in other oil-related activities

It is not possible to describe in detail the nature of the wide range of employment associated with exploring for, producing and processing North Sea oil and gas. Both space and resources dictate a more limited approach. Here, we attempt to provide a view of the differing composition of the labour forces attached to different functions of the oil and gas industries. The analysis of employment in production platform construction has shown a heavy reliance on labour drawn from the construction industry and a marked tendency to draw the great bulk of the labour force from the working population adjacent to the site itself. However, production platform fabrication is more or less unique in its locational and labour requirements: most oil and gas-related activities require labour forces of a very different character.

We can illustrate this through a survey of the male labour force employed by ten firms located in the Aberdeen area and accounting, in Spring 1976, for a male employment of some 1,750. These firms provided access to their personnel records, and these have been used to analyse the male labour force, in respect of age, marital status and geographical origins. The results are shown in Table 3. For the purpose of the analysis, the data have been grouped by operational functions since it is these, rather than the identity of the employing unit, which are influential in determining the characteristics of the labour force. Five functional groups have been distinguished: exploration and drilling; supply boats and helicopters; administration; manufacturing; and production platform operation. For each function we show the distribution of the labour force by (a) age, (b) marital status, (c) residence on application for employment, and (d) place of birth. The numbers covered in each functional group, shown in the bottom row of each table, vary through (a) to (d) because of a fluctuating 'not known' category. However, except with place of birth the number of this category is generally small.

The first thing to notice is that those functions involving work offshore employ relatively few people in the older age groups: only one in five males employed in exploration and drilling and on production platforms is aged 40 years or more. In the other offshore activity, supply boats and helicopters, about one in every four males is in this age group, and the ratio rises to one in three for the largely land-based function of administration and manufacturing. Offshore activities, therefore, are very much the province of younger males, offering limited employment opportunities for males in their 50s and 60s. Rather surprisingly, at least at first sight, the differing age structure of offshore and onshore activities is not reflected in a differing composition of marital status. Manufacturing and exploration and drilling have a relatively low proportion of married males, and the highest proportion of married males is found amongst production platform crews. The latter fact is probably a consequence of the long-run stability of employment, offered by production platform operations, which could be expected to appeal particularly to married men.

The most noticeable differences, and the most important differences viewed from the economic standpoint, arise in the geographical composition of the labour forces attached to the different functions. The area of recruitment evidently varies from function to function. Thus, manufacturing concerns associated with North Sea oil and gas appear to have recruited the great bulk of their employees from within the locality: no less than nine out of ten were resident in Aberdeen and district when they applied for work, and although the information on place of birth is much more limited, it does imply a predominantly local labour force. In contrast, less than one in five of the production platform crews were recruited within Aberdeen City and its environs, and almost two-thirds were previously resident outside Scotland. Of course, at the time of the survey, the recruitment of production platform crews was in its early stages and this must preclude any strong conclusions from these figures. Nevertheless there is one feature of them that enjoins caution in the inference drawn from the 'residence on application' figures. In the case of production platform crews comparison of this characteristic with place of birth suggests that a non-negligible proportion of the group covered in this survey was recruited from Scots returning to Scotland to take up work. Indeed, return migration seems to be a feature associated with *all* the functions surveyed, since the proportion born in the rest of Scotland outside Aberdeen is always substantially higher than the proportion whose residence on application was in this area.

More generally, it is evident that, of the functional groups, only manufacturing resembles production platform fabrication in drawing heavily on the local labour force. In the other four functions, local recruitment always accounts for less than one-half of all employment and, in each case there is significant recruitment from outside Scotland. Supply boats and helicopters, administration and production platform crews all draw quite heavily from other areas of the UK, and exploration and drilling appears to have the most 'international' labour force, measured either by residence on application or by place of birth.

For these four functions, the impact of recruitment on the local labour market will be different from that either of production platform fabrication or manufacturing. In the latter cases, recruitment has a pronounced local bias and the recruitment of a largely Scottish labour force will have an immediate effect on the labour market (e.g. leading to a direct reduction in unemployment) and a continuing effect on income levels through the increase in income and consumption within Scotland. For exploration and drilling, supply boats and helicopters, administration, and production platform crews, a given level of recruitment will have less direct impact on, say, the Scottish level of unemployment, given the tendency to recruit from a wider geographical area. However, unemployment will be reduced indirectly to the extent that the additional incomes created are spent within Scotland. Yet, the regional multiplier is not high, certainly not greater than two and in some cases much lower since only a small part of any increase in incomes will have an impact on the Scottish economy. It is clear that much of the labour force recruited for the exploration phase has not resulted in any permanent in-migration to the east coast ports which serve as the land bases for the activity. The general pattern of work on rigs, two weeks on and two weeks off, has meant that men recruited outside of Scotland have tended to return to their home bases for leave. Again many of the skilled workers on the rigs (e.g. toolpushers) are foreign nationals

Table 3

Analysis of male labour force in ten oil-related firms in Aberdeen

	Exploration and drilling	Supply boats and helicopters	Administration	Manufacturing	Production platforms	All function groups
Distribution by age				*per cent*		
Aged 29 or less	41.6	22.5	32.0	38.8	28.4	
30–39	36.0	49.9	30.0	23.3	52.1	
40–49	16.4	23.5	26.4	17.8	16.0	
50–59	5.8	3.7	10.0	15.5	3.6	
60 or more	—	0.4	1.6	4.6	—	
				number		
Total covered in group	291	485	250	219	505	1,750
Distribution by marital status				*per cent*		
Married (and other)	72.0	83.4	82.9	73.6	86.5	
Single	28.0	16.0	17.1	26.4	13.5	
				number		
Total covered in group	296	481	251	227	513	1,768
Distribution by area of residence on application				*per cent*		
Local area	43.7	35.7	39.1	92.3	8.2	
Rest of Scotland	11.6	22.8	6.7	5.9	28.8	
Rest of UK	14.8	38.1	30.7	1.4	41.1	
Rest of World	30.0	3.4	23.5	0.5	21.9	
				number		
Total covered in group	277	473	238	221	219	1,428

Distribution by place of birth				*per cent*		
Local area	21.4	26.4	34.4	76.2	12.2	
Rest of Scotland	25.5	29.0	21.9	9.5	41.4	
Rest of UK	20.4	38.3	28.1	7.1	38.1	
Rest of World	32.7	6.3	15.6	7.1	8.5	
				number		
Total covered in group	196	269	192	42	181	880

who may never be resident in Scotland, their only contact being at an airport in transit. The same situation arises with the crews of the laybarges working on the pipelines off Peterhead and Shetland. Most of these barges are foreign owned and are largely crewed by foreign nationals: for example, the ETPM 160 which worked off Peterhead and is French owned had a complement of 380 men, most of whom came from Djibouti, whilst even the Viking Piper barge, which worked on the Ninian Pipeline and is partly British owned, had a mainly Spanish crew.

The same pattern of specialised recruitment is shown by the supply boat operators. Most of the crews were previously employed in the Merchant Navy or in offshore servicing and tend to retain their homes in the areas out of which they previously operated, for example the Home Counties or Great Yarmouth. Most firms insist on their recruits having a seagoing ticket which restricts the impact on the local labour market, though some of the unemployment caused by the recession in the fishing industry has been mopped up.

Although activity offshore has been largely concentrated in the exploration phase to date, it is unlikely that the increasing importance of production will have significantly different implications in terms of direct labour market impact. The skills required of production platform crews are of a highly specialised nature and, hence, the area of recruitment is likely to be wide in geographical terms. The immediate impact on the local labour market may not be significantly different from that experienced during exploration and drilling. However, there is one important difference—the continuity of employment offered to production platform crews as opposed to the short-term nature of employment in exploration and drilling. This fact seems likely to result in permanent in-migration in a fashion never necessary during the exploration stage, as residence adjacent to the site of a permanent production platform will yield significant economic benefits. Originally, British Petroleum applied a rule that production platform crews must live within a 70 mile radius of Aberdeen and, although other firms have not applied a similar measure, permanent in-migration is still likely to result. Hence, a given volume of employment and income generated for production platform crews is likely to have more substantial secondary effects on the Scottish economy than the same level of income and employment generated in, say, exploration and drilling.

Impact on the labour market

As we have seen, the employment arising from North Sea oil activities has a geographical distribution very different from that of Scotland's economically active population. Most communities in Scotland have been little affected by North Sea developments in the past and will be little affected in the future. However, for some communities, especially those on the eastern seaboard of North-East Scotland, and in the Highlands and the Islands, the impact of oil has dominated all other economic changes in the 1970s. This has carried with it both advantages and disadvantages. In the short-run, the creation of additional income and employment has led to difficulties in providing necessary social services and infrastructure. In the longer-term, there is at least a danger, implicitly present in much of this discussion, that the introduction of sizeable amounts of high-paid employment might adversely affect the long-run viability of established, indigenous industry. Up to now, little evidence has been presented to allow the evaluation of this possibility, but the following section provides information on one important aspect of the debate—the movement of wage levels in indigenous industry in the Grampian Region.

The data are taken from a postal questionnaire carried out in each quarter (April, July, October and January) over 1974–76. The inquiry was based on a classified random sample of all firms operating in the area of North-East Scotland now contained in the Grampian Region. The survey included questions on the level and skill composition of employment; the number, earnings and hours worked by male and female manual employees; and labour turnover, recruitment and shortages. The initial questionnaire (in April 1974) was completed by 126 firms and each survey obtained a response from more than 100 firms. However, to maintain consistency, we analyse below the questionnaires completed by those 90 firms which co-operated in each of the quarterly surveys over the period April 1974– April 1976. At April 1976 these firms employed 11,448 males and 5,974 females, giving total employment of 17,422 about one-tenth of the Grampian Region's employed labour force over 1974–76.

It proved impossible to obtain information on wage earnings from a significant section of those companies directly engaged in, or closely associated with, North Sea oil and gas activities. Hence, the following analysis is based almost exclusively on companies established in the Grampian Region before the onset of oil and gas. This does have the merit, however, of gauging the levels and movement in the wage levels of indigenous concerns operating within the geographical area which has the most important concentration of oil-related employment.

Table 4 shows gross and standard weekly earnings for male and female manual employees over each quarter April 1974–April 1976. Gross weekly earnings measure all payments, including overtime payments. Overtime earnings may show substantial variation over the short-term, since adjustment of the number of hours worked is usually the most immediate response to a change in the demand for labour. Hence, changes in gross weekly earnings are quite a sensitive indicator of the pressure of labour demand, particularly in male-dominated industries.[2] For example, a rapid rise in gross weekly

---

[2] As Table 4 indicates, there is little difference between gross and standard weekly earnings for females.

Table 4

Quarterly labour market survey: Grampian Region

£

	1974			1975				1976	
	April	July	October	January	April	July	October	January	April
Gross weekly earnings: males									
Manufacturing	36.1	39.0	41.5	45.7	45.3	49.3	50.2	49.9	54.2
Construction	37.7	47.1	49.2	46.6	55.6	63.0	59.9	49.3	57.1
Services	30.4	30.9	36.4	37.7	39.0	42.2	46.4	44.6	48.1
Allied Industries	35.6	38.3	41.6	43.8	45.6	49.5	51.1	48.9	53.1
Standard weekly earnings: males									
Manufacturing	28.9	30.3	31.9	37.4	37.9	40.5	40.5	41.4	43.9
Construction	28.8	34.2	37.3	38.1	43.2	50.4	47.5	43.9	46.1
Services	26.6	26.7	30.0	34.1	34.4	35.3	38.3	40.2	41.6
Allied Industries	29.0	30.0	32.5	36.6	38.0	40.6	41.3	42.1	43.7
Gross weekly earnings: females									
Manufacturing	21.3	22.6	25.4	27.8	28.1	28.9	32.1	33.0	33.1
Construction	—	—	—	—	—	—	—	—	—
Services	20.5	20.9	22.6	25.7	27.2	29.9	30.9	36.3	34.1
Allied Industries	21.0	22.1	24.5	26.9	27.8	29.1	31.3	34.1	33.6
Standard weekly earnings: females									
Manufacturing	20.2	21.3	24.1	26.7	27.4	28.1	31.3	32.5	32.1
Construction	—	—	—	—	—	—	—	—	—
Services	20.1	20.7	21.9	24.9	26.6	28.9	29.0	33.7	32.7
Allied Industries	20.1	21.0	23.4	25.9	27.1	28.2	30.0	32.7	32.5

earnings usually reflects an increase in labour demand, where the labour supply, measured in terms of the *number* of persons of the required skill available, is not very elastic. In these circumstances, labour supply can be augmented by increasing the number of hours worked and this will then be accompanied by further increases in gross earnings as employers compete for the scarce labour supply by raising bonus earnings etc. Short-term movements in gross weekly earnings are, thus, a useful barometer of the degree of competition faced in the labour market.

For other purposes, standard weekly earnings may be more informative. As the earnings returns relate to a particular week in each quarter,[3] and as the amount of overtime can vary significantly over the short-run, a measure of gross weekly earnings may not be representative of long-run changes in the wage structure. A change in gross weekly earnings may simply disclose a transient situation caused by variations in overtime working. In measuring secular trends, therefore, changes in standard weekly earnings are generally more informative. Together, measurements in gross and standard weekly earnings provide a reasonably comprehensive picture of developments in the wage structure.

Some conclusions emerge clearly from Table 4. Over the period, female earnings (gross and standard) advanced more quickly than male earnings, but for both sexes the similarities across industrial groups are more obvious than the differences—a fact which is perhaps unsurprising in a period of such rapid inflation. However, male wage movements in the construction industry do stand somewhat apart from the rest, showing more seasonal and cyclical fluctuation and a stronger upward trend over the two-year period. The labour market pressure on the industry is reflected in a rapid increase in gross weekly earnings over 1974, a relapse with the seasonal downturn in January 1975, a further sharp spurt in earnings to the summer (July) of 1975, another seasonal relapse and, again, a recovery from the January 1976 low. Clearly, in the summer of 1974, in the spring-autumn of 1975 and, possibly, again from spring 1976, competition for construction labour was fierce and earnings rose sharply in consequence. In the longer term, too, this has had some effect as male standard weekly earnings, excluding overtime, rose by 60 per cent in the construction industry over April 1974–April 1976, compared with an increase of 50 per cent for all industries.

The data allow some comparison of wage movements between indigenous North-East firms and Scottish and British/UK averages. Table 5 summarises the available information. The April data for Scotland and Great Britain are derived entirely from the *New Earnings Survey* (analysed in *Scottish Economic Bulletin*, No. 9, Winter 1976) and the October data for Scotland and the UK from the *Department of Employment Gazette.*[4] The basis of the calculation

---

[3] National data are usually collected on the same basis.
[4] At the time of writing the 1976 data for Scotland and the UK were not available.

Table 5
Comparative weekly earnings: Scotland, Great Britain and Grampian Region

	April 1974	April 1975
Average gross weekly earnings, full-time adult males	£	£
(1) Scotland	42.9	56.7
(2) Great Britain	43.6	55.7
(3) Grampian Region	35.6	45.6
	%	%
(4) (3) as % of (1)	83.0	80.4
(5) (3) as % of (2)	81.7	81.9
Average standard weekly earnings, full-time adult males	£	£
(1) Scotland	35.7	47.8
(2) Great Britain	36.6	47.7
(3) Grampian Region	29.0	38.0
	%	%
(4) (3) as % of (1)	81.2	79.5
(5) (3) as % of (2)	79.2	79.9
	October 1974	October 1975
Average gross weekly earnings, adult male manual employees	£	£
(1) Scotland	48.4	60.7
(2) United Kingdom	48.6	59.6
(3) Grampian Region	41.6	51.1
	%	%
(4) (3) as % of (1)	86.0	84.2
(5) (3) as % of (2)	85.6	85.7
Average standard weekly earnings, adult male manual employees[a]	£	£
(1) Scotland	40.7	53.3
(2) United Kingdom	40.8	52.5
(3) Grampian Region	32.5	41.3
	%	%
(4) (3) as % of (1)	79.9	77.5
(5) (3) as % of (2)	79.7	78.7

[a]Estimated from data on gross weekly earnings and hours worked by assuming (a) that standard working week is 40 hours and (b) that all overtime working is paid at time and one half. Past experience indicates that these assumptions allow very accurate estimation of standard weekly earnings.

differs slightly between the two sources. The New Earnings Survey excludes those whose pay is affected by absence from work during part of the working week, whereas this category is included in the Department of Employment returns and in our survey of Grampian firms.

Both sets of comparisons point to much the same conclusion.

Grampian firms offered average earnings significantly below the UK and Scottish averages in 1974 and there was some slight tendency for the gap to widen, and not narrow, over the year to 1975. The gap in earnings is quite substantial and is wider for standard weekly earnings than for gross weekly earnings. This may suggest that competition for labour has resulted in some increase in overtime working, but that the basic structure of wage levels, reflected by standard weekly earnings, has not been much affected by labour market pressures. For our purposes, the Department of Employment return is the more valuable as it is on the same basis as our survey. Using it as the point of reference, gross weekly earnings in indigenous firms in the Grampian Region were some 14 per cent below the Scottish and UK average in October 1974 and the gap relative to the Scottish average widened slightly by October 1975. For standard weekly earnings the Grampian average was 20 per cent below the Scottish and UK levels in October 1974 and, once again, the difference increased slightly by October 1975.

There are no detailed Scottish or British data for the period after October 1975, but there is one further guide as to movements in earnings—the index of average earnings for all employees, which is published on a monthly basis. The British index shows an increase in average earnings of 53.9 per cent over April 1974—April 1976. This compares with an increase in gross weekly and standard weekly earnings of 49.2 per cent and 50.7 per cent respectively, for Grampian males. The comparable increases for Grampian females are 60.0 per cent and 61.7 per cent and the weighted increases for males and females are 59.6 per cent and 61.2 per cent. Our sample includes only manual employees, and may contain a higher weighting for female employees, for whom earnings increased more quickly, than the British index.[5] Taking these differences into account, there is no reason to alter our earlier conclusion that, on our data, there has been no apparent tendency for earnings in indigenous firms in the Grampian Region to rise relative to the Scottish or British averages.

To some extent, this may appear to be a surprising conclusion. The number of oil-related jobs created in the Grampian Region is greater than in any other Scottish region [. . .] and this employment is significant given the size of the indigenous labour force. [. . .] It is true that a high proportion of the jobs concerned are off-shore and are filled by men who are not resident in the area; nevertheless, the actual resident labour force, especially taking account of multiplier effects, is substantial. Moreover, although we have not been able to obtain detailed data, it is clear that many of the job opportunities in directly oil-related work offer wages which are high, even by Scottish or UK standards. Yet, many indigenous firms still continue in business and are able to recruit and maintain labour at

---

[5] It is not possible to be more precise as very little information has been published on the composition of the British index.

wage levels which are significantly below the Scottish and British averages. There are certainly points of pressure. For example, competition is sharp for skilled workers in metal-using trades and some firms in the Peterhead area have had extreme recruitment difficulties, but evidence from the earnings survey suggests that this is not general. This suggests further that the labour force may be highly segmented—that much of the labour force of indigenous firms is unable, because of location, aptitudes, skills or attitudes to compete for work in oil-related sectors. Hence wages in indigenous firms remain low. The one exception is in construction where, as we have seen, wages were quickly subject to upward pressures. However, the exception tends to lend weight to our general rule, for construction labour is highly mobile between different types of work and sites within the industry. The lack of segmentation means that an increase in the demand for labour in one sector is quickly transmitted to other employers in the industry. The same argument may not apply to wide sectors of manufacturing and service employment in the Grampian Region.

4

The Economic Impact of North Sea Oil

(ii) The Impact on Scottish Infrastructure

by T. M. Lewis and I. M. McNicoll

Introduction

This chapter assesses the impact of oil-related developments on the infrastructure[1] of affected regions. Generally, as discussed below, the oil industry's demands for public and private infrastructural services have greatly exceeded existing local capacity, and therefore have generated considerable pressure for expansion in infrastructural capacity. Section 1 examines, by empirical examples, the major areas of infrastructure affected by oil in Scotland and the differences in specific impacts among various Scottish regions. Section 2 discusses the immediate implications of these oil-induced demands for infrastructure. [. . .]

Section 1 Oil-Induced Infrastructural Developments

Most activities associated with the incoming oil industry make demands on various areas of the local infrastructure with the region in which they are located. Whether these demands lead to expansion of this infrastructure depends, of course, on the existence or otherwise of excess capacity within this sector. As discussed below (pp. 77–79), with a few exceptions, the oil industry in Scotland has tended to locate in outlying areas whose pre-existing infrastructure (geared to the needs of small, rural communities) was totally inadequate for the requirements of a large-scale, technologically advanced, industrial development. Thus, in the main, oil-related demands for infrastructural services have been met by expansions in the provision of the latter. Table 1 indicates qualitatively some components of infrastructure affected by various oil activities.[2]

Table 1 is not comprehensive in coverage either of oil activities or of infrastructural services, and furthermore the categorisation in Table 1 of services needed or not needed by each oil sector should not be regarded as definitive, but rather as indicative. In spite of these caveats Table 1 clearly demonstrates that generally any oil

From *North Sea Oil and Scotland's Economic Prospects* pp. 41–48 (Croom Helm, London, 1978). Reprinted by permission.

Table 1
Infrastructural Requirements of Various Oil Activities

Infrastructural Service	Accommodation		Transport			
	Housing	Camps, etc.	Good Harbour	Rail	Heavy-duty road	Air service
Oil Sector						
Ocean exploration			✓			✓
Construction of bases, ports, etc.		✓			✓	✓
Rig operation	✓		✓	✓	✓	✓
Pipe laying LAND		✓			✓	
SEA			✓		✓	✓
Platform construction	✓	✓		✓	✓	✓
Platform operation	✓		✓	✓	✓	✓
Management of exploration and production	✓				✓	✓

activity will demand a variety of infrastructural services, and conversely that demands are placed on any given infrastructural service by a variety of offshore oil activities.

Given the qualitative impression from Table 1 that the infrastructural impacts of North Sea oil activities may be substantial and diverse, it is possible to confirm this quantitatively by examining oil-induced infrastructural developments which have been, and are, occurring in Scotland. Infrastructural developments are examined under 5 headings: *Housing, Transport, Education, Health and Social Services*, and *Professional Services*. Considering each in turn:

(a) Housing

The onshore developments associated with North Sea oil exploration and production have already caused and will continue to cause significant geographical movements of workers and their families within Scotland. One of the most immediate requirements in most oil affected areas therefore has been the provision of adequate housing for the incoming population attracted by the prospects of highly paid employment in the 'oil towns'.

The Scottish Information Unit[3] estimates that oil-created demand for housing in the North of Scotland could be 10,000 houses or more. In addition to this oil affected regions will face non-oil induced demands for housing; in particular replacement demand may be substantial.[4] Estimates have been made of the number of houses needed in individual regions as a result of local oil developments, e.g. 16,500 (oil *plus* non-oil needs) in Aberdeen 1972–6 (Mackay & Mackay (1975)), 5,400 (oil only) in Buchan 1971–81 (Francis & Swan (1974)), 4,000 in Cromarty Firth (oil only) by 1975 (Hutcheson & Hogg (1974)) and 1,200 (oil only) in Shetland by 1971 (Llewellyn-Davies (1975)).

As these single region estimates are obtained by different methods and at different points in time, they are not necessarily strictly comparable; however they indicate clearly the substantial, if varying, oil-induced housing requirements in affected regions.

Construction of houses in numbers of this magnitude involves a substantial cash investment. Implicit in the Scottish Information Office discussion[5] is a cost per house of £12,000 (1974 prices), though this substantially underestimates the cost in outlying areas such as Shetland, where £17,000 (1974 prices) per house is regarded as a more reasonable figure (Llewellyn-Davies, op. cit.). Based on the lower cost per unit figure, and an estimated 10,000 houses, total housing investment created by oil developments in the North of Scotland can be conservatively estimated at £120 million (1974 prices).

A summary of progress made in providing the housing requirements estimated above is given in Table 2. Comparing these figures with those given above on estimated regional needs is interesting, although again difficult because of differences in treatment, etc. However, it seems clear that in most regions the number of houses completed by mid-1977 was reasonably close to estimated needs to that date; so that if the latter are reasonable then instances of serious housing shortages should by now be fairly isolated. In addition, the figures for housing under construction and awaiting start suggest that, unless changing circumstances cause a radical upward revision in housing requirements, a further easing of any regional housing shortages can be expected during 1977–8.

Table 2
*Summary of Housing Completions in Oil Affected Regions
of Scotland*[6]

Region	1974	1975	1976	January–June 1977	Total 1972–7	Under construction and awaiting start at June '77
Moray	1,410	2,499	1,259	408	7,341	1,834
Aberdeen/ Peterhead	2,126	3,362	4,613	1,586	14,462	3,778
Zetland	180	327	391	186	1,165	344
Lewis	12	96	178	57	356	378

In addition to actual dwellings, of course, housing provision generally requires complementary infrastructural improvements in access roads, electricity and water provision, sewerage, etc. Examples of this type of infrastructural development are common throughout oil-affected regions.

(b) Transport

Oil-related developments have caused considerable alterations in the transport network in Scotland. The impact has been felt in all forms of transportation and has included the construction of new transport infrastructure, the improvement of existing transport services and the creation of entirely new services. Specific examples can be discussed according to transport mode:

(i) Air   The demand for air services has increased greatly since, and because of the advent of North Sea oil,[7] and local air transport networks have expanded accordingly. New services have been provided in Aberdeen and the Northern Isles improving the links between these areas themselves and with other areas such as North America and Norway. Physical improvements have been effected at Dyce (e.g. new offices and hangars (£10 million) built for BA), Dalcross (improved to provide jet capability), and most spectacularly, at Sumburgh where a complete overhaul of the existing airport has resulted in improved accommodation, runway extensions, all-weather landing facilities and 24-hour operational capability.

(ii) Sea   Developments in sea transport facilities associated with North Sea oil activities have followed a similar pattern to those in air services discussed above, i.e. improvements in services (e.g. new freight lines between Aberdeen and the Northern Isles) and physical infrastructure. If anything, the latter has been even more significant in the case of sea transport since the oil operators themselves have required additional facilities for the operation of supply bases, etc. Some of the more important port developments include the reconstruction and realignment of quays, and the deepening of Victoria and Upper Docks, in Aberdeen harbour. The harbour is now able to operate 24 hours a day in all weather conditions. Similar improvements have taken place at Peterhead (extension of harbour by provision of quays and jetties), Montrose (dredging of the mouth of the South Esk river, land reclamation and the construction of 50ft quay and 1,300ft frontage), and Lerwick (construction of roll-on, roll-off ferry facilities). In addition to these improvements in general harbour facilities, a number of developments specifically designed for oil requirements have also taken place in affected regions.

(iii) Roads   As suggested above, developments in the improvement of existing, and in the provision of new, road networks in the North of Scotland have occurred both through the needs of oil-related traffic directly and indirectly through the needs of new housing communities created by local oil developments. Some of the major trunk road developments associated with oil activities are as follows:[8] first, substantial improvements in the A9 Perth-Inverness road include provision of dual carriageway along one quarter of its 137 miles, and re-routing across the Black Isle to reduce the travelling distance between Inverness and Invergordon. Secondly, the Perth-Dundee A85 dual carriageway is near completion and related construction of a new bridge at Friarton and a link with the M90 Inverkeithing-Perth motorway is well under way (August 1976).

Finally, improvements to the Aberdeen-Inverness A96 bypass Inverurie and Huntly and eliminate bottlenecks at Elgin and Forres. In addition, a very large number of non-trunk road developments are under way.

(iv) Rail Oil-induced developments in rail infrastructure have been more restricted than those in other transport modes, but include the construction of a new railway line to the pipecoating plant at Nigg, the re-opening of certain Northern stations (e.g. Alness), the retention of the Kishorn line, and a general increase in service provision.

(c) Education, Health and Social Services

The immigration of workers and their families into oil-affected regions of Scotland requires not only the provision of housing for them discussed above, but also the provision of complementary services in education, health, etc. Developments in this area follow the pattern of those in housing closely, and therefore need not be catalogued in detail. To summarise, the oil-induced expansion in demand for community services has been met by various combinations of more intensive utilisation of existing facilities, additions to personnel (i.e. teachers, nurses, social workers, etc.), and increases in physical infrastructure (through the construction of new schools, hospitals, etc.).

(d) Professional Services

The development of oil-related industries in Scotland has generated 'multiplier' developments in a number of tertiary industries through backward linkage effects,[9] including the establishment in oil areas of professional service capabilities. Mackay and Mackay (op. cit.) discuss the oil-induced expansion in financial facilities (e.g. in Aberdeen, the establishment of merchant banks such as the Bank of Nova Scotia and Finance for Industry), and office capacity. Other developments [. . .] have taken place in the provision of technical services and training facilities. Whether this type of expansion in local capacity is termed 'infrastructural' or not is largely a matter of semantics. For the purposes of assessing the development stimulus generated by local infrastructural expansion [. . .], it will be useful to employ a broad definition of infrastructure which includes scientific, technical and other professional capacities.

Section 2 The Immediate Impact of Oil-Induced Infrastructural Expansion

The development paths of oil-related activities within Scotland have typically demonstrated very rapid growth from negligible (or non-existent) beginnings to substantial levels. This has resulted in a simultaneous rapid expansion in demand for infrastructural services within affected areas. As suggested above (p. 73) much of the oil-induced expansion in demand has occurred in localities where

existing local capacity was totally inadequate to meet it. Before discussing the implications of this, however, it should be noted that in
certain areas sufficient excess capacity existed pre-oil to meet readily
the new demands imposed by oil developments.

Areas which have tended to have few difficulties in meeting oil
infrastructural demands are those with large existing infrastructural
capacities relative to oil needs; so that the latter are only a marginal
addition to existing demand which can be met easily by slightly
more intensive resource use.[10] This has generally been the case in
oil-affected areas such as Ardersier, Portavadie, Leith, and, to a lesser
extent, Aberdeen, where substantial infrastructural facilities exist
within, or within easy travelling distance of, the region.[11]

In other areas, existing industry had been in decline in the period
immediately prior to oil development so that substantial excess
capacity had been created in infrastructural services within the
locality. In such circumstances, the demands imposed by emergent
oil activities have been relatively easily met by re-employment of
existing indigenous facilities. Scottish areas where this had broadly
been the experience are Methil, where Redpath Dorman Long have
replaced the declining coal industry, and Clydebank where Marathon
and McAlpine have re-employed capacity left idle by declining
indigenous shipbuilding, etc.[12] Ironically, Glasgow, with the largest
indigenous infrastructural base in Scotland *and* substantial excess
capacity in that base as traditional industries decline, has virtually
been bypassed by major oil-related developments, though it may act
as a 'central' service provider for various oil activities in the west.

Frequently, however, oil-created demands for infrastructure in
Scottish regions have greatly exceeded local supply,[13] and significant
problems have resulted from this. Before illustrating the type of
problems which have arisen, it is worthwhile examining briefly the
reasons why any problems in the provision of needed infrastructure
should have arisen in the first place.

First, the planning authorities in many regions at the time of initial
oil developments were small or even non-existent.[14] Reflecting the
needs of the pre-oil community, resources were limited and sophisticated knowledge and expertise lacking. Shetland and Sutherland,
indeed, did not have a development plan for the local economy
without oil developments when they were affected by oil. The strain
on local expertise was exacerbated in many regions by the fact that
local government re-organisation coincided with the upsurge of
oil-related activity.

Secondly, the forecasting of oil-related infrastructural needs has
often been inadequate and inaccurate. Partly this has been caused
by the lack of appropriate expertise within local authorities mentioned above, but, in addition, problems have also undoubtedly
arisen through misleading information provided by oil operators. A
classic example of this is in Cromarty where Highland Fabricators'
planning application made provision for 600 employees, but by 1974

the company were employing over 2,000.[15] M. K. Shand, in the same locality, similarly grossly underestimated their employment requirements.

Finally, given the almost instantaneous increase in infrastructural demand created by oil developments, a disparity between supply and demand in these services is inevitable, since at the very least, time must be spent in the construction of needed facilities. In reality the lag will be even greater since planning applications must be processed and approved, manpower hired to construct and staff facilities arranged.

Given the above difficulties, the emergence of 'bottlenecks' was inevitable and duly occurred. In many regions, housing supply was totally inadequate for the increased demand. Perhaps the most striking example of this was at Nigg, where for a period Highland Fabricators had their labour force housed in two Greek liners specially imported for the purpose.[16] In other areas, however, the situation has been similar if less dramatic and the excess demand has inevitably led to greatly increased prices for accommodation and land and to 'queueing' for available accommodation.[17] Apart from significant income redistribution effects which surprisingly are seldom mentioned, the housing shortage has *itself* exacerbated the shortage in supply of infrastructural facilities through what Taylor[18] has called 'the vicious circle of oil development'. More specifically, the shortage and expense of available accommodation has made it difficult to attract not only the construction workers needed to build new facilities (including ironically housing) but also the professional staff needed to provide the expanded services.[19] Similar difficulties have occurred in the provision of health, education, police, roads, etc.

Further difficulties have arisen in financing these infrastructural improvements. Initially, most of the burden fell on the local authorities themselves and there were considerable anxieties concerning the effect such substantial expenditure would have on local rates. However, in November 1974, the Secretary of State announced an additional element to rate support grant to assist affected areas.[20] In the longer term, [...] the financing of the expanded infrastructure may create fresh problems.

Notes

1. The problem of defining infrastructure (or social overhead capital) functionally by the use of specified criteria to include or exclude any given item is discussed in Youngson (1967), Chapter 2. For present purposes it is sufficient to have a listing of infrastructural items; typically, as is again discussed in Youngson, such a list includes housing, transport, health and education services, water and power.
2. Adapted from Hutcheson and Hogg (1974).
3. *Factsheet*, March 1975.
4. E.g. in the Buchan area alone, replacement needs are estimated at 1,400 houses between 1971 and 1981. Francis & Swan (1974).
5. *Factsheet*, March 1975.

6. Adapted from Scottish Information Office, *Factsheet*, RF 12 1977. Figures include private and public housing.
7. E.g. traffic at Dyce Airport (Aberdeen) has doubled since the discovery of North Sea Oil (Mackay and Mackay, op.cit.), while at Sumburgh Airport (Shetland) aircraft movements increased five-fold between 1971 and 1976 (see Marshall (1977)).
8. Source: Scottish Information Office, *Factsheet*, August 1976.
9. See Chapter 5 for a fuller discussion.
10. In addition, a large settlement is likely to have a more diverse industrial base within which particular industries may be in decline at any point in time and therefore *decreasing* their demands for infrastructural services. The incoming oil industry can therefore 'mop up' this unemployed capacity.
11. Refs: Baldwin and Baldwin (1975); Fernie (1976).
12. See Taylor (1974).
13. E.g. in Shetland, Nigg, Kishorn, Orkney, etc. pre-oil indigenous infrastructure was very limited and totally inadequate to meet the demands of oil.
14. Taylor (op.cit.) points out that ten local authorities did not have planning departments at all in 1971. Milne (1973) makes similar points on the small scale of planning departments in many affected regions at the onset of the oil boom.
15. See Rosie (1975).
16. Ibid.
17. Virtually every commentator on North Sea oil developments has noted this point and many give specific examples of accommodation or land prices increasing dramatically as a result of oil developments. See e.g. Mackay and Mackay (op.cit.) Francis & Swan (1974), Rosie (op.cit.) etc.
18. Taylor (op.cit.).
19. Francis & Swan (1974).
20. SIO, *Factsheet*, August 1976.

References

Baldwin, P. L. and Baldwin, M. F. (1975), *Onshore Planning for Offshore Oil*, Conservation Foundation University Books.
Fernie, J. (1976), *North Sea Oil: A Review*, Huddersfield Poly, Occasional Paper No. 4.
Francis, J. and Swan, N. (1974), *Scotland's Pipedream* (The St. Andrew's Press, Church of Scotland, Edinburgh).
Hutcheson, A. and Hogg, A. M. (1974), *Scotland and Oil* (Oliver & Boyd).
Llewellyn-Davies (1975), '*A Structure Plan for Shetland*', unpublished consultants' report.
Mackay, D. I. and Mackay, A. G. (1975), *The Political Economy of North Sea Oil*, (Martin Robertson, London).
Marshall, E. (1977), *Shetland's Oil Era*. Thuleprint.
Milne, R. (1973), 'Scottish Planners Strike Oil', *Surveyor*, January.
Rosie, G. (1975), *Cromarty: The Scramble for Oil*, Canongate Publishing Edinburgh.
Youngson, A. J. (1967), *Overhead Capital: A Study in Development Economics*. Edinburgh University Press.

PART II

DEMAND

Introduction to Part II

The establishment of demand relationships is a flourishing area of applied microeconomics. The reasons for this are not difficult to understand. First the theory which is being tested is a reasonably simple one. Whilst there are different approaches to demand theory—utility, indifference curve, revealed preference etc.—they are all concerned to speculate on the effect on demand of changes in key variables such as price and income.

A second reason is that, unlike other areas of microeconomics, data on demand behaviour are reasonably accessible. As Baumol in the first reading in this section points out, there are different ways of obtaining these data. There is the questionnaire or interview approach often used in market research. Alternatively a firm may initiate a direct experiment in a particular market or markets, changing some variables under its control and observing consumer reaction. Finally there is the observation of consumer behaviour, a method which seeks to establish the importance of particular variables by using statistical techniques. This last approach is the one most widely used and is represented by the other three readings in this section.

A further factor in the encouragement of empirical studies of demand relationships is the evident interest of firms and governments in such studies. Firms have an obvious interest in obtaining information on the broad variables such as price and income which affect the demand for their products. Whilst the firm is principally interested in its own share of the market and is likely to use industry demand studies as a starting-point, governments are more interested in the operation of an industry as a whole. Empirical demand studies may give governments some indication of the effects on particular industries of changing macroeconomic variables such as credit controls, tax rates, or interest charges.

The readings chosen in this section all appeared in the first edition. Clearly, later readings could have been substituted and the choice is a reasonably large one. The existing readings, however, are useful in indicating different aspects of demand estimation. Moreover, the Open University has incorporated these readings into its course texts, and there is some benefit therefore in retaining them.

Baumol's contribution is a well-known chapter from his popular text demonstrating how economic theory—largely micro but also macro—can be operationalized to provide guidance for decision-making. The core of the reading is a clear explanation of the identification problem. This problem, first raised by E. J. Working in 1927, refers to the need to separate out or 'identify' the specific demand relationship in observed market price changes which reflect the simultaneous interaction of both supply and demand relationships. Baumol indicates how the correct relationship can be identified.

The paper by Koutsoyiannis reports on an international study of the demand for tobacco. The author points out that the establishment of price and income elasticities is of great practical relevance to governments in countries where tobacco is an important source of tax revenue.

The study looks at fourteen countries over the period 1950-9, with individual demand functions being estimated for each country. The author considers five variables as possible influences on the demand for tobacco, namely income, the price of tobacco, the price of other goods, the adult population, and time (measured in calendar years).

Least squares regression is used to estimate price and income elasticities and, as might be expected, these were generally found to be low. The prices of other goods were generally found not to have any significant effect on demand and these three results seem consistent with the view that tobacco is a 'necessity' commodity in the sense that there are no substitutes able to meet the demand to smoke. The study of course relates to the period 1950-9 since when there have been concerted campaigns in many countries to make smokers aware of health risks and to reduce their smoking habits. In this connection an additional conclusion of the study, namely that 'tobacco consumption in most countries seems to be influenced mainly by changes in the number of smokers', is particularly important. It would seem that reductions in tobacco consumption are less likely to occur through reductions in the amount smoked by each consumer as a result of price and income movements than through reductions in the number of consumers brought about by health campaigns.

Koutsoyiannis's study is important not only for its conclusions but for its methodology. The analysis gives a very full discussion of the preliminary work necessary before any empirical demand study is undertaken. It sets out the *a priori* reasoning clearly and the expected outcome of the hypothesized relationships and assesses the strengths and weaknesses of the data and the methodological procedures. The study does raise some statistical questions. For example, the price and income data are measured in 'current money' rather than real terms. The price of tobacco is an average price for all tobacco products, which might disguise some demand shifts between different tobacco qualities. Instead of aggregating the ten-year observations for fourteen countries and thus providing 140 observations, the author calculates separate demand functions for each country relying on only ten observations in each case. However, these and other statistical questions are explicitly raised and discussed and the particular decisions taken are justified.

One problem which Koutsoyiannis does not deal with is the identification of the demand curve. However, this is a central concern of Allan in his paper on the demand for herrings. He argues that the quayside market for herrings features a fixed exogenously determined supply of a highly perishable product where no stocks are kept and the market is cleared. In any market period, therefore, it is possible to identify and specify the demand curve using observed market equilibrium quantities and prices.

One of Allan's concerns is methodological, to show that under certain supply and market conditions a single-equation model can be used to estimate demand functions. He admits however that 'the applicability of this type of simple one-equation model to problems of demand estimation is likely to be limited.' His results in this particular case, however, are also of interest. They show that the price-elasticity for this particular fish is rather high and that it is higher in periods when the fish is of poorer quality.

The final reading in this section by Buxton and Rhys is interesting in a number of ways. It is concerned with the demand for a consumer durable, uses cross-section rather than time-series data, examines the demand for a stock rather than a flow of goods, and is concerned with a disaggregated model. As the authors point out, most estimates of car demand are concerned with aggregate demand functions rather than the variations in demand response between regions or areas. These aggregate models identify car price and income levels as independent variables and the results indicate a higher income than price-elasticity.

Buxton and Rhys however are concerned with the demand for car ownership in different licensing authorities in England and Wales and identify as their independent variables income density and age structure of the population. The results support the hypothesis that car ownership is positively related to income and inversely related to population density. The authors point out that the latter may in fact be a proxy variable for public transport provision or home to work/shopping, etc., distances. The results on the influence of age structure are less clear. In most instances the coefficient was not statistically significant, and where it was significant seemed to indicate a negative relationship. In other words car ownership was lower in areas with a higher proportion of persons in the potentially car-owning age bracket. This seems to contradict the results of other studies and whilst the authors point out possible explanations they also suggest that further analysis is required.

5

On Empirical Determination of Demand Relationships

by W. J. Baumol

Why Demand Functions?

Demand functions, as they are defined in economic analysis, are rather queer creatures, somewhat abstract, containing generous elements of the hypothetical and, in general, marked by an aura of unreality. The peculiarity of the concept is well illustrated by the fact that only one point on a demand curve can ever be observed directly with any degree of confidence, because by the time we can obtain the data with which to plot a second point, the entire curve may well have shifted without our knowing it. A more fundamental but related source of our discomfort with the idea is the fact that the demand relationship is defined as the answer to the set of hypothetical questions which begin, 'What would consumers do if price (or advertising outlay, or some other type of marketing effort) were different than it is in fact?' We are, then, dealing with information about potential consumer behaviour in situations which consumers may never have experienced. And, since we have very little confidence in the constancy of consumer tastes and desires, all of these data are taken to refer to possible events at just one moment of time —e.g., consumer reactions to alternative possible prices if any of them were to occur tomorrow at 2.47 p.m.

In view of all this, there should be little wonder that people with an orientation towards applied economics occasionally become somewhat impatient with the economic theorist's demand function. Yet no matter how ingenious the circumlocutions which may have been employed, they have been unable to find an acceptable substitute for the concept. For the demand function must ultimately play a critical role in any probing marketing decision process, and there is really no way to get away from it.

For example, to decide on the number of salesmen which will best serve the interests of the firm, it is first necessary to know what difference in consumer purchases would result from alternative sales force sizes. But this is precisely the sort of odd and hypothetical information which goes to make up the demand relationship. It is for exactly the same reason that many large and reputable firms in

From *Economic Theory and Operations Analysis* (Prentice-Hall, Inc., 1972), pp. 234–54. 3rd ed. Copyright © 1972. Reprinted by permission of Prentice-Hall, Inc., Englewood Cliffs, New Jersey.

diverse fields of industry are conducting ambitious research programmes whose aim is the determination of their advertising-demand curves, that is, the relationship between their advertising outlays and their sales. So far, these efforts have met with varying degrees of success, and it must be admitted that many of them have not come up with very meaningful results. For the empirical determination of demand relationships is no simple matter and there are many booby traps for the amateur investigator and the unwary. It is no trick at all, on looking over a small sample of the published demand studies, to come up with horrible examples of just about every available type of mis-step.

This chapter is designed primarily to point out some of the pitfalls which threaten the investigator of demand relationships. Its aim is to warn the reader to proceed with extreme caution in any such enterprise. No cut-and-dried solutions are offered to the problems which are discussed. This is true for two reasons. First, because many of the methods for dealing with these difficulties are highly technical matters of specialized econometric analysis. Second, and more important, solutions are not listed mechanically because there simply are no panaceas; the problems must be dealt with case by case as they arise, and the effectiveness with which they can be handled is still highly dependent on the skill, experience, and judgement of the specialist investigator.

Interview Approaches to Demand Determination

Before turning to statistical methods for the finding of demand functions, it is appropriate to say a few words about a more direct method for dealing with the problem—the consumer interview approach. In its most blatant and naive form, consumers are simply collared by the interviewer and asked how much they would be willing to purchase of a given product at a number of alternative product price levels.

It should be obvious enough that this is a dangerous and unreliable procedure. People just have not thought out in advance what they would do in these hypothetical situations, and their snap judgements thrown up at the request of the interviewer cannot inspire a great deal of confidence. Even if they attempt to offer honest answers, even if they had thought about their decisions in advance, consumers might well find that when confronted with the harsh realities of the concrete situation, they behave in a manner which belies their own expectations. When we get to the effects of advertising on demand, the problems of such a direct interview approach become even more apparent. What is the consumer to be asked—how much more of the company's product he would buy if it were to institute a 10 per cent increase in its spot announcements to its television budget?

Much more subtle and effective approaches to consumer interviewing are indeed possible. Indirect, but far more revealing, questions can be asked. Consumers may, for example, be asked about the difference in price between two competing products, and if it turns out that they simply do not know the facts of the matter, one may be led to infer that a lower product price may have a relatively limited influence on consumer behaviour, just because few consumers are likely to be aware of its existence. A clever interview designer may in this way build up a strategy of indirect questions which gradually isolates the required facts.

Alternatively, consumers may be placed in simulated market situations, so-called consumer clinics, in which changes in their behaviour can be observed as the circumstances of the experiment are varied. An obvious approach to this matter is to get groups of housewives together, give them small amounts of money with which they are offered the opportunity to purchase one of, say, several brands of dishwasher soap which are put on display at the clinic, and observe what happens as the posted prices on the displays are varied from group to group. Here again, much more subtle variants in experimental design are clearly possible.

But even the best of these procedures has its limitations for our purpose, which is the determination of the precise form of a demand relationship. Artificial consumer clinic experiments inevitably introduce some degree of distortion because subjects cannot be kept from realizing that they are in an experimental situation. In any event, such clinics are rather expensive and so the samples involved are usually extremely small—too small for confidence in any inferences which are drawn about the magnitudes of the parameters the demand relationships for the body of consumers as a whole. And large sample interviews which approach the determination of consumer demand patterns by subtle and indirect questions are often highly revealing, but they rarely can supply the quantitative information required for the estimation of a demand equation.

Direct Market Experiments

A second alternative approach which is sometimes considered as a means for finding demand relationship information is the direct market experiment. A company engages in a deliberate programme of price or advertising level variation. Suppose it increases its newspaper advertising outlay in one city by 5 per cent, in another city it increases this outlay by 10 per cent, and in still a third metropolis a 10 per cent reduction is undertaken. In some ways such a direct experimental approach must always be the most revealing. It gives real answers to our formerly hypothetical questions and does so without subjecting the consumer to the artificial atmosphere of the interview situation or the consumer clinic.

However direct experimentation has its serious limitations as well.

1. It can be very expensive or extremely risky for the firm. Customers

lost by an experimental price increase may never be regained from competitive products which they might otherwise never have tried, and a 10 per cent increase in advertising outlay for any protracted period may be no trivial matter.

2. Market experiments are almost never *controlled* experiments, so that the observations which they yield are likely to be coloured by all sorts of fortuitous occurrences—coincidental changes in consumer incomes or in competitive advertising programmes, peculiarities of the weather during the period of the experiment, etc.

3. Because of the high cost of the experiments and because it is often simply physically impossible to try out a large number of variations, the number of observations is likely to be unsatisfactorily small. If, for example, it is desired to determine the effects of varied advertising outlay in a national periodical, the company cannot increase the size of its ads which are seen by Nashville readers and simultaneously reduce those which are seen in Lexington, Kentucky. This difficulty has been eased to some extent by the fact that a number of national magazines now put out several regional editions, but by and large the problem remains: market experiments usually supply information only about a very limited number of alternatives.

4. For similar reasons, market experiments are often of only relatively brief duration. Companies cannot afford to permit them to run long enough to display much more than impact effects. And yet the distinction between impact effects and long-run effects of a change are often extremely significant, as was so clearly demonstrated by the sharp but very temporary drop in cigarette sales when the first announcement was made about the association between smoking and the incidence of cancer. How often has a rise in the price of a product caused a major reduction in purchases for a few weeks, with customers then gradually but steadily drifting back?

Market experiments do have a role to play in demand relationship determination. They can be important as a check on the results of a statistical study. Or they can provide some critical information about a few points on the demand curve in which past experience is entirely lacking. In some special circumstances experimentation is particularly convenient and has been used in the past, apparently with a considerable degree of success. For example, some mailorder houses have employed systematic programmes in which a few special experimental pages were bound inconspicuously into the catalogues distributed to customers within restricted geographic regions, thus permitting observation of the effects of price, product, or even catalogue display variations. However, it should also be clear that market experiments cannot by themselves be relied upon universally to provide the demand information needed by management. Economics is just not a subject which lends itself readily to experimentation, largely because there are always too many elements beyond the control of the investigator and because economic experimentation is often inherently too expensive, risky, and difficult.

Standard Statistical Approaches

The third, and generally most attractive, approach to demand function determination attempts to squeeze its information out of sources such as the accumulated records of the past (a time-series analysis), or a comparative evaluation of the performance of different sectors of the market (a cross-sectional analysis). The available statistics on sales, prices, advertising outlays of the most relevant varieties, and other marketing data are gathered together and then analysed with the aid of the standard statistical techniques.

The basic procedure is simple enough; in fact as we shall see presently, it is often far too simple. Suppose, for example, that the data in Table 1 on company sales and advertising outlays have been accumulated.

Table 1

Year	1950	1951	1952	1953	1954	1955	1956	1957
Sales (millions of dollars)	67	73	54	62	70	75	79	83
Advertising (millions of dollars)	12	15	13	14	18	17	19	15

Once the figures have been plotted, the pattern formed by the dots can be used in an obvious manner to fit a straight line (see Figure 1) or a curve to them. This line is then taken as the desired advertising-demand curve. Its slope can be used as a measure of advertising effectiveness, that is, it measures the marginal sales productivity of an advertising dollar, Δ sales/Δ advertising outlay. This line can be determined impressionistically simply by drawing in a line that appears to fit the dots fairly well, or any one of a variety of more systematic methods can be used.

The most widely employed and best known of these techniques is the method of least squares, in which the object is to find that line which makes the sum of the (squared) vertical deviations between our dots and the fitted line as small as possible, where the deviations are defined as the vertical distances such as AB or CD in Figure 1. The idea is inherently attractive. We wish to minimize deviations because a line which involves very substantial deviations from the dots representing our data surely does not represent the information in a very satisfactory way. But if, in our addition process, a large negative deviation such as AB (that is, a case where the line

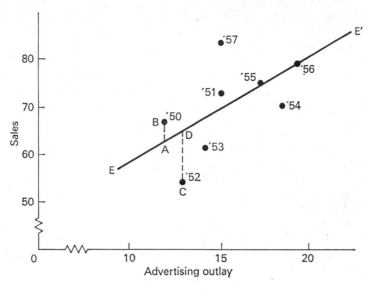

Figure 1

underestimates the vertical co-ordinate of our dot) happens to be largely cancelled out by a positive deviation, *CD*, the sum of the deviations can turn out to be small. This is surely not what we want in looking for a line which does not deviate much from the dots. One can avoid ending up with a line which fits the facts rather badly but in which the positive and negative deviations add up to a rather small number, by squaring all the deviation figures before adding them together. Since the square of a negative real number as well as that of a positive real number is always positive, large, squared negative deviations cannot offset large squared positive deviations, and the sum of squared deviations will never add up to a small number unless our line happens to fit the dots closely.

Omission of Important Variables

Clearly, sales are affected by other variables in addition to the company's advertising expenditure. Prices, competitive advertising, consumer income variations, and other variables also play an important role in any demand relationship. If, therefore, we try to extract from our statistics a simple equation relating sales to advertising outlay alone, and in the process we ignore all other variables, our results are likely to be very badly distorted. We may ascribe to the company's advertising outlays sales trends which are really the result of the behaviour of other economic changes. The behaviour of other variables can thus conceal and even offset the effects of advertising. To show how serious the results can be, consider the illustrative demand equation

$$S = 50 + 4A + 0.02\gamma \qquad (1)$$

where S represents sales, A advertising expenditure, and γ consumer income. The values given in Table 2 can easily be seen to satisfy the equation precisely, and any standard estimation procedure based on such information can be expected to yield the correct equation.

Table 2

Date	1956	1957	1958
γ	3,000	4,000	3,500
A	2	3	2.5
S	118	142	130

But a *two*-variable, straight, least-squares line which gives us a (perfect!) correlation between S and A alone (ignoring γ) and which is based on these same values will yield the equation

$$S = 24A + 70. \qquad (2)$$

This equation asserts that each added dollar of advertising expenditure brings in $24 in sales, instead of the true $4 return shown by equation (1). In addition, because of the perfect correlation there is, in this case, no residual unexplained variation in S which is left to be accounted for by a subsequent correlation between S and γ, i.e., *this incorrect procedure appears to show that consumer income has absolutely no influence on demand*! The advertising coefficient has been inflated by usurping to itself the influence of γ on sales.

Incidentally, if, instead of proceeding as we just did, we had started off by finding a least-squares equation relating sales to consumer income alone, we would have obtained from the same statistics the equation

$$S = 0.024\gamma + 46$$

which this time overvalues the influence of income on sales and ascribes absolutely no effectiveness to advertising.[1]

It is clear, then, that more than two variables must usually be taken into account in the statistical estimation of a demand relationship. And, in fact, this is ordinarily done, the estimation usually employing what is called a least-squares *multiple regression* technique. However, it should be remembered that, even if we include five variables in our analysis but omit a sixth rather important variable, precisely the same difficulties will be encountered. That is,

[1] The correlation between γ and A creates another difficulty in this example. The resulting problems are discussed in the next section.

the omission of any important variable, however defined, from the statistical procedure can lead to serious distortions in its results.

This might appear to constitute an argument for the inclusion in the analysis of every variable which comes to the statistician's mind as a factor of possible importance, just as a matter of insurance. Unfortunately, however, we are not at liberty to go on adding variables willy-nilly. The more variables whose influence we want to take into account, the more data we require as a basis for the estimation. If we only have statistical information pertaining to three points in time, it is ridiculous to try to disentangle the influence of fifteen variables. In fact, the statistician requires many pieces of information for every variable he includes in his analysis, if he is to estimate his relationship with a clear conscience.

However, large masses of marketing data are not easily come by. Records are often woefully incomplete; additional data can sometimes be acquired only at considerable expense, and in any event, statistics which go too far back in time are apt to be obsolete and irrelevant for the company's current circumstances. We must, therefore, very frequently be contented with skimpy figres which force us to be extremely niggardly in the number of variables which we take into account, despite the very great dangers involved.

Inclusion of Mutually Correlated Variables

Another difficulty which, to some extent, can help to make life easier as far as the problem of the preceding section is concerned arises when a number of the relevant variables are themselves closely interrelated. For example, one encounters advertising effectiveness studies in which income and years of education per inhabitant are both included as variables. Now education is itself very closely related to income level both because higher-income families can afford to provide more education and larger inheritances to their children and because a more educated person is often in a position to earn a higher income.

It may nevertheless be true that education and income do have different consequences for advertising effectiveness. For example, an increase in income without any change in educational level could increase the person's willingness to purchase more in response to an ad, whereas more education not backed up by larger purchasing power might have the reverse effect. But, in general, there is no statistical method whereby these two consequences can be separated, because, for the bulk of the population, whenever one of these variables increases in value, so does the other. Hence, the statistics which can merely exhibit directions of variation might show that, other things remaining equal, whenever sales increased, income also increased, and so (as a consequence?) did education.

In such circumstances if we include both the income and the educational level variables in the statistical demand-fitting procedure, the chances are that the mechanics of the procedure will provide a perfectly arbitrary ascription of the sales changes to our two causal variables. And sometimes the results may turn out completely nonsensical because the standard computational procedure has no way to apply common sense in imputing the total sales change to the separate influences of education and income changes.

Therefore, if in a demand relationship there occur several variables which are themselves highly correlated,it is usually wise to omit all but one of any such set of variables in a statistical study. If this is not done, another powerful source of nonsense results is introduced.

Simultaneous Relationship Problems

The difficulties which have so far been discussed, while they can be extremely important and are often overlooked in practice (with rather sad consequences) may, by and large, be considered rather routine and in retrospect, fairly obvious matters.

We come now to a far more subtle and perhaps a far more serious problem which was only brought to our attention in 1927 by E. J. Working and which has only received serious and systematic attention quite recently, largely as a result of the work of the Cowles Foundation. The problem in question, in a sense, follows from the difficulty which was discussed in the previous section. If there is a close correlation between two variables, it is likely to mean that they are not independent of one another and that there is at least one other relevant equation in the system which expresses the relationship between them. For example, in our illustrative case there might be an equation indicating how income level is ordinarily increased by a person's education. We then end up having to deal with not just a single demand equation, but with a system of several equations in which a number of the variables interact mutually and are determined simultaneously.

Economics is characterized by such simultaneous relationships. The standard example is the price determination process in which a supply equation is involved as well as our demand relationship. Similarly, simultaneous relationships constitute the core of national income analysis. National income depends on the demand for consumer's goods which helps determine the level of profitable production. But the consumption demand equation, in turn, involves national income (as a measure of the public's purchasing power) as a variable. To mention another simultaneous relationship example, the coal mining industry is a customer for steel whose volume of demand depends on coal sales, but the demand for coal itself depends heavily on the amount of coal to be used in producing steel. It is possible to expand the list of simultaneous relationships in economics indefinitely.

The empirical data which are generated by such a set of equations are the information source on which the statistician must base his estimates of the relationships. But since these data are the result of a number of such relationships, the difficult problem arises of separating out the relationships from the observed statistics.

Unless steps are taken to make sure that the influences of the several simultaneous relationships on the data can be and have been separated, there is not the slightest justification for the use of any estimation procedure, such as that depicted in Figure 1, to compute a statistical relationship. Yet it will readily be recognized how frequently this completely fallacious procedure is employed in practice in the form of simple or multiple correlations computed without any attempt to cope with the simultaneous relationship problem. Let us see now how serious are the distortions which can be expected to result.

The Identification Problem

In rather general terms our basic problem can conveniently be divided into two parts.

1. In some circumstances the simultaneous relationships (equations) will be so similar in character that it will be impossible to unscramble them (or at least some of them) from the statistics. Such relationships are said to be *unidentifiable.* Presently it will be shown how such an unhappy situation can arise, and it will be indicated that it is unfortunately not unheard of in marketing problems. Clearly, in such a case, we are wasting our time in a statistical investigation of the equation in question. There do exist some mathematical tests which show whether or not an equation is *identified* (i.e., whether or not it is in principle possible to separate it from the other relationships in the system). These tests should always be applied before embarking on the type of statistical investigation under discussion. It must be emphasized that if an equation happens not to be identified, it is impossible even to approximate the true equation from statistical data alone. Market experiments or other substitute approaches must be employed to obtain this information.

2. Even if an equation turns out to be identified, precautions must be taken to ensure that a statistically estimated equation is not distorted by the presence of the simultaneous relationships. We will see in the next section that an ordinary least-squares procedure is likely to lead to precisely this sort of distortion.

In this section we deal with the first of these, the identification problem—the circumstances under which it is, at least in principle, possible to unscramble our simultaneous relationships statistically.

To illustrate, let us consider what is involved in finding statistically an advertising-demand curve such as the one which Figure 1 attempted to construct in a rather primitive fashion. Now while sales are doubtless affected by advertising, as the advertising-demand function assumes, this function is often accompanied by a second relationship in which what we might call the direction of causation is reversed. It is well known that a firm's advertising budget is frequently affected by its sales volume. In fact, many businesses operate on a rule of thumb which allocates to advertising expenditure a fixed proportion of their total revenues. For such a business, then, we will have two advertising expenditure demand relationships: (1) the demand function which shows how quantity demanded, Q is affected by a firm's advertising budget, $A : Q = f(A)$ and (2) the budgeting equation which shows how the firm's advertising decisions are affected by the demand for its product: $A = g(Q)$.

Both of these relationships may actually be of interest to the businessman. The first, as already stated, is directly relevant to his own optimal expenditure decision. The second, if obtained from industry records, will give him vital information about the behaviour patterns of his competitors.

The firm's actual sales and its actual advertising expenditure will, of course, depend on both its advertising budgeting practices (the budgeting equation) and on the demand-advertising relationships. In Figure 2 the graphs of two such hypothetical relationships are depicted.

In Figure 2a we show the two curves which the statistician is seeking. We make ourselves, as it were, momentarily omniscient and thus have no difficulty envisioning the true relationships. However, the information available to the statistician is much more restricted as we shall now see. In our situation the actual advertising expenditure, A, and the volume of sales, Q are determined, as for any simultaneous equation, by the point of intersection, P of the two curves.

We now can describe two cases of non-identification.

Case 1: *Neither curve identified*. If the two curves were to retain their shape from year to year, that is, *if neither of them ever shifted*, all the inter-section points P would coincide or at least lie very close together (Figure 2b). There would only be a single observed point, as in the figure, or the tightly clustered points would form no discernible pattern, and so the shape of neither curve could even approximately be found from the data. We see then, though it may be a bit surprising, that curves which never shift are from this point of view the worst of all possibilities.

Case 2: *One of the curves not identified* (but the other curves identifiable). This is a case frequently encountered in practice when the demand curve of one firm is investigated. The data form a neat and simple pattern, but what they describe is the firm's inflexible advertising budgeting practices rather and the nature of the demand for its product. In such circumstances what happens is that the budget curve never shifts but the demand curve does. There will then be a number of different intersection points, such as P, P', and

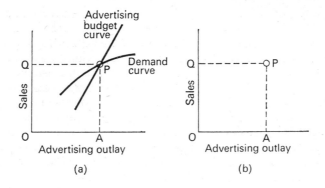

Figure 2

P'', but they will always describe only the shape of the advertising budget line (Figure 3). The reader can well imagine how often statistical attempts to find the advertising-demand curve have produced neat linear relationships (and spectacularly high correlation coefficients), though what the triumphant investigator has located (without his knowing it) is a totally different curve from the one he was seeking. The situation which we have just examined is really ideal from the point of view of the statistician, *provided the relationship which is not shifting happens to be the one he is seeking.* But the question remains; How is he to know when one relationship is standing still, and even if he somehow knows this, how does he determine which one it is? We will see that in the answers to these questions lies the key to the solution of the identification problem.

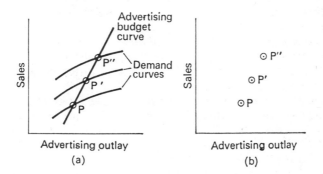

Figure 3

It will be shown presently that only where both curves shift over time or from firm to firm or from geographical territory to territory can they ordinarily both be identified. However, in this case the difficult task of unscrambling the two relationships becomes particularly acute. Figure 4 illustrates how three points, *A*, *B* and *C*, in a diagram

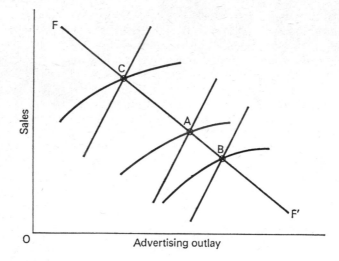

Figure 4

similar to Figure 1 might have been generated by three different (shifted) pairs of our curves. It is noteworthy that the negatively sloping (!) 'advertising curve' *FF'* estimated statistically from these points bears not the slightest resemblance to any of the true curves. Nor, since it is merely a recording of points of intersection, is there any reason why it should. *The shape of* FF' *is not even any sort of 'compromise' between those of the budget and advertising demand curves*! We conclude that where simultaneous relationships are present the standard curve-fitting techniques described in Section 4 and Figure 1 may well break down completely. *Their results are likely to bear absolutely no resemblance to the equations which are being sought*! Such a naïve approach may therefore well be worse than no investigation because misleading information is usually worse than no information at all.

Let us now see how one can, in principle, test whether the relationship we are seeking is identified (potentially discoverable by statistical means).

First we note that, as the model has so far been described, there is no way of accounting for any shifts in either relationships which, as we have observed, are crucial for our problem. The reason is that only two variables, A and Q, have been considered in the relationships $Q = f(A)$ (the demand relationship) and $A = g(Q)$ (the advertising budget equation).

There must, in fact be some other influences (other variables) which disturb the relationships between Q and A and produce the shifts in their graphs. These additional variables must be taken explicitly into account. As we know, the demand relationship is likely to involve many variables in addition to A. For example, consumer's disposable income is a variable which affects the volume of sales resulting from a given level of advertising expenditure though, very likely, it does not enter the firm's budget calculation explicitly but only indirectly via the effects of income on the sales of the company's product. Similarly, the firm's budget policy may be affected by its past dividend payments, which determine how much it can currently spare for advertising expenditure, but this dividend policy will have little or no effect on the demand curve for its products. Suppose, for the sake of simplicity, that the four variables Q, A, γ (the disposable income), and D (the total dividend payments in the preceding year) are the only ones that are relevant to the problem. Our two relationships then become:

$$\text{the advertising-demand function } Q = f(A, \gamma) \tag{3}$$

and

$$\text{the advertising budget equation } A = g(Q,D). \tag{4}$$

Here changes in the value of γ are what produce the shifts in the graph of the demand equation which have been discussed. Similarly, changes in D produce shifts in the advertising budget curve.

Now that we have examined how shifts in the two curves are produced we can return to the question of identification. Let us see, intuitively, how the presence of the shift variables in equations (3) and (4) makes it possible, in principle, to separate the relationships from the statistics (i.e., how the shift variables identify the equations). It will be shown now that γ and D permit the statistician, at least conceptually, to divide up the statistical information in such a way that he is left with situations like that depicted in Figure 3. Such a situation gives him the information that permits him to infer which of the relationships is shifting and which is standing still. That is, he can determine when one graph is not moving while the other shifts around, so that the resulting dots trace out the graph of the equation which is not shifting, the equation he is trying to estimate. The reader should first be warned, however, that the procedure which is about to be described is not usually a practical estimation (curve-finding) procedure and that other, more sophisticated measures are normally employed for the purpose.

In Figure 5 we replot the data of Figure 1. Let us, in addition, determine for each point the level of income γ for that particular year. Suppose this information is as shown in Table 3 (the corresponding sales and advertising figures are in Table 1).

We note that the income values for the points representing 1951, 1952, 1953 and 1957 are fairly close together. Hence, if we are convinced that γ is the only variable which makes for sizeable shifts in the advertising-demand curve, it is reasonable to assume

Table 3

Advertising Demand point	1950	1951	1952	1953	1954	1955	1956	1957
Disposable Income γ ($ billions)	360	297	295	307	428	381	420	300

that all four points lie on (or close to) the same curve; that is, among these points there has occurred little or no shift in the curve. We may, therefore, use these four points (ignoring the others) to locate a demand curve UU' (for income level approximately 300 billion) as shown. Similarly, we can use points for years 1954 and 1956 alone

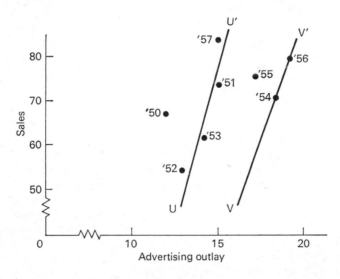

Figure 5

to find the shape of the advertising-demand curve VV' which pertains to income level approximately 420 billion, etc. In other words, the additional information on the value of γ for each point has permitted us, in principle, to ignore all points which contain information irrelevant to a given advertising-demand curve.

We see, then, that if variable γ is present in one equation but not in the other it permits us, in principle, to discover statistical points over which the budget line has shifted but through which the demand curve remains unchanged, thus enabling us to trade out the corresponding *demand curve*.

In an analogous way we were able to trace out a *budget line* in Figure 3, for there the position of the demand curve changed while the budget line remained stationary. But while this enabled us to find the budget line in Figure 3, there the demand curve was unidentifiable because the budget relationship postulated at that point which moves the budget line about and yet permits the demand curves to stay still. This gives us the following result: *one of a pair of simultaneous relationships will be identified if it lacks a variable which is present in the other relationship.* A change in the value of that variable will not affect the position of the curve corresponding to the relationship we are seeking, but it will shift the other curve.

The relevance of the shift variables γ and D for identification can also be seen in another way. Assume that on the basis of *a priori* judgement we have already constructed our model consisting of equations (3) and (4) in which we postulate in advance that the variable γ is present only in the first of these equations and the variable D appears only in the second. Suppose now that we use any simultaneous-equation estimation procedure to find some statistical relationships among the variables Q, A, γ and D. The system is identified if it is possible, in principle, to obtain one such statistical relationship which is known to be an approximation to equation (3) (the demand function) and another statistical function which approximates (4) (the budget function), and if it is possible to find out whether any given statistical curve derived in the process represents (3), (4) or neither. Suppose, then, we have obtained some such statistical function from our data on Q, A, γ or D. How might we be able to tell whether it represents a demand function, a budget function or a hodge-podge combination of the two? There are three possibilities:

1. Suppose, after our calculations are completed, we discover that the statistical relationship turns out to take the form $Q = (A, \gamma, D)$ in which all four variables are present (*all* of their coefficients are significantly different from zero). In that case we know that the statistics have given us a mongrel function resembling neither of the relationships we are seeking, for the equations of our model tell us that neither of the *true* relationships contains *both* variables γ and D.

2. Suppose now that the statistical relationship turns out to have an equation of the form $F(A, \gamma) = Q$; i.e., D plays no role in the equation. Then we can be fairly sure that no budget function component has sneaked into our statistical equation; for, if the budget equation had somehow gotten mixed into our calculation, the variable D would have shown up in our calculated equation, since it is present in the budget curve (4). The presence of the variable D would have shown at once that the budgeting relationship had intruded into our computation. But since, in the case we are discussing, we obtain an equation $Q = F(A, \gamma)$ *from which D is absent*, we conclude that our statistical equation must be an estimate of the demand relationship (3) alone.

3. Similarly, if the form of the statistical equation is $F(A, D) = Q$, it must represent the budget relationship (4) alone.

Thus the two variables γ and D, each of which appears in one and only one of the two *a priori* relationships in our model, have permitted us to identify both equations. For example, the presence of the variable D, which occurs only in the budget equation, acts as a warning signal which notifies us at once when the budget equation has somehow got itself mixed in with our demand information.

Least-squares Bias in Simultaneous Systems

Even if it transpires that a set of simultaneous relationships is identified so that it is appropriate to investigate them statistically, the analyst's troubles are not yet over. For the statistical methods which yield satisfactory results in determining the nature of a single relationship are apt to yield seriously biased results in the presence of simultaneous equations.

To show one way in which they may come about notice first that any economic relationships are constantly subject at least to small shifts as the result of minor random occurrences. A sudden change in the weather or a newspaper strike affects department store sales, rumours of a price rise may lead housewives to stock up on a product, and so on. Consequently, a demand curve can never be expected to stand still for very long. Rather, it is likely to shift back and forth so that its position will (at least) vary within a (more or less) narrow band.

Figure 6a illustrates the band within which our illustrative advertising-demand curve usually varies as the result of random disturbances. Suppose first that this is a single relationship situation so that the advertising-demand curve is the only relevant curve. Observed statistics are then likely to fall throughout this band as shown by the points in Figure 6a. The dots form a pattern very similar in shape to the demand curve itself. A least-square line fitted to these data will then tend to follow the same pattern and it will be a rather good representation of the true demand curve which the statistician is seeking.

Now let us contrast this with what happens when there is a second relationship present—our advertising budget line. The range of variation of these two curves is shown in Figure 6b, where both curves may be expected to shift about simultaneously. This means that the intersection points of the two curves are likely to move about within the diamond-shaped region $ABCD$. The dots within that region, then, represent the information which the statistician observes.

This time it will be noted that the pattern of dots does not resemble either curve closely. Moreover, a least-squares line, LL', fitted to these dots will generally pass approximately through a diagonal of the diamond moving upward and to the right from corner A to corner C. It should be clear to the reader that a diagonal line of this sort should appear to yield a good fit to such a diamond-shaped collection of dots (see Figure 6c). But from our state of omniscience

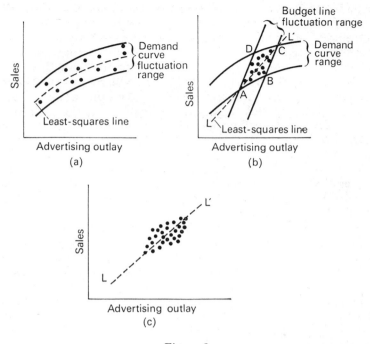

Figure 6

in Figure 6b we can easily see that this least-squares line is really a very poor approximation to the advertising-demand curve.

All sorts of alternative methods have been devised for simultaneous-equation estimation to avoid these difficulties of the standard least-squares approach. Aside from the full maximum-likelihood method, which is generally too expensive and cumbersome to be employed in practice, several alternatives have been designed and employed extensively. Noteworthy are the limited-information method, the instrumental variables method, and the multiple-stage least-squares method (which employs several repeated applications of the least-squares technique, designed to correct for its deficiencies). All of these are intended to serve as approximations to the maximum-likelihood method.

There is no point in trying to describe these methods here. It is enough for our purpose that the reader has been made aware of the statistical problems caused by the presence of simultaneous relationships and of the fact that methods exist for dealing with these difficulties.

Concluding Comments

We have seen, then, how difficult it is to find actual demand relationships in practice. These problems are, to a large extent, a consequence of the very peculiarity of the demand function concept itself—the fact that it represents the answers to a set of purely hypothetical questions and that the information is taken to pertain simultaneously to the same moment of time. Unfortunately, this odd demand relationship turns out to be indispensable to sophisticated decision-making within the firm. We simply have to learn to live with it, and to face up to the difficulties involved in its empirical determination. An essential part of this process is knowledge of the pitfalls which await the unwary investigators who set out to beard the demand function in its lair.

6

Demand Functions for Tobacco

by A. P. Koutsoyiannis

In this article[1] an attempt is made to establish the demand function for tobacco manufacturers for fourteen countries; the United States, the United Kingdom, France, Italy, the Netherlands, Belgium, Sweden, Norway, Austria, Finland, Greece, Canada, Australia and Ireland, a group which includes some of the world's most important tobacco consumers. These countries were the ones for which data were available.

The demand function for tobacco manufacturers has considerable theoretical interest. Tobacco manufactures have no direct substitutes, except other kinds of tobacco manufactures, mainly because of the extraordinary nature of the need which tobacco fulfils. Thus there are strong *theoretical* implications as to the price- and income-elasticities of demand for tobacco products. Furthermore, tobacco is such an important source of tax revenue to almost all countries, even those where there is no tobacco monopoly, that these elasticities assume a great *practical* importance.

Although tobacco might be considered a 'luxury' compared with the more basic needs of food, drink, etc., the consumption of tobacco products seems to be far more widespread than that of most other 'luxuries'. The smoking habit can be found in all income groups, and it is generally recognized that for many people the habit is extremely difficult to break. This is one of the reasons why demand for tobacco products may show a much smaller price- and income-elasticity than the demand for other 'luxuries'.

A further reason for low elasticities of demand for tobacco manufactures is the fact that there is no similar commodity that could be used as a 'direct substitute' to meet the demand to smoke. Moreover, tobacco has only one possible function as a part of final consumption, namely to be smoked. Of course there are indirect substitutes for tobacco, in the sense that all commodities purchased by the consumer compete for part of his income. Tobacco manufactures, however, are extraordinary to such a degree that the extent to which other goods compete for the consumer's income is likely to be small

From *The Manchester School*, 1963, pp. 1-20. Reprinted by permission of the author and the editor of the journal.

[1] This article arose out of research undertaken as part of the thesis requirement for the degree of Ph. D. in the Faculty of Economics and Social Studies at the University of Manchester. I am indebted to my supervisor, Prof. C. F. Carter, to Prof. J. Johnston and Mr. D. D. Bugg.

over a much wider range of incomes and prices than in the case of almost any other 'luxury' commodity.

One suspects that there is some substitution between the various types of tobacco products (cigarettes, pipe, etc.) and an even greater substitution between the many varieties of the same product (cigarettes of various brands, tobacco of various qualities, etc.). But this type of substitution raises questions different from those of substitution between tobacco goods and other goods in the consumer's final 'basket of goods', and these are not relevant to the present study.

Basic Procedures

For each of the fourteen countries we estimated a demand function of the form

$$Q = aM^\beta P^\gamma \, \pi^\delta \, n^\epsilon \, e^{rt} \tag{1}$$

where: Q = quantity of tobacco demanded, M = money income, P = price of tobacco goods, π = index of prices of other commodities, n = adult population, e = base of natural logarithms, and t = time in calendar years.

Such a relation assumes that:

1. The relationship between the dependent and the explanatory variables is non-linear. By taking logarithms we come to the following function (linear in logarithms):

$$\log_{10} Q = \log_{10} a + \beta \log_{10} M + \epsilon \log_{10} M + \ldots \ldots$$
$$\gamma \log_{10} P + \delta \log_{10} \pi + rt \log_{10} e \tag{2}$$

the parameters of which we estimated by least squares.
2. $\beta, \gamma, \delta, \epsilon$, are constant elasticities. In other words the elasticities of demand for tobacco with respect to income, price of tobacco, prices of other commodities, and population are taken as constant over time.
3. The trend takes the form of a constant rate of change per unit of time.

Our analysis covers the ten-year period 1950–1959. The time series of the variables used in the study of the consumption function are taken mainly from United Nations' statistics.[2]

Regarding the variables included in the demand function the following points should be noticed:

First, in empirical demand analysis it is customary to work with real prices and real income.[3] The theory of consumer demand rests

[2] See Koutsoyiannis and Kokkora, *An Econometric Study of the Leaf Tobacco Market of Greece* (Athens, 1962).

[3] See H. Wold and L. Juréen, *Demand Analysis*, Wiley publications in statistics, 1953, pp. 15–16.

on the assumption that money is a scale factor. Thus inflationary or deflationary pressures are regarded simply as changes in the monetary unit and are therefore assumed to have no influence on consumer behaviour. However, we decided to use money income series in our analysis. We made the assumption that consumers react to changes in money incomes and are much less conscious of changes in the real purchasing power of those money incomes. Experience suggests that this is a reasonable assumption, at least in periods where there are no violent movements in price levels, and therefore in real incomes. It is observed that in periods of depression consumers, and especially wage and salary earners, are influenced in their consumption patterns by money income, and the same seems to be true in periods of slow increases in prices. It is only when price increases take the form of rapid inflation that money income ceases to be the predominant guide in consumption patterns.[4] Therefore it is money income which is important for the demand function, especially for the countries studied and the period under consideration, during which increases in prices were moderate and never took the form of uncontrolled inflation.

Furthermore we believe that during this period there has been money illusion at work. Using nominal prices and income, the condition for the absence of money illusion would be indicated by $\beta + \gamma + \delta = 0$. If one uses nominal prices and real income[5] then the absence of money illusion would be indicated by the sum of the two price-elasticities being equal to zero. However, for reasons which will be explained below, we will make use of formulations using relative prices P/π as an explanatory variable. In such cases the use of real income in the relation would explicitly rule out the possibility of money illusion. Consequently when P/π appears in the relation, the use of money income M is essential, when in fact it is believed that money illusion has not been absent.

A third reason for using money income in our analysis is the fact that it is easier for economic interpretation and more convenient for practical computations to have the whole price effect (substitution plus income effect) measured by a single coefficient for each of P (price of tobacco) and π (prices of other commodities). We normally are interested in measuring the percentage change in the quantity demanded of a commodity as a result of a percentage change in its own price (P) or in prices of other commodities (π), not bothering to split this change into an 'income effect' and a 'substitution effect'.

In other words we are usually interested in the type of question: 'What will the change in Q be when we change P and/or π by a

---

[4] See also R. P. Congard, *Étude économetrique de la demand de tabac* (Paris, 1955).

[5] See, e.g. R. Stone, 'The Analysis of Market Demand', *Journal of the Royal Statistical Society*, vol. cviii (1945).

given percentage?' The answer to this question necessitates measurement of the elasticities of P and π by a single coefficient. This is not feasible if we introduce in the formulation real income and absolute prices, as for example in Stone's relation:

$$Q = aR^b P^c \pi^d e^{rt} \tag{3}$$

where: Q = quantity demanded, R = real income, P = price of the commodity, π = prices of other commodities, e^{rt} = trend factor, b,c,d = constant elasticities.

In Professor Stone's formulation P and π appear explicitly and they also enter into the function for a second time in computing real income. Thus the coefficients c and d reflect only part of the effect of price changes, namely the substitution effect. The income effect of a price change is lumped together with the 'pure' income-elasticity,[6] and thus the coefficient b measures partly the 'pure' income-elasticity and partly the income effect of a price change.

If we call money income M, and Π the cost of living index, which for simplicity we can assume is the simple form $\Pi = P^{w_1} \pi^{w_2}$ (and $w_1 + w_2 = 1$), we have $R = \dfrac{M}{\Pi} = \dfrac{M}{P^{w_1} \pi^{w_2}}$, and substituting in equation (3) we get:

$$Q = aM^b P^{c-bw_1} \pi^{d-bw_2} e^{rt} \tag{4}$$

In equation (4) the coefficients of P and π, namely $c - bw_1$ and $d - bw_2$ respectively, clearly comprise the whole price effect in the change in prices, i.e. a substitution effect (measured by c or d) plus the income effect of the price change (measured by $-bw_1$ or bw_2). These income effects, however, are absorbed into the coefficient of real income R in Stone's formulation (3). (Our formulation $Q = aM^\beta P^\gamma \pi^\delta e^{rt}$ is in fact identical with (4) with $\beta = b$, $\gamma = c - bw_1$ and $\delta = d - bw_2$.)

Second, our equation $Q = aM^\beta P^\gamma \pi^\delta e^{rt}$ involves absolute prices P and π. In other words the coefficients γ and δ (which we have seen represent total price-elasticities) are left to 'float free' without restriction. *A priori* we expect, in fact that $-\gamma > \delta$; i.e. that demand for tobacco is more sensitive to changes in the price of tobacco than to changes in other prices. By leaving γ and δ unrestricted, such a hypothesis can be tested directly, in terms of the estimated values of $\hat{\gamma}$ and $\hat{\delta}$.

An additional indirect examination of the hypothesis may be made by examining the results of calculations on a relation involving relative prices P/π, i.e. $Q = aM^h (P/\pi)^f e^{rt}$. Here the restriction is imposed upon the coefficients of P and π that $-\gamma = \delta = f$. We shall compare results of this 'restricted' formulation with those of our 'unrestricted' form.

[6]i.e. the percentage change in Q as a result of a percentage change in money income.

Third, in our analysis the variable 'price of tobacco products' is an average price for all tobacco products, computed by dividing total expenditure on tobacco during each year by the quantity consumed. The average price computed in this way will be a weighted average of the retail prices of all varieties during the year in question.

Thus the regression coefficient of P will be an average price-elasticity for one time period of a year. It is impossible to measure point elasticity, because of lack of data for short periods. One should know the retail prices over the whole year, the consumption figures and the changes in stocks. But even if it were feasible to measure the short-run elasticity, it would be of limited practical value. It is the long-run elasticity which is important for empirical analysis.[7] The reaction of consumers to any change in price in the short run is usually capricious. In particular for tobacco, experience shows that the immediate effect of a change in retail prices tends to be a turning to lower quality types of tobacco goods, so that the total quantity will be practically unaffected. After a short period (perhaps one to three months) consumers resume the old pattern of their demand.[8] Thus it is the long-run elasticity which is most significant from an economic point of view.

Similar considerations hold for the regression coefficient of income, which is the long-run income-elasticity (average elasticity of demand with respect to income over one time period).

Fourth, since tobacco has no obvious direct substitutes, we need not concern ourselves with the influence on tobacco consumption of the change in price of any other *particular* product. Instead, we examine the influence of changes in the prices of all other commodities as reflected by a general price index which should, of course, exclude the price of tobacco. Unfortunately we had to use the cost of living index of each country, which includes the price of tobacco, because we could not obtain an index excluding the weight of the tobacco price. However, the error introduced from this source can be expected to be small. Even if the price of tobacco could be extracted from the cost of living index, it would make no perceptible difference to the price index of the remainder.[9]

Fifth, the distribution of income has been suggested by economic theory as an important factor for demand analysis. In the post-war period in most Western countries there may well have been a tendency towards greater equality in the distribution of income. We think, however, that the influence of this factor on consumption cannot be important in the short run. If there has occurred any variation in Q because of changes in the distribution of income, we assume that it will be absorbed by the coefficient of income and the trend factor.

Sixth, there is the problem of population. One should take into

[7] See also H. Wold and L. Juréen.
[8] See also *Tobacco*, published by Barclays Bank D.C.O. (London, 1961), p. 62.
[9] See also R. Stone.

account in a demand function changes of population and its distribution by age and sex. This might be done either by working with *per capita* data, or by introducing adult popultion as a separate variable in the equation. The two methods differ in that the inclusion of population as a separate variable implies an attempt to measure directly the influence of population change upon quantity demanded Q; while the use of *per capita* data (of consumption and income) is equivalent to the assumption that the coefficients of income and population—in the formulation involving populaion 'n' explicitly—sum to unity.[10]

Alternatively, over the period considered one might reasonably expect any influence of the 'population' factor to be absorbed by the trend factor introduced in the equation, since in most cases 'n' and 't' are highly correlated. In fact, our series of population 'n' and 't' show a high correlation, as do the 'n' and M series (money income). The dangers here are, therefore, that singularity of the moment matrix of explanatory variables may make regression calculations impossible, or worse, that a slightly less than perfect correlation between, say, 'n' and 't' may cause rounding errors in the computations to yield spurious (though apparently valid) results.

Thus, we decided to attempt the measurement of the influence of population 'n' on Q using *per capita* data (which assumes that the coefficients of n and M sum to unity, a hypothesis which might not be true), though in some cases we also experimented with functions including 'n' as an explicit variable.

In general, where the function is expressed in aggregate, as distinct from *per capita*, terms, we assume that the influence of population is absorbed by the residual trend factor. We prefer to drop n out of our relation rather than t, since we anticipate that t should reflect other 'autonomous' factors which may be important for the consumption of tobacco, e.g. changes in the proportion of smokers to non-smokers which may not correspond exactly to changes in 'n'.

Seventh, we introduced time as an explanatory variable in our equation, in order to take care of continuous variation of variables which have not been introduced explicitly into the relationship. In particular in our analysis we expect this factor to account for changes in consuming habits, changes in the distribution of income, changes in the age and sex distribution of population etc. Furthermore, t is expected to absorb the influence of factors like income, population etc., which have a strong trend in them, in formulations where such factors are not explicitly included.

---

[10] For consider a formulation involving *per capita* consumption and income

$$Q/n = a(M/n)^\beta P^\gamma \pi^\delta e^{rt}$$
$$= aM^\beta P^\gamma \pi^\delta n^{-\beta} e^{rt}$$
$$Q = aM^\beta P^\gamma \pi^\delta n^{1-\beta} e^{rt}$$

i.e. this *per capita* form is identical with a formulation involving population 'n' explicitly, with the sum of the coefficients of M and n equal to unity.

Expected Elasticities

We come now to our *a priori* expectations about the signs, magnitudes or relative magnitudes of the regression coefficients.

(*a*) The income-elasticity of demand for all tobacco goods is expected to be positive. Tobacco is not an inferior good. This may be so for some of the lower-grade types of tobacco manufactures, but it is not true for tobacco as a whole.

(*b*) The elasticity of demand with respect to the price of tobacco is expected to be negative. In our relation, which is formulated in terms of nominal income and absolute prices, the coefficient of the price variable measures both the substitution effect and the income effect of the price change. The substitution effect is always negative as a necessary consequence of the 'preference hypothesis'.[11] The income effect is positive for normal goods, but negative for inferior goods. If the good is inferior and the substitution effect is smaller in absolute value than the income effect, i.e. if $|c| < |bw_1|$, the whole price effect will be positive. For this 'Giffen' case to arise, firstly the good must be inferior, secondly a considerable proportion of income must be spent on it, so that the income effect of a price change is important, and finally the substitution effect must be small. The first two conditions clearly do not apply to tobacco and consequently we must expect the price-elasticity to be negative.

(*c*) The elasticity of demand with respect to the average level of all other prices (π) is expected to be positive, since a rise in all other prices will render the commodity in question relatively less expensive and vice versa. However, as we shall see below, the influence of π on the quantity of tobacco demanded is expected to be unimportant.

As regards the magnitudes of the coefficients, we expect none of the elasticities to be large. In other words the demand for tobacco goods is expected to be inelastic with respect to their own price, income and prices of other commodities. On the other hand we expect the influence of population—especially the increase in the proportion of smokers to non-smokers—on the quantity demanded to be important.

First, the elasticity of demand with respect to tobacco price is expected to be low: (1) because smoking has become a very powerful social habit, so that tobacco is considered among the 'necessity' products; (2) because of lack of direct substitutes; (3) a third reason derives from the fact that the average price computed above is a 'statistical' price and the elasticity of demand with respect to changes

---

[11] See J. R. Hicks, *A Revision of Demand Theory* (Oxford: Clarendon Press, 1956), pp. 59–68.

in this 'computed price' cannot be high, and is not a 'true' elasticity. A *fall* in the 'statistical' average price may be due to a shift of the demand to lower quality products, due either to a fall in income or even to *increases* in the retail prices of the various tobacco goods, which attracts consumers to lower (cheaper) brands of tobacco manufactures. Similarly an *increase* of the 'statistical' average price may disguise either an increase in income, with no price change, or a *fall* of the retail prices of the various types of tobacco manufactures, both factors leading to a shift of the demand to higher quality—more expensive products.

Second, as regards income-elasticity, we notice that tobacco, being a 'necessity', is bought in quantities adequate to satisfy more or less the need of smoking. Thus when income increases tobacco consumption may be expected to increase less than proportionally, especially in the countries under consideration where income is already high. A low income-elasticity might be expected for an additional reason. Unlike most other 'necessity' products, tobacco is offered at a very wide variety of prices, according to the quality of the type of tobacco goods. When income decreases, the consumer has the alternative of turning to cheaper brands without being obliged to curtail the total quantity consumed. Thus when income falls, the quantity of tobacco consumed may not be much affected, though there may be a shift of consumption to lower quality tobacco products. Similarly when income increases the effect on the quantity of tobacco consumed may well be expected to be small, while it may be expected to cause a shift of the demand to higher quality (more expensive) varieties. This substitution cannot be measured because of lack of data. One would need analytical data of 'real' consumption by types, retail prices of each type, changes in stocks etc. One would, of course, expect that such influences would reflect themselves in a positive correlation between the time series of money income and average tobacco price. However, the inverse observation, that the observed correlation does reflect such influences, need not be valid, since it ignores other 'trend' influences on both series.Thus we content ourselves with the *a priori* expectation of a low income-elasticity.

Third, as for the prices of other commodities, tobacco does not have direct substitutes, and cannot substitute for other commodities, so that changes in the prices of other commodities are expected to have practically no influence on the demand for tobacco, at least in the fourteen countries examined.

Fourth, the influence of changes in adult population which we are assuming to be reflected in 't', is expected to be important for the consumption of tobacco. Furthermore, one of the most important factors in the increase of tobacco consumption has been the increase in the proportion of smokers to non-smokers, mainly because of the extension of smoking among women and members of lower age groups.

Statistical Procedure

In our calculations we adopted a procedure which combined the theoretical considerations discussed above with empirical observations, designed to extract the maximum of information from our observed statistical series. That is, we performed least squares regression calculations on a demand function (linear in logarithms) of the form of (2) above. However, we began by calculating the regression of Q on just one explanatory variable, namely money income M (which on *a priori* grounds we believed to be the most significant variable in explaining variations in tobacco consumption). As calculations were then carried out by adding other explanatory variables in various combinations, we were able to observe the statistical effects of such additions in an attempt to use our data to the full in throwing light on our function. Each time a new variable is introduced because it is thought to explain a significant part of the variation in the dependent variable of the relation, three statistical effects on the relation will normally result.

1. The new variable will have some effect, minor or major, on the 'systematic part' of the relation. In other words, the new variable will or will not be shown to explain a significant part of the variation of the dependent variable.
2. It will affect the 'non-systematic' (residual) part of the relationship, for example because of errors of observation in this new variable.
3. It will have some minor or major effect upon the *coefficients* of the variables already included in the equation. We should notice that if an important variable is omitted, not only may the overall fit of the relation be worse, but the coefficients of the included variables may well be distorted from the values which would be obtained from a complete analysis. In this case the introduction of the new variable will 'correct' the value of the coefficients of the other explanatory variables.[12]

Clearly we need some criteria to decide whether the introduction of a new variable or variables into our relation has proved 'significant' and meaningful, or not.

The criteria, which we used for deciding whether to accept or reject the newly introduced variable, were the following.

1. A new variable was judged useful if it improved the multiple correlation coefficient (R^2), thus indicating a better fit of the regression plane. This is an important indicator for acceptance of the new variable, but not a sufficient one.
2. The introduction of the new variable should furthermore affect the coefficients of the other explanatory variables in a meaningful

[12] See R. Stone.

way. By this we mean that the new variable would not be acceptable if it gave the 'wrong' signs to the other coefficients, or ascribed to them unreasonably high or low values. There is always the question of the *a priori* expectations about the parameters. In most cases these are rather restrictive, so that if we find 'wrong' signs of the coefficients, for example, we must look elsewhere for a better formulation of our model, irrespective of the apparent goodness of fit of the expression in which these results are found.

3. The new variable must not be linearly correlated with the other independent variables. If the explanatory variables are perfectly intercorrelated it is not possible to partition the variation in the *dependent* variable between the explanatory variables: in other words the structural coefficients of the regression will be arbitrary, although the over-all relation may still be useful for prediction. If the explanatory variables are highly but not perfectly intercorrelated, estimates of the structural coefficients can be obtained, but they will be subject to large sampling errors. Here the decision to retain the new variables will depend on *a priori* economic criteria as well as statistical considerations.

4. The '*F*' tests on the estimated coefficients must show that the new variable is significant, though in attempting to apply tests of significance, especially when the number of observations is small, we should bear in mind that by introducing additional variables we lose degrees of freedom, a fact that is expected to render the statistical tests of significance less reliable. Thus in this case also the *a priori* expectations about the signs and values of the coefficients will be important in deciding about the acceptance or rejection of the new variable.

Autocorrelated residuals in any of our formulations are a possible source of error, casting some doubt upon the validity of the '*F*' tests used as a criterion for choosing between the various formulations. However, in all our computations the number of observations is small. Consequently we do not consider the Durbin-Watson '*d*' statistic to be sufficiently reliable, either as an additional criterion for choice between relations, or to suggest further statistical investigation of the structure of the residuals.

The Results

We carried out regression calculations on the following combinations of factors for each of the fourteen countries.

A. Absolute prices—Money income. Aggregate data of Q and M.

$$1. \quad Q = f(M)$$
$$2. \quad Q = f(M,P)$$
$$3. \quad Q = f(M,t)$$

    4. $Q = f(M,P,\pi)$
    5. $Q = f(M,P,t)$
    6. $Q = f(M,P,\pi,t)$

B. Absolute prices—Money income. *Per capita* data of Q and M.

    7. $Q/n = f(M/n)$
    8. $Q/n = f(M/n,P)$
    9. $Q/n = f(M/n,P,\pi)$
  10. $Q/n = f(M/n,P,t)$
  11. $Q/n = f(M/n,P,\pi,t)$

C. Relative prices—Money income. Aggregate data of Q and M.

  12. $Q = f(M,P/\pi)$
  13. $Q = f(M,P/\pi,t)$

D. Relative prices—Money income. *Per capita* data of Q and M.

  14. $Q = f(M/n,P/\pi)$
  15. $Q/n = f(M/n,P/\pi,t)$

We started by computing models including only income as an explanatory variable. Countries with high income rates are the heaviest consumers of tobacco. Consumption per adult tends to be lower in the less industrialized countries with generally lower *per capita* incomes. On the other hand, high proportions of smokers are found even in the low income groups of the United States and the United Kingdom, both heavy consuming countries, and this is probably true also for most other countries with high total consumption.

Experience, furthermore, suggests that changes in price have little permanent effect on consumer demand for tobacco. Despite the very high levels to which taxes on tobacco have risen in many countries, demand has survived and consumption has, in general, increased. The immediate reaction against an increase in price is often a falling off in the quantity consumed, but it is common experience that within a short period demand recovers. It also seems true that when price rises, or when incomes decline, the consumer tends to turn to a cheaper 'smoke' rather than cut down his smoking, so that even in the short run the quantity consumed is not seriously affected.

Thus it seems justifiable on empirical grounds to consider income as the main factor determining the demand for tobacco.

Starting with aggregate money income as a single explanatory variable, $Q = f(M)$, we obtain a fairly good fit in most countries. Only in the case of Belgium and Austria is R^2 very low, and in Ireland and Austria the coefficient of M takes the 'wrong' (negative) sign. The value of the income-elasticity is in all cases less than unity (with the exception of Australia) but is significantly different from zero according to the 'F' test.

If we introduce price of tobacco as a second explanatory variable, $Q = f(M,P)$, we obtain an improved fit in the case of the United States, France, Italy, Belgium, Sweden, Finland, Ireland and Australia. The coefficients of price and income acquire expected signs and values, with the exception of Italy, where the price-elasticity is rather high, and Australia, where the coefficient of M is higher than expected. Furthermore, the income-elasticity is significant in all these countries except Ireland, while the coefficient of P satisfies the 'F' test only in four cases, France, Italy, Finland and Ireland (significant at least at 5 per cent level).

In the remaining six countries the coefficient of price takes the 'wrong' (positive) sign and is insignificant. In most cases the over-all correlation coefficient is slightly higher, though less significant than in the formulations including only aggregate income as independent variable. In the case of Austria both coefficients acquire unexpected signs. In general the results of aggregate models in the case of Austria do not give plausible results.

The formulations including aggregate income and a trend factor as explanatory variables, $Q = f(M,t)$, give in general worse results than the previous formulation involving P and M, with the exception of the Netherlands.

If we introduce π (prices of other commodities) as a third explanatory variable, $Q = f(M,P,\pi)$, we obtain in all cases a slightly higher but less significant R^2. The coefficient of π acquires in some cases the 'wrong' sign, while in all countries it is statistically insignificant. The only case in which the coefficient of π seems to be somehow significant, despite its negative sign, is Greece, where special conditions permit the formulation of different expectations about the sign and significance of the coefficient of π. Greece has the lowest income per head of all the fourteen countries under consideration. Thus it would seem realistic to expect the demand for tobacco to be sensitive to changes in the cost of living, and, moreover, for Q to change in the opposite direction to changes in π. As prices of other commodities increase, low income consumers cannot afford to spend as much of their income as before on tobacco, and consequently reduce the quantity smoked.

If instead of π we introduce time as a third explanatory variable, $Q = f(M,P,t)$, in an attempt to reflect mainly the influence of population changes on the demand for tobacco, we obtain in general 'better' results for Italy, the Netherlands, Sweden, Finland, Ireland and Australia. In the cases of the United States ($Q = f(M,P,n)$) and the United Kingdom ($Q = f(M,P,n,t)$), introduction of adult population (n) as a direct explanatory variable appears to yield quite satisfactory results.

In the remaining countries neither 't' nor 'n' seems to improve the results obtained from the formulation containing P and M as explanatory variables. Despite a higher (though less significant) R^2, the sign of at least one of the coefficients of the explanatory variables cannot be accepted on theoretical considerations.

If we introduce all four explanatory variables M, P, π, t, simultaneously in the equation, once more we reach the conclusion that π (prices of other commodities) is not a significant factor in the explanation of the variation of the quantity of tobacco demanded, with the exception perhaps of Greece.

The formulations involving *per capita* data give in most cases worse results than the equivalent combinations of aggregate data from the statistical point of view. The only exceptions are Austria and Canada, where the results obtained from the models including *per capita* data are considerably more satisfactory. In all other cases, however, the conclusions about the significance of the explanatory variables, their signs, values and their interpretation in general are broadly the same as those derived from the equations expressed in terms of aggregate consumption and income.

On the basis of the above considerations, we arrive at the functions shown in Table 1 as the most satisfactory explanation of the variation in the quantity of tobacco demanded for each of the 14 countries examined.

Comments on the Tests of the Hypotheses $-\gamma \neq \delta$ and $-\gamma > \delta$

The formulations including absolute prices P and π permit a direct comparison of the coefficients of P and π. This comparison shows that $-\gamma \neq \delta$ in all models. Furthermore:

1. in 7 countries (the U.S.A., France, Italy, Finland, Austria, Greece and Australia) our hypothesis that consumers are more sensitive to changes in price of tobacco than in prices of other commodities is true; in other words for these countries we found that $-\gamma > \delta$;
2. in two countries (Norway and Ireland) the opposite seems to be true, in other words consumers appear to be more sensitive to changes in π than in P; thus $-\gamma < \delta$;
3. in the remaining countries (the U.K., the Netherlands, Belgium, Sweden and Canada) in some models we observed $-\gamma > \delta$, while in others we found that $-\gamma < \delta$.

Another indirect test of the hypothesis that $-\gamma \neq \delta$ is to compute models including relative prices P/π. Such formulations assume that $-\gamma = \delta$. Thus if these models yield 'worse' results than the relations including absolute prices P and π, this suggests that the two price-elasticities are different.

The results of the models including P/π show that: In eight countries (France, Italy, the Netherlands, Sweden, Finland, Austria, Canada, Australia) the formulations with relative prices give 'worse' fits, in general. In three countries (the U.S.A., Norway, Ireland) the models including relative prices seem to give a better fit. Finally in three countries (the U.K., Belgium and Greece) the results of models with relative prices are equally as 'good' as those of formulations including absolute prices. Thus, in most cases, our results suggest that consumers of tobacco do not act according to the usual suggestions of economic theory. Though the evidence is by no means unambiguous it seems plausible to accept that $-\gamma \neq \delta$.

In analysing our results, we should notice several possible sources of error.

1. The number of observations is small. Sampling errors in a ten-year period may be expected to be considerable.
2. Errors in the variables have been inevitable in our study and may well give misleading estimates of the true parameters. Thus: (*a*) the data for consumption of tobacco are in fact figures of the manufacturing production of tobacco goods. Unfortunately data of tobacco consumption, like most consumption statistics, are scarce. Of course, demand is not the same as supply, since consumption and production in general are not in perfect equilibrium, especially if we consider data for a limited period. Thus, production data should be corrected to account for changes in stocks, as well as for imports and exports.[13]

However, the error introduced from this source is probably unimportant. For one reason, changes in stocks of tobacco manufacturers are negligible. Tobacco products cannot be stored for a long time without losing their special characteristics (flavour, humidity, etc.); thus manufacturers stockpile leaf tobacco instead, with which they can fairly easily meet abrupt changes in demand, since the manufacturing process is rather short. Imports and exports of tobacco manufactures on the other hand offset each other to a certain degree. Furthermore, they are relatively unimportant when compared with total consumption in each country. Despite that, some error cannot be avoided from the use of production data, since in particular any error may be amplified and carried through into the 'average statistical price', which, as we saw, is computed by dividing total expenditure on tobacco by the total manufacturing production of tobacco goods.

(*b*) Ideally, one should use personal disposable income in a demand function. Unfortunately the required series of disposable personal income were not available, and we used 'total national income at factor cost' instead.

(*c*) The cost of living index used as an index of changes in prices of other commodities, includes the price of tobacco. However, the weight of a single commodity is usually small in the cost of living index. Thus, even if we extracted the price of tobacco, it would make no perceptible difference to the price index of the remainder.

---

[13] See also H. Wold and L. Juréen.

3. Some distortions of the parameter estimates may well be expected, because most time series used in the formulation of the demand function are highly correlated. We tried to detect and take into account such distortions by introducing each explanatory variable separately into the equation and studying its effects on the other coefficients and the over-all fit, both statistically and in relation to our *a priori* economic criteria. However, because of multi-collinearity we must view the actual numerical values of our estimates with a certain amount of suspicion.

4. The observed '*d*' statistic often suggests autocorrelation in the 'disturbance term', a fact which invalidates statistical tests on the coefficients. Another reason for suspecting that the statistical tests are not reliable is the limited number of observations, which leaves very few degrees of freedom.

However, bearing in mind these deficiencies, we can draw the following tentative general conclusions regarding our hypotheses postulated above.

First, the assumption of constant elasticities has yielded plausible results. In all fourteen countries the formulation finally selected is capable of explaining the greatest proportion of the variation in consumption of tobacco (i.e. R^2 is fairly high in all cases).

Second, price- and income-elasticities are low. Demand for tobacco manufactures in the countries and the period under review has been rather inelastic to changes in price of tobacco or in incomes. In all countries both price- and income-elasticities are well below unity.

Third, in all countries (except Greece) the prices of other commodities do not appear to have influenced the consumption of tobacco manufactures. In all countries it seems true that $-\gamma \neq \delta$, in other words consumers do not react to relative prices. Furthermore, in most cases tobacco consumers tend to be more conscious of changes in the price of tobacco than in the prices of other commodities, i.e. $-\gamma > \delta$. This result is supported both directly by the results of the formulations including unrestricted prices (P, π), and indirectly by the 'poorer' results of most relative price models.

Fourth, the results of our analysis gave inconclusive evidence concerning the existence of money illusion. In our formulation the absence of money illusion would be indicated by $\beta + \gamma + \delta = 0$. However, the variable π was dismissed as insignificant to the relation for all countries excepting Greece, reducing the condition for the absence of money illusion in the final formulation for each of those thirteen countries to $\beta + \gamma = 0$. ($\beta + \delta = 0$ in the case of Greece.)

Significance tests based on the estimated variance–covariance matrix of parameters in each case showed $\beta + \gamma$ to be significantly different from zero (at the 5 per cent level) in only six out of the final fourteen formulations selected. Further investigation based on wider information as it became available would therefore seem to be necessary before we can (*a*) produce more satisfactory significance

Table 1

Final Results for the Demand Function of the Fourteen Countries

	Countries	$\log_{10}a$	γ_P	β_M	δ_n	ϵ_n	r_t	R^2	d
1	U.S.A. $\quad Q = f(P,M,n)$	-11.84419 (2.13)	-0.93726 (5.63)	0.33698 (1.18)	—	2.18760 (3.20)	—	0.722 (5.21)	1.134
2	U.K. $\quad Q = f(P,M,n,t)$	-30.43041 (45.93)	-0.03647 (0.17)	0.06628 (1.07)	—	4.26654 (28.24)	0.00637 (1.28)	0.997 (493.1)	1.633
3	France $\quad Q = f(P,M,t)$	19.40504 (2.06)	-0.54394 (14.90)	0.82818 (12.87)	—	—	-0.02351 (1.60)	0.937 (30.23)	1.887
4	Italy $\quad Q = f(P,M,t)$	-14.20161 (1.18)	-0.82040 (4.61)	0.48480 (2.11)	—	—	0.02213 (1.32)	0.989 (186.3)	1.540
5	Netherl. $\quad Q = f(P,M,t)$	-9.73522 (1.08)	-0.07837 (0.16)	0.10303 (0.82)	—	—	0.01913 (2.37)	0.986 (147.4)	2.526
6	Belgium $\quad Q = f(P,t)$	-19.26284 (4.80)	-0.67797 (7.04)	—	—	—	0.03332 (9.07)	0.574 (4.72)	1.048
7	Sweden $\quad Q = f(P,M,t)$	-14.87188 (0.34)	-0.41373 (1.83)	0.26324 (0.17)	—	—	0.02339 (0.40)	0.789 (7.49)	1.292
8	Norway $\quad Q = f(M)$	4.82726 (209.9)	—	0.18124 (31.21)	—	—	—	0.796 (31.21)	2.627
9	Finland $\quad Q = f(P,M,t)$	-22.99165 (10.57)	-0.41495 (30.03)	0.13224 (2.65)	—	—	0.03493 (14.05)	0.918 (22.58)	2.715
10	Austria $\quad Q/n = f(P,M/n,t)$	-29.24782 (31.02)	-0.95120 (98.72)	0.11482 (3.42)	—	—	0.03684 (31.53)	0.987 (160.3)	1.698
11	Greece $\quad Q = f(M,\pi,t)$	-22.13187 (12.73)	—	0.06545 (0.36)	-0.36525 (4.96)	—	0.03430 (17.78)	0.965 (55.77)	1.698
12	Ireland $\quad Q = f(P,M,t)$	24.17338 (1.76)	-0.14709 (1.04)	0.55557 (1.07)	—	—	-0.02595 (1.00)	0.722 (5.19)	2.996

| 13 | Canada | $Q/n = f(P,M/n,t)$ | −16.53282 (6.08) | −0.20938 (0.30) | 0.08983 (0.17) | — | 0.02008 (5.38) | 0.902 (18.35) | 2.015 |
| 14 | Australia | $Q = f(P,M,t)$ | −32.46265 (2.54) | −0.36186 (3.43) | 0.42580 (0.81) | — | 0.04232 (2.08) | 0.977 (86.84) | 1.445 |

Note: The numbers in brackets are the values of the '*F*' tests on the estimated parameters.

tests after a more serious investigation of serial correlation in the residuals, and (*b*) arrive at firmer conclusions concerning our money illusion hypothesis.

Fifth, tobacco consumption in most countries seems to be influenced mainly by changes in the number of smokers either as a result of increase in total population or of increase in the proportion of smokers to non-smokers. Such influences in the functions for many countries have adequately been absorbed by the residual trend factor.

The above conclusions about the magnitudes and the significance of the regression coefficients are confirmed by computations with *per capita* data of consumption and income.

Thus for most of the countries examined the results obtained appear fairly unsatisfactory, though more confident conclusions, based upon more satisfactory functions, must await further investigation with more observations when they become available.

7

The Demand for Herring: A Single-Equation Model[1]

by Charles M. Allan

This article reports on the successful estimation of demand equations for herring. This work claims the attention of economists on two grounds. First the prices observed, unlike the vast majority of prices, are *equilibrium* prices being achieved by auction. And secondly because the *identification problem* is avoided, which enables demand to be estimated using a simple one equation model.

Since H. L. Moore[2] investigating the demand for pig-iron found a positive sign on the regression line of Price on Quantity the problem of separating and identifying supply and demand has been recognized. As E. J. Working in his famous article[3] showed, what Moore observed was a series of market equilibria. Each point represented the intersection of *a* supply curve with *a* demand curve but there was no reason for thinking that the same demand or supply curve was common to any two observed equilibria. Moore either observed a supply curve (Figure 1) or a regression line produced by the movement of the demand and to a *lesser* extent also the movement of supply (Figure 2). This regression line has no meaningful equivalent in the static theory of price.

One can never be quite sure in the statistical measurement of the demand that what one is measuring is 'demand'. Indeed one only has to consider that both demand and supply are functions of price to see that the problem of identifying which blade is doing the cutting is considerable.

The most usual approach to the problem is to estimate demand and supply using simultaneous equations. This procedure is subject to stochastic variation and does not often yield convincing estimates of demand. This paper gives an interesting example of the successful statistical estimation of demand using two simple single-equation three-variable models not unlike those used by Moore.

A second barrier to the successful estimation of demand curves

From *Scottish Journal of Political Economy* (Feb. 1973), pp. 91–8. Reprinted by permission of The Scottish Economic Society and the editor.

[1] I am indebted to the Herring Industry Board for statistical information and the opportunity to do this work. I should also like to acknowledge the technical help I received from Mustafa A. Ali and the helpful comments of A. B. Jack, A. J. Phipps and E. Ramm.

[2] *Economic Cycles: Their Law and Cause* (1914).

[3] 'What Do Statistical "Demand Curves" Show?', *Quarterly Journal of Economics*, vol. 41 (1927), pp. 212–35; reprinted in H. Townsend (ed.), *Price Theory* (Harmondsworth: Penguin, 1971).

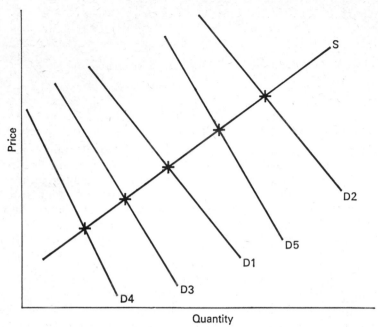

Figure 1

is the fact that by far the majority of prices are not equilibrium prices at all. Market analysis of the classical type, which forms such a large part of undergraduate training and which lies at the back of so much of economists' thinking about market, assumes that prices are made by the intersection of demand and supply schedules and that prices will be determined on the basis of market-clearing; that there will be equilibrium prices. Whilst we all believe that something, not altogether unlike the classical market mechanism does exist statistical investigation is not easy. The only statistical information available is actual prices paid and received and quantities bought and sold. Most prices are not in fact equilibrium prices. They may reveal points which are neither on the supply curve nor on the demand curve: stocks are normally being increased or decreased and queues are common. As Eckstein and Fromm[4] have observed, 'the continuous clearing case where production equals supply and supply equals demand is probably an exception. Disequilibrium is the more common situation.' Market clearing is achieved in this case of the British quayside market for herring as there are no stocks and all of each day's catch is sold immediately by auction.

One set of conditions sufficient for the successful statistical estimation of demand using single-equation estimating techniques is:

[4] O. Eckstein and G. Fromm, 'The Price Equation', *American Economic Review*, vol. 58, No. 5, Part 2 (1968), pp. 1159–83.

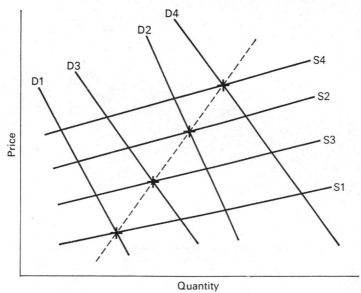

Figure 2

1. A highly perishable product
2. A unified market
3. A homogeneous and divisible product
4. Adequate accurate statistical information
5. Supply which varies in response to exogenous influences
6. Demand which remains constant for long enough to enable a sufficient number of observations to be made.

If these conditions are met it will be possible to identify demand by plotting successive market equilibrium quantities and prices as in Figure 3.

These conditions were all met to a satisfactory degree in the case of the British Quayside Market for herring.

1. The herring is very highly perishable. Herring must be sold on the day of landing. Sale is by auction which ensures market clearing. If a glut forces the price down the meal manufacturers will buy (at a low minimum price of 75p per cran) any surplus for making into fish meal.
2. The British market for herring consists of several major and several minor centres. They are linked by an efficient transport system and the buyers of all but a few fish consumed locally have efficient telecommunications with all major ports. Thus price differentials are principally determined by differences in transport costs. A change in landings may be expected to have the same effect on prices irrespective of where it occurs.
3. The quality of herring varies considerably due to variation in size,

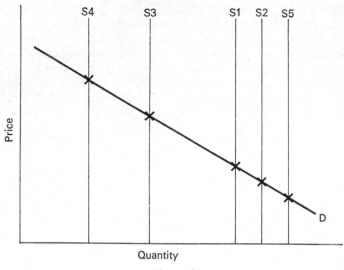

Figure 3

time since catching and oil content. Although each catch is described by the Herring Industry Board representative at the port, it proved impossible to use this information on quality. The principal difference in quality appeared to be between summer (oily) and winter (dry) fish. It was therefore decided to estimate two demand equations per year—one for summer quality fish and one for winter quality. Herring is a divisible product.

4. A great deal of statistical information was available from the Herring Industry Board. But the only usable material giving both quantity and price for the same fish is the annual figures and the weekly figures for *all ports* together. This then was the information from which demand was estimated.

5. Supply is determined by the number of boats going out to hunt herring. This is vitally affected by the day of the week. There is nothing on the Sabbath as most of the boats are Scots. There is nothing on Monday because catching fish for Monday means setting out on Sunday. Tuesday is a good day and so is Thursday because this gets the fish into the shops for Friday. Saturday is less good, demand being less as Saturday's fish can't be sold until Monday and discriminating housewives will know that the fish is not fresh. The problem then is that, on this account supply *is* determined by demand to some extent—we do have some identification problem.

It was attempted to overcome this problem by estimating demand separately for each day of the week. The information necessary to do this was not available. The problem was then overcome by taking weekly average sales and average prices. In this case supply in any one week is very largely determined by the biology of the herring and the weather. These are exogenous factors which affect supply and indeed alter it daily.

6. It is 'common knowledge' that the quality of herring increases dramatically in early June each year and stays high until around Christmas when quality declines drastically. This is reflected in the demand for herring at the ports. It was therefore assumed that demand was stable between June and December and between January and May. There may be some circularity here but the veracity of this assumption is supported by the high R^2 achieved in the equations 1–16 estimated in this paper.

To a greater or lesser extent the conditions 1–6 have not been completely fulfilled. It was felt that they were sufficiently nearly met to make the attempt to estimate statistical demand equations worthwhile. The proof of this matter rests largely on what extent the models tested proved to be statistically significant.

The Models Tested

Two, three-variable equations were estimated.
The first:

$$P_t = f(Q_t, Q_{t-a})$$
$$\text{where } P_t = \text{Price in period } t$$
$$Q_t = \text{Quantity in period } t$$
$$Q_{t-a} = [Q_{t-1} - \text{antilog } 4.2] \text{ Zero if negative.}$$

Q_{t-a} was included because it was widely held that landings of over 26,000 crans (=antilog 4.2) in $t-1$ reduced P_t. The asymmetry of the effect of Q_{t-1} on price—having a negative effect on price above 26,000 crans but no effect if smaller—is related to the size of the cold storage capacity. Thus landings in Q_{t-1} will have no effect on price as long as there is plenty of storage space. However, a Q_{t-1} of over 26,000 crans has the effect of causing a shortage of available storage and so of reducing the quantity demand for freezing.

$$U_t \text{ is an error term.}$$

The estimating equation was:

$$\log P_t = \log a + b \log Q_t + c \log Q_{t-a} + U_t$$

	$\log a$	$b \log Q_t$	$c \log Q_{t-a}$
1964 1st half	1.492 —	0.232	— 0.662
SE	(0.296)	(0.079)	(1.130)
t	5.04	2.94	0.59
R^2	0.396		
1964 2nd half	2.798 —	0.490	— 0.360
SE	(0.404)	(0.098)	(0.215)
t	6.91	4.99	1.67
R^2	0.608		

1965 1st half	1.500	−	0.217	−	0.686
SE	(0.121)		(0.034)		(0.301)
t	12.41		6.36		2.28
R^2	0.814				
1965 2nd half	1.502	−	0.173	−	0.673
SE	(0.204)		(0.051)		(0.472)
t	7.37		3.42		1.43
R^2	0.398				
1966 1st half	2.311	−	0.429	+	0.116
SE	(0.266)		(0.075)		(0.352)
t	8.69		5.69		0.33
R^2	0.792				
1966 2nd half	2.673	−	0.473	−	0.482
SE	(0.209)		(0.051)		(0.147)
t	12.81		9.27		3.28
R^2	0.814				
1967 1st half	0.925	−	0.047	−	0.940
SE	(0.109)		(0.029)		(0.198)
t	8.48		1.69		4.78
R^2	0.687				
1967 2nd half	2.741	−	0.492	−	0.503
SE	(2.731)		(0.068)		(0.202)
t	10.04		7.24		1.81
R^2	0.787				

The second:

$$P_t = f(\dot{Q}_t, Q_{t-n})$$

where $Q_{t-n} = (0.6\,Q_{t-1} + 0.3\,Q_{t-2} + 0.1\,Q_{t-3} - \text{antilog } 4.2)$
Zero if negative. Q_{t-n} was a weighted average of the previous three quantities as it seemed plausible to suppose that past quantities would affect price and that such effects would diminish through time. Like Q_{t-a} in the previous equation this variable was specified in such a way that only the effects of large landings on price were estimated.

Here the estimating equation was:

$$\log P_t = \log a + b \log Q_t + c \log Q_{t-n} + U_t$$

1964 1st half	1.490	−	0.232	−	0.351
SE	(0.327)		(0.088)		(1.187)
t	4.56		2.63		0.30
R^2	0.329				
1964 2nd half	2.945	−	0.530	−	0.128
SE	(0.506)		(0.124)		(0.421)
t	5.82		4.28		0.30
R^2	0.569				

1965 1st half	1.381	—	0.175	—	0.790
SE	(0.117)		(0.035)		(0.216)
t	11.84		5.04		3.65
R^2	0.896				
1965 2nd half	1.508	—	0.175	—	0.812
SE	(0.206)		(0.051)		(0.658)
t	7.33		3.44		1.24
R^2	0.387				
1966 1st half	2.179	—	0.386	—	0.195
SE	(0.340)		(0.101)		(0.376)
t	6.42		3.84		0.52
R^2	0.801				
1966 2nd half	2.629	—	0.462	—	0.371
SE	(0.211)		(0.052)		(0.112)
t	12.43		8.92		3.30
R^2	0.814				
1967 1st half	1.721	—	0.275	—	0.058
SE	(0.255)		(0.729)		(0.218)
t	6.74		3.78		0.27
R^2	0.785				
1967 2nd half	2.739	—	0.491	—	0.503
SE	(0.254)		(0.063)		(0.224)
t	10.9		7.79		2.25
R^2	0.800				

Both models give results which are acceptable. All show high R^2s and have at least one explanatory variable which is highly significant and in all but one case the sign is as expected. Although the R^2s are roughly the same with the two models the second is preferred for the following reasons.

1. With the first model 1966 1st half there is an unexpected sign for Q_{t-a}.
2. With the first model an odd result for 1967 1st half emerges. The result that Q_t is not significant is unlikely.
3. The variance of the constant term (a) and the price-elasticity of this demand is much smaller in the case of the second model. This is shown in Tables 1 and 2.

It seems intuitively more plausible that the more stable relationships are produced by the most appropriate model although there is no *a priori* proof that it is so.

Because of the paucity of equilibrium prices in modern economies the possibility of deducing demand curves by observation of price changes is confined to such cases where market clearing is achieved. Indeed the applicability of this type of simple one-equation model to problems of demand estimation is likely to be limited. Its chief interest is that of the limiting case where supply is determined

Table 1
Values of Constant Term (a) by Model

	First model		Second model	
	Jan.–June	July–Dec.	Jan.–June	July–Dec.
1964	1.5	2.8	1.5	2.9
1965	1.5	1.5	1.4	2.2
1966	2.3	2.6	1.5	2.6
1967	0.9	2.7	1.7	2.7

Table 2
Price-Elasticities of Demand by Model

	First model		Second model	
	Jan.–June	July–Dec.	Jan.–June	July–Dec.
1964	4.3	2.0	4.3	1.9
1965	4.6	5.2	5.2	5.2
1966	2.3	2.1	2.6	2.1
1967	21.3	2.0	3.6	2.0

exogenously. However there will be other cases where, because the product is perishable and subject to supply variations in response to natural phenomena like the weather, where such an approach may be worth attempting. Fresh fruit, such as strawberries, and of course all other fish come near to fulfilling the conditions mentioned above— conditions sufficient for overcoming the identification problem and the need for models using simultaneous equations.

8

The Demand for Car Ownership: A Note

by M. J. Buxton and D. G. Rhys

Existing statistical estimates of the aggregate demand for cars suggest that the main explanatory variables are price and some measure of *per capita* income. Whilst other factors, such as socio-economic indices of various kinds and variables relating to credit conditions have been tried, none of these have tended to add much to the explanatory power of the models involved. In fact price and income variables alone, in some cases, have been found to explain up to 95 per cent of the variation in demand.[1]

These main econometric studies have yielded values for the long-run elasticity of demand in the range 1.1 to 4.2. For instance Evans[2] suggests that a 1 per cent change in income would lead to a 1.1 per cent change in the expenditure on cars (although he measures the short-run elasticity as 2.2). At the other end of the scale, Suits[3] estimates the income elasticity of the demand for new cars as 4.2. Similarly the empirical studies place the long-run price-elasticity of the demand for cars between −0.6 and −1.5, although Evans calculates a short-run coefficient of −3.1. These studies however, were concerned with aggregate demand functions, and were not intended to examine variations in demand response according to area, or on a regional basis. A study by Bennett[4] introduced the rural or urban location of the family unit as an explanatory variable. He found that the higher the ratio of rural to urban families the higher the level of the demand for cars.

From *Scottish Journal of Political Economy* (June 1972), pp. 175–81. Reprinted by permission of The Scottish Economic Society and the editor.

[1] For example, G. C. Chow, 'Statistical Demand Functions for Automobiles and Their Use for Forecasting', in A. C. Harberger, *The Demand for Durable Goods* (Chicago, 1960), expressing the stock of automobiles in new-car equivalent units finds that price and disposable income variables together explain 85–90 per cent of the variance in the stock of cars. Using expected income instead of disposable income the function can explain 90–95 per cent of the variance.

[2] M. K. Evans, *Macroeconomic Activity, Theory, Forecasting, and Control* (New York: Harper and Row, 1969).

[3] D. Suits, 'The Demand for Automobiles in the U.S.A., 1929–1956', *Review of Economics and Statistics* (1958), pp. 273–80.

[4] W. B. Bennett, 'Cross-Section Studies of the Consumption of Automobiles in the United States', *American Economic Review* (Sept. 1967), pp. 841–50

Our basic model followed upon the work of Sleeman[5] and Tanner,[6] and consists of a cross-section analysis, on a geographical basis, of the level of car ownership. Basically it uses car ownership per 1,000 population as the dependent variable and population density, average income *per capita*, and an index of the age structure of the local population as independent variables. A stepwise multiple regression programme[7] was used to computer analyse the data which was for 1968 and 1969.

Car ownership: This is the average number of 'private cars and private vans' licensed in the particular licensing authority in the relevant year per 1,000 population (Ministry of Transport, *Highway and Statistics, 1968* and *1969* (London: H.M.S.O., 1969 and 1970)).

Population density: Estimated population per square mile in June of the relevant year (General Register Office, 1969 and 1970).

Average income: This is perhaps more accurately described as an *index* of average income. It uses the official figure for the counties' total net personal incomes (excluding persons with an income of less than £275), divided by the counties' population figures (Board of Inland Revenue, *Inland Revenue Statistics, 1968* and *1969* (London: H.M.S.O., 1970 and 1971)).

Age structure: This figure was perforce the same for each of the two years analysed, being based on the 1966 Sample Census of Population. It represents the percentage of the local population between the ages of 15 and 60 at the census date (General Register Office, *Sample Census, 1966, County Reports* (London: H.M.S.O., 1967)).

In addition a fourth independent variable was used for part of the analysis: as no Inland Revenue figures for incomes were available that distinguish between administrative counties and the county boroughs, the main part of the analysis had to use population statistics for counties including their county boroughs. However, it was appreciated that the population density of some county boroughs might be considerably higher than that of the administrative county with which they had to be included.

Skew variable. This was therefore introduced and defined as the percentage of the total population of the county living in the county borough(s) divided by the percentage of the total area of the county lying within the county borough(s). Where there was no county borough the variable was given the value 1.0. The value of this

[5] J. F. Sleeman, 'The Geographical Distribution of Motor Cars in Great Britain', *Scottish Journal of Political Economy* (Feb. 1961), pp. 71–81; and 'A New Look at the Distribution of Private Cars in Britain', ibid. (Nov. 1969), pp. 306–18.

[6] J. C. Tanner, 'Car and Motorcycle Ownership in the Counties of Great Britain in 1960', *Journal of Royal Statistical Society*, Series A, Part 2 (1963), pp. 276–84.

[7] Stepwise Regression Programme (BMD02R), from *Biomedical Computer Programs*, University of California Press, 1970.

variable thus ranges upwards from 1.0 as the population density of the county boroughs increasingly deviates from that of the administrative county with which they have been included. Thus it can be said to give a measure of the variance of the population density from the mean figure used basically.[8]

This analysis was carried out on the data for England and Wales: both together and separately. Table 1 summarizes these results. What seems immediately noteworthy (though in no way unexpected) is the consistency of the direction of the relationship between the dependent variable (car ownership) and the independent variables of average income and population density. This clearly supports the hypothesis that car ownership is positively related to income and inversely related to population density. (It is not claimed that the latter is necessarily a causal relationship. It may well be that the density of population is in effect a 'proxy' variable for the adequacy of public transport service, or the distances involved in home-to-work, business, shopping or social journeys.) The R^2 (or apparent explanatory power of the models) varies from a weak 28 per cent to a fairly strong 78 per cent. The log-linear models (which used logs of all variables) are neither consistently better nor worse than the arithmetic-linear models. It is interesting, however, to note that in all the Welsh models population density is a better explanatory variable than average income. In all cases the 'T' statistic (viz. the coefficient divided by its standard error) for average income is superior to that for population density. One reason for this is the higher significance of the skew variable in the English models, reflecting the importance of the county boroughs. The R^2 is also higher in the Welsh cases. One possible reason for this is that the dichotomy between urban and rural administrative counties is much more clear-cut in Wales than in England, where in the latter a seemingly rural county may have a number of significant urban areas, which this analysis cannot distinguish. In Wales, however, the rural counties include only small towns which are less significant than the English ones in terms of the proportion of the population of the administrative county they account for.

A further analysis was also carried out disaggregating administrative counties and county boroughs, so eliminating the need for the skew variable. These results are summarized in Table 2. Unfortunately, no figures for average income are available on this basis, so the results are not totally comparable; however, it is interesting to see that the 'T' statistic for population density is much higher.

Sleeman (1969) also comments upon the relationship between car density and population density; however the sensitivity of his analysis is reduced by his consideration of regions rather than counties (a result again of the availability of data at the time of his writing)

[8] There seems intuitively a strong possibility that there may be a relationship between 'skewness' as measured here and the distribution of total income: the greater the 'skewness' the greater the influence of the county borough(s) in the county as a whole, and possibly the greater the concentration of incomes.

Table 1

Ref.	Area	Year	Transf.	R^2	Constant	Av./Inc.	Pop./Dn.	Age/St.	Skew.
1.	E. + W.	1968	—	0.3543	18.5402	0.2028 (0.0532)	−0.0090 (0.0025)	n.s.	−1.4765 (0.4207)
2.	E.	"	—	0.4032	−71.7770	0.2761 (0.0712)	−0.0083 (0.0025)	n.s.	−1.0556 (0.4580)
3.	W.	"	—	0.7815	28.9457	0.2159 (0.0717)	−0.0709 (0.0123)	n.s.	n.s.
4.	E. + W.	"	LOG.	0.5171	−1.3499	1.2973 (0.2506)	−0.0874 (0.0169)	n.s.	−0.0402 (0.0123)
5.	E.	"	LOG.	0.4851	−2.0701	1.5374 (0.3654)	−0.0925 (0.0229)	n.s.	−0.0370 (0.0149)
6.	W.	"	LOG.	0.7139	2.6171	n.s.	−0.1125 (0.0215)	n.s.	n.s.
7.	E. + W.	1969	—	0.2795	558.5928	0.1531 (0.0588)	−0.0052 (0.0032)	−8.4403 (2.9394)	−1.2525 (0.5449)
8.	E.	"	—	0.5623	407.0872	0.4733 (0.0716)	−0.0048 (0.0025)	−12.7709 (2.5411)	n.s.
9.	W.	"	—	0.4944	265.7790	n.s.	−0.0681 (0.0208)	n.s.	n.s.
10.	E. + W.	"	LOG.	0.4380	1.7504	1.3262 (0.3004)	−0.0921 (0.0232)	−1.8112 (0.6341)	−0.0324 (0.0151)
11.	E.	"	LOG.	0.5759	−0.1814	2.5595 (0.3790)	−0.0620 (0.0229)	−2.9334 (0.6346)	n.s.
12.	W.	"	LOG.	0.6868	2.6613	n.s.	−0.1250 (0.0255)	n.s.	n.s.

Notes: (i) The data for E. (England) is based upon 46 observations and that for W. (Wales) upon 13 observations.
(ii) n.s. Not statistically significant at the 5 per cent level.
(iii) Figures in parentheses are the appropriate standard errors.

Table 2

Ref.	Area	Year	Transf.	R^2	Constant	Av./Inc.	Pop./Dn.	Age/St.
13.	E. + W.	1968	—	0.4327	234.4135	N.A.	−0.0063 (0.0006)	n.s.
14.	"	"	LOG.	0.4185	2.5964	N.A.	−0.0909 (0.0090)	n.s.
15.	E. + W.	1969	—	0.4101	243.2905	N.A.	−0.0064 (0.006)	n.s.
16.	"	"	LOG.	0.3856	2.6207	N.A.	−0.0877 (0.0094)	n.s.

Notes: (i) The data for E. + W. (England and Wales) are based upon 142 observations.

(ii) N.A. Relevant data not available.

(iii) n.s. Not statistically significant at the 5 per cent level.

(iv) Figures in parentheses are the appropriate standard errors.

By looking at the level of car ownership in regions, important variations within these regions are averaged out and so the exact nature of the relationship is further obscured. In a footnote[9] he gives some details in his statistical analysis which looks at the relationship between car density, and population density and/or average income in two groups of regions, which he describes as 'more urbanised' and 'less urbanised'. For comparative purposes the present authors ran similar regressions on the basis of 'more urbanised' *counties* and 'less urbanised' *counties*, using the same operational dividing point as used apparently by Sleeman (viz. 450 persons per square mile). Unfortunately, Sleeman does not give his figures for the values of R^2, but as far as is possible Table 3 includes details of his published results and summarizes our own.

The most surprising aspect of Sleeman's findings is that although he obtains the now familiar relationship of car density being positively related to average income and negatively related to population density in his 'more urbanised regions', in the 'less urbanised regions' he finds car ownership positively related to both these variables. Furthermore, the 'T' statistic for the population coefficients suggests that neither are in fact significant. Using the county basis, however, this unexpected sign reversal does not appear, and indeed although income is still the more significant, the population density variable is in each case significant at the 5 per cent level. However, it is clear that for the less urbanised counties the model has a low explanatory power (viz. $R^2 = 0.24$) and other factors must be important. For instance, socio-economic groupings social ethos may vary considerably within the group of counties, and perhaps in these essentially rural (or at least non-urban) areas the skewness of the distribution of incomes may be greater. By

[9] Sleeman, 1969, p. 315.

this last point we mean that the income distribution deviates from the normal pattern with perhaps a greater discontinuity between low and high income groups. Thus as incomes increase, the low-income groups may still consider the car outside their effective demand, whilst the high-income groups have already achieved their optimal

Table 3

Ref.	Area	Year	Transf.	R^2	Constant	Av./Inc.	Pop./Dn.
17.	L.U.R.	1966	LOG.	V.N.S.	V.N.S.	1.76 (0.45)	0.02 (0.03)
18.	M.U.R.	"	LOG.	V.N.S.	V.N.S.	2.89 (0.96)	−0.10 (0.10)
19.	L.U.C.	1968	LOG.	0.2398	0.8094	0.5793 (0.3276)	−0.0849 (0.0342)
20.	L.U.C.	1969	LOG.	0.2413	1.1175	0.5200 (0.3447)	−0.1380 (0.0483)
21.	M.U.C.	1968	LOG.	0.7749	−6.6475	3.0621 (0.3366)	−0.1334 (0.0271)
22.	M.U.C.	1969	LOG.	0.5617	−6.2341	2.9198 (0.5453)	−0.1407 (0.0447)

Notes: (i) Sleeman's data for L.U.R. (less-urbanised regions) is based on 6 observations, that for M.U.R. (more-urbanised regions) on 9 observations. The data for L.U.C. (less-urbanised counties) is based on 30 observations, that for M.U.C. (more urbanised counties) on 29 observations.
　　(ii) V.N.S. Values not stated.
　(iii) Figures in parentheses are the appropriate standard errors.

level of per capita car ownership (at least in terms of numbers of vehicles, even if not in terms of quality or type of unit).

Our findings are much more in line with the results of the study carried out by Tanner (1963), using much earlier data (1960). He obtains, however, a very strong correlation for car-ownership against his variable 'distance north'. The biggest problem in using this in our particular context is to understand its causal significance. Clearly it is a proxy variable: but a proxy for what? If indeed it is, as he suggests, an expression of difference in climate, it seems surprising that so simple a proxy for such an intricate variable as climate has such a high explanatory power. Certainly as far as transport policy is concerned, it gives little help in anticipating or being able to influence future trends in car ownership in any particular area. However, one point of his that we investigated further was the effect of the age structure of the population. He suggests that 'Sussex has a low number of cars probably because the proportion of the population over the age of 65 is particularly high' (Tanner, p. 281). The implication of this is presumably that persons over that age are unlikely to own or drive cars. (The question of financial ability of old-age pensions to run vehicles should be covered by the average income variable.) Clearly, however, there is also the question of young persons unlikely to own, or indeed prohibited from owning, motor vehicles. Thus our age structure variable measured the percentage of the population within the likely car-owning age brackets. For the most part, however, the resulting coefficient was not statistically significant at the 5 per cent level. However, where it was significant, the relationship was negative, i.e. car ownership was lower in areas with a high proportion of persons in the potentially car-owning age bracket! This perhaps deserves further analysis: one tentative explanation may be that families with a large number of children consider the car as more of a necessity than other sectors of the community. From an economic point of view it is true that the larger number of persons travelling in a vehicle the lower the average costs per person per mile. This cost saving is not fully reflected in public transport fare structures as far as the family is concerned, and so makes the car relatively cheaper the larger the family.

Clearly this type of analysis is severely restricted by the limitations of the available statistics. Unfortunately, county boundaries do not enclose areas with a homogeneous population density; average income is a poor indicator of the diversity of actual income distributions. Aggregate studies suggest that a meaningful price variable (including perhaps a measure of the relative costs of private and public transport) would increase the explanatory power of the functions. However, our results show that even the use of county statistics improves the explanatory power of such disaggregated models, as compared with earlier studies, and leads to theoretically more acceptable results.

PART III

PRODUCTION AND THE THEORY OF THE FIRM

Introduction to Part III

The development of theory on the supply side of the market equation has been concerned with the theory of production and costs and the theory of the firm. Assuming that a firm seeks to maximize its profits (and thus to minimize its costs), the shape of its cost and revenue curves could be postulated. Whilst the shape of its cost curves would be affected principally by the factors of production it employs and its production techniques, the structure of the markets it operates in would be the main determinant of its revenue curves. The interaction of these costs and revenue curves would then show the output and price at which the firm would maximize its profits.

One of the main concerns of the traditional theory is to predict the influence of particular market structures on firms' behaviour and in particular the difference between competitive and non-competitive markets. Assuming profit maximization, it is postulated that more output at a lower price will be supplied to a market if there is perfect competition than if supply is dominated by a monopolist or a small group of firms.

These basic theoretical formulations have been developed, extended, and adapted in a number of ways. Thus the argument that the monopolist will supply less at a higher price resulted from postulated differences in his revenue curve. The firm in a perfectly competitive industry being unable to influence the price of its products by its own actions is faced with a horizontal average revenue curve as output increases. By definition the monopoly firm is the industry, and variations in its output can affect price. The profit-maximizing output for the monopolist will be one that is lower than the aggregate output that a group of firms in competition will produce and it will be provided at a higher price. This combination of price and output will produce excess profits for the monopolist. From the point of view of allocation perfect competition seems a more efficient structure.

But might not the average cost curve for the monopolist be lower as a result of economies of scale? It is certainly possible to show theoretically that, if concentration of production in a single unit reduced average costs sufficiently, a monopolist might well produce at a lower price and a higher output than a large number of small firms in competition. The monopolist might still make excess profits, but the consumer will be better off in terms of price and output than if the same market is a competitive one supplied by a large number of small firms. From the point of view of production a monopoly structure might be more efficient.

The empirical question, therefore, is the existence of such economies of scale and their significance in relation to the over-all size of a particular industry. For competition policy purposes it is important to establish the extent to which the domination of a particular industry by one or two large firms might be justified by the existence of sufficiently large economies of scale.

The pioneering work on economies of scale in UK industry was undertaken by Pratten and his colleagues at the University of Cambridge Department of Applied Economics in the 1960s. Extracts from Pratten's work appeared in the first edition of these readings. Since then the results of others' work in this area have been published and they are conveniently summarized in the first reading in this section. Significantly this reading comes from a background paper published by the Department of Prices and Consumer Protection in 1978 as part of a review of monopolies and merger policy.

The paper covers the effects on costs of both economies of scale and of learning and experience over time. As far as scale economies are concerned, the basic information for some 49 different products is provided in Table 1, which presents estimates of the minimum efficient plant size (MEPS) in terms of a rate of physical output per period of time. In effect the MEPS is equivalent to the minimum point on the average cost curve. As the paper is mainly concerned with the implication of economies of scale for competition policy, the MEPS figure not surprisingly is linked to the total UK production for the same period of time. The results suggest 'that in a number of UK industries high concentration may be required if scale economies are to be realised'.

The paper points out deficiencies in the data which might both over- and under-estimate the extent of scale economies. It also discusses the less quantifiable question of the extent of economies of scale at the level of the firm (managerial, financial, risk aversion, etc.). Case-study evidence points to these type of economies as being significant in recent merger activity in the UK.

Perhaps more important for competition policy is the extent to which large scale is *necessary* for cost economies to be achieved. What is required is some information on the slope of the average cost curve as it falls to its minimum point. If the slope is steep it indicates sharp falls in average cost as output increases and the importance of achieving rates of production close to the minimum average cost point. If the slope is more gentle it implies little change in average cost over quite a large range of output.

It is disappointing that relatively little empirical work is available on this question. Scherer's study is mentioned, and on the evidence of his small sample it would seem that 'the cost penalty of operating below MEPS is quite small'. If this conclusion could be generalized it might be found that reducing concentration might not lead to significantly increased average costs even in those industries where MEPS is a high proportion of total output. Productive efficiency might not be greatly affected and might be compensated for by the improvement in allocative efficiency which increased competition would bring about. This is all highly speculative, however, and the empirical evidence is such that any judgement on the respective claims of productive and allocative efficiency must be an agnostic one.

In studying the effect of different market structures on behaviour, particular attention has been given to oligopoly markets. These markets are characterized as having a small number of suppliers (in the limiting case just two) each of whom has to take account of its competitors' reactions in deciding its own market behaviour. A number of reaction models have been produced seeking to explain such oligopoly behaviour, one of the most long-standing and durable being the kinked demand curve.

This is the subject of the provocative paper by Stigler, who uses the development of the theoretical and empirical literature on the kinked demand curve as a case study to illustrate the factors which determine the survival of particular economic ideas. His own antipathy for the theory, established by his 1947 paper, is soon made clear and he puts forward a convincing case highlighting the paucity of empirical support for the theory.

Stigler has to admit, however, that despite its weaknesses the kinked demand curve has led an active life in all four decades since its first formulation. It has been mentioned in over 100 articles and, on Stigler's calculations, appears in over 50 per cent of general economics or price-theory texts published in the last twenty years. His explanation for this is a conservative snowball effect of continuing reference in the textbooks. Each cohort of graduate economists emerges believing the theory to be an important part of the literature so that it continues to be referred to without theoretical development or empirical justification. It is a rather dispiriting conclusion, but the paper itself provides a good survey of the relevant literature and the occasion to reflect on the insights the kinked demand theory provides.

Shaw and Sutton's study of the effect of new entry on competition in the petrol supply industry includes a passing reference to the kinked demand theory. The evidence of the period 1953–9 is more consistent with a price-leadership or collusive model than the predictions of the kinked theory. They point out that all price changes, increases as well as decreases, were matched by competitors.

This paper complements the shorter and more contemporary study by the Monopolies Commission included in Part I. The interest there is in the short-run effects on price of changes to supply and demand curves. The study here is a longer-run one on the effect of potential and actual new entry on existing firms' behaviour. This potential new entry began to make itself felt about 1960.

Shaw & Sutton examine whether behaviour is consistent with a limit-pricing approach, whereby existing firms reduce prices to a level which will reduce the attractiveness of entry for potential competitors. They divide the period into two parts: spring 1960 to spring 1967 when supply conditions were easy; and from summer 1967 onwards when rising costs and periodic supply difficulties were encountered. They argue that whilst prices were reduced by existing firms, their main purpose was not to prevent the entry of new competitors but to limit their rate of penetration. In a period of surplus supply and expanding and relatively price-inelastic demand, this was the most profitable strategy. In the changed market conditions of post 1967 the industry reverted to the price leadership behaviour characteristic of the 1950s. With higher costs affecting all firms, price increases were generally followed. The shortage of supply reinforced this tendency by making it difficult for individual firms to take advantage of rivals' price increases to extend their market share. Shaw & Sutton conclude that despite this, 'the long-term effect of entry, reflected in the increased number of firms and reduced shares of the leaders, had been to reduce retail prices (net of taxes) relative to costs. Entry had largely performed its competitive function—the reduction of monopoly power and profit.'

An important criticism of the traditional theory concentrates on the assumption that firms seek to maximize profits. In the main these alternative theories argue that firms may seek to maximize other variables. Baumol (1959), for example, suggested that firms might seek to maximize sales revenue rather than profits, although some minimum acceptable profits level might be built in as a constraint. The result is likely to be a higher level of output at a lower price from the sales maximizer compared to the profits maximizer.

Marris (1964), on the other hand, postulated that firms would seek to maximize growth of capital assets subject to a job security constraint on the management. This job security is obtained by a combination of low-risk investment policy and a correct balance between the need for retained profits as an important source of finance for internal growth and the level of distributed profits necessary to keep shareholders happy.

Williamson (1963) argues that managers pursue their own utility rather than that of the shareholders. A minimum level of profits acts as a constraint on managers but, once this is met, the purpose of their behaviour is to enhance their own salaries, expenses, status, etc. This takes the form of large offices, expense accounts, company cars, etc., none of which are necessary for the carrying-out of their functions. Williamson's arguments in part are close to those which Leibenstein (1966) later formulated as X-inefficiency. According to Leibenstein, the problem of monopoly behaviour is that higher prices result not from an attempt to maximize profits but from the absence of any pressure to minimize costs. The large firm with some control over its markets is characterized by 'slack' as management disburse some of the excess profit created into their own work environment, rather than to the shareholders.

Whilst all three models criticize the profit-maximization hypothesis, they still assume that firms seek to maximize something. An alternative approach pioneered by Cyert & March (1963) is that firms have to follow satisficing behaviour. The firm is seen as a coalition of competing groups whose goals will often be in conflict. As it is not possible to achieve all goals simultaneously, the firm as a whole does not seek a maximum level of attainment but a satisfactory one instead. This approach concentrates on the internal behaviour and resource-allocating processes within the firm rather than the allocation of resources between firms which is the starting-point of the traditional theory.

All these critiques, however, share one important premiss. They are predicated on an assumed divorce between ownership and control within the modern firm. The traditional theory with its concept of the entrepreneur started from the premiss of a simple owner-manager and adapted to the development of large firms by some assumption of continuing owner control of major decisions. The various alternative maximization theories and the satisficing theory all assume that for most firms' control has passed from owners to managers. The latter take the major decisions and are subject to minimum constraints on their freedom by the need to satisfy the owners.

It is the empirical evidence for this assumption which is the subject of the study by Nyman & Silberston. Their work is based on a study of the top 250 firms in the UK of whom twenty have been intensively investigated. The authors provide a useful review of the existing (rather scanty) evidence as well as a discussion of the criticism of the general view that control has now passed from owners to managers. Their approach is to assume that an owner's presence is expressed either through shareholding percentage and/or significant representation on the board of directors or by occupying the key position of Chairman or Managing Director. They also distinguish between different forms of ownership control ranging from private (usually family) holdings to ownership by other industrial concerns or by financial interests.

Their main premiss is that where an ownership presence exists, as defined above, managerial discretion is severely limited. In such situations the major decisions, including the important one of the hiring and firing of senior executives, is taken by the owners rather than the managers.

Of the top 250 companies in 1975 they found that some 56 per cent were owner-controlled in these terms. This is a higher figure than had previously been assumed, and they point out that, even using the definitions of previous studies, there seems to have been an increase in ownership control of major UK companies over the previous fifteen years. Moreover, over half of the ownership-controlled companies arise through family shareholdings or directorships rather than through industrial or financial holdings. Their studies also indicate a differentiation between different industrial sectors in the extent of owner control: 'It is apparent, for example, that non-manufacturing industries are predominantly owner-controlled.'

At first glance these results would seem to argue against the view that ownership and control have been largely divorced and that as a result management discretion is sovereign. However, it can be argued that the criteria used by Nyman & Silbertston for ownership control are too weak. For example, they accept a minimum share-holding of 5 per cent or less than this if there is a family chairman and managing director as evidence of owner control. The authors might counter on the other hand, that, according to Table 1, even if these categories were ignored, the figures for ownership control would still be a respectable 40 per cent plus.

Ultimately, however, the crucial question for the theory of the firm is the nature and extent of ownership control. The case studies of Vickers and Debenhams cited by the authors are not conclusive. It would seem from the evidence presented that these were firms where managerial failure precipitated the rescue actions of owners just as the managerial theories with their built-in minimum profit constraints predict.

The threat of take-over is another important element of the theory of the firm. Those supporting the profit-maximization thesis argue that this threat forces firms to maximize profits whether they wish to or not. Non-maximization of profits will lead to an increased probability of take-over. Those supporting alternative hypotheses argue that the threat acts only as a constraint to produce some minimum acceptable level of profits. Firms, however, are interested in other goals than profit maximization.

Singh attempts to provide some empirical evidence relevant to these arguments by studying the characteristics of acquiring, acquired, and surviving firms in four major UK industries between 1967 and 1970. Although, as he admits, his results are suggestive rather than conclusive, they are nevertheless of some interest.

They indicate that whilst the characteristics of acquiring and acquired firms are significantly different in terms of profitability, for example, the difference is far less marked between acquired and surviving firms. Moreover, whilst unprofitability may be an important influence on vulnerability to take-over for smaller firms, it is far less so for larger firms. Size itself is an important defence against take-over; the evidence shows that the larger the firm within its industry the less vulnerable it is to take-over for any given rate of profit. Singh concludes:

'Rather than forcing them [large firms] to improve profitability, the take-over process may well actually encourage salaried managers in large corporations to concentrate even more on size rather than profitability. Altogether, therefore, for larger firms the empirical evidence about the nature of the take-over mechanism supports the new managerial and behavioural theories of the firm, and gives very little support for the strict requirements of the neo-classical theory.'

References

W. J. Baumol (1959), *Business Behaviour, Value and Growth* (New York: Macmillan).

R. M. Cyert & J. G. March (1963), *A Behavioural Theory of the Firm* (Englewood Cliffs, NJ: Prentice-Hall).

H. Leibenstein (1966), 'Allocative Efficiency vs X-Efficiency', *American Economic Review*, 56, June.

R. Marris (1964), *The Economic Theory of 'Managerial' Capitalism* (London: Macmillan).

O. E. Williamson (1964), *The Economics of Discretionary Behaviour* (Englewood Cliffs, NJ: Prentice-Hall).

9

Economies of Scale and Learning Effects

by Department of Prices and Consumer Protection

Introduction

1. For many industries the larger the size of the firm the greater the opportunities for achieving lower unit production costs. There are three principal sources of such cost reductions:

  (i) plant level scale economies,
  (ii) firm level scale economies, and
  (iii) the effects of learning and experience.

The cost reductions that can theoretically be achieved tend to peter out beyond some point (although this point tends to move forward over time) and in practice there will usually be sound economic or commercial reasons for not going to the limits of what is technically achievable. Nevertheless, in a number of industries, the scale economies that are feasible warrant the existence of firms that are large in relation to the size of the industry and thus tend to lead to a high degree of concentration. In such cases, the policy issue is whether the benefits of lower costs outweigh the possible disadvantages of high concentration.

2. In part 1 [. . .] the available evidence on scale economies is examined with a view to establishing whether this issue is likely to be of importance for competition policy in the UK. In Part 2 the implications for competition policy of the dynamic process of achieving cost reductions over time through changes in the scale and technique of production and through the acquisition of experience are considered.

Plant Level Scale Economies

3. The main sources of scale economies at plant level are well known and include such factors as increased possibilities for the division of labour, better utilisation of indivisible items of plant, and

From *A Review of Monopolies and Mergers Policy*, Appendix C (Cmnd 7198 May 1978) pp. 77–96. Reprinted by permission of the Controller of Her Majesty's Stationery Office.

capital cost savings on large plant (e.g. through the operation of the so-called 'cube law'[1] in respect of process-type plant).

4. Attempts to establish the likely extent of plant level scale economies in particular industries have produced a substantial literature. The second and third columns of Table 1 present estimates of 'minimum efficient plant size' (MEPS)[2] for forty-nine different products taken from a number of sources. These estimates are of an 'engineering type' in that they attempt to estimate costs for plants of different sizes on the basis of current design, cost and performance standards. The viewpoint is thus similar to that of a firm which is undertaking new investment at a point in time. The advantage of this approach is to produce fairly precise numerical estimates which relate well to the *a priori* arguments for the existence of scale economies. In practice however firms will be constrained in their choice of plant by existing capacity and by demand prospects while actual unit costs will be determined by the quality of management, the enthusiasm of the workforce, fluctuations in demand and a host of other factors as much as by the intended capability of the plant so that these estimates will tend to overstate the overall economic advantages of large scale plant, although they do indicate the potential for achieving cost savings in ideal circumstances.

5. For those products for which estimates of minimum efficient plant size are available some assessment can be made of the extent to which high concentration is likely to be necessary if plant level scale economies are to be realised. The assessment is hampered by the degree of aggregation in industrial statistics Minimum List Headings (MLH) normally cover a wide range of products, albeit in related areas of production) but figures for sales of the more important products can be gleaned from the appropriate Business Monitors and from other published sources so that in most cases a reasonable indication can be obtained. Column 4 of Table 1 shows UK production in 1973 (a peak year) of the relevant products insofar as it has proved possible in the time available to muster them. The final column of Table 1 then shows what proportion of UK production

[1] The volume of a vessel is roughly proportional to the cube of its radius while its surface area is proportional to the square. Thus as the volume capacity of plant increases, the material requirements tend to increase less fast. Also, associated pipework, valves, motors and controls do not need to be duplicated while staffing requirements increase little if at all.

[2] Minimum efficient plant size is defined by Pratten, one of the authors whose work has been drawn on heavily in Table 1, as 'the minimum scale above which any possible subsequent doubling in scale would reduce total average unit costs by less than 5 per cent and above which any possible subsequent doubling in scale would reduce value added per unit by less than 10 per cent'. Not all the figures quoted in Table 1 are based on this definition—for example, Scherer's concept is 'minimum optimum plant scale' defined as that plant output volume at which the long run unit production cost curve attains its global minumum. Other authors are less precise in their definitions.

would be accounted for by a plant of the size shown in column 3. Where this figure is above about 20 per cent there is an implication that efficient production in the supply of that product is likely to require an appreciable degree of concentration. Products for which this is the case include cigarettes, sulphuric acid, ethylene, ammonium nitrate, aluminium semi-manufactures, small diesel engines, electronic calculators turbo-generators, small electric motors, TV tubes, electric cookers, electric refrigerators, tractors, motor cars, aircraft and rubber contraceptive sheaths. Products for which the figure is close to 20 per cent include sugar, detergent powder, steel, pig iron, synthetic fibres and plasterboard. Insofar as it is possible to generalise, it appears that plant level scale economies are particularly likely to be found in bulk chemicals (sulphuric acid, ethylene) and in asseembly operations where mass production methods can be applied (e.g. electronic calculators, refrigerators, motor vehicles).

6. There are a number of qualifications to be kept in mind in considering the figures in Table 1. Understatement of the significance of scale economies in UK manufacturing may have arisen for three reasons. Firstly, MEPS estimates are only available for a small proportion of manufactured products. While it is likely that many of those products for which scale economies are particularly important will have been studied by researchers, further research would certainly reveal more products for which MEPS is above 20 per cent in UK production. Secondly, many of the estimates are rather dated now, relating mostly to best practice in the 1960s, so that in some cases MEPS may have increased since then. Thirdly, UK production includes production for export so that MEPS in relation to home market sales will generally be larger than indicated by the final column of Table 1 although significant import competition would offset this. On the other hand, the figures in Table 1 may overstate the significance of scale economies for a number of reasons. The MEPS estimates generally refer to the bulk version of a product whereas for most products there is also a market for versions of a more sophisticated or specialist type (e.g. special steels, sports cars, real ale) and hence a role for smaller scale production. In some cases (e.g. motor vehicles) the scale economies may be as readily realisable in a number of closely associated plants as in a single plant. In many cases, the cost penalty of operating below MEPS is quite small—only Scherer among the authors cited in Table 1 gives systematic information on this point but his figures show a cost penalty of less than 5 per cent for operation at ½ of optimum scale in the case of 5[3] out of the 12 products he studied and of less than 10 per cent for a further 4[4] products. Finally, there are a number of more practical considerations which are likely to limit the extent to

[3] Cigarettes, paints, oil refining, shoes and automobile storage batteries.
[4] Beer, cotton and synthetic broadloom textiles, anti-friction bearings and refrigerators.

which it is worth seeking to obtain maximum scale economies, including:

(i) the need to maintain flexibility in the presence of changes in demand, particularly where fashion plays an important part in consumer choice;

(ii) the problems of managing large plants, a symptom of which in UK is the strong positive correlation between plant size in terms of employment and incidence of labour disputes;

(iii) transport costs which for some products (e.g. bricks, cement, beer) may effectively limit the size of the market that can be economically served by a large plant; and

(iv) prudence- where production is concentrated in a small number of plants the consequences of production failure, from whatever cause, are more costly.

7. These qualifications notwithstanding, the figures in the final column of Table 1 do suggest that in a number of UK industries high concentration may be required if scale economies are to be realised. Production of many of the products identified in paragraph 5 above is in fact highly concentrated in the UK—for example, the 5-firm concentration ratio (not available for some products) is over 90 per cent for sugar, ethylene, cigarettes, detergent powder, ammonium nitrate, diesel engines, TV tubes, electric cookers, re-frigerators, auto batteries, tractors, motor cars and plasterboard—an observation which is consistent with the existence of economies in these cases. This observation may also be interpreted as showing that for the most part the structure of British industry is sufficiently concentrated to take advantage of such scale economies as are available. This interpretation is substantially confirmed by an internal study[5] which attempted to assess for the products included in Table 1 the proportion of UK output which was produced in plants of at least minimum efficient size. For only 8 products (16 per cent of cases) did less than 25 per cent of output appear to be produced in such plants, including aluminium semi-manufacturers, turbo-generators, small electric motors, electric refrigerators, motor cars and cotton and synthetic broadloom textiles.

8. Thus far, reliance has been placed on the engineering-type estimates of scale economies given in column 3 of Table 1. It is relevant to note that a number of researchers into industrial concentration have chosen an alternative approach which attempts to infer minimum efficient plant size from the observed distribution of plant sizes within industries. Information on the size distribution of establish-ments by employment is available from the census of production reports and these provided the starting point for such estimates. Using this data imposes three serious difficulties; first, the census

[5] G. Walshe and J. Graham—*Scale Economies in UK Manufacturing Industry.*

information is largely at MLH level so that plants producing a variety of products tend to be included in each division; secondly, the size classification is by employment whereas output would be more appropriate; and thirdly, it is unlikely, particularly in industries subject to rapid technical progress, that many existing plants will actually be of optimum size. For these reasons, particularly the first, statistical measures of optimum plant size tend to indicate a much smaller need for concentration than the figures in Table 1. A further criticism of the statistical measures that have been used in the literature is that they tend to embody preconceptions about scale economies rather than provide evidence for their existence—for example, Comanor and Wilson *define* 'minimum optimum size' as the average size of plant in the top 50 per cent of an industry's employment size distribution. Such numbers may be useful indicators of the importance of scale effects in comparative industrial studies but they would seem to be of little help where the problem is to determine the nature and extent of scale economies in particular lines of production.

Firm Level Scale Economies

9. Firms can take advantage of whatever plant level economies of scale are available. In addition, there are a number of possible economies associated with increasing firm size independently of plant size. The sources of firm level scale economies include economies in overheads (e.g. top management, R & D), economies due to bulk handling, economies in stocks and work in progress through spreading of risks, marketing economies and financial economies. Such economies may accrue to single plant firms as plant size increases or to firms which increase in size by increasing the number of plants under their control. In the latter case, there are additional considerations and the nature and extent of the economies available will be affected by the type of multi-plant operation concerned. Where the multi-plant operation involves horizontal or vertical integration, it is the interaction of plant level scale economies with overhead costs, transport and marketing costs which determine optimum firm size. In addition firms may gain advantages from the stronger market position that goes with increasing firm size. In the case of conglomerates, the economic issues are much less clear. There may be benefits arising from the pooling of resources across industries with different cyclical patterns, different levels of risk or serving different markets; on the other hand, there may be disadvantages due to cross-subsidisations, use of leverage in one market to obtain benefits in another or other effects arising when transactions across industry boundaries are internal to a firm. Unfortunately these possibilities have not been the subject of any systematic research to date so that it is not possible to say how important these effects might be or which way the balance of advantage might in general be expected

to lie. The following remarks should therefore be understood to apply principally to firms which are large within a single fairly narrowly defined industry.

10. The fact that the increase in concentration in the UK since the war has mainly been through an increase in the number of plants owned or controlled by firms rather than through increasing plant size (although the average size of plants has increased over the period) suggests that the inducement for firms to increase in size in this way is strong. How far this is due to economic factors (firm level scale economies on the one hand and ability to exploit markets more effectively on the other) and how far to factors such as ambition for status and power among business executives, or advantages in terms of taxation or legal status and so on remains an unresolved issue. Researchers have been able to find little positive association between firm size and profitability on average and recent studies of mergers show that increases in firm size through the acquisition process often fail to realise any obvious advantages, although some firms which are both large and profitable can be found, as can instances of successful mergers.

11. Some of the issues can be clarified by considering particular cases. In some industries, the potential for achieving cost savings through larger plant and firm size may be frustrated by circumstances. In the British steel industry for example, nationalisation has provided a framework within which a policy of rationalisation and high investment aimed at increasing the scale of bulk steel making plants could be pursued. Even so, ten years after nationalisation the process is by no means complete, the financial strains of the investment programme in the face of slow growing demand and the political difficulties of phasing out obsolete plant having proved to be powerful constraints. In the case of the motor industry, even many years after the Leyland–BMC merger, the CPRS report noted that 'In comparison with the structure of the industry on the Continent, there is a large number of manufacturers in Britain and an even larger number of plants in relation to the number of cars produced.' Similarly in the aircraft manufacturing industry, the merging of manufacturing facilities under the management of a single firm has taken a long time to lead to rationalisation of capacity and the development of a coherent commercial strategy. In the turbo-generator industry, the CPRS has argued that 'To be in a position to produce a full range embodying the latest technology, it will be necessary to have in this country only one company, with one turbo-generator technology, offering the full range of sets which the market requires'—but bringing about this situation is attended by many difficulties. These cases illustrate the importance of the practical realities which estimates of scale economies tend to ignore. Nevertheless in all these cases the prospective cost savings associated

with large scale production can reasonably be argued to justify the efforts that have been made to increase the size of firms and plants although this has tended also to increase concentration. Nor have efforts to obtain the advantages of large scale production always been frustrated. Bulk supply of electricity provides an instance of an industry successfully reorganised (admittedly over a fairly long period) to take maximum advantage of scale economies. More recently, the GEC-led mergers in the electrical industry are generally considered to have been successful in lowering unit costs through determined rationalisation of capacity. Another successful case is the restructuring of the bearings industry resulting in a reduction in the range of standard bearings produced from 45,000 to 15,000, yielding substantial cost savings through longer runs and reduced manpower requirements. Similarly, developments in the brewing industry which have reduced the number of breweries from 399 in 1958 (average output 60,000 barrels p.a.) to 162 in 1973 (average output 228,000 barrels) must have produced significant cost savings if the estimates of scale economies in brewing cited in Table 1 are accepted.

Implications for Competition Policy

12. In the light of this brief survey of the available evidence on scale economies, it appears that there are industries in which scale economies are sufficiently large to be likely to warrant high concentration, at least at the product level. In these cases, high concentration can lead to lower production costs which it would be in the public interest to promote.

Learning Effects

13. In the course of their evolution most industries expand their scale of plant to achieve real-terms reductions in unit costs. This process is reinforced by two other factors; technological advances, which are usually embodied in newer, larger plants; and a process whereby managers and operators learn from experience how to operate particular technologies and facilities more effectively. The combined effect of these three factors—scale, technology and learning—have been observed across a wide spectrum of industries, including such widely differing technologies as steel, oil refining, power generation, machine tool manufacture, electronics and life insurance.

14. A leading authority in this area, the Boston Consulting Group, which has documented these combined effects for many industries, has proposed a general observation based on its consulting work, that the characteristic decline in the unit cost of value added 'is consistently 20 to 30 per cent each time accumulated production is doubled. This decline goes on in time without limit (in constant prices) regardless of the rate of growth of experience. The rate of decline is surprisingly consistent, even from industry to industry.'[6] The exhibits 1–6 appended

[6] Boston Consulting Group, *Perspectives on Experience* (1970), pg. 12.

to the Annex indicate the kind of relationship the Boston Group have documented for fifty or so industries; they are referred to as 'experience curves' and are characterised according to the extent to which unit costs (often measured for convenience in terms of prices) decline with each successive doubling of output (an 80 per cent curve indicating a 20 per cent unit cost reduction per doubling, and so on).

15. Disentangling the contributory factors in this process is not easy or always possible. The learning effects themselves have been isolated in a number of cases, beginning with the US aircraft industry in which it was noted in 1936[7] that reduction in unit costs were related to *cumulative* output of particular aircraft. It was here that the term 'learning effects' was coined, because these particular unit cost reductions derived not from changes in technology or scale but from the repetition of a complex task. The Stanford Research Institute and the Rand Corporation carried out extensive studies of these learning effects in the late 1940s, concluding that doubling cumulative airframe output was accompanied by an average reduction in average labour requirements of about 20 per cent. In 1956, Hirsch[8] investigated the same effects in machine tool production, for eight products, finding that successive doublings led to unit labour reductions of 16–25 per cent. Interestingly, the learning effect was found to be roughly twice as large in assembly (26 per cent) as in machining (14 per cent), the difference being attributed to the basic similarity of many machined parts, regardless of the model they are used for, and the relatively prescribed task involved in machining, whereas assembly work involved greater novelty and complexity.

16. Later work by Nadier and Smith[9] generalised this result further by showing that learning is related to the proportion of manual to mechanical effort in a given operation, e.g. labour requirements per unit decline 15 per cent with successive doublings of output when the ratio of assembly workers to machining workers is 50/50, and by only 10 per cent when the ratio is 25/75. It is also important for budgeting purposes to know whether the learning resides in the organisation concerned or with the individual workers. A study by Harvey[10] in the British Aircraft Corporation indicated that the contribution of individual operators was substantial but not overriding. Thus if all workers remained on a particular complex task without

[7] T. P. Wright, 'Factors Affecting the Cost of Airplanes', *Journal of the Aeronautical Sciences*, vol. 3, 1936.

[8] W. Z. Hirsch, Firm Progress Ratios, *Econometrica*, vol. 24, 1956.

[9] G. Nadler and W. D. Smith, Manufacturing Progress Functions for Types of Processes, *International Journal of Production Research*, vol. 2, 1963.

[10] R. A. Harvey, Learning in Production, Paper presented to the Royal Statistical Society Conference, Swansea, September 1976.

interruption, a 75 per cent learning curve (25 per cent labour unit cost reductions per doubling of cumulative volume) obtained; if a new assembly line were set up by the same company with new workers a flatter 84 per cent curve obtained. More generally, learning effects have become commonplace in industry and are frequently used as an aid to budgeting and rate-fixing.

17. Whereas learning is highly significant in labour-intensive operations, scale becomes the important factor in capital-intensive industries' experience curves but even here, it is not the whole story. Exhibit 7 illustrates how increases in plant scale, contributed to cost reductions in plastic resin manufacture. With each plant scale, it was possible with experience to move down a 90 per cent learnng curve. Successive increases in plant size increased the overall slope of the curve to 75–80 per cent.

The Impact of Experience Curves on Companies and Industry Structure

18. How do these curves relate to individual companies? The Boston Consulting Group argues that in the early stages of an industry's development, each company makes its own way down a broadly similar path, without much benefit from the experience of its competitors (there are exceptions to this, witness the information exchange in the embryonic California electronics industry). For example, each of the three leading US steam turbine manufacturers in exhibit 8 follow a similar path which reflects a common underlying experience curve in the industry. This phenomenon is of great strategic significance for companies because the company which, like General Electric in this exhibit, secures the market leadership also moves fastest down the experience curve, so securing a cost advantage over its competitors further back up the curve.

19. If the market leader or dominant producer has a real cost advantage over other producers it may be expected that this would show up in higher profitability, given that all producers in competition charge broadly similar prices. Moreover, since prices reflect the unit costs of the marginally profitable and usually small-scale manufacturer it is likely that the profitability of concentrated industries as a whole will be higher than in fragmented industries simply because they contain some companies very much larger than the marginal producer, with significantly lower costs. The positive association between profitability and the degree of industry concentration noted by many researchers in the field of industrial organisation is consistent with this expectation. More specific evidence on the significance of individual companies' market shares is provided by the Profit Impact of Market Strategy programme of the Harvard Business School. The heart of the programme is a cross-section analysis of data from some

600 'businesses' (mainly American but replicated since with similar results for 80 businesses in the UK). A business is product-centred, defined in the programme as 'a division, product line or other profit centre within its parent company, selling a distinct set of products and/or services to an identifiable group of customers in competition with a well-defined set of competitors'. As Table 2 indicates, the analysis found a strong positive correlation between market share and profit margins; businesses with less than 10 per cent market shares made losses and those with market leadership earned healthy margins exceeding 10 per cent.

20. The origins of this difference lie largely in relative costs. Groups 1–4 charged very similar prices, and offered products of comparable quality (line 6) so that it is clear that the progressively higher returns of Groups 2, 3 and 4 reflect increasing cost advantage *vis-a-vis* smaller competitors in the same market. It is less easy to compare Group 5 companies with the rest because they claimed significantly higher quality of product and charged relatively higher prices. Higher quality entails higher costs and hence justifies higher prices but the study does not make clear to what extent this is so. If, for ease of comparison, one simply ignores the quality difference and adjusts the profits of the Group 5 businesses to take account of their higher prices (even though these may be jutified in part or entirely by the costs of achieving higher quality) it turns out that even on this unflattering comparison Group 5 businesses are the most profitable of the sample on a price-adjusted basis (see line 4), implying a corresponding cost advantage over their competitors.[11] Thus the predicted relationship between market share and profitability and its origins in relative positions on the experience curve finds strong empirical support.

21. Further evidence of a different kind is available to test whether the superior profitability of concentrated industries reflects efficiency rather than the exploitation of market power. This evidence can be found in the relationship, if any, between concentration and international competitiveness. If the relative profitability of concentrated industries is a reflection of superior efficiency, one would expect that these industries would also be relatively competitive internationally, allowing for the other factors which have a bearing on a country's trade structure. Conversely, if their relative profitability derived from the exploitation of market power in their domestic market, and/or this market power provided a cover for a sluggish

[11] This finding is not at all inconsistent with the finding that company *size* and profitability are unrelated. Most companies operate in several markets and their profitability will therefore reflect some average of their market shares. Moreover company size does not correlate necessarily with market shares in relevant markets; it is not uncommon that within a particular industry, the industry leaders earn higher returns than medium-sized companies in the main product markets of the industry but a few small firms, with dominant positions in specialist markets, also earn high returns.

performance in terms of efficiency and innovation, one would expect to find an inverse relationship between concentration and international competitiveness. A recent study in the Department of Industry which attempts to explain the competitive performance of British manufacturing industries points towards the former explanation. In Britain's trade with the world as a whole and with OECD countries taken together in 1970, 1975 and 1976—the three years studied—industrial concentration was found to contribute to a statistically significant extent to an industry's trade performance as reflected in its ability to generate a positive trade balance. In Britain's trade with the EEC and Less Developed Countries this effect was also positive but less significant. If international competitiveness is regarded as a good index of industries' performance, these results suggest that concentration makes a positive rather than a negative contribution.

22. Concentration is not equated with lack of competition in the Boston Consulting Group analysis either. BCG argue that the realisation of cost reductions through experience is not automatic but depends crucially on a competent management that seeks ways to force costs down as volume expands. Effective competition has an important role to play in the process. 'The interaction of competitors over time provides a guarantee that superior cost improvement by one competitor will result eventually in the displacement of the less effective competitor.'[12] In fact many of the price curves used by BCG to illustrate their thesis show a period of relatively slow decline followed by a period of much faster decline.[13] BCG interpret this as instances of the leading producer (whose costs are lowest owing to having the greater experience) deciding to go for a larger market share at the expense of the weaker producers who were previously able to shelter under the 'price umbrella' of the market leader.[14] BCG suggest that such breaks in price trends are more likely the faster the growth of the product, the larger the number of producers and the greater the difference between price and cost for the lowest cost producer. These circumstances would seem to correspond to the middle phases of the product cycle. It seems clear however that effective competition must be reduced in the later stages of the cycle as the product matures and market growth slows down. On the other hand, at this stage of the product cycle when product characteristics have stabilised and technology can be

---

[12] Boston Consulting Group, *Perspectives on Experience*, pg. 23.

[13] See exhibits 9 and 10.

[14] The process described here refers to the majority of industries which are highly fragmented in their early stages, becoming more concentrated with maturity. There are reverse sequences in certain, technology-based industries such as pharmaceuticals and photocopiers, in which the technological originator dominates the market from the outset and is eventually threatened by entrants as patents expire.

acquired by purchase, international competition particularly from lower cost producers is likely to develop, as is indicated below.

23. In many businesses which have reached their mature, slow-growth phase in the US and Europe, the increase in international trade has significantly changed the nature of competition. Techno-logy is often openly available in these industries; that is, scale, pro-duct design, technology advances, etc, can be purchased, enabling new competitors in new locations to enter the business. Sometimes a new entrant enjoys fast growth in its home market, and thus accumu-lates experience more rapidly than its larger competitors in Europe and the US. Experience is accumulated and eventually, since the new entrant starts from a position well down the experience curve, it can overtake the dominant US or European producers in cost reduction. Often, lower labour and materials factor costs accelerate this process. These trends have been most noticeable in the case of Japan par-ticularly in the motor cycle and motor vehicle industries, to the UK's cost, but are increasingly becoming characteristic of many less developed countries. In many products, such as motor vehicles, construction equipment, TVs, and appliances, which had reached maturity in their domestic markets, an international shakeout is now under way, analogous to the national and regional shakeouts which occurred earlier. To dominant producers in Europe or the US, this new rapid-growth phase in other countries provides an oppor-tunity for changing competitive position and a threat inasmuch as producers based in these fast-growth countries have an opportunity to overtake internationally established competitors by acquiring experience. The Japanese Government has contributed to this process by promoting competitive oligopolistic structures; by a strategy of correctly anticipating the experience effect in these industries and by aggressively pursuing growth and market share gains, the companies concerned have been very successful in ob-taining low-cost world positions.

The Significance for Competition Policy

24. A consideration of the combined effects of learning, scale and technology, their apparently systematic operation, their possible links with market share and their predictable consequences for profitability via cost advantage, underlines the critical roles assigned to market share and concentration in competition policy literature but suggests a rather different interpretation of their significance. The Boston Consulting Group argues that, not only does this incentive drive industries towards concentrated structures; it has highly bene-ficial results. Thus, 'there is an implication that the consumer is best served by letting the dominant producer emerge, or even encourage his development and the concentration of production'. The diver-gence of this interpretation from the traditional economic analysis

of concentration is fundamental: According to the latter, concentration confers opportunities to exploit consumers via higher prices; according to the experience curve approach, concentration is the outcome of a process which confers on the leading producer a real cost advantage and it is this real cost advantage which maintains its superior profitability rather than exploitative behaviour in the market or improper restraints on competition. To the extent that monopoly references and investigations hinge on the profitability of dominant suppliers, they may need to give due weight to the latter interpretation.

25. The implications for mergers are less clear. The accumulation of experience and the achievement of cost reductions have been assumed to occur within companies. In fact, industry concentration and gains in market share often occur through merger. Under these circumstances, it would not be valid to assume that the greater combined accumulated experience achieved through merger can be translated effectively into lower costs. To some extent, experience can be effectively transferred through merger, the specific advantage depending on the phase in the product cycle. The advantages of marketing and distribution scale can be more readily shared; these considerations are likely to be particularly important in the mature, slow-growth phase of a business, when competition is directed to specific segments of the market. Scale advantages, on the other hand cannot be immediately transferred, although future investments can exploit the increased size and experience of the company. This means that scale advantages have more impact in high-growth businesses because the future investments to be undertaken by the combined companies are relatively more important than those already in place. In contrast, the problems of rationalizing two large capital-intensive companies with different plants, engineering and management styles are considerable and may require many years to resolve.

Table 1

*Some engineering-type estimates of minimum efficient plant size**

MLH	Product	Estimates of MEPS with author reference	UK produced sales of product in 1973	MEPS as % of UK produced sales
001	Broiler fowls	80,000 birds p.a. [30]		Small (?)
211	Flour	40–60 sacks per hour [22] 100 sacks per hour (narrow range of flours)	3.7 million tonnes (29 million sacks)	0.7–1.0% 1.8%
212	Bread	30 sacks per hour [26] 12–18 sacks per hour [22]	2.2 million tonnes (17.3 million sacks)	about 1% about ½%
214	Sausages	Very small [15]		Very small
216	Sugar, refined	450,000–500,000 tpa [14] 190,000 [1]	2.5 million tonnes	18–20% 8%
218	Potato Crisps	30,000–35,000 tpa [3]		About 10%
231	Beer	1 million barrels p.a. [26] 4.5 million barrels p.a. [31] 1–1.5 million barrels p.a. [4] 600,000 barrels p.a. [2]	35 million barrels	About 3% (About 13% (3–4% (About 2%
240	Cigarettes	36 billion cigarettes p.a. [30]	276 million lbs. (approx. 170 billion cigarettes)	21%

*Minimum efficient plant size is defined by Pratten, one of the authors whose work has been drawn on heavily in Table 1, as 'the minimum scale above which any possible subsequent doubling in scale would reduce total average unit costs by less than 5 per cent and above which any possible subsequent doubling in scale would reduce value added per unit by less than 10 per cent'. Not all the figures quoted in Table 1 are based on so precise a definition and it should be noted that the products listed cover a relatively small proportion of total UK manufacturing output and that the comparability of the various estimates is not high in view of the variety of authors and dates of the studies.

Table 1 (continued)

MLH	Product	Estimates of MEPS with author reference	UK produced sales of product in 1973	MEPS as % of UK produced sales
262	Oil Refining	10 million tpa [27] [26] 10 million tpa (200,000 bls per day) [31]	114 million tonnes (crude imput)	9% 9%
271	Sulphuric acid	5 million tpa [32] 1 million tpa [26]	3.9 million tonnes (production)	4% 26%
271	Ethylene	300,000 tpa [26]	887,000 tonnes	34%
274	Paint	10 million US galls p.a. [31]	528.3 million litres (140 million US galls)	7%
275	Soap	10,000 tpa [26]	240,000 tonnes	4%
275	Detergent powder	70,000 tpa [26]	342,000 tonnes	20%
278	Ammonium nitrate	300,000–350,000 tpa [9]	about 1.12 million tonnes (379,227 tonnes Nitrogen)	27–31%
279	Diazo copying materials	Very small [23]	n.a.	Very small
311	Steel	2–3 million tpa [27] 4–9 million tpa [26] 4 million tpa [31]	about 24 million tonnes (production)	8–12% 17–37% 17%
313	Pig iron	2–3 million tpa from blast furnaces [12]	about 15 million tonnes (production)	13–20%
313	Iron castings	50,000 tpa (cylinder blocks) [26] 10,000 tpa (small engineering castings) [26]	n.a.	
321	Aluminium semi-manufactures	200,000 tpa [24]	550,000 tpa	36%
332	Machine Tools	Various [26]		
334	Diesel engines (industrial)	100,000 units (engines of 1–100 bhp) [26]	179,000	56%

Page	Product	Output / Capacity	Ref	Market size	%
338	Electronic calculators	3–4 million units	[16]	About ½ million units (?)	Probably well over 100%
349	Anti-friction bearings	800 employees	[31]	34,100 (employment)	2%
361	Turbo-generators	6,000 MW p.a.	[26]	5,000 MW approx	120%
361	Electric Motors	8–10,000 MW p.a.	[8]		160–200%
		60% of UK market (1–100 hp)	[26]	8.4 million (less than 0.75 kw)	60% (?)
				740,000 (over 0.75 kw)	
364	TV tubes	750,000 p.a.	[10]	n.a.	Around 100%
		1½ million p.a.	[11]		
368	'White goods'	500,000 units	[26]	About 2½ million units	20%
368	Electric cookers	300,000 units	[5]	1.04 million units	30%
368	Electric refrigerators (part of 'white goods' above)	250,000–500,000 units	[5]	1.13 million units	22–43%
		800,000 units	[31]		69%
369	Automobile storage batteries	1 million units	[31]	About 7 million units (?)	14%
370	Large marine diesel engines	100,000 HP	[26]	769,000 HP (engines over 1,500 bhp)	13%
380	Tractors	90,000 units p.a.	[13]	119,000 units	76%
381	Motor Cars	½–1 million units p.a.	[26]	1.75 million units	29–57%
		See also [28] and	[17]		
381	Commercial Vehicles	20–30,000 units p.a.	[29]	416,000 units	5–7%
381	Clutch mechanisms	300,000 p.a.	[18]	About 2½ million units (?)	12%
382	Bicycles	160,000 units p.a.	[26]	2 million units	8%
383	Aircraft	'Substantial economies of scale are available'	[26]		At least 100% (?)
411	Synthetic fibres	80,000 tonnes p.a. polymer manufacture	[26]	454,000 tonnes (production)	18%
		40,000 tonnes extruded filament yarn	[26]		

Table 1 (continued)

MLH	Product	Estimates of MEPS with author reference		UK produced sales of product in 1973	MEPS as % of UK produced sales
413	Cotton and synthetic textiles	37.5 million sq. yds. (288 Sulzer looms) 1,000 conventional looms	[31]	771 million sq. metres (production)	6%
417	Hosiery	Small	[26]	776 million pairs	Small
450	Shoes	300,000 pairs p.a.	[26]	189 million pairs	0.2%
		1 million pairs p.a.	[31]		0.5%
		1,200 pairs/day	[7]		0.2%
461	Building bricks	25 million p.a.	[26]	7,000 million bricks (5,580 million ?)	0.4%
		50–62.5 million p.a.	[20]		0.7–0.9%
463	Glass beer bottles	133,000 tons p.a.	[31]	1,781 million bottles (including wine and spirit and cider bottles)	?
464	Cement	200,000 tpa (kiln capacity)	[25]	17.8 million tonnes	1%
		2 million tpa	[26]		11%
		1.2 million tpa	[31]		7%
469	Plasterboard	18–20 million sq. metres	[19]	104 million sq. metres	17–19%
489	Books	10,000 p.a. (hardback)	[26]		
		100,000 p.a. (paperback)	[26]		
491	Rubber tyres	5,000 tyres/day	[6]	30.3 million tyres (car and van)	About 6%
491	Rubber contraceptive sheaths	500,000 gross p.a.	[21]	About 1 million gross	About 50%

Sources (for Col. 4): Mostly Business Monitors (Census of Production reports). Also Monthly Digest of Statistics & Monopolies Commission reports.

1 R. M. Auty — Factory Size & Economies of Scale in Commonwealth Carribbean Sugar In Industry 1930-70 (Ph.D. Thesis, London, 1973).

2 G. Bannock — *The Smaller Business in Britain & Germany* (1976) Appendix I.

3 A. Bevan — The UK Potato Crisp Industry 1960-72: A study of New Entry Competition. (*Jul of Ind Ec* 1974).

4 A. Cockerill — The Merger Movement in the Brewing Industry (*Jul of Ind Affairs* 1976).

5 J. E. Cousin & P. I. Freeman — The UK Domestic Appliance Industry (Mintech study, 1968).

6 D. J. Daly et al. — *Scale & Specialisation in Canadian manufacturing* (Economic Council for Canada, 1968).

7 Economists Advisory Group — *British Footwear—The Future*, vol. II II (1976).

8 B. Epstein (& D. Burn) — *Realities of Free Trade* (Allen & Unwin for TPRC, 1972).

9 *European Chemical News* — *Major New Fertilizer Plants* (1976).

10 *Financial Times* — Why normal service may never be resumed (27 Oct. 1975).

11 *Financial Times* — New colour tube poses problems for TV makers (22 Oct. 1976).

12 B. Gold — Evaluating scale economies: the case of Japanese blast furnaces (*Jul of Ind Ec* 1974).

13 J. B. Heath, N. Owen et al. — *The Evaluation of concentration in UK mechanical engineering* (1975).

14 l. Hjalmarrson — Reply (*European Economic Review No. 7*, 1976).

15. D. Lees & J. Morley — Competition in the sausage market (*Jul of Ind Ec* 1970).

16 R. Levine — Calculating on cheap labour and high volume (*Financial Times*, Jan 19 1976).

17 J. S. McGee — *Jul of Law and Economics* (Oct. 1973).

18 Monopolies & Mergers Commission — *Report on Clutch Mechanisms* (1968).

19 Monopolies & Mergers Commission — *Report on Plasterboard* (1974).

20 Monopolies & Mergers Commission — *Report on Supply of Building Bricks* (1975).

21 Monopolies & Mergers Commission — *Report on Contraceptive Sheaths* (1975).

22 Monopolies & Mergers Commission — *Report on Flour & Bread* (July 1977).

23 Monopolies & Mergers Commission — *Report on Diazo copying materials* (1977).

24 National Board for Prices & Incomes — *Cost & Prices of Aluminium semi-manufactures* (Report No. 39, 1967).

25 National Board for Prices & Incomes — *Portland cement prices* (Report No. 133, 1965).

26 C. Pratten — *Economics of scale in Manufacturing Industry* (Cambridge University, DAE occasional paper 28, 1971).

27 C. Pratten & R. M. Dean —*Economics of large scale production in British Industry* (Cambridge University, DAE occasional paper No. 3, 1965).

28 D. G. Rhys —*The Motor Industry: an economic survey* (London 1972).

29 D. G. Rhys —Heavy Commercial Vehicles (*Jul of Ind Ec* 1971).

30 S. Richardson —*The UK Broiler Industry* 1960–75 (University of Manchester, Agriculture Enterprise Studies No. 42, July 1976).

31 F. M. Scherer The Determinants of International Plant sizes in six Nations (*Rev of Ec & Stats* 1973).

32 N. A. White —*The Economies of scale in the International Petroleum Industry* (Ph. D. Thesis, London, 1973).

Table 2

*Estimated relationship between market share and unit cost advantage**

	Group 1	Group 2	Group 3	Group 4	Group 5
1. Number of Businesses Investigated	145	179	105	67	87
2. Market Share	Less than 10%	10–20%	20–30%	30–40%	Over 40%
Costs and Margins					
3. Pretax profits/Sales	—0.2%	3.4%	4.8%	7.6%	13.2%
4. Pretax profits/sales adjusted for effects of price premia charged by each group†	—0.2%	3.3%	4.1%	7.0%	9.6%
5. Implied unit cost advantage relative to businesses with less than 10% market share	—	3.5%	4.3%	7.2%	9.8%
6. Quality index‡	15	20	20	20	43

*Derived from Harvard Business School's Profit Impact of Market Share Analysis.

†The average price charged by each Group, relative to its competitors, is provided in the Harvard analysis on a 5-point scale. These results are interpolated and used to adjust profit margins in relation to those of the Group 1 businesses.

‡This index is based on each business's estimate of relative superiority/inferiority of its own product. Group 5 businesses have noticeably superior products. This is *not* taken account of in calculating their unit cost advantage; because higher quality implies higher cost, the cost advantage of the Group 5 businesses is certainly higher than the figure indicated if quality differences are taken into account.

The following exhibits were prepared by the Boston Consulting Group

Exhibit 1. Japanese Time Recorders 1962–72

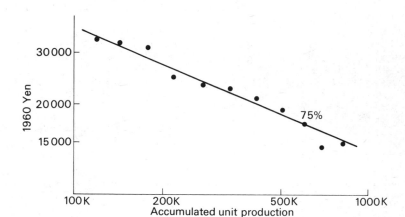

Exhibit 2. Bottle Caps (West Germany)
Value added cost-constant 1974 D-Marks

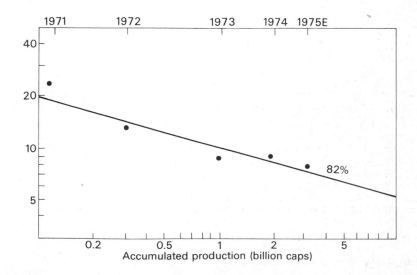

Exhibit 3. Life Insurance Industry (US)
Operating expense per policy-year

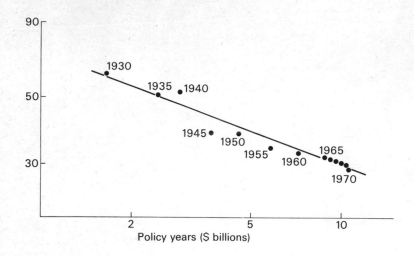

Source: Institute of Life Insurance

Exhibit 4. Pilkington Brothers Float Glass (1962–67)
Total cost per square foot

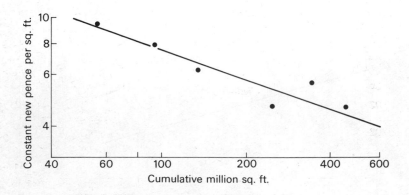

Source: The Monopolies Commission

Exhibit 5. Electric Shavers

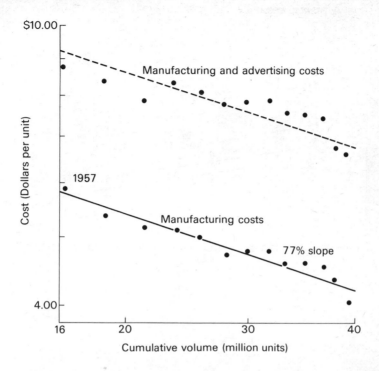

Exhibit 6. Advertising per Case VS Volume (US) 1974

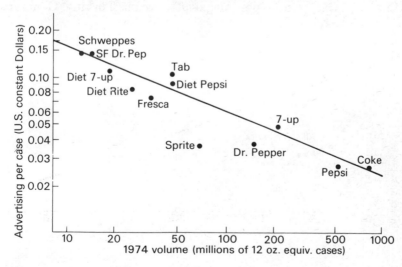

Source: Beverage Industry Annual Manual

Exhibit 7. Scale Evolution Over Time
               A plastic resin

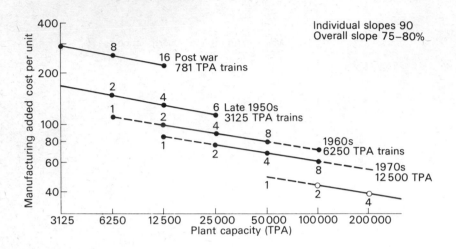

Exhibit 8. Direct Costs per Megawatt Steam Turbine Generators
               1946–63

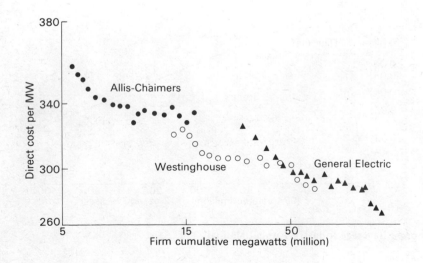

Exhibit 9. Refrigerators UK, 1957–71

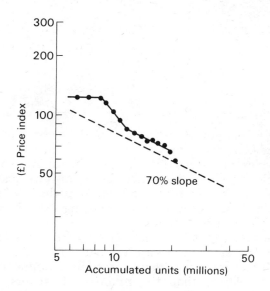

Source: Association of Manufacturers of Domestic Electrical Appliances

Exhibit 10. US Silicon Transistors

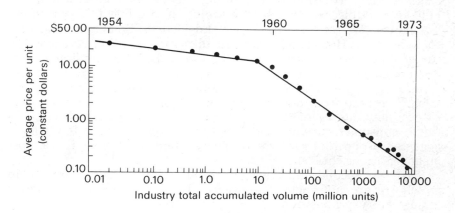

10

The Literature of Economics: The Case of the Kinked Oligopoly Demand Curve

by George J. Stigler*

The literature of economics is the accumulated product of innumerable economists. In a recent year nearly 6000 different economists published articles or books in English, and another (overlapping) group, possibly as large, published book reviews, pamphlets and other papers. The former group produced perhaps 800 books and 5000 articles, and the addition to the existing stock of literature in a year is on the order of 5 percent.

It is a literature that no one person could possibly read—the limits imposed by sanity are stricter than those imposed by time. Indeed it is a literature that perhaps is read by a number of economists only moderately larger than the number of writers. The best of memories can accurately recall only a tiny fraction of this literature, and if the literature were irrevocably destroyed, most of it would utterly perish from human knowledge.

Most of us, I suspect, have two very different views of this literature, views suited to different portions of the literature we have studied. There is a sweeping historical survey, in which the main stages in the evolution of the ruling theory are contemplated. To take an example, we consider the evolution of utility theory through Jevons and Walras, Pareto, Fisher, Edgeworth, Slutsky-Hicks-Allen, to Samuelson, Houthakker, and the ultra-moderns. In that account—the standard fare of histories of economic thought—the literature is dominated by major figures and major advances. The backing and filling, the digressions and confusions, the sometimes acrimonious debates, recede from memory and the major advances form the stuff of economic literature. The scores of articles on integrability conditions, consumer surplus, and the like coalesce into a few widely accepted propositions to which, if any name is attached, it is almost an adventitious christening.

There is, second, the view we hold today of the literature in which we are now actively engaged. Here if controversy is active almost every proposition seems open to debate, and the course of

From *Economic Inquiry*, vol. 16, part 2 (Apr. 1978), pp. 185-204. Reprinted by permission of the author and editor of the journal.

*University of Chicago. I wish to express my debt to Claire Friedland for indispensable assistance. I also have benefitted from comments by Gary Becker and Robert K. Merton. An oral version of this paper was presented in April 1977 at a UCLA symposium in honor of Armen Alchian.

controversy shifts as rapidly as the situs of a fox hunt—indeed, a series of simultaneous and intersecting fox hunts. The participants are numerous, so the debate takes place simultaneously in many journals and a large number of economists enter the discussion. Occasionally the whole literature may have proved to be unfruitful— the theory of monopolistic competition is a truly major example —in which case the episode will never coalesce into a new example of scientific evolution described in the first view of the literature.

Of course most economic literature falls in neither category. It is not lively and rapidly shifting, because there are only a few topics which at any time capture the interest of a considerable number of active economists. It is not historical and masterly, because only a few topics achieve such scope, persistent importance, and breadth of professional acceptance and use as to dominate a generation or more of our literature. Most literature deals with the experimental, the temporarily relevant, the special (in scope) application of general knowledge, the idiosyncratic interests of writers and the whimsies of editors.

It is to this routine literature that this essay is devoted. I seek to determine why it exists,—that is, why that subject is being discussed —who is interested in the literature, how if at all, it changes over time, and what finally terminates its course. The goal is to understand the nature of 'normal' literature.

To this end, a reasonably full canvass has been taken of the literature of the kinked oligopoly demand curve. It is a literature to which I made one contribution in 1947 and then put aside as of no further interest to me. I have returned to it now with the wholly different purpose of examining the course of normal scientific literature in dealing with a particular topic. There is no way of knowing whether it is an atypical literature, since I know of no other similarly intensive study of economic literature.[1] The choice was commended to me by these attributes:

1. The literature began at a definite time—1939—and any precursor work was unknown. At least one partial anticipation was found.[2]

---

[1] I have since been introduced by Stephen Stigler to Kenneth O. May's history of the literature of determinants, partly reported in 'Growth and Quality of the Mathematical Literature' (1968–69), with additional material in 'Who Killed Determinants?' (n.d.).

[2] Joseph Spengler (1965) has found earlier kinked demand curves, but none has the economic content of asymmetrical oligopolistic behavior studied here. R. F. (Lord) Kahn (1937, pp. 8–9) sketched the essentials of the kinked demand theory without drawing the demand curve. But he did not accept the lower branch of the demand curve. For it violated (for him) the assumption. 'the backbone of the theory of duopoly.' that 'no firm has any trust whatever in its competitors.' A discontinuous oligopoly demand curve based upon different prices being charged by the rivals was used in R. H. Coase (1934, p. 139) 'The Problem of Duopoly Reconsidered.'

2. The theory of the kinked demand curve has attracted the attention of a substantial fraction of the leading economists for nearly 40 years, as we shall see. But the literature was not monopolized by prominent economists.
3. The literature is both theoretical and empirical.
4. The theory has run its course and is dying, so it is possible to treat it in a disengaged manner.

The last attribute proved, in fact, to be wholly mistaken, but I am prepared to derive some useful information about economic literature from this very fact.

1. The Genesis of the Kinked Demand Curve

This is a study of economic literature, not of references to the literature (citations), so we must concern ourselves with the scientific content as well as the literary pedigree of the work on the subject. So first a brief restatement of the kinked demand theory.

Paul Sweezy (1939) proposed the theory in a brief, wholly theoretical paper in 1939.[3] He proposed a demand curve for an oligopolist which takes account of the expected behavior of his rivals at each price he sets (which he termed an 'imagined' demand curve, although he believed that it would be confirmed by experience). The typical rival responses will be to match price decreases (to prevent the loss of business) but not to follow a price increase (because a gain of business 'is a pleasurable feeling'). The kink thus produced in the oligopolist's demand curve at the ruling price produces a discontinuity in the corresponding marginal revenue curve. The sharpness of the kink, and as a result the length of the gap in marginal revenue, was less when demand for the oligopolistic industry was strong; the converse was expected with a decrease in market demand. As a result, price reductions would be most uncommon in periods of low demand, price increases would become more common in periods of increasing demand. The rigidity of prices in oligopolistic markets appeared to be nicely explained by this construct. Sweezy explicitly rejected the hope that a theory of oligopoly could explain the level of prices; it could only seek to explain the process of price change.

Nearly simultaneously, Robert Hall and Charles Hitch (1939) presented another, related kinked demand curve under oligopoly. The Oxford version of the theory departs in one major respect from that of Sweezy. Hall and Hitch believe that the level of prices will be set at 'full cost:; the average cost (including a 'conventional allowance for profit') of producing at a normal rate of output. This full-cost price becomes the ruling price under oligopoly, apparently as a result of diverse influences such as collusion, long run tenability of price, moral notions of fairness, and ignorance of demand elasticities. It is

---

[3] It is interesting to notice that Sweezy (1938, pp. 113 ff.) drew an *industry* demand curve with a kink the preceding year.

enforced, so to speak, by the belief of oligopolists that rivals will not follow price increases but would match price decreases, thus producing a kink in each firm's demand curve. The main difference from Sweezy is the element of full cost pricing: 'any circumstance which lowers or raises the average cost curves of all firms by similar amounts . . . is likely to lead to a re-evaluation of the full cost price' (ibid. p. 25).

The Oxford version thus has the advantage over Sweezy's version of explaining the level of prices, but this advantage is dearly bought: a fundamental conflict exists between a kinked demand curve and full cost pricing. If the kink does not exist so far as industry-wide cost changes are concerned, this means that firms succeed in acting jointly and harmoniously, and are not prevented from adjusting to the new cost level by kinks in their individual demand curves. Similarly, then, the kink should not exist so far as response to any other industry-wide change in circumstances is concerned. One of these industry-wide circumstances is that all firms will have larger profits by varying prices when industry demand changes—but the very purpose of the kink is to explain why such price changes do not occur. There are elements of slack in the Oxford version (e.g., the desire of firms to maintain large outputs, and irrational behavior leading to price reductions in deeply depressed times), and the subsequent literature shows a clear and correct preference for Sweezy's version.

The existence of a literal kink, it should be observed, was not necessary to either version of the theory. Even in a fully deterministic world there would presumably be some buyers who would obtain homogeneous goods from an oligopolist who charged slightly more than his rivals (perhaps because of costs of buyer search). With a probabilistic (or empirically determined) demand curve, continuity of slope would be all the more probable. The effects would be minor, however, if a literal kink were replaced by a very sharp bend in the demand curve at the ruling price.

2. The Scientific Evolution of the Theory

The theoretical evolution of the kinked demand curve has been remarkably meager, and despite the wide attention to the theory, the empirical testing has been almost equally meager. The main stages in the scientific evolution of the theory are quickly summarized.

1. *Bronfenbrenner (1940) and Efroymson (1943).* Bronfenbrenner, in the first article devoted to the kink after it appeared, developed more explicitly its implications: (i) that prices under imperfect competition will be rigid; (ii) that open price agreements (advance notification of price changes to rivals) accentuate the inelasticity of demand with respect to price reductions, (iii) cutthroat competition is an exaggerated form of behavior leading to kinks, and (iv) kinks will appear in supply curves with oligopsony. The internal logic

of the theory and the possibility of (or necessity for) testing it empirically are not considered.

C. W. Efroymson became perhaps the leading supporter of the theory. The already conventional kinked demand curve is given priority over the full-cost principle, I think correctly, even in the Hall and Hitch version. The main contribution consists of a cyclical analysis of oligopoly demand curves.When sales volume is cyclically low, an oligopolist will realize that his rivals are extremely loathe to lose volume, and hence will match price decreases but not price increases. But when volume is cyclically high and capacity is approached, the situation is reversed. Now a price rise will not lead customers to shift to a rival, for that rival will also be operating at a high rate of output and be unable to accommodate many more customers, and similarly be unwilling to follow a price reduction. A 'reflex' demand curve, elastic for price reductions and inelastic for price increases, will emerge.[4] The shift from one state of demand to the other is usually 'sudden and decisive.' With the reflex demand curve, profits are minimized at the kink, and prices change—how much, and in what direction, are questions left unexplored. Equilibrium is possible only after the conventional ('obtuse') kink is restored in the oligopolist's demand curve.

2. *Stigler's Critique*. My appraisal of the theory in 1947 was stimulated more by a growing interest in the empirical testing of theories than by the intrinisic interest of the kinked demand curve.

On the formal side, my chief criticism was that if price rises were indicated by the theory, they would contradict the existence of the kink. Hence the kink could, perhaps, explain the persistence of a given price, but not the reappearance of a kink. In retrospect I should have emphasized (and not merely mentioned) instead the arbitrary asymmetry of the behavioral pattern attributed to each firm. Price decreases were promptly matched to preserve market share, whereas the rivals would not follow price increases in hope of increasing their share of the market. But surely the price increaser would usually promptly restore the former price if he was not followed, so that non-following rivals would in fact not get appreciable sales increases if they did not follow the price increase.

The main task of the article, however, was a test of the empirical fruitfulness of the theory. A modest direct test was first applied: price histories in seven industries were examined to see whether in fact price increases were not followed and price decreases promptly followed. The vast majority of the recorded price episodes were not in keeping with the assumption of the theory.

The larger test, however, was a study of BLS wholesale prices from June 1929 to May 1937. The following implications of the theory were tested:

1. Monopolies had no kink, so these prices should be more flexible than those of oligolistic industries. (Here and later the impact

---

[4] A reverse kink had already been suggested by E. T. Grether (1939, p. 23ln).

of demand fluctuations was measured by the coefficient of variation of output, and used as a control.) The reverse was the case.

2. The fewer the number of firms, the less probable the kink, because of the realization that price increases that were not followed would quickly be rescinded. The facts were the reverse: price changed more often and more widely, the larger the number of firms.

3. Price leaders who were dominant firms (I proposed also a 'barometric' price leader whose function was to adjust price to changing market conditions) should have no kinks and hence have more flexible prices. The reverse was true.

4. The kink is sharper, the more elastic the upper branch, so prices should be more flexible with oligopoly with differentiated products than those with homogeneous products. This prediction was also contradicted.

5. The kink disappears when the firms collude. Prices proved to be more rigid in periods of known collusion.

3. *The Rejoinders.* A considerable number of economists have objected to some or all of the tests I made. The objections will be inventoried, but first a comment should be made on one characteristic these defenders of the theory of kinked demand curves all share: the belief that they need not provide evidence to support the theory. If my criticisms could be rejected, apparently there has been a presumption that the theory is acceptable: theories, like other citizens, are presumed innocent until shown to be guilty.

The main lines of criticism of my tests have been:

1. Since the kink is based upon *expected* responses of rivals, and expectations may be independent of previous experience, and possibly geared to future experience, or even irrational, therefore actual experience cannot be used to prove the non-existence (or existence?) of the kink (Smith 1948, pp. 204–6). As Paul Streeten (1951, p. 109n.) put it,

As long as oligopolists believe in the kink, prices will not be altered. Only when they abandon this belief will they change prices, but these changes are no evidence of their disbelief in the kink at other times.[5]

I would like to think that this type of criticism is no longer publishable.

2. When a cost increase is common to all firms in the industry, they may reasonably assume that the rivals will follow a price increase. This is the single most popular criticism of my tests: they failed to include changes in variable costs (Smith 1948, p. 207 and Shepherd 1962, p. 423n). Needless to say, no one actually introduced this variable to rerun the tests. The response is remarkably ad hoc: if industry-wide phenomena are

[5] The same point is made with more restraint by J. M. Clark (1961, p. 287) who then asks for an independent determination of when the kink exists.

responded to jointly by all firms, then there *is no kink*. Industry-wide phenomena include changes in demand, and what, besides changes in industry supply and demand, could influence market price appreciably?

3. The reflex demand curve explains the price changes, so a different kink explains price increases (Efroymson 1955, pp. 119-22, 128 ff).
4. The seven price histories were too few in number to support a criticism (Shepherd 1962, p. 423n). Individual circumstances —collusion, memory of a previous episode, price leadership— had smoothed out the kink (Efroymson 1955, p. 127).
5. The tests relied on BLS list prices, which are notoriously inflexible relative to transaction prices (ibid., pp. 130ff). One would think that the denial of the phenomenon the kink theory was designed to explain was an unhappy defense.[6]
6. Collusion may be incomplete, and fail to remove the kink (ibid., p. 132). It is not explained how collusion makes for a sharper kink.
7. The lesser price flexibility of monopolies than of oligopolies, and of heterogeneous than of homogenous product oligopolies, shows only that other forces in addition to the kink explain price behavior (ibid., pp. 133-35; Clark 1961, p. 288).
8. One needs objective standards of competitive price behavior in order to judge patterns of oligopolistic price behavior Shepherd 1962, p. 423n).

4. *Later Empirical Tests.* A second empirical test of the kinked demand curve was made by Julian in 1969. The advertising rates in business magazines are compared for 'groups' (journals serving the same markets), and the rates of monopolists are found to change less often than those groups with two or more magazines. This is of course contrary to the prediction of the theory.

A third empirical test, by W. J. Primeaux Jr., and M. R. Bomball (1974), examines electrical rates in cities with one and two independent electric utilities. Again monopolists changed rates less often than duopolists, and duopolists more commonly followed rate increases (with or without a lag) than rate decreases. W. J. Primeaux Jr. and M. C. Smith (1976) made a similar test of the price movements of prescription drugs of monopolists and oligopolists, and also found that the predictions of the kinked demand curve theory were contradicted. Both studies are weakened by the use of annual data on prices.

Although no other quantitative studies have been made, there are many assertions in the literature of the existence of a kink in

---

[6] Efroymson (1955) finds discrepancies from list price most likely under oligopoly because of secret price cutting with ostensible collusion—which surely is inconsistent with the assumption that price reductions will be matched.

the demand curve of a particular industry, perhaps at a particular time. Two examples are:[7]

1. Rayon. Markham (1952) found weak evidence of a kink (weak because price leadership was well established): the average delay of firms in following a price increase was 10 days, a price decrease 7 days.[8]
2. Steel. The cited passage states that U.S. Steel will not (cannot?) increase its market share by 'undercutting' prices (Kaplan et al. 1958, p. 174). Yet the company led price moves frequently (ibid., p. 167).

These examples are not cited to show that there are no price episodes consistent with kinked demand curve theorizing: of course there are many episodes where a price increase by one firm has not been followed by others, or where price decreases have been followed. The examples suggest only that no extensive, careful search for supporting evidence has been made by anyone.

5. *Elaborations of the Theory.* The paucity of additional theoretical work on the kinked demand curve has been remarked. Only two suggested extensions seem worthy of note here. The first suggestion, by Cohen and Cyert (1965, pp. 251ff), is that until a firm has learned the behavioral pattern of its rivals, a kink is quite likely, so rigid prices are more likely to be found in (1) young industries, and (2) industries experiencing new entry.[9] An illustrative episode from the potash industry is given.

The second extension, this time by Cyert and DeGroot (1971),[10] can be viewed as an extension of the previous proposal: the learning behavior of the firm is allowed to produce kinks under certain

---

[7] These were cited by F. M. Scherer (1973, p. 147n); repeated by A. A. Thompson (1973, p. 400n).

[8] Markham (1952, pp. 88, 143, 199). The significance of the difference could not be calculated but since the reports carried a 15 to 30 day uncertainty of date (ibid., p. 86), it is improbable that a significance test would be passed.

[9] It is instructive to set against this conjecture the contrary one of the National Bureau of Economic Research, Committee on Price Determination (1943), in a report which bears the imprint of the Committee's chairman, E. S. Mason:

'There is no doubt that this [the kinked demand curve] is a realistic picture of the demand situation as envisaged by individual firms in a great number of industrial markets a large part of the time. It goes a long way toward explaining some important aspects of industrial price behavior. There is rather strong reason for believing that leading firms in the automobile, steel, agricultural implement, and many other industries act upon approximately this view of the situation. As a working hypothesis, however, it is probably limited to industrial markets which have attained something like long run stability in the sense that demand is mainly for replacement and the entry of new firms is unimportant' (ibid. p. 278).

Characteristically, the remainder of the paragraph restricts the claims for the kink.

[10] A later article suggests by its silence on the kink that it played only a temporary role in their work; see 'An Analysis of Cooperation and Learning in a Duopoly Context' (Cyert and DeGroot 1973, 24–37).

conditions. For example, firm A believes that B will match price increases up to a certain level Θ, which is not known precisely, so it experiments with price increases to learn Θ. The extension is potentially interesting, but the behavior of the oligopolists is not related to ordinary profit maximizing parameters so in its present form this extension has no empirically graspable handles.

6. *The Extension to Limit Pricing.* The theory of limit pricing—the setting of oligopoly or monopoly prices that will make entry into the industry unattractive to prospective rivals—has an ancient history in economics.[11] The modern formulation, especially that of Paolo Sylos-Labini (1962),[12] bears a close affinity to kinked demand curve theory. In the more precise statement by Modigliani (1958) a definite price exists above which rivals will be attracted. The limit price is so chosen by the existing firms that after entry a new firm, if the existing firms maintain their output and the new entrant enters at the smallest remunerative output, his average costs will equal the after-entry price. Hence the existing demand curve of the combined oligopolists has a kink (or at least sharply increased elasticity for price increases) at the limit price. This kink price should closely follow long run costs of production of entrants.

The similarities between the two kinds of kink are evident, as is also the crucial absence of oligopolistic uncertainty in the limit price version. There is no direct evidence that limit price theory was influenced by the kinked demand curve literature.[13] Neither Bain nor Sylos-Labini was an enthusiastic supporter of the kinked demand curve theory.[14] We have noticed, however, that Sweezy presented a limit price kink before he published the kinked oligopolistic demand curve.[15]

7. *Other Kinks.* Any asymmetry in the response of rivals to increases and decreases of a variable may lead to a kink in the relevant function. Hence one could readily have extended the theory to other dimensions of rivalry in addition to price. This was not done.[16]

Some economists have apparently been led to attribute kinks to quite different demand phenomena. L. Fouraker and W. Lee (1956) in an under-appreciated performance, managed to find a kink in the demand curve of individual Pennsylvania apple growers. Other variants have been proposed by H. R. Edwards (1952), Hieser (1953), M. Farrell (1954), Grossack (1966), Hawkins (1954), McManus (1962), Greenhut (1967), Levitan and Shubik (1971), and Douglas (1973). Of course Edgeworth's theory of duopoly (1925, I, p. 118ff)

---

[11] One classic exposition is J. B. Clark's in (e.g.) *The Control of Trusts* (1901, Ch. IV).

[12] J. S. Bain (1956) offers a similar theory.

[13] Joan Robinson (1933, p. 81) used the situation of a monopolist who faced entry of rivals above a certain price as a possible source of kinks.

[14] Sylos-Labini (1962, pp. 98–99) rejected the theory; Bain (1960, p. 203) gave it little scope.

[15] See above note 3.

[16] Doyle (1968) attributes an advertising kink to Kaldor, but I have not been able to find it.

which rested on capacity constraints on the rivals, produces a kinked demand curve which has often been reproduced.

8. *Dynamics of Individual Firm Prices.* An Important potential service of the kinked oligopoly demand curve literature would have been to advance, or at least to arouse economic theorists' interest in, the problem of how the prices of individual firms change when market price changes. The kinked demand curve theory indeed contains a rudimentary, if unprepossessing, version of such a theory. No such catalytic role was served: the rapidly growing modern literature of the dynamics of price movements is intimately related to the economics of information but the kinked demand curve literature had no apparent influence.

3. The Reception of the Kink

The year 1939 was inauspicious for the launching of a new economic theory, but even a World War did not prevent a fairly wide acceptance of a plausible explanation for the existence of the pervasively inflexible ('administered') industrial prices for which Gardner Means had successfully argued.[17] Already by 1940 Bronfenbrenner had spelled out various implications of Sweezy's note, and in 1942 there were no less than 9 articles mentioning the theory (4 by Sidney Weintraub).

There is a measure of paradox in this marriage of the literatures of oligopoly and price inflexibility, because there was a serious incompatibility between the partners. The phenomenon that Means emphasized in the 1930's was the *downward* rigidity of prices. (In the late 1950's Means shifted his emphasis, indeed, to the upward aggressiveness of the price policies of oligopolies.) But the kink argues primarily against *upward* price changes: the kinked demand curve of an oligopolist for price reductions is the same as that with full collusion, so if a price were at the (industry) profit-maximizing level, it would be fully responsive to a large class of subsequent downward movements of cost and demand, and the upper branch of the firm's demand curve and the kink would be irrelevant. This was apparently seldom remarked.[18]

A statistical history of the references to the kinked demand curve is given in Table 1. This canvass of the literature underlies our discussion of its nature, so it is necessary to describe how it was compiled. An extensive search was made of all articles in the *Index of Economic Journals* under appropriate headings in microeconomic theory, price and market theory of firm and industry, and public policy towards monopoly and competition. Undoubtedly there are other articles in which the kink appeared: anyone using oligopoly price theory in fields such as international trade, labor markets or

[17] Beginning with the celebrated monograph, *Industrial Prices and their Relative Inflexibility*, (Means, 1935).

[18] See, however, D. H. Whitehead (1963, pp. 187-95) and W. Hamburger (1967, p. 268).

Table 1
References to the Kinked Demand Curve, 1939–76

Year	Total Number of Articles	Articles Primarily on Kink*	Number of Books (1st ed. only)
1939	2	2: Sweezy; Hall & Hitch	—
1940	3	2: Bronfenbrenner; Mikesell	—
1941	2		1
1942	9		—
1943	2	1: Efroymson	1
1944	—		1
1945	—		—
1946	1		—
1947	6	1: Stigler	4
1948	4	1: V. Smith	4
1949	—		3
1950	1		—
1951	4	1: Streeten	4
1952	3		2
1953	3	1: Hieser	—
1954	8		—
1955	7	1: Efroymson	4
1956	1		—
1957	1		2
1958	1		2
1959	1		2
1960	2		4
1961	2		4
1962	2	1: Shepherd	3
1963	1		3
1964	1		5
1965	2	1: Spengler	5
1966	1		4
1967	5		2
1968	5		5
1969	2	1: Simon	3
1970	6		7
1971	3	2: Smith & Neale; Cyert & DeGroot	2
1972	3	1: Peel	2
1973	4		4
1974	3	2: Primeaux & Bomball; Murphy & Ng	—
1975	3	1: Coyne	1
1976	1	1: Primeaux & Smith	2
1940's	27		14
1950's	30		16
1960's	23		38
1970's	23		18

*See starred items in list of references.

public finance would be overlooked by this procedure. The foreign-language literature is omitted. Our search of books was even more narrowly confined to textbooks in principles and theory and works in industrial organization and price behavior.[19]

The canvass reported in Table 1 yields a respectable total of 103 articles in which the kinked demand curve is at least mentioned, 18 articles (not including those of Sweezy and Hall and Hitch) of which it was the main subject, and some 86 books. The latter count pertains only to the first (post-1939) edition in which the theory appeared (thus Samuelson's text is counted only in the 6th edition, 1964, when the kink was introduced, although it persists in all later editions). In terms of individual specimens of economic literature displaying a kinked demand curve, in recent years the *annual* count has probably been on the order of 300,000 or more (in many of the leading textbooks on principles or price theory) plus another 15,000 specimens in the two or three articles in journals. There is little evidence of abatement of the number of references; in fact the theory seems to have reached a steady state.

Unless an author explicitly sets out to refute a theory, one should characterize his attitude toward that theory as favorable, or at worst neutral, if he actually refers to the theory. For he is reviving its currency and advertising its existence. In classifying the attitudes in references to the kinked demand curve I have therefore leaned in the direction of classifying discussions as favorable unless they were fairly explicitly otherwise. Of the 189 references to the kink, 143 were favorable, 29 neutral, and 17 unfavorable (see Table 2). The favorable and neutral references have dominated throughout the period since 1939, but recently the unfavorable references have become moderately more common.[20] The theory has received no systematic empirical support and virtually no theoretical elaboration in these decades, but these lacks have been no handicap in maintaining its currency.

The *uses* made of the kink by various economists are difficult to classify in a reproducible fashion. Most references are simple 'mentions' of the theory, for example:

The commonest market situation is one of oligopoly with product differentiation, in which case the demand curve must be regarded as kinked (and the marginal revenue curve as discontinuous) at the existing price. In this case one cannot really say that output and employment are determined by the intersection of the (horizontal) marginal cost curve and the (discontinuous) marginal revenue curve. The causal sequence starts rather with the determination of a price for the product . . . . (Reynolds 1948, p. 297)

The difficulty arises in setting a level of elaboration or application of the theory that involves some element of novelty, a category of use I label 'analysis.' It contains all (20) full-length articles devoted to the kinked demand curve, whatever their contribution, since surely analysis (professional development of the subject)

[19] I am indebted especially to Maurice Schiff and Herminio Blanco for compiling the basic canvass of the literature. *The Journal of Economic Literature* was used for years in which the *Index* was unavailable.
[20] This article can be so classified!

Table 2
*Classification of Attitude Toward and Use Made of
Kinked Demand Curve*

Year	Attitude			Use Made of Theory		
	Favorable	Neutral	Unfavorable	Economic Analysis	Mention	Exposition
1940	3	—	—	3	—	—
1941	3	—	—	—	3	—
1942	9	—	—	2	7	—
1943	3	—	—	2	1	—
1944	1	—	—	1	—	—
1945	—	—	—	—	—	—
1946	1	—	—	—	1	—
1947	9	—	1	2	6	2
1948	7	—	1	1	3	4
1949	2	—	1	1	2	—
1950	1	—	—	—	1	—
1951	5	1	2	1	5	2
1952	2	3	—	—	4	1
1953	1	—	2	1	2	—
1954	7	1	—	3	5	—
1955	6	4	1	1	8	2
1956	1	—	—	1	—	—
1957	2	1	—	—	2	1
1958	2	1	—	—	1	2
1959	1	2	—	—	3	—
1960	5	1	—	—	2	4
1961	5	1	—	1	2	3
1962	3	2	—	2	1	2
1963	4	—	—	1	—	3
1964	4	2	—	—	2	4
1965	7	—	—	2	1	4
1966	4	1	—	—	2	3
1967	6	—	1	2	3	2
1968	9	1	—	1	5	4
1969	3	1	1	1	1	3
1970	10	2	1	1	8	4
1971	3	2	—	2	2	1
1972	4	—	1	2	2	1
1973	6	—	2	1	4	3
1974	1	—	2	2	1	—
1975	1	3	—	1	2	1
1976	2	—	1	1	—	2
1940's	38	0	3	12	23	6
1950's	28	13	5	7	31	8
1960's	50	9	2	10	19	32
1970's	27	7	7	10	19	12
	143	29	17	39	92	58

was their purpose. In addition there are a large number of references
of this type:

A rise in costs 'justifies' a price increase in the sense that, if profit margins are left unchanged as a result of the cost-price alterations, no encouragement is given to potential competitors, suppliers, purchasers, the Government, trade unions, or anyone else to vary the incipient or actual pressures they are exerting in their various ways. However this does not fully explain why price changes would occur. Would it not be possible for the first firm raising its prices to be forced into an embarrassing and costly re-shuffle as a result of other firms failing to move? In most cases it is easy to see that the answer is in the negative. If the cost increase is large, any satisfaction over the embarrassment of a competitor would ring hollow in the face of substantially reduced profit margins in the other firms that failed to increase prices; also a dangerous precedence would have been created. Moreover, in many industries some minimal degree of collusion in such matters exists. Where the cost change is small the chances of its being absorbed are increased because uncertainty about the reaction of other firms is multiplied and in any case there are often costs attached to price changes . . . .

The analysis suggests that there is even more chance that a fall in costs will be quickly translated into price cuts. This is because there is no fear on the part of the first mover that he may not be followed—if he is not followed, so much the better! . . . It seems paradoxical in the extreme that economists have suggested that prices are more likely to be 'sticky' downwards than upwards in the face of cost variations (Whitehead 1963).

This discussion of the kink is fuller than most, but it does not constitute a new formulation nor does it introduce new variables, new relationships, or new kinds of facts. I have consistently labelled such discussions 'analysis,' nevertheless, because they represent at least a conscious rethinking of the theory.

Even with this undemanding criterion only 39 of the 189 references could be labelled analytical: all the remainder of the uses were mentions or textbook expositions. The kinked demand curve has not been part of the arsenal of the working economist.

The final category of use I have labelled 'exposition' and it is restricted to textbooks plus one expository statement by B. F. Haley (1948). The treatment here is essentially didactic. As the count in Table 3 indicates, a steadily rising number of textbooks have devoted their 2 or 3 pages to the subject, and I have encountered no case in which the kinked demand curve, once introduced, is deleted.[21] At the present time two-thirds of the textbooks in print in principles and price theory that we examined contain a more or less routine exposition (see Table 3).

The geometrical implications of kinks are the chief subject of these textbook discussions: hardly ever do they even go so far as to compare the expected price behavior of monopolists and oligopolists under the theory. Yet if the instruction of students on the implication for marginal curves of kinks in curves of average quantities is the *raison d'être* of the discussion of the kinked demand curve, the textbook writers could do that at least as well with the analyses of

[21] The textbook collection of the Regenstein Library of the University of Chicago was supplemented to some degree by the library of Northwestern University, but the survey is far from complete.

Table 3
*Frequency of Appearance of the Kinked Demand Curve in
Textbooks on Principles and Price Theory In Print**

Period	No Kink	Kink	Total in Print	Percent With Kink
1947–49 (incl.)	12	4	16	25.0%
1950–52 "	13	6	19	31.6
1953–55 "	14	6	20	30.0
1956–58 "	15	7	22	31.8
1959–61 "	16	10	26	38.5
1962–64 "	19	15	34	44.1
1965–67 "	17	23	40	57.5
1968–70 "	13	25	38	65.8
1971–73 "	14	24	38	63.2
1974–76 "	13	22	35	62.9

*We exclude instances in which a text does not contain a kinked demand curve but the later known edition is unavailable, and those in which a kinked demand curve is present but an earlier edition is not available. If no revisions appear, a book is assumed to be out of print seven years after its publication.

legal maximum and minimum prices. Nevertheless one must concede that the spread of textbook presentations is strong evidence of (kinky?) market demand.

In fact, the failure to use the theory as a source of hypotheses on the differential behaviour of firms in different market structures and associations, is the very hallmark of the kinked demand curve literature. One would expect the theory to explain phenomena such as:
—the nature of the industries in which periods of price rigidity are observed.
—the lengths of the periods of price rigidity.
—the conditions under which frequent price changes occur under oligopoly.
—the price rigidity observed in industries with numerous producers, or a single producer.
Instead the theory is a piece of scripture: it is to be taught and it is to be quoted in suitable contexts, but it is not to be tampered with.

4. Some Hypotheses on Professional Literature

This review of the literature of the kinked demand curve suggests several hypotheses on the nature of scientific discourse.

The first and most fundamental hypothesis is that a theory need not be used in order to remain current. The fundamental 'use' of the kinked demand curve in the literature is to suggest a reason for the observed fact that many prices do not appear to change frequently. But of course this is not a real use, since the theory is not related to the prices to be explained. No one, with almost no exceptions, uses the pattern of differences in price change frequency which the theory contains to explain differences in observed price changes.

There is then no particular need for a special theory for so limited an explanation: literally *no* scientific function is now performed by the kinked demand curve theory that would not equally well be supplied by the simple argument that price changes cannot be made without cost.

A second hypothesis is that the textbooks of a discipline play a powerfully conservative role in the transmission of doctrine. The kinked demand curve is a meager theory and yet there surely cannot have been a new Ph.D. in economics in America in the last ten years who has not been exposed to it. Some textbook writers are scarcely authorities on any branch of economics, but economists of the stature of Samuelson, Lipsey and Steiner, Baumol, Henderson and Quandt, Cyert, Kuenne, Hirshleifer, Mansfield, and Ferguson and Gould repeat the scripture in each edition; the young economist must naturally consider it a necessary part of the mystery of the craft. The writing of textbooks is apparently not a thought-intensive activity: the modal number of changes of *any* sort between editions of a textbook in its discussion of the kinked demand curve is zero.

The third and most general hypothesis is that theories never perish. There is a belief, widespread but implicit, that one theory 'supplants' another. Of course ruling theories undergo change, but the supplanted theory never vanishes completely.

It is seldom and perhaps never the case that two theories are in exact rivalry, so that the acceptance of one implies the complete rejection of the other. Consider a famous example in the history of economics. The theory of value of Ricardo and Mill asserted that for freely producible goods their relative prices were determined by their relative costs of production. Jevons, Menger, Wieser and Böhm-Bawerk asserted that the foundation of relative value was in the relative marginal utilities of the goods. The latter theory was more general, for it embraced goods that were not freely producible, but it was also less informative, for it did not even explain why a house sells for more than a banana or even why two pounds of bananas sell for twice as much as one pound. One can combine the two theories, and indeed Marshall and Walras did so, but that is hardly displacing one theory by another.

Even when one theory *includes* the second as a special case, it is not inevitable that the acceptance of the former leads to the abandonment of the latter. A simple example from oligopoly theory will suffice. The revenue of a duopolist, I, is

$$q_1 f(q_1 + q_2) \tag{1}$$

where f is the demand function and q_i the output of firm i, and Cournot wrote the marginal revenue of firm I as

$$q_1 f'(q_1 + q_2) + f(q_1 + q_2) \tag{2}$$

treating q_2 as a constant. The output of II, q_2 may however be treated as a function of q_1 and then I's marginal revenue becomes

$$q_1 f'(q_1 + q_2)(1 + (dq_2/dq_1)) + f(q_1 + q_2),\qquad(3)$$

and dq_2/dq_1 (sometimes called the conjectural variation) is not necessarily zero. The predictions of the Cournot model are much more definite, so many modern economists still use this model: the more general theory has not driven out the less general theory.

There is no obvious method by which a science can wholly rid itself of once popular theories, logical error aside (and even this may not be a true exception). This is not to deny that theories decline in currency: the fraction of scientists working on the subject to which the theory pertains who *know* a theory will decline with time, and eventually the fraction will become so small that the theory is no longer a part of the working knowledge of the science. The fraction of scientists working on a subject to which a theory applies who actually *use* the theory will of course decline sooner, and is near zero for the kinked demand curve. If at this stage a theory is revived, it is much more likely to be rediscovered than refurbished from the past.

The study of a single theory, which has not yet entered the long decline in currency, does not equip us to understand the rate of decline of a theory. The literature surveyed here suggests that adverse empirical evidence is not a decisive factor. It is a plausible conjecture that when a theory is actively and frequently used, its susceptibility to displacement is much greater than when it performs essentially ceremonial functions.

A final, and rather morbid, observation is that there is a simply enormous amount of unprogressive publication: articles which certainly add nothing to the accumulation of rigorous theory or tested findings. Of the hundred-odd articles which I have had occasion to read in part or whole in preparing this paper, it is a conservative estimate that two-thirds *at a minimum* made no positive contribution to received knowledge on oligopoly behavior: they contain neither a new idea nor a new fact.[22] In the case of the kinked demand curve this judgment is not based upon hindsight since scarce any progress has been made in the theory in thirty years. Do the articles

---

[22] Kenneth May (1968–69, p. 367), in the history of determinants referred to (note 1), classified 1995 titles (sometimes into several categories) as follows:

New ideas and results	14%
Applications	12
Systematization and history	12
Tests and education	15
Duplications	21
Trivia	43
Total	117%

serve as a poll of the views of the more communicative branch of a profession? Or can it be that ordinary scientific discourse is like ordinary social discourse: simply practice in communication, so that, when an important message needs to be communicated, the faculties for communication will not be impaired by atrophy?

References

(Starred items are those referred to in Table 1.)

Bain, Joe S., *Barriers to New Competition*, Harvard University Press, 1956.
——, 'Price Leaders, Barometers, and Kinks,' *Journal of Business*, July 1960, 33, 193-203.
*Bronfenbrenner, Martin, 'Applications of the Discontinuous Oligopoly Demand Curve,' *Journal of Political Economy*, June 1940, 48, 420-27.
Clark, J. B., *The Control of Trusts*, New York: Macmillan, 1901, Ch. IV.
Clark, J. M., *Competition as a Dynamic Process*, Brookings, 1961.
Coase, Ronald H., 'The Problem of Duopoly Reconsidered,' *Review of Economic Studies*, February 1935, 2, 137-43.
Cohen, K. J. and Cyert, R. M., *Theory of the Firm*, Prentice Hall, 1965.
*Coyne, John, 'Kinked Supply Curves and the Labour Market,' *Journal of Economic Studies*, November 1975, 2, 139-51.
*Cyert, Richard M. and DeGroot, M., 'Interfirm Learning and the Kinked Demand Curve,' *Journal of Economic Theory*, September 1971, 3, 272-87.
—— ——, 'An Analysis of Cooperation and Learning in a Duopoly Context,' *American Economic Review*, 1973, 63, 24-37.
Douglas, Evan J., 'Price Strategy Duopoly with Product Variation—A Comment,' *Kyklos*, 1973, 26, 608-11.
Doyle, Peter, 'Advertising Expenditure and Consumer Demand,' *Oxford Economic Papers*, N.S. 20, November 1968, 394-416.
Edgeworth, F. Y., *Papers Relating to Political Economy*, London: Macmillan, 1925, I.
Edwards, Harold R., 'Goodwill and the Normal Cost Theory of Price.' *Economic Record*, May, 1952, 28, 52-74.
*Efroymson, Clarence W., 'A Note on Kinked Demand Curves,' *American Economic Review*, March 1943, 33, 98-109.
*——, 'The Kinked Oligopoly Curve Reconsidered,' *Quarterly Journal of Economics*, February 1955, 69, 119-36.
Farrell, Michael J., 'An Application of Activity Analysis to the Theory of the Firm,' *Econometrica*, July 1954, 22, 291-302.
Fouraker, Lawrence E. and Lee, W. A., 'Competition and Kinked Functions in the Marketing of Perishables,' *Southern Economic Journal*, January 1956, 22, 367-70.
Greenhut, Melvin L., 'A Theory of the Micro Equilibrium Path of the Firm in Economic Space.' *South African Journal of Economics*, September 1967, 34, 230-43.
Grether, E. T., *Price Control Under Fair Trade Legislation*, New York: Oxford University Press, 1939.
Grossack, Irvin M., 'Duopoly, Defensive Strategies, and the Kinked Demand Curve.' *Southern Economic Journal*, April 1966, 32, 406-16.
Haley, B. F., 'Value and Distribution,' in *A Survey of Contemporary Economics*, Howard S. Ellis, editor, Irwin, Homewood, Ill., 1948, vol. I.
*Hall, Robert L. and Hitch, C. J., 'Price Theory and Business Behaviour,' *Oxford Economic Papers*, No. 2, May 1939, 12-45.
Hamburger, William, 'Conscious Parallelism and the Kinked Oligopoly Demand Curve,' *American Economic Review Supplement*, May 1967, 57, 266-68.

Hawkins, Edward R., 'Price Policies and Theory,' *Journal of Marketing*, January 1954, **18**, 233–40.

*Hieser, Ron, 'A Kinked Demand Curve for Monopolistic Competition,' *Economic Record*, May 1953, **29**, 19–34.

Kahn, Richard F., 'The Problem of Duopoly,' *Economic Journal*, March 1937, **47**, 1–20.

Kaplan, A. D. H., Dirlam, Joel B. and Lanzilotti, R. F., *Pricing in Big Business*, Brookings, 1958.

Levitan, Richard E. and Shubik, M., 'Price Variation Duopoly with Differentiated Products and Random Demand,' *Journal of Economic Theory*, March 1971, **3**, 23–39.

McManus, Maurice, 'Numbers and Size in Cournot Oligopoly,' *Yorkshire Bulletin of Economic and Social Research*, May 1962, **14**, 14–22.

Markham, Jesse W., *Competition in the Rayon Industry*, Harvard University Press, 1952.

May, Kenneth O., 'Growth and Quality of the Mathematical Literature,' *Isis*, 1968–69, **59**, 363–71.

——, 'Who Killed Determinants?' *The Mathematical Association of America*, *Film* Manual No. 4 (n.d.).

Means, Gardiner C., *Industrial Prices and their Relative Inflexibility*, Senate Document 13, 74th Congress, 1st Session, January 17, 1935.

*Mikesell, Raymond F., 'Oligopoly and the Short-Run Demand for Labor,' *Quarterly Journal of Economics*, November 1940, **55**, 161–66.

Modigliani, Franco, 'New Developments on the Oligopoly Front,' *Journal of Political Economy*. 1958, **66**, 215–32.

*Murphy, T. A. and Ng, Y. K., 'Oligopolistic Interdependence and the Revenue Maximization Hypothesis—Note,' *Journal of Industrial Economics*, March 1974, **22**, 227–33.

National Bureau of Economic Research, Committee on Price Determination, *Cost Behavior and Price Policy*, 1943.

*Peel, David A., 'The Kinked Demand Curve—The Demand for Labour,' *Recherches Economiques de Louvain*, September 1972, 3, 267–73.

*Primeaux, Walter J. Jr., and Bomball, Mark R., 'A Reexamination of the Kinky Oligopoly Demand Curve,' *Journal of Political Economy*, August 1974, **82**, 851–62.

*—— ——, and Smith, Mickey C., 'Pricing Patterns and the Kinky Demand Curve,' *Journal of Law and Economics*, April 1976, **19**, 189–99.

Reynolds, Lloyd G., 'Toward a Short-Run Theory of Wages,' *American Economic Review*, June 1948, **48**, 289–308.

Robinson, Joan, *Economics of Imperfect Competition*, Macmillan, 1933.

*Shepherd, William G., 'On Sales-Maximising and Oligopoly Behaviour,' *Economica*, N.S. '29, November 1962, 420–24.

*Simon, J. L., 'A Further Test of the Kinky Oligopoly Demand Curve,' *American Economic Review*, December 1969, **59**, 971–75.

*Smith, D., Stanton and Neale, Walter C., 'The Geometry of Kinky Oligopoly: Marginal Cost, the Gap, and Price Behaviour,' *Southern Economic Journal*, January 1971, **37**, 276–82.

*Smith, Victor E., 'Note on the Kinky Oligopoly Demand Curve,' *Southern Economic Journal*, October 1948, **15**, 205–10.

*Spengler, Josph J., 'Kinked Demand Curves: By Whom First Used?' *Southern Economic Journal*, July 1965, **32**, 81–84.

*Stigler, George J., 'The Kinky Oligopoly Demand Curve and Rigid Prices,' *Journal of Political Economy*, October 1947, **55**, 432–49.

*Streeten, Paul, 'Reserve Capacity and the Kinked Demand Curve,' *Review of Economic Studies*, 1951, **18**, 103–13.

Sweezy, Paul M., *Monopoly and Competition in the English Coal Trade, 1550–1880*, Harvard University Press, 1938.

*Sweezy, Paul M., 'Demand under Conditions of Oligopoly,' *Journal of Political Economy*, August 1939, 47, 563–73.

Sylos-Labini, Paolo, *Oligopoly and Technical Progress*, Harvard University Press, 1962.

Thompson, A. A., *Economics of the Firm*, Prentice Hall, 1973.

Whitehead, Donald H., 'Price-Cutting and Wages Policy,' *Economic Record*, June 1963, 39, 187–95.

11

Competition and Entry—Petrol Retail Supply[*]

by R. W. Shaw and C. J. Sutton

The main purpose of this study is to examine the impact of entry into a tightly oligopolistic market. The competitive process is examined largely in terms of the theories of entry-deterrent pricing, and dominant-firm price leadership though various forms of non-price competition are also discussed.

The study is divided into three main sections discussing: the development of the structure of the industry between 1953 and 1973; competitive behaviour in the period 1953-9 prior to the emergence of the entry threat; and the effects of potential and actual entry, 1960-73.

1 Changing Structure of the Industry, 1953-73

Number and size distribution of firms

In 1953, when branded petrol was reintroduced and price control ended following the post-war restrictions, there were three major groups: Shell-Mex and B.P., Esso and Regent. Together with two newcomers, Mobil and Petrofina, these shared virtually the whole of the retail petrol market in the United Kingdom. This remained substantially true until about 1960 when Jet, V.I.P. and other smaller independent suppliers either entered or became a noticeable force in the market. Thereafter the position changed significantly as both integrated international oil companies, for example Total and Gulf, and further wholesale distributors, for example Curfew and Heron, entered the market. Whereas in the 1950s there were only five petrol groups with significant market shares, by the early 1970s there were in total around forty firms (*Petroleum Review*, Apr 1974). As a result the major firms' shares, which had remained fairly stable in the 1950s, progressively declined thereafter (see Table 1).

Vertical integration

The five major firms supplying petrol in the 1950s were vertically integrated with access to sources of crude oil and owning or having interests in refineries. They also owned some retail outlets but most

From *Industry and Competition* (Macmillan, London, and Basingstoke, 1976), pp. 23-43. Reprinted by permission of the publishers.

[*]Much of the analysis contained in this study was presented in a paper by Shaw [1974].

manufacturer–retailer integration involved long-term supply contracts, or *solus tie* arrangements, in which a retailer undertook to
take his total petrol requirements from a specific supplier. These
were initiated by Esso in 1950. Regent, and Shell-Mex and B.P.
retaliated almost immediately so that by spring 1951 over 50 per

Table 1
Percentage shares of the U.K. retail petrol market**

Firm	1953	1960	1964	1972
			(per cent)	
Shell-Mex and B.P.	51.4	49.4	45.0	38.2
Esso	28.4	29.8	27.5	20.0
Regent/Texaco	14.0	12.5	11.1	8.4
Mobil	1.1	4.2	5.9	7.6
Petrofina	2.2	2.5	2.5	2.5
Continental (including Jet)	—	0.7	3.5	4.3
Burmah	—	—	0.4	2.0
V.I.P.	—	. . .	0.8	3.0
Total	—	—	1.0	3.0
Others	2.9	0.9	2.4	10.8

*'—' indicates that the group had not entered the retail market; and '. . .' in-
dicates that the market share was trivial.
 Sources: Monopolies Commission (1965); and Lowe (1976).

cent of petrol outlets had some form of tie to one company or
another. By early 1953 the proportion of tied outlets had risen to
83 per cent, and by 1960 95 per cent of all outlets were tied. This
included a growing number of company-owned petrol stations
(Dixon [1962]). In exchange for the agreement to take supplies
from only one firm, the retailer obtained a lower wholesale price
for petrol as well as a variety of loans, advertising material and
advice. Thus, although the vast majority of petrol stations were independently owned in the 1950s, the *solus tie* constituted a weak
form of forward integration for suppliers.
    The new entrants to the petrol market in the late 1950s and 1960s
were of two main types: first there were subsidiaries of international
oil companies which had not previously been active in the U.K. retail
market; and second there were non-integrated petrol wholesalers
who bought petrol from oil refiners at home or in Europe. Some
independent wholesale distributors remain but most of the important
ones, including Jet and V.I.P., were later absorbed by the integrated
oil companies. This occurred as the independents sought to secure
their petrol supplies as their commitments rose, and as the oil companies—particularly the new entrants—sought outlets to establish a
foothold and to increase their market share.
    Forward vertical integration into retail outlets increased in the
1960s. Both the established majors and the new entrants bought
and built petrol stations. For the majors this was a way of both

rationalising their distribution networks and defending their market positions. For the new entrants this was a major means of obtaining and securing their market penetration (Monopolies Commission [1976]).

Joint supply

Petrol is a product in joint supply with diesel oil, fuel oil, naphtha and others. Thus it is only within technologically defined limits and at increasing cost that the balance of products can be altered. The difficulty of matching this balance to the demand for the various products may lead to the excess supply of individual products, and firms may then be willing to off-load this supply at reduced prices.

Barriers to entry

In the early post-war years entry to the petrol-supply industry in the United Kingdom was difficult. There were several reasons for this. Supplies of oil were largely controlled by the established firms. There was a shortage of tankers, and high charter rates placed independent firms without their own tankers or long-term contractual arrangements at a cost disadvantage compared with the larger established firms. Further, there was a shortage of independent storage facilities in the United Kingdom. Finally, the development of the *solus tie* system and planning restrictions on building new petrol stations made it difficult for a new entrant to build up a distribution network sufficiently rapidly to justify the construction of refinery capacity.

In the later 1950s and early 1960s, the supply difficulties disappeared as a result of the discovery of new oil reserves in Africa and the Middle East, often by firms without existing market outlets. Since imports of oil to the United States were restricted, a surplus of oil developed in Europe, and the suppliers were anxious to expand their own market outlets and willing to sell petrol on the open market to independent wholesalers. Nevertheless, the *solus tie* system and consumer preferences for existing brands of petrol remained as barriers, particularly to large-scale entry.

Finally, restrictions of supply as a result of the Six-Day War in 1967 and by members of the Organisation of Petroleum Exporting Countries (OPEC) in the 1970s led to soaring petrol prices on the open market and substantial difficulties for the non-integrated petrol wholesaler.

Product differentiation

The degree of product differentiation achieved by the major firms seems to have been limited. This was reflected in the near uniformity of prices between equivalent brands of the major firms which arose from their belief that there was a high cross-elasticity of demand between them. However, in the early 1960s at least the established major firms did succeed in achieving a significant degree of differentiation between their products and those of the cut-price entrants. Thus the major firms felt that they could maintain a small differential in their favour and still retain the larger part of the market. This of course was reinforced by the then relatively small number of outlets controlled by entrants which itself was a major force restraining their market penetration.

The extent of the differentiation almost certainly declined in the 1960s as consumers became familiar with the new brand names. This was encouraged by increased knowledge following the publication of the Consumers' Association *Which* report [1964], and the introduction of the star-grading system for petrol in 1967, both of which reduced the credibility of product-differentiation claims.

Other market characteristics

Petrol deliveries to retailers increased every year between 1953 and 1973 apart from 1957 during the Suez crisis. However, there were some fluctuations around the average 7.5 per cent per annum rate of growth and considerable differences in growth between the various grades of petrol.

The high cross-elasticity of demand between brands of petrol contrasted strongly with the over-all market price elasticity of demand which remained low throughout the twenty-year period despite the considerable changes in actual prices. This was partly because the cost of petrol was only one element in the cost of running a car, and partly because the substitutes for car travel were felt to be poor (see Lowe [1976], Schendel and Balestra [1969]).

Wholesale prices to retailers depended on the grade of petrol, the geographical area (lower prices were charged near the ports and main centres of population than in more remote areas), *solus agreement* discounts, bargaining power, and latterly on the size of the delivery. Apart from the outlets owned by the petrol companies, the retailers were independent businesses with freedom to determine their own pricing policy. However, this freedom was restricted up to 1962–3 by resale-price maintenance practised by most suppliers though not the market leader. All suppliers at least recommended prices until 1964. Thereafter Esso and Regent/Texaco stopped recommending prices but Esso soon resumed the practice. Finally, all the major petrol companies stopped recommending prices towards the end of the 1960s.

2 The Competitive Process, 1953–9

Market characteristics in this period made price competition most unattractive to the major firms. A high inter-brand cross-elasticity of demand ensured, in a highly concentrated oligopoly, that competitive price cuts by any major supplier would be followed and so be self-defeating. Consequently we would expect firms, recognising this high degree of interdependence and the low market price elasticity of demand,* to avoid price competition. They might achieve this either by collusion or by the price leadership of one or more firms. The potential weakness in this prediction is the behaviour of the minor firms, Mobil and Petrofina. They might have risked price competition if they believed that the major firms would not find it worthwhile to retaliate.

In these circumstances four possible types of pricing behaviour seem worth investigating. First, the oligopolists could resolve the competitive problem by collusively setting prices. Second, they could allow one or more firms to act as price leaders. Third, they could avoid price competition and opt for the security of price rigidity as suggested by the kinked demand curve hypothesis. Finally, they could engage in price competition. Unfortunately we cannot distinguish from observed price movements between collusion and price leadership/followership. However, it seems probable that they would lead to similar results in the petrol-supply industry. Since either of the giants, Shell–B.P. or Esso, acting as a price leader would seek to choose a price acceptable to the other, it is probable that the price would not differ significantly from that chosen by explicit collusion between them.

The pricing consequences of the alternatives are shown in Figure 1.

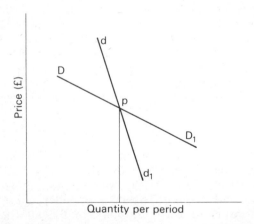

Figure 1

Assume that P is the initial price. DPD_1 is the demand curve for a firm that changes its prices while rivals' prices remain constant at P. dPd_1 is the demand curve for a firm that changes its price with its

---

*Although a short-run profit-maximising monopolist might be expected to choose a price where market price elasticity is greater than one, uncertainty, imperfect oligopolistic co-ordination, fear of political interference, and concern for the long run, might cause the existing market price to have a point price-elasticity of demand of less than one.

rivals making an identical change. In the price-leadership or collusive case the relevant demand curve is dPd_1 since the initiator(s) price changes, upwards or downwards, are matched by the other firms. In the kinked demand curve case, the relevant demand curve is DPd_1 since firms pessimistically expect rivals to match their price reductions but not to follow their price increases. In the 'competitive' case, for the market situation described, the small firms, Mobil and Petrofina, might anticipate that the relevant demand curve is DPD_1. In contrast with the kinked demand curve case, the larger firms might allow the small firms to reduce their prices without retaliating because the impact on the sales of the larger firms remains small. Conversely, the larger firms will probably not be expected to follow a small firm's upward price initiative.

Between 1953 and 1959 the industry's pricing behaviour seems to have been consistent with the price-leadership or collusive model. The eighteen price changes to the main grades were usually announced on the same day, or thereabouts, by all five groups. *Significantly, price increases were matched as well as price reductions:* that is, firms moved along demand curve dPd_1. Recommended or maintained retail prices were adjusted upwards for either premium, standard grade, or both, on eight, and downwards on ten occasions during the period. While this is a far cry from freely fluctuating prices it represents a significant degree of flexibility within the context of administered prices. Any price rigidity due to the fear that competitors would follow downward but not upward price adjustments, associated with the kinked demand curve theory, seems at most to have reflected hesitancy over adjusting prices to reflect changing supply and demand conditions. Further, the persistent unanimity of upward price adjustments suggests the absence of a kink at the existing price with the leaders at least being able to anticipate parallel changes by other firms.

The second characteristic of pricing behaviour in this period was its restraint. Both price increases and decreases were generally small, the only exceptions being during the period of the 1956–7 Suez crisis when consultations with the government preceded the changes (Shaw [1974]). There is also no evidence either of a firm making a deep price cut so as to embarrass rivals or of a price cut leading to a series of retaliatory moves. Finally, the two smaller firms seem to have refrained from experimenting with price competition.

Although not conclusive, the evidence suggests the avoidance of price competition by the collusive or price-leadership technique. However, this does not mean that there was a complete absence of rivalry. Indeed the initiation and development of the *solus tie* system and the outright buying of petrol stations represented keen competition for market shares. Some indication of this is given in the Monopolies Commission's *Report on Petrol* ([1965] para. 158ff.):

Regent began buying stations in 1952 'in order not to lose ground in the market'

. . . . Esso has told us [Monopolies Commission] that . . . 'certain of our competitors were determined to acquire further outlets by purchasing service stations' . . . and that it was therefore compelled to purchase certain stations belonging to its own solus customers in order to secure its exclusive outlets.

In addition there were continuing efforts to differentiate products and promote favourable brand images.

3 The Effects of Potential and Actual Entry, 1960–73

In the late 1950s easier supply conditions made entry easier. This posed two new competitive problems for the existing oligopolists: first how should these firms react to actual new small-scale competition from both wholesalers and subsidiaries of integrated oil companies; and second, how should existing firms react to the potential competition of possible new entrants. Theoretically these may be treated as distinct though related problems. The existing small-scale competition is, by definition, certain: the major established firms had to decide on the emphasis to be placed on price, product differentiation and other forms of competition in the light of the existing and possible competitive strategies of the minor firms. Potential competition, on the other hand, may not materialise as actual competition, and hence the established major firms had to decide whether to let their policies be influenced by the possibility of entry prior to its occurrence, or to ignore the possibility and adjust policies if and when the competition materialised. Potential competition is considered first.

Pricing and potential entry

Two types of potential entrant are relevant: the large integrated international company previously unrepresented in the U.K. retail petrol-supply market, and the usually small petrol wholesaler. The first line of defence against both types of entrant is to establish and maintain barriers to entry. Predictably it was adopted: 'not merely are most of the pumps under contract, but the majority of existing storage capacity and the best sites for bringing oil into Britain have been pre-empted by the majors operating here already' (*The Economist*, 28 May 1960). Further, the established firms were buying some of the best petrol-station sites and striving to reinforce the brand loyalty of their customers. Nevertheless, the U.K. market could not be completely insulated from the world market and there were continuing reports of possible entry by Total, Tidewater Oil and E.N.I. (*The Economist*, 28 May 1960 and 3 Sep 1960).

The second line of defence might have been to practice entry-deterrent pricing: that is, reducing prices to a level which would make potential entrants believe that entry would be unprofitable (Bain [1956] and Scherer [1970]). Such a policy would have had the disadvantage that it entailed sacrificing certain present profits for uncertain future profits. The policy would only have been attractive if the expected present value of profits over the planning horizon was higher with lower prices immediately, thus deterring entry and providing a larger market share over the future, than with higher prices and a higher probability of entry and lower market share in the future. The profitability of an entry-deterrent policy depended on its credibility as seen by potential entrants, the opportunity cost of the lower prices and the threat to profits should entry actually take place.

Its credibility in the petrol-supply case was doubtful. It seems likely that potential entrants would have expected the established oligopolists to pursue the most profitable policy for themselves in the changed circumstances after entry had taken place. This would probably have involved pricing policies which made prospective entry seem profitable. The low market price-elasticity of demand would have continued to make co-operative high prices much more profitable for the industry as a whole than competitive low prices. Further, so long as entrants' ability to capture the established firms' market was restrained by brand loyalty and the small number of retail outlets available to the entrants, the established firms' share in those profits would remain large. The established firms would hardly reduce these profits merely to spite a new entrant. Rather they would be expected to accommodate the entrant into the oligopoly unless there was a strong prospect of forcing the intruder to leave the market at not too great a cost. [. . .] The threat of predatory competition designed to eliminate such intruders must have seemed implausible in the case of the integrated international oil firms with large financial resources and the ability to retaliate in other markets. This would have been particularly the case for those entrants whose primary interest was not in petrol sales but in other oil products: for these firms it was the joint-supply relationship between petrol and other oil products that made participation in the petrol market seem desirable (Lowe [1976]).

The opportunity cost, in terms of reduced profits, of a limit-price entry-deterrent policy would probably also have been high. Because of the growth of oil supplies relatively to demand in the late 1950s and early 1960s, the presence of excess refining capacity in Europe, and the situation where variable costs attributable to individual petroleum products were low, an entry-deterrent price would have had to have been kept extremely and unprofitably low for an indefinite period.

Finally, even if entry occurred, the reduction in profits was unlikely to be large for several years. It would take an entrant a considerable time to build up storage facilities and a distribution network of retail outlets—particularly the latter because of the long-term petrol-supply contracts between the established firms and the petrol stations. This last point is significant because it meant that entry had initially to be on a small scale, and consequently the cost of entry deterrence by price reduction was likely to be very large relative to the potential gain.

Despite the apparent unattractiveness of entry-deterrent pricing, there were a series of small price reductions between the spring of 1960 and 1963. Although these demonstrably failed to deter potential entrants, in the case of the 1963 price reduction the initiator, Shell–B.P., gave as one of the reasons 'to make the United Kingdom market less attractive to newcomers and potential newcomers' (Monopolies Commission [1965] para. 69). Here perhaps is a clue to an optimal entry-deterrent policy: prices should indeed be modified by the threat of entry not so as to deter entry entirely but to control its rate (Gaskins [1971]). In this way abnormal profits may continue to be earned while market share is only surrendered slowly. This aspect is taken up later.

Pricing and actual competition: price leadership

Since entry was not deterred, the established firms had to decide how to react to the consequent new competition. Once again the response was twofold: an attempt to reinforce existing market positions by the continuing policies of buying retail outlets, maintaining long-term *solus tie* contracts with retailers, and extensive brand advertising; and a measured price response attempting to balance current profitability with restraining the growth of the entrants and so maintain long-term profitability. It is to the analysis of this price response that we now turn; first, by examining the applicability of the price-leadership model in a general sense in the changed circumstances; and, in the next section, by analysing the direction and timing of the price changes themselves.

In the normal dominant-firm price-leadership model it is assumed that a leading firm sets a price and allows the minor firms to sell all they can at that price. Normally, if the leading firm raises or lowers its price, other firms follow with parallel changes. The short-run equilibrium price and output position is outlined in Figure 2. The market demand curve is DD_1; S_m is the minor firm's supply curve; and MC is the marginal-cost curve of the dominant firm.

The demand curve of the dominant firm, ABD_1, is derived by subtracting the amount the minor firms supply from the market demand curve. MR is the dominant firm's marginal-revenue curve derived from its demand curve. AC_m is the minor firms' average-cost curve. This is drawn showing abnormal profits being earned by the minor firms. At price OR the minor firms sell nothing and the total market demand, RB, is satisfied by the dominant firm. At price OA the minor firms satisfy the total market demand, AC, and the dominant firm sells nothing. At intermediate prices the dominant and minor firms share the market. For the dominant price leader the short-run profit-maximising price is OP with sales of OM ($= PQ$) given by the intersection of the marginal-cost and marginal-revenue curves. The minor firms, being price takers, sell PT where their horizontal average- and marginal-revenue curve cuts their supply curve, S_m.

The post-entry period is conveniently split into two parts: spring

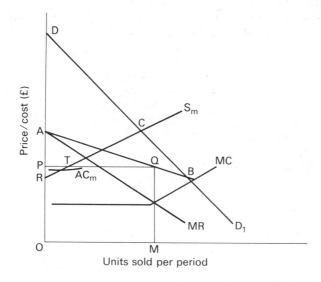

Figure 2

1960 to spring 1967, when supply conditions were easy; and from summer 1967 onwards when costs were rising sharply, periodic supply difficulties were encountered, and government price control was intermittently applied.

In the first period there were seven significant price reductions and one price increase. The price-leadership model again receives some support though it is its dynamic instability that is perhaps its most striking feature. Before considering this, however, some modification to the model is necessary. First, some new entrants such as Jet and V.I.P. set significantly lower prices for their brands than those set by the dominant firm(s). Despite this clear initiative taken by the cut-price firms, however, the price-leadership model may still be usefully retained. First, because many of the new-entrant integrated firms, for example Total and Agip, did in practice accept the prices of the leaders. Second, because even the cut-price firms were using the major company prices as reference points, and their prices tended to move in parallel and after the initiating change of the leaders.* A second modification concerns the assumption of a single price leader. This role was at best shared between Shell–B.P. and Esso so that a more plausible specification of the model is to see the two firms as joint profit maximisers with the remainder of suppliers acting as followers. Even this is a simplification however. The two leaders showed keen rivalry in advertising, the signing of long-term *solus tie* contracts with retailers and the purchase of petrol stations, while

---

*There were, however, some independent price moves as in June 1962 when Jet raised its prices by 1d. a gallon.

minor price discrepancies, reflecting their differing price preferences, persisted as they had in the 1950s. The third and final modification concerns the degree of co-ordination of policy achieved by the leaders. The impressive unanimity of price changes which had been a feature of the 1950s and the beginning of the 1960s later began to break up. In the early and mid-1960s the strains of new entrants aggressively seeking to establish themselves were added to the more decorous competition of the established firms, and consequently initiatives by the leaders were less well co-ordinated and the rivalry much more pronounced.

The price cuts initiated by either Shell–B.P. or Esso were made by all the established firms and were generally accepted by the new entrants, although some cut-price firms made smaller changes. However, the character of the price-leadership model had changed: it was now partly a vehicle for competitive rivalry rather than just a means of avoiding an unprofitable form of competition. The disciplined price uniformity adopted by the majors enabled the cut-price firms to practice price followership at consistently lower prices so long as these exceeded their unit costs. Thus they maintained a competitive advantage which gradually extended their market share. Further, the restraint shown by the established firms in the 1950s diminished with initiatives reflecting individual firms' interests and with price cuts increasing in size. Thus in 1962 Esso gained a competitive advantage over Shell–B.P. by cutting the price of mixture grade, which was not sold by the latter, along with the standard-grade reduction. In turn the Shell–B.P. price cut of premium grade in 1963 was partly designed to meet the increased competition from the mixture grades (Monopolies Commission [1965]). Whereas the typical price cut in the 1950s was only 1d. (one old penny) or less, the 1960s saw an escalation: 1d. in 1962; 1½d. in 1963; 1½d. and 2d. in 1965 and up to 4½d. in 1967. The last price cut in particular was clearly an aggressive move by Esso and marked the apparent abandonment of price restraint. Most other firms responded with only smaller cuts (Shaw [1974]).

The single price increase for all brands, initiated in 1964 by Shell–B.P., also provides evidence of the strains caused by entry. Although Total, Mobil and Petrofina and some other smaller suppliers also increased retail prices, Esso and Regent, by stopping recommending prices, let their retailers decide for themselves. This failure to respond fully represented a significant departure from behaviour predicted in the price-leadership model. It was an acknowledgement of the competitive pressures at the retail level: by 1964 over 1000 outlets were supplied by cut-price firms, and since these tended to be concentrated in the more densely populated areas where other retail outlets were similarly concentrated, several thousand garages must have been subjected to the price competition stimulated by the cut-price firms. Indeed it seems that the rapid growth in the practice of offering trading stamps (*The Economist*, 7 Dec 1963), which began in about 1960, partly reflected the defensive reactions of retailers faced with cut-price competitors.

In the second period, spring 1967 onwards, all the price changes were upwards. Although the interpretation of identical price increases is somewhat confused by the need to obtain either government or Price Commission approval, for some parts of the period, the evidence is consistent with the price-leadership model. Only two rounds of price increases involving Esso and a few other firms (in winter 1968–9 and autumn 1969, bringing the prices of those making the deepest cuts in spring 1967 back into line with the market leader, Shell–B.P.) did not involve a general upward shift in the prices of all the major firms. The remaining ten increases up to the end of 1973 were parallel price adjustments made by the major firms within a few days of the lead given by Shell–B.P. or Esso.*

The direction and timing of price changes

Although the generally downward direction of price changes between 1960 and 1967 and the subsequent upward trend are clear, the causes of these trends and the timing of the changes still require analysis. For the later period, when prices were rising, the trend is explained by rising costs and supply shortages which made increased prices seem desirable while reducing the competitive threat of the entrants and so making the increases possible.

For the earlier period the essence of the argument revolves round the dynamic consequences of the price leaders setting a price which allowed abnormal profits for potential entrants and existing minor firms, thus encouraging their entry and expansion (Worcester [1957]). It was argued earlier that the major firms had avoided price competition in the 1950s and that they would not have chosen to set an entry-deterrent price. Consequently the price chosen by the leaders, OP in Figure 2, offered prospects of abnormal profits to the minor firms: $OP > AC_m$ at output PT. Given a constant industry demand the effect of expansion by minor firms would have been to shift their supply curve, S_m, progressively to the right, and conversely shift the dominant firms' demand curve to the left. However, this would probably be offset by the rapid expansion in over-all petrol demand so that the effect would only be seen as a loss of market share by the leaders and not as an absolute decline in sales. The subsequent argument shows both why the dominant firms accepted this long-run decline in market share, and how they might be expected to reduce prices progressively to control the rate at which the fringe suppliers expanded. A central feature of the argument was the tendency for the rate of decline in their market share to accelerate as both cut- and full-price entrants were encouraged to expand by the prospect of attractive profits.

*This excludes the merging of the cheapest central zones, created in 1967, with the inner price zones in 1969–70 which, in effect, constituted selective price increases. These adjustments were not made simultaneously.

The pricing problem for the established leaders facing such a challenge from new entrants is illustrated in Figure 3. For simplicity a constant total demand is assumed. The short-run cost of a retaliatory price cut is equal to the reduction in price, $\Delta P = AD$, multiplied

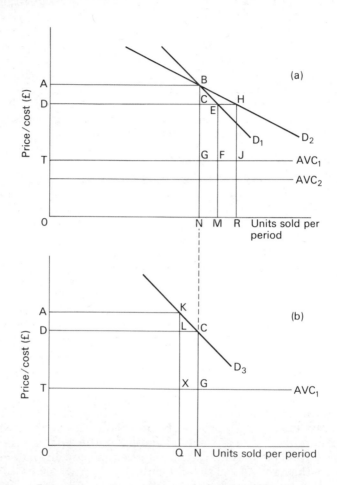

Figure 3

by the volume of sales, ON, that would have been made even at the old higher price: that is area $ABCD$. The short-run gain to the firm is equal to the contribution to profit earned on the additional sales volume, NM, that is retained by cutting price: area $CEFG$. In a single-product firm with spare capacity this contribution is calculated as follows:

$$\text{contribution} = (P - AVC)\Delta Q = (OD - OT)NM,$$

where $P \equiv$ price; $AVC \equiv$ constant average variable costs; $\Delta Q \equiv$ change in quantity sold as a result of the price change. Hence the change in profit due to a retaliatory price cut is

$$Q_2 \Delta P - (P - AVC)\Delta Q = (AD \times ON) - (OD - OT)NM,$$

where Q_2 is the quantity that is sold at the unchanged high price.

In the case of oil companies where two or more grades of petrol are produced along with fuel oil and other products, the contribution has to be adjusted to allow for changes in the sales, costs and hence contributions of other products. If other product sales have to be reduced because sales of petrol are low, then the gain from cutting price is increased. Conversely, where other product sales can be substituted for petrol the gain from cutting price is reduced.

It is clear from Figure 3(a) that higher product and brand price-elasticities of demand increase the gain from cutting price: instead of *CEFG* for a volume difference of *NM*, in the case of demand curve D_1, the gain would be *CHJG* for a volume difference of *NR*, in the case of demand curve D_2, and hence the greater the incentive to reduce price. Similarly, the larger the contribution per gallon as indicated by lowering the average-variable-cost curve from AVC_1 to AVC_2, the greater the incentive to cut price.

This analysis is extended in Figure 3 (b) by assuming that the market leader continues to lose a constant volume of sales each year if he does not cut price. We continue to assume constant total demand. In year t the established leader fails to cut price and so his sales are reduced from *OM* to *ON* (Figure 3(a)). In year $t + 1$ he must reduce price to maintain sales *ON* and can only achieve *OQ* sales at the existing high price. The cost of a price reduction is now only *AKLD* (Figure 3(b)) instead of *ABCD* (Figure 3(a)), and the gain is *LCGX* (= *CEFG*). Hence for a given potential loss of sales, the incentive to cut price is increased annually as the cost of the change in price is reduced.

So far the analysis has been based on the calculations of short-run gains and losses from cutting price. Clearly, this requires extension to take account of the long-term consequences. Suppose a failure to reduce price entails a loss of 1 per cent of the total market in each succeeding year. A decision to maintain price now, therefore, leads to an annual loss which increases with time: in terms of Figure 3(b), this is given by *LCGX* in year $t + 1$; *2LCGX* in year $t + 2$; *3LCGX* in year $t + 3$, and so on. The annual gain from maintaining the high price is a series of savings based on the difference between the high and low price multiplied by the sales at the former price with the sales volume declining each year. A simple illustration is given in Table 2 based on the hypothetical question of whether Shell–B.P. could have profitably reduced prices in 1960 to avoid the growth of Jet and V.I.P. The following assumptions are made:

(1) A 3d. (old pennies) price cut of all grades of petrol by all

Table 2

The effect of cutting price by 3d. in 1960 on the annual profits of a firm with a 50 per cent market share

Year	Expected total market sales (000 gallons)	Gain from cutting price		Loss from cutting price		Net gain from price cut (£)
		Market share increase (per cent)	Contribution × extra gallons sold (£)	Market share without price cut (per cent)	Price cut × market share × market sales (£)	
1960	1,887,000	1	1,336,625	49	11,557,875	−10,221,250
1961	2,037,960	2	2,887,110	48	12,227,760	− 9,340,650
1962	2,200,996.8	3	4,677,118	47	12,930,856	− 8,253,738
1963	2,377,076.5	4	6,735,050	46	13,668,190	− 6,933,140
1964	2,567,242.7	5	9,092,318	45	14,440,740	− 5,348,422
1965	2,772,622.1	6	11,783,644	44	15,249,421	− 3,465,777

major established firms would have successfully prevented the gain in total market share of 2 per cent per annum by the price-cutters;

(2) The Shell–B.P. group with approximately 50 per cent of the market would avoid losses proportionate to its share of the market, that is it would avoid a loss of 1 per cent per annum of the total market;

(3) The market growth rate was expected to be 8 per cent per annum;

(4) The contribution per gallon after the 3d. price cut is set at 17d. which is approximately equal to the net sales receipts per gallon of the oil companies (recommended retail price 4s. 8d. per gallon premium grade, less tax 2s. 6d. less retailers' margin 6d., less price cut 3d. = 17d.) and hence as a limiting case assumes zero variable costs! This gives the maximum incentive for price cutting by established firms: the incentive would be less for positive variable costs.

As is apparent from Table 2 the Shell–B.P. group would have lost heavily despite the limiting assumptions of zero variable costs and complete success in the defence of market share. Obviously the protection of a small proportion of a firm's market share by across-the-board price cuts is too costly. Indeed, general price cuts could only be justified as a means of reducing expectations of profitability of entry by other firms and expansion by the existing intruders. Further, since the actual competition by new entrants was necessarily limited to the areas where they had been able to acquire retail outlets, a blanket response would have been inefficient. A more limited regional price cut would have been less costly but initially it, too, would probably have been unprofitable.

An alternative response by the established firms might have been to allow, and perhaps to encourage, their *solus tied* retailers to meet the competition of the individual rival cut-price outlets. This, however, might have set up an ever-spreading chain reaction of price competition by retailers with claims for reduced wholesale prices to compensate, and hence led to the undermining of the general price structure. In this case the oil companies would have found the position similar to that achieved by a general price cut but with the added disadvantage of the rapid breakdown of control over the retail price structure, and the loss of favourable publicity arising from the formal announcement of a price cut.

Thus the obvious measures of price retaliation were of limited use to the established oligopolists. The most that could be done was to take mild action to discourage other potential entrants and to try to increase the difficulty of entry and expansion for newcomers by reinforcing brand loyalty and extending the network of tied retail outlets. Indeed for the two years between August 1960 and August 1962 no further price reductions were made despite the increase in market share by the minor firms from 1.6 to 5.0 per cent.

However, the major firms did go on to make a series of price cuts.

One reason was probably a threatened acceleration in the rate of decline in their market share due to the expansion of both cut- and full-price entrants. In the case of the former this can partly be represented by a progressive pivoting of the 'demand' curve shown in Figure 3(a) from D_1 through D_2 as customers got used to the new brand names and as the credibility of product differentiation decreased. This reinforced the effect of the increase in the number of retail outlets supplying cut-price petrol which was shifting the major firms' demand curve to the left. A two-stage process was involved. A large price differential favouring cut-price firms would, first, increase their sales at existing outlets, and second, this success would encourage more retailers to transfer their custom to a cut-price brand. In the case of full-price entrants the process was probably largely confined to the transfer of business from existing brands due to the expansion of the newcomers' distribution networks. A series of price cuts by the established firms would combat both threats by reducing the potential profitability of entry and expansion. For the cut-price firms either their price differential would be narrowed, and so their petrol's relative attraction to customers, and therefore to retailers, would be reduced; or if the price differential were retained the cut-price firms' profits would be squeezed and hence their incentive, and possibly their ability to expand would be reduced. For the full-price entrants the reduced prices would lower profits and hence reduce their incentive to expand.

Although possibly insufficient on its own, the success of Jet and other cut-price firms was a major factor in the August 1962 price cut led by Esso (*The Times*, 15 Aug 1962). Jet's standard grade marketed at both a higher octane rating and a lower price than the majors' equivalent brands. By 1961 it had already achieved a market share for standard grade of about 6 per cent, and with continuing expansion of its outlets the rate of progress could have accelerated further. This threat was strengthened by Jet having become a subsidiary of Continental Oil in June 1961, thus securing Jet's sources of oil and capital. Similarly, Shell–B.P. acknowledged a desire 'to reduce the gap between its own price . . . and those of companies supplying cut-price petrol' (Monopolies Commission [1965] para. 69) as one of the reasons for its June 1963 premium-grade price cut. However, it was also intended to combat competition from the cheaper mixture grade whose price Esso had reduced the previous year; to make expansion in the United Kingdom less attractive to the integrated oil companies such as Total, Agip, Murco and Gulf, which had already entered the market; and to deter others from following. It is also possible that the Shell–B.P. 1965 price cut was partly caused by a threatened expansion by cut-price firms whose outlets were sharply increasing. Further, a 6d. increase in petrol duty in November 1964 had badly hit demand for the most expensive grades and possibly this provided a boost to cut-price firms as consumers became more price conscious.

Finally, the March 1967 price cut, initiated by Esso, seems to have been very largely precipitated by fear of the possible growth of the cut-price firms. According to one report, the market share of the cut-price competition of just over 10 per cent at the end of 1966 would increase to 13 per cent by the end of 1967, and to over 25 per cent by the end of 1970 if nothing was done to restrain it (*Petroleum Times*, 17 Mar 1967). If these estimates are accepted, then an acceleration in the market penetration of the cut-price firms was anticipated and some response was to be expected. Certainly such an acceleration was plausible. The star-grading system introduced in the spring of 1967 reduced the credibility of product differentiation. Arising from the Monopolies Commission's *Report*, the petrol firms had agreed to limit the duration of *solus ties* with retailers to five years, and to accept restrictions on the construction and purchase of petrol outlets by the larger firms selling more than 15 per cent of their petrol through company-owned stations. Together these meant that entrants could more easily acquire new outlets while the activities of the established firms were restricted. Lastly, new entrants attracted by falling wholesale petrol prices on the international open market, including some with even lower prices than the existing cut-price firms, were continuing to appear adding their impact to the expected growth of earlier entrants.

However, it would be wrong to regard fear of cut-price entrants as the only cause, or indeed to accept the particular price reductions that occurred as being necessarily optimal responses (Simmonds and Leighton [1973]). At least two other causes already referred to were significant: first, the threatened entry and expansion of full-price integrated firms reinforced the challenge posed by the cut-price firms; and, second, the rivalry between established suppliers was increased by the strains caused by new-entrant competition. Behind these immediate threats was of course the underlying problem of the general excess supply situation which still persisted (Lowe [1976]). In so far as this led to sagging prices on the international open market for petrol, the incentive to enter and expand in the U.K. retail market was enhanced. Indeed the timing of the various U.K. price cuts, which roughly reflected movements on the international open market, is consistent with the hypothesis that the price leaders were responding to the threat of minor-firm expansion.

After Esso's aggressive price cut in March 1967 the trend of prices turned upwards. Although at first sight this new trend appears to run counter to the earlier argument on the effects of competitive pressure, it is probably consistent with it. It was argued that the incentive to reduce prices increased directly with the threatened rate of expansion of both cut- and full-price entrant firms. However, when the price increases occurred, the entrants' rate of expansion was a much less serious threat than it had been during the period of price cuts because of rising costs and supply shortages. With profits squeezed by rising costs, all firms were anxious to raise prices. The cut-price entrants who, at other times, might have taken advantage of any increase in price by the market leader(s) to widen the price differential were often particularly hard pressed by the increase in costs and consequently were willing to follow the price increases. Further, with profits squeezed and petrol in short supply, there was little danger to established firms from new entry and aggressive expansion. Thus the July 1967 2d. surcharge on prices allowed by the government, following the Six-Day War and the closure of the Suez Canal, was gratefully adopted by all firms (*The Times*, 1 July 1967). Similarly, prices were raised four times between July 1970 and February 1971 when supplies were disrupted, following the closure of the Trans-Arabian pipeline and restrictions on Libyan oil production. At the same time costs rose sharply with a doubling of tanker-freight rates and higher prices paid to oil-producing governments. Finally, in both 1972 and 1973 rising prices paid to the oil-producing governments, production cut-backs, and a rapid growth in demand for imports by the United States again pushed up the cost of oil (*Petroleum Press Service*, May; June; Nov 1973). Dramatic evidence of the difficulties of the independent firms relying on open-market purchases of surplus petrol was provided by the announced withdrawals from the retail supply market of Trident (200 retail outlets) and Redwing (22 outlets) as a result of 'being priced out by the high international cost of oil products' (*The Times*, 31 Aug 1973). In addition Conoco (Jet) was allowed a larger price increase by the Price Commission in October 1973 under a loss provision of the Price Code than Shell–B.P., Esso, Mobil and Burmah.

In the market conditions described above, the leaders were able to place more emphasis on attempting to maintain their profitability by increasing prices than on protecting their not too vulnerable market shares. However, there were periods between 1967 and 1973 when supply shortages were not a problem, and although costs in the United Kingdom were rising the newcomers were proving a serious threat to established firms. Thus, although there were no formal price cuts in 1968 and 1969 there was an escalation in sales-promotion expenditure on gift offers. Further, between 1969 and the end of 1970, the major suppliers were forced to abandon the practice of recommending retail prices. Competitive pressures were also probably responsible for the absence of any price increases between February 1971 and April 1972.

Entry and non-price competition

So far the analysis for the post-entry period has focused largely on the pricing behaviour of entrants and established firms. This was only one aspect of market rivalry. Two other forms of competition were important: competition for retail outlets; and brand advertising and gift-promotion schemes. These are briefly discussed in turn.

The emergence of the single-brand petrol station in the 1950s meant that firms had to compete for the patronage of retail outlets.

This was partly done by suppliers building and buying their own petrol stations and partly by competition for the trade of the independent retailers. As indicated earlier, the established firms began to acquire their own outlets in the 1950s so that by 1964 Shell–B.P., Esso, Regent/Texaco and Mobil owned 12.4, 11.7, 16.0 and 23.5 per cent respectively of all the stations they supplied. Despite being handicapped for a short time by the government's restriction on their acquiring petrol stations, their ownership proportions had risen to 23.7, 23.1, and 47.4 per cent respectively by 1973 for Shell–B.P., Esso and Mobil* providing increased market security (*Petroleum Review*, Apr 1974). For some entrants, particularly the integrated international oil firms, ownership of stations provided the basis for their assault on the market. By buying and building their own outlets they were effectively buying a captive share of the market. Among the entrants relying particularly heavily on ownership were Amoco and Gulf with 92.2 and 80.1 per cent of their outlets company owned in 1973 (*Petroleum Review*, Apr 1974).

Competition for the trade of the independent retailers centred on the margin between wholesale and retail price, and the likely volume of sales for each outlet. Jet originally built up its share through its low retail price, giving retailers a large sales volume thus compensating for their smaller retail margin: in 1964 the average sales of petrol at Jet stations was over twice that of standard price stations. Although the established firms generally offered relatively large margins between their wholesale and recommended retail prices, their outlets increasingly used stamp offers and cut prices in their own struggle for market share so that the cut-price suppliers' advantage was eventually much reduced. While this competition for outlets was of immense importance in determining market shares, it should be remembered that by reducing prices relative to costs the leaders were seeking to lessen the attraction of expansion by the newcomers whether by building and buying more petrol stations or by competing for the trade of the independent retailers.

Advertising has also been used as a competitive weapon. Although as a proportion of sales it has tended to be unimportant, Shell–B.P., Esso, and to a lesser extent Regent/Texaco, have at times spent large absolute sums—Shell–B.P. spent over £2 million in 1969 (Lowe [1976]). In the middle and late 1960s in particular the market leaders seemed to be trying advertising (for example Esso's 'Tiger' campaign) as a means of stemming their loss of market share. The leaders continued to lose ground to firms spending relatively little on advertising (Lowe [1976]), but whether advertising reduced the rate of decline from an otherwise higher level is unknown. The subsequent fall-off in advertising expenditure in 1970 might have been partly due to the reduced threat to market shares as supply conditions tightened. However, it is difficult to avoid the conclusion

*Regent/Texaco have not released details of company-owned sites for 1973.

that product differentiation supported by advertising expenditure was essentially a failure. It demonstrably was largely ineffective as a barrier to entry, and with the increase in consumer knowledge its effectiveness in retaining custom for higher-priced petrol undoubtedly sharply declined. Indeed this apparent failure of general promotional advertising seems to have been reflected in its replacement by gift offers (for example water tumblers) in the petrol firms' promotion campaigns. However, since gift offers are a form of indirect price competition, their use may be interpreted as a partial breakdown of price discipline.

4 Summary and Conclusions

The tight oligopoly dominated by Shell–B.P. and Esso which had carefully avoided price competition among established firms in the 1950s was threatened at the end of the decade by new entry. Despite this threat the leaders chose to set prices which promised abnormal profits for new entrants and minor firms, and consequently the leaders had to accept a continuous decline in their market share. This policy was dictated by the unprofitability of adopting a full-scale limit-pricing policy to deter small-scale entry. Nevertheless, the established firms did try to control the rate of entry and their loss of market share partly by advertising and trying to control retail outlets and partly by a series of price cuts which reduced the incentive to entry and further expansion by minor firms. However, the losses in market share placed considerable strains on the pricing discipline of the established firms, and the restraint which had characterised competition in the 1950s almost disappeared.

In summer 1967, and after 1970, market conditions were changed by the rapid escalation of costs and periodic supply shortages. Although competitive pressures remained strong, the earlier pattern of price leadership/followership was largely restored. This was made possible both by the common interest of all firms in higher prices to combat rising costs and, during supply shortages, by the inability of aggressive firms to take advantage of any price increases by rivals to extend their market share. Despite this, the long-term effect of entry, reflected in the increased number of firms and reduced shares of the leaders, had been to reduce retail prices (net of taxes) relative to costs. Entry had largely performed its competitive function—the reduction of monopoly power and profit.

References

J. S. Bain [1949], 'A Note on Pricing in Monopoly and Oligopoly', *American Economic Review*, 39 (2), Mar., pp. 448–64.
—— [1956], *Barriers to New Competition* (Harvard University Press).
Consumers Association [1964], 'Petrol', *Which* (London), Jan.
D. F. Dixon [1962], 'The Development of the Solus System of Petrol Distribution in the United Kingdom 1950-1960', *Economica*, N.S. 29 (133), Feb., pp. 40-52.

D. W. Gaskins [1971], 'Dynamic Limit Pricing: Optimal Pricing under Threat of Entry', *Journal of Economic Theory*, 3 (3), Sep., pp. 306-22.

J. F. Lowe [1976], 'Competition in the U.K. Retail Petrol Market 1960-73', *Journal of Industrial Economics*, 24 (3), Mar.

Monopolies Commission [1965], *Petrol, A Report on the Supply of Petrol to Retailers in the United Kingdom* (London: H.M.S.O.).

D. E. Schendel and P. Balestra [1969], 'Rational Behaviour and Gasoline Price Wars', *Applied Economics*, 1 (2), May, pp. 89-101.

F. M. Scherer [1970], *Industrial Market Structure and Economic Performance* (Chicago: Rand, McNally).

R. W. Shaw [1974], 'Price Leadership and the Effect of New Entry on the U.K. Retail Petrol Supply Market', *Journal of Industrial Economics*, 23 (1), Sep., pp. 65-79.

K. Simmonds and D. Leighton [1973], 'Esso Petroleum Company Ltd.' in their *Case Problems in Marketing* (London: Nelson).

D. A. Worcester [1957], 'Why "dominant firms" decline', *Journal of Political Economy*, 65 (4), Aug., pp. 338-46.

12

The Ownership and Control of Industry[1]

by Steve Nyman and Aubrey Silberston

1 Introduction

The ownership and control of large firms has been a continuing, if sporadic, interest of economists, and of industrial economists in particular, since Berle and Means (1932) wrote their pioneering work. There is now a widely held opinion that a majority of large firms are controlled by professional managers, that the proportion of large firms controlled by ownership interests is declining, and that, in any event, there is very little difference in behaviour between managerially and owner-controlled firms. In this paper we suggest that this view is misleading to a considerable extent. It is based on too narrow a conception of the forms which ownership takes and on too simple a theory of the relationship between ownership and corporate behaviour.

We shall present new evidence on the extent of ownership control in British industry which shows that the extent of managerial control is more limited than has been thought and may not have an inexorable tendency to increase. However, the situation differs very much by industry and this may have affected the results of previous empirical studies on the relationship between control and behaviour. This differentiation by industry is of course of interest in itself and a topic that needs investigating. A further differentiation is that between different types of ownership control. Firms which are controlled by professional managers, by families, by other industrial firms, or by financial institutions may display very different behaviour characteristics. These differences have not been discussed much in the literature, nor have the ways in which the control of firms changes over time.

This work forms part of the Growth of Firms project at Nuffield College[2] and is very much based on ideas and information gathered from intensive case studies of twenty large U.K. firms as well as less intensive studies of the top 250 firms. We believe that it is this kind

From *Oxford Economic Papers*, vol. 30, No. 1 (Mar. 1978), pp. 74–101. Reprinted by permission of the authors and Oxford University Press.

[1] This paper is a revised version of one presented to the Nijenrode Conference on Industrial Organisation, August 1976. We should like to thank our colleague Arthur Francis for the many discussions and ideas which have helped us with this paper. We should also like to thank fellow participants at the Nijenrode Conference, R. W. Bacon, and two anonymous referees, for their helpful comments on earlier drafts.

[2] Financed by the Social Science Research Council.

of study which is needed to bring out the continuing importance of ownership. In recent years a good deal of new work has been done elsewhere on this issue, much of it published outside conventional economic journals, and this too helps to throw a light on data and hypotheses concerning the ownership structure of industry and its implications.

2 Previous studies

Two of the most widely used textbooks in industrial economics are George (1974) and Scherer (1970). George devotes only a few paragraphs to the question of the divorce between ownership and control in large U.K. firms and quotes the conclusion of Sargent Florence (1961) that 70 per cent of the large firms he studied were characterized by a divorce between ownership and control. George suggests that this is an overestimate of the extent of the divorce because of the stringent criteria used, and adds that ownership control is normal for smaller firms. Nevertheless he concludes that: 'a very important part of the private enterprise sector of the economy is characterised by management control' (p. 103).

Scherer devotes more space to the question of the ownership and control of industry—some four pages out of over five hundred. On the basis of Berle and Means's (1932) and Larner's (1970) data he suggests that managerial control has been increasing and quotes Larner's conclusion that by 1963 over 80 per cent of the largest 200 U.S. corporations were management-controlled. However, he adds that this may be an over-simplification, and that considerable power may be wielded by families and by financial institutions. Control of several corporations may also be exercised via interlocking directorates. Scherer concludes his review of the topic by saying:

. . . our ignorance on this subject is great, and we can scarcely afford the complacent assumption that interlocking directorates and other corporate affiliations have no significant behavioural effects. (p. 47).

The so-called 'divorce' between ownership and control has also been the starting-point for recent managerial theories of the firm. Perhaps the most comprehensive discussion of these has been in *The Corporate Economy*, edited by Marris and Wood (1971), which, however, contains no discussion of ownership and control in eleven chapters and three appendices. The authors rely on earlier works such as Marris (1964) which assume that most large corporations are managerially controlled, on the basis of evidence from Berle and Means, Gordon (1961), Larner, and Sargent Florence.

The criteria which these and other writers have used to classify corporate control have differed, but in general they have mainly been mechanical. They have defined a percentage of the total votes which an individual or clearly defined group must own, to class a company as effectively controlled by a minority. Majority control, of course, presents no problem. The relevant percentages as definitions of minority control are as follows:

20–50 per cent—Berle and Means;
10–50 per cent—Larner;
5–50 per cent—Patman Committee (1968), Chevalier (1969).

In his study of the ownership of large U.K. companies Sargent Florence used several alternative criteria which a company had to satisfy to be considered owner-controlled. These were:

A. That the largest single shareholder had 20 per cent of the votes or more.
B. That the largest twenty shareholders had 30 per cent of the votes or more.
C. That either A or B was satisfied, but these shareholders were companies, or, if persons, were connected.
D. That the directors, between them, had 5 per cent or more of the ordinary shares. (Florence (1961), p. 111.)

For the U.K., on the basis of the tests mentioned above, Florence identified thirty out of the ninety-eight largest companies as being probably owner-controlled or marginally so. Including a sample of smaller companies, he found that eighty-nine out of 268 were owner-controlled, or 33 per cent. He concluded that: 'Two thirds of the large companies in 1951 was thus probably not owner-controlled' (p. 85). Furthermore he concluded that between 1936 and 1951 the trend towards a divorce of ownership from control was very clear (p. 186). He called the trend a 'managerial evolution' (p. 187).

On the basis of the criteria mentioned, Berle and Means classified 44 per cent of the largest 200 U.S. firms in 1929 as under management control. Even after lowering the definition of 'minority control' to 10 per cent or more of the shares, Larner classified 84 per cent of the top 200 in 1963 as being management-controlled. He concluded that the 'managerial revolution', in process in 1929, was now 'close to complete'.

Gordon's study, based on secondary analysis of the TNEC data (Goldsmith and Parmelee, 1940), came to very similar conclusions for 176 out of the largest 200 U.S. corporations.

The real revolution (in property rights) has already largely taken place; the great majority of stockholders have been deprived of their property through the diffusion of ownership and the growth in the power of management. (Gordon (1961), p. 350.)

The TNEC report used the cut-off point of 10 per cent of the votes to define a dominant stockholding interest. They used less than 10 per cent only when there was evidence that the stockholding group had representatives in management. On this basis the TNEC concluded that, in 118 of the 176 corporations, control was exercised through ownership (see Gordon, pp. 40 and 41, for the TNEC results). However, Gordon disputes the significance of this figure. He subtracts those corporations where the dominant stockholder is another corporation, and also those where a multi-family group is the dominant holder, especially as nearly two-thirds of the combined multi-family holdings total less than 30 per cent of the voting stock. On this basis he suggests that probably in less than one-third of the 176 corporations does a small compact group of individuals exercise control, i.e. 'possession of the power to select management' (p. 43). However, he argues that active leadership does not necessarily go with substantial ownership. He concludes by saying that:

Probably no more than a fifth, perhaps less, of the stock of the giant concerns is owned by those in a position to exercise a strong influence on management. Most important, however prevalent may be substantial minority holdings, the mere existence and size of these holdings tell us little or nothing concerning the extent to which stockholding groups actually participate in the function of business leadership. It is practically certain that those actively engaged in exercising the leadership function do not own, on the average, more than a small minority of the stock of the large corporations with which we are concerned. As we shall see in later chapters, corporation executives are today primarily responsible for the exercise of business leadership in the large corporation. To the extent that this is true, there can be no doubt that leadership and ownership are very largely in different hands. (p. 45.)

3 A critique of the general view

It is on the basis of the evidence of Berle and Means, Larner, Gordon and Florence that current beliefs are based. The typical large modern corporation is viewed as being run by professional managers with little proprietary relationship to their firm. Its actions are constrained, to the extent that they are, by product, labour, and capital markets, and not by ownership interests, internal or external to the firm. This view underlies the models of corporate behaviour of Marris (1964), Galbraith (1967), and others.

The methods and conclusions of previous research into the issue of ownership control have been strongly challenged in recent papers by Fitch and Oppenheimer (1970), Zeitlin (1974), and Scott and Hughes (1976). These papers have not yet been taken into the thinking of most economists, and they suggest that current beliefs are incorrect for the following main reasons:

1. The suggestion by Gordon and others—most importantly Galbraith—that even if we find interest groups owning large blocks or having seats on the board of directors, this does not amount to business leadership is not convincing. Fitch and Oppenheimer point out that the Board controls finance, capital expenditure, dividends, and broad objectives, and that it chooses the Chief Executive. It controls operations by financial standards and does not need to

concern itself with questions—considered by Galbraith to be the basis for management control—such as product technology. Evidence from intensive case-studies of large U.K. companies in our research project supports this view.

2. Berle and Means, Gordon, and Larner's conclusion that there has been a managerial revolution is based on a particular approach to empirical data, or simply on a lack of relevant data. Gordon excluded from ownership control holdings by other corporations, even though this may clearly reduce managerial autonomy. Similarly Berle and Means excluded control by share-pyramiding, although this device actually reduces the percentage of shares needed for control.

The difference between the methodologies of Berle and Means, Gordon, *et al.*, and Zeitlin, Fitch and Oppenheimer, *et al.*, may be partly explained by a difference of emphasis. The former group were more concerned with the disenfranchisement of the vast majority of shareholders and the ultimate location of control of large corporations. The latter group have been more concerned with the presence of ownership or external control from the point of view of any given large corporation. Thus Berle and Means excluded from their definition of owner-control, control by legal devices. They also classified companies according to their ultimate control. Thus if company A was minority-controlled by company B but the latter was management-controlled, company A was also considered to be management-controlled (Berle and Means (1932), p. 94), even though there was clearly an external locus of control.

Berle and Means classified 88 out of the largest 200 corporations as under management control in 1929. However, Zeitlin has pointed out that they actually provided no information on 44 of these, which they called 'presumably management controlled' (Zeitlin, p. 1081). Of the 43 (from a total of 106) *industrial* corporations classed as under management control, Berle and Means classified 39 as 'presumably under management control'. Of these 43 industrial corporations, no less than 33 were identified as having a definite centre of ownership control by later studies (see Goldsmith and Parmelee, 1940; NRC, 1939; Perlo, 1957).[3] Thus only a very small number of industrial corporations can be identified as definitely under management control in the 1930s in the U.S.A.

3. To locate control in any given corporation, it is not adequate to set up arbitrary statistical criteria such as the percentage of shares which must be owned by the largest holder or the largest twenty holders. Rather a case-by-case approach is necessary. Any individual firm may be related to other corporations, banks, financial institutions, and family owners via complex patterns of shareholdings, interlocking directorates, and kinship networks. Using such an approach in a study which appeared at about the same time as Berle and Means, Lundberg (1937) concluded that a small group of families,

---

[3] These studies are reported by Zeitlin (p. 1084).

via their control of the major banks, were still in control of the
U.S. industrial system. More recently the Patman Committee suggested
that banks were becoming much more important as trustee holders
of corporate stock and that control of a corporation could be exercised
with 5 per cent or sometimes even less of the total shares. 147 out of
the Fortune 500 had more than 5 per cent of their shares held by
one of the forty-nine banks surveyed by the Patman Committee.
Although these shares are held by the banks for a variety of beneficial owners, there is little doubt that in practice they provide the
banks with potential control over a number of large corporations.
Furthermore, the largest banks are themselves very closely linked.
For the six largest New York City banks in 1966, between 12 per
cent and 20 per cent of their stock was held by the same six banks,
and these proportions had markedly increased since 1962 (Fitch and
Oppenheimer, Part 1, p. 98).

The importance of banks—although not necessarily as shareholders—has very much increased in recent years as large corporations
have increasingly relied on external funds to finance expansion
(Meeks and Whittington, 1975). Of particular importance for the
U.K. is the role of merchant banks in the issuing of new equity, in
the arranging of loans, and the giving of general financial advice.
Many large U.K. companies have at least one merchant banker on
the board. The increase in the degree of external financing has also
resulted in the rise of institutional shareholders, such as pension
funds and insurance companies (see Moyle, 1971).

4. A very important means of control by interest groups has been
interlocking directorates, and these have not been given sufficient
attention in the past. Their importance is, however, stressed by both
Fitch and Oppenheimer and Zeitlin. Particularly important again is
the role of the banks. Of the 2,350 outside (i.e. non-executive)
directorships of the largest 500 U.S. corporations, 361 came from
another of the top 500 firms and 491 from commercial and investment banks; for over 40 per cent of outside directors with three or
more directorships, a bank was their principal employer (Zeitlin,
p. 1104). For the U.K., Stanworth and Giddens (1975) have shown
how the extent of interlocking directorships, between the top fifty
industrial companies and the largest utilities and financial institutions,
has increased markedly since 1900. Whitley (1973) has shown how
for the largest twenty-seven financial institutions in the U.K., the
directors not only interlock, but come from a common educational
background, belong to the same social institutions, and have many
family connections. Family connections may spread both to financial
institutions and large industrial corporations: Zeitlin has shown how
families such as the Rockefellers and the Mellons are heavily involved
in both spheres in the U.S.

Another factor which has led to an underestimation of the extent
to which ownership interests may dominate industrial corporations
is the existence of nominee shareholders, about whom there is little

information. There is also the exclusion from lists of the largest companies of certain large private companies. These private companies are obviously owner-controlled, and in 1966 Fortune estimated that there were twenty-six private corporations that it believed would qualify for inclusion in the top 500 U.S. list, and that there might be others which had escaped its notice. For the U.K. we have no such comparable data for firms which are not listed in the *Times* 1000. However, there are at least two private companies which do not appear in the *Times* 1000 but whose sales would warrant inclusion in the top 250, i.e. the Littlewoods organization controlled by the Moores family, and the Vestey organization.

This critique of earlier studies does not invalidate one of Berle and Means's central findings: that the vast majority of shareholders do not control the corporation which they own. Nor does it provide a solution to the debate on the legal rights of shareholders and the general role of ownership in the industrial structure, which was one of Berle and Means's prime concerns. However, it does suggest that the position taken by Galbraith, Marris, and others—that most large corporations are controlled by managements with little proprietary interest in their companies—is not warranted by the evidence.

What is stressed here is that for many firms there is an effective locus of control connected with an identifiable group of proprietary interests. The exercise of this control may be actual or potential. In the last analysis, even a managerially controlled firm is under the potential control of its shareholders, via a take-over bid, for example. So is a firm which is 'controlled' by a family holding of 5 per cent of the shares. It makes sense to call the latter firm owner-controlled, however, since the family is likely to be able to exercise actual control unless the firm performs disastrously badly. It has considerable *discretion* in its behaviour, including the power which we regard as the key one—the power to change senior management. It is less obvious that a firm can be 'owner-controlled' by a small shareholding held by another industrial company or by a financial institution, since in such a firm the managers may be able to exercise great discretion for considerable periods of time. However, control can be made actual, rather than potential, more readily and more speedily in this case than when there is no identifiable locus of control. The proprietary group may be reluctant to change the senior management but is able to do so with an ease denied to the scattered shareholders of a managerially controlled company.

We share Zeitlin's view that

When the concrete structure of ownership and of intercorporate relationships makes it probable that an identifiable group of proprietary interests will be able to realise their corporate objectives over time, despite resistance, then we may say that they have 'control' of the corporation. (Zeitlin, p. 1091.)

Since 'corporate objectives' have to be realized by the senior management of a company, it is the power to select and change senior management that we consider to be the main indicator of control, rather than any specific company behaviour.

We are suggesting, therefore, a structural rather than a behavioural analysis, and emphasizing potential rather than observed control. This is important, since an analysis of observed power struggles in individual corporations, for example, will not disclose the numerous situations where control is exercised but never challenged.

4 Recent studies

The implication of this critique is that a full investigation of the extent of ownership control of industrial firms must take a case-by-case approach and investigate the wide range of factors discussed above. For the U.S. this has been partially done by Burch (1972) who systematically searched through business and financial journals over the period 1950–71 for evidence of control (reported in Zeitlin (1974)). One reason why he did this was that he believed, and indeed showed, that stockholding reports to the Securities Exchange Commission had been deliberately falsified. His condition for classifying a firm as owner-controlled was that 4–5 per cent of the voting stock was owned by a family, group of families, or an individual, and that he found representation of a family on the board of directors over an extended period. For the top 300 he found that 45 per cent were probably under family control in this sense, 40 per cent probably under management control, and a further 15 per cent *possibly* under family control. He did not study control by financial institutions, but it is difficult to conclude, on the basis of this evidence, that most U.S. corporations are managerially controlled.

Similarly Chevalier (1969) looked at the 200 largest U.S. manufacturing corporations in 1965 and included data gathered from the financial press. He defined 'minority-control' as a group or individual holding more than 5 per cent of the shares of a corporation. He also included a category of control called 'Dominant Influence' where 'There is a group, represented on the board of directors, which seems to wield a decisive influence on the corporation.' Included in this group were companies such as IBM where the Watson family was dominant but held only 3 per cent of the shares, and General Electric controlled by Morgan Guaranty via four interlocking directorships. Of the 200 he found that 69 corporations were controlled by individuals or families, 31 by banks and other financial institutions, and 20 by other groups. Thus only 80 could be said to be management-controlled. Chevalier believed some of these to be owner-controlled, but he lacked the necessary information to prove this.

Scott and Hughes's investigation, following Zeitlin's methodology for the largest Scottish registered companies, found the vast majority to be owner-controlled, via either large shareholding blocks or interlocking directorates. Most of these companies would not be very large in terms of the U.K. economy. However, Scott and Hughes have shown what can be achieved by looking very closely at large companies which on the surface appear to have no important proprietary interest. For example, Burmah Oil was ranked sixteenth in the 1975-6 *Times* 1000. In 1974 its board of directors owned only 0.09 per cent of the shares, and no single person or institutional investor owned a substantial percentage of the shares. Yet Scott and Hughes showed how six of the largest institutional holders in Burmah (two unit trusts, three investment trusts, and an assurance company) were intimately linked via shareholdings, directorships, management, and other associations. Most importantly, Burmah's six non-executive directors had six other directorships with four of these institutional holders. Burmah and one of the most important of these, the Murray Johnstone group, were founded by the same man, and Murray Johnstone's chairman was also chairman of Burmah until 1974 and then became deputy chairman. Similar studies for other U.K. companies which appear to be management-controlled would probably produce similar evidence.

No comprehensive study of the ownership and control of large U.K. companies has been carried out since Florence's investigation of the 1951 position, referred to above. The following section describes a study we have carried out of the largest 250 companies in 1975. This goes some way, but by no means all the way, towards utilizing the methodology implied above.

5 Ownership and control of the 'Top 250' U.K. firms

A comprehensive study of the patern of proprietary interests in an individual company should, in our view, look at the following factors. Our aim in drawing up this list is to attempt to define circumstances in which an individual, or a group of individuals (whether incorporated or not), are probably able to exercise control over a firm, in the sense of being able to select its senior management.

1. The percentage of votes held by the largest shareholder and his identity;
2. The percentage of votes held by the largest twenty shareholders and their identities, the percentage of votes they hold in each others' companies, and the extent of interlocking directorships among them;
3. The percentage of votes held by the board of directors and their families;
4. The presence on the board of directors of either the founder of a company, a member of his family, or his descendants;
5. The other directorships of directors, and the relationship of these to major institutional shareholders;
6. The identities of the Chairman and Managing Director, their career history, and the manner by which they came to be appointed.

The last of these has not been explicitly mentioned by previous writers[4] but we believe it to be very important in deciding the location of control in any given company. Detailed studies of large companies co-operating with the Growth of Firms project have emphasized the power wielded by the Chairman of the board of directors. Even if he is not the Chief Executive or a full-time executive, his control of board meetings, his contacts with major shareholders, and his monitoring of company performance, normally make him the key person in appointing or dismissing senior management. The latter may make the operating decisions, but the Chairman in most cases has 'possession of the power to select management' (Gordon, p. 43). In some cases, of course, he may be a figurehead, and this power may lie with the Managing Director or Chief Executive. This may be the case with G.E.C., for example, where Sir Arnold Weinstock refused the position of Chairman, but is obviously more powerful than the current Chairman, Lord Nelson. However, how the Chairman was appointed is clearly an important matter to investigate.

If the Chairman is the founder of a company, or if he is a member of the founder's family or one of his descendants, then we may well be able to designate the firm as 'family', even if the family are not large current shareholders. Similarly if the Chairman has come to his position after a career as a merchant banker rather than as a full-time executive in the company, for example, and has been appointed after institutional intervention, then proprietary interests can be said in some sense to 'control' the company. We have come across more than one example of both these phenomena. It is, however, important to differentiate between these and other forms of control as they may well have very different implications.

A comprehensive study of the factors we have listed above for the largest 250 U.K. companies would be a very time-consuming exercise. To obtain at least some estimate of the extent to which large U.K. companies are effectively controlled by proprietary interests at present, we have looked at the following:

1. The percentage of votes held by a known individual, institution, or cohesive group;
2. The percentage of votes owned by the board of directors and their families;
3. The identity of the Chairman and Managing Director, and their relationship to the firm's founder and his family.

Potential control is assumed to be present with a shareholding of more than 5 per cent.

This information has been gathered from the *Times* 1000 (1975/6), Moodies Investment Handbook (July 1975), Company Annual Reports for 1974, and *Financial Times* articles in 1975 and 1976. We have defined the 'Top 250' as being all those companies ranked in

[4] Except in Francis (1976).

the top 250 by the *Times* 1000 by either net assets or sales (276 firms were actually involved). We have then excluded all those companies wholly owned by foreign firms, and also those firms whose assets or sales were less than half those of the 250th by either assets or sales respectively. We also had to exclude three companies which appeared in the *Times* 1000 but which were, in fact, subsidiaries of other firms appearing in the list—British Aluminium, Carrington Viyella, and Amalgamated Metal. Table 1 presents a summary of our results.[5] It can be seen that 56.25 per cent of our 'Top 250' firms have at least some proprietary interest and can be classified as 'owner-controlled' according to one of the factors we consider important.[6] We have included in the total fifteen companies which have family chairmen but with less than 5 per cent of the voting shares held by an individual or known group. Since the power of these Chairmen is based on, at least, a former family ownership of the company's shares, we feel justified in including these firms. Also in some cases the family or board shareholding is only just below 5 per cent. Our usage is similar in this respect to that of Chevalier (1969).

It may be argued that seven of our 'owner-controlled' firms should be omitted from the analysis since they are majority-controlled by another industrial company, or are unquoted and controlled by another industrial company, i.e. they are really subsidiaries of other firms. However, of these seven, three are jointly controlled by two other firms and can thus be thought of as independent corporate entities. Another four are public companies in which foreign firms own more than 50 per cent of the shares, but since foreign control is not absolute, we have considered them still to be U.K. firms which should be included in the analysis.

The figure of 56.25 per cent quoted above is an underestimate of the extent of ownership control for the following reasons:

1. There are an unknown number of private firms such as Little-woods and the Vestey organization which are certainly large enough to come into the top 250 but for which sales or assets figures are not available. These firms are obviously owner-controlled.
2. For many individual companies large blocks of shares are held by nominees. Sometimes these are acting on behalf of many individuals, but they also act for companies, individuals, or financial institutions who wish to remain anonymous. It is virtually certain that in some cases these nominee shareholdings would enable us to categorize a company as owner-controlled,

---

[5] These results are slightly different from those presented at Nijenrode as we have become aware of information which has led us to recategorize several firms.

[6] Interested readers can obtain from the authors a list of the companies involved, their industrial and ownership classification, and the information which led us to place them in a particular category.

Table 1
Ownership control of the U.K. 'Top 250'[a] *in 1975*

% of voting shares held by a single, institution or by the board of directors and their families	Type of holder								
	I	F	D	C	G	M	O	N	Total
Unquoted company	3	..	8	1	1	..	..	3	16
Over 50%	4	..	15	1	1	..	1	..	22
40%–50%	1	..	5	1	..	..	1	..	8
30%–40%	1	..	8	1	1	..	..	..	11
20%–30%	8	1	2	..	..	..	..	1	12
10%–20%	5	4	17	..	..	..	..	..	26
Other holdings greater than 10%[b]	..	..	2	..	..	4	..	..	6
5%–10%	1	4	5	..	..	..	..	..	10
Total	23	9	62	4	3	4	2	4	111

Family Chairman or M.D. (but less than 5% shareholding by individual or group)	15
Total owner-controlled	126
No known control	98
Total firms	224
% owner-controlled	56.25

[a]For an explanation of how these firms were selected see Section 5 of the paper.

[b]Two cases where it was not possible to calculate the exact percentage of the votes controlled by the board of directors, but where it was clearly over 10%. Four cases where there was more than one holding greater than 10% and it was not possible to allocate control to any one holder.

Types of Holder I = Another industrial company.
　　　　　　　　F = Financial institution.
　　　　　　　　D = Directors and their families.
　　　　　　　　C = Charitable trust.
　　　　　　　　G = Government or quasi-Government agency.
　　　　　　　　M = Mixed control type.
　　　　　　　　O = Other control type.
　　　　　　　　N = Not classifiable due to lack of information.

if we knew the identity of the individuals concerned and their relationship to other shareholdings.

3. We have little data for the 'Top 250' on shareholdings by other than the largest shareholders, on interlocking directorships, on family directors who do not bear the name of the firm, or on the career history and circumstances of appointment of all Chairmen and Managing Directors. Knowledge of these would certainly add to the number of firms where there is found to be a controlling proprietary interest. For example we have gathered such data as part of the Growth of Firms project, and for three of the nineteen firms concerned (Debenhams,

Associated Biscuits, and Vickers), all in the 'Top 250', a change of control status is indicated.

Thus the first component of the beliefs held by managerial theorists such as Galbraith and Marris—that control of large corporations is by and large not in the hands of proprietary interests—is not true for the U.K. However, as we can see from Table 1, there is a wide variety of proprietary interests. It is important to distinguish between different types of ownership control since, as we shall argue later, they may have a different impact on company behaviour. Of 126 companies classified as owner-controlled, 77 are controlled via either the shareholding of their board of directors or through family Chairmen or Managing Directors. Of the rest, 23 companies are controlled by other industrial firms, and 7 by charitable trusts or government organizations. One interesting point to note is the relative lack of ownership by financial institutions. Only 9 cases were found, 4 of these being holdings of between 5 and 10 per cent by the Prudential Assurance Company. This is a very different situation from the U.S., where Chevalier found 15½ per cent of his companies to be controlled by financial institutions: our figure is 4 per cent.

It is difficult to assess the impact of government agencies or charitable trusts, but we do know that the holdings of at least two of the latter must be important sources of actual or potential control. Some 18.5 per cent of Unilever's equity is owned by the Leverhulme Trust, which has five trustees—Lord Leverhulme, the current Chairman and Vice-Chairman of Unilever, and two past Chairmen of the company. Fifty-one per cent of the voting shares of Great Universal Stores is held by the Wolfson Foundation, which is known to be controlled by Sir Isaac Wolfson, Chairman of G.U.S.

The second component of the generally held view is that the proportion of large firms which are management-controlled has been increasing over time. For the U.S., this had been disputed by Fitch and Oppenheimer and by Zeitlin, who point to the increasing influence of financial institutions, particularly banks. They suggest that at some point families may have given way to professional managers but that the latter in turn have been forced to cede control to financial forces. Chevalier has compared the control position in the eighty-five corporations common to his 1965 study and that of Berle and Means for 1929. He found little change in the over-all degree of ownership control but he did find a significant increase in the number of companies controlled by banks and other financial institutions. For the U.K. it is difficult for us directly to compare our evidence for 1975 with that of Florence for 1951, since our methodology and research effort have differed widely. He found 30 per cent of very large companies to be owner-controlled, a substantially lower figure than our own for 1975. A rough calculation for Florence's categories A and D gives 45 per cent in 1975 for our whole sample as owner-controlled, and 35 per cent for the top 100

Table 2
Ownership control and company size

Rank in Times *1000* by turnover	Number of companies			% Owner-controlled
	Owner-controlled	Management-controlled	Total	
1–50	23	19	42	54.7
51–100	24	19	43	55.8
101–150	22	15	37	59.4
151–200	19	20	39	48.7
201–250	24	13	37	64.9
251–	14	12	26	53.8
Total	126	98	224	56.25

firms. On this basis, the figures suggest an increase over the period 1951 to 1975.

Other evidence used to suggest increasing management control of industry is the increasing dominance of very large firms in the economy, and the fact that larger firms are more likely to be management-controlled. Table 2 shows that the latter does not appear to be true within the current U.K. Top 250.

There is little evidence to show conclusively that management control of British industry is increasing. If anything the tendency may be the other way—towards a greater degree of ownership control, particularly by financial and other industrial interests. However, we have suggested above that the distinctions between different forms of ownership may be just as important, in their behavioural consequences, as the distinction between owner and mangement control. This can best be looked at not cross-sectionally at one point in time, but as part of the evolution, or life cycle, of companies. We have therefore tried to develop a typology of stages of corporate control which we discuss in the next section.

A final important point about our research into the ownership of the Top 250 is that it has revealed great industrial differences in the extent of ownership control. This is important partly because much empirical work on the relationship between ownership and control and company performance has looked at the question on an industry basis, ignoring the fact that industries differ widely in the extent to which they are owner-controlled. Table 3 shows the number of firms in each industry we have classified as owner-controlled.

We can divide industries into groups, as follows:

Industries predominantly owner-controlled—Food, Electrical engineering, Construction, Retailing, Merchanting, Miscellaneous services.

Industries predominantly non-owner-controlled—Chemicals, Metal goods (n.e.s.), Building materials.

Table 3
Ownership control and industry

Industrial group	Total no. co's in 'Top 250'	No. co.'s owner-controlled
Food	15	12
Drink	7	4
Tobacco	3	1
Oil	5	2
Chemicals	12	3
Metal manufacturing	5	3
Mechanical engineering	15	8
Electrical engineering	13	8
Vehicles	8	5
Metal goods (N.E.S.)	9	3
Textiles	6	3
Building materials	12	4
Paper, printing and publishing	7	4
Other manufacturing	6	3
Construction	9	7
Transport	8	3
Retailing	17	13
Merchanting[a]	17	11
Miscellaneous services	7	7
Conglomerates[b]	24	11
Unclassified	19	11
Total	224	126

[a]Wholesaling, Merchanting, and Overseas Commodities.

[b]Companies with significant business in three or more industries, without 50% or more in any.

The remaining industries appear to fall somewhere between these two extremes.

There must be many factors which account for these differences. It is apparent, for example, that non-manufacturing industries are predominantly owner-controlled. This may be because they are less capital intensive than manufacturing industries and there is therefore less need for firms to raise outside finance and dilute their equity holdings. A good many other influences are relevant, however, and we hope to carry out further work on this question.

6 The stages of corporate control[7]

We have suggested above that to classify firms simply as owner- or management-controlled does not do justice to the wide variety of ownership forms which we have encountered in the Growth of Firms case-studies. Such a classification may also serve to hide important

[7]In this section we are very much indebted to the ideas of Arthur Francis. Figure 1 is taken from Francis (1976).

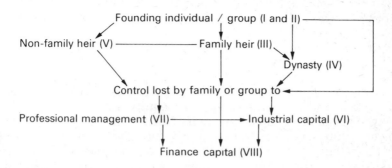

Figure 1. Stages of corporate control

differences in performance which are related to the ownership position. The different control situations we have found in our studies of firms relate very much to the historical evolution of individual companies, and can best be described as stages in some kind of life cycle, following one of the several paths shown in Figure 1.

The placing of any given company at a point in time will depend on the proportion of the voting shares held by particular groups, the career pattern and circumstances of appointment of the senior management, particularly the Chairman of the board, and relationships with external institutions. The mechanisms by which control may progress from the founding individual or group to another location have been described and rationalized in Francis (1976) and will not be discussed in detail in this paper. However, we shall spend a little time discussing categories VI and VIII—control by industrial or finance capital.

Industrial capital is sometimes used to mean capital in the form of commodities, i.e. bricks, mortar, stocks of materials and semi-finished goods, and machinery, and finance capital to mean capital in the form of money. Here we mean industrial companies and financial institutions respectively. Control may pass to industrial capital if the family prefer to have their interests looked after by other industrialists rather than by professional managers who may well have different objectives. It may also pass to industrial capital involuntarily as a substitute for a takeover bid. The presence of large blocks of shares held by industrial firms in each other may also indicate collusive practices, or simply technical co-operation.[8] One example

---

[8] They may also be a device by which managers—with or without substantial individual shareholdings—seek to protect their own position against potential interference by other shareholders. Such cases would work against our argument.

of cross-shareholding is British Insulated Callenders Cables, where General Cable Co., U.S.A. owns 10.8 per cent of the shares with an option to purchase a further 9 per cent. B.I.C.C. in turn owns 20 per cent of General Cable Co.

Control by finance capital may appear in the form of large blocks of shares owned by financial institutions, such as pension funds or insurance companies, or in the form of a Chairman or Chief Executive effectively appointed by financial institutions with interests in the firm. Banks do not normally own equity capital directly but they may manage such capital on behalf of nominees, pension funds, etc. In addition, their control of credit may give them effective control for substantial periods of time. Control may pass to finance capital (possibly in the form of a new Chairman with a financial background) if the family cannot find professional managers or other industrial capitalists they trust to look after their interests. It may also pass to finance capital if professional management or industrialist owners run into a profitability or liquidity crisis and need funds to survive. This was the case at Debenhams and at Vickers in 1970. Finance capital control appears to be much more prevalent in the U.S. (see Zeitlin, Fitch and Oppenheimer, Chevalier) and other countries than the U.K. However, even in the U.K. it seems to be increasing, as industrial profitability has declined and equity investment by financial institutions has increased. In recent years intervention by financial institutions has occurred in several large U.K. companies. We have not classed all of these as controlled by financial institutions in Table 1, for example Distillers Co. (identified by Scott and Hughes as controlled by financial institutions) and the Rank Organization. The latter company is majority-controlled by the Rank Foundation but the holding of 13 per cent of the votes by Eagle Star Insurance was important in facilitating the institutional intervention which occurred during 1976.

Finance capital has been shown in the diagram as the 'ultimate' form of control, since it might prove difficult (although not necessarily impossible), in contrast to the other forms, for it to be displaced once it has taken hold. As early as 1959, Berle, for example, suggested that once the stages of majority, minority, and management control have been gone through, a fourth stage of control, by fiduciary institutions, might be reached, through which dispersed stockholdings would once more become concentrated.

In the light of this analysis, we would not often expect to find professional or career managers in effective control, since their power base for gaining control is very small compared with families, other firms, or financial interests. This is borne out by Table 4 which shows who founded the firms which have co-operated in the Growth of Firms project, and also who controls these firms at present. Thus of the eighteen firms for which we have information only four can be classified as under professional management control.

Table 4

The founding and control of firms co-operating with the Growth of Firms project

Company	Rank in 1975 Times 1000 by turnover	Industry	Founder	Current control stage
Albright and Wilson	124	Chemicals	Quaker	VI
Associated Biscuits	187	Food	Quaker	IV
Baker Perkins	359	Mech. Eng.	Quaker	IV
British Home Stores	144	Retailing	American businessmen	VII
Cadbury Schweppes	37	Food	Quaker (on Cadbury side)	IV
Debenhams	105	Retailing	English drapers	VIII
Dixons Photographic	367	Retailing	Jewish	I
E.M.I.	64	Elec. Eng.	··	VI
G.E.C.	12	Elec. Eng.	Jewish	I/VIII
I.C.I.	4	Chemicals	German, Jewish, Swedish, Swiss	VII
I.T.T. Consumer products	(Not ranked)	Elec. Eng.	American subsidiary	·iv
J. Lyons	58	Food	Jewish	I
Mothercare	363	Retailing	Iraqi Jewish	I
Sears Holdings	34	Retailing	Jewish	IV
W. H. Smith	117	Retailing	English	VII
Stone Platt	206	Mech. Eng.	Defensive Merger	III
Tesco	61	Retailing	Jewish	VII
Unilever	5	Food	English: Nonconformist	VII
Vickers	97	Mech. Eng.	Defensive Merger	VIII

7 The behavioural consequences of types of control

At least ten empirical studies have been published in the last fifteen years which have investigated the effect of the nature of control on company performance. Almost without exception they have been based on the managerial models of the firm developed by Baumol (1962), Marris, and others. These have suggested that owner-controlled firms should have higher rates of profit but lower rates of growth than management-controlled firms. Predictions have also been made about the effect of control on other measures of performance. Empirical studies have almost all been cross-sectional and based on categorizing firms as either owner- or management-controlled. A summary of their findings is shown in the Appendix. The only clear pattern which emerges from these studies is that without exception owner-controlled companies have a higher rate of profit than management-controlled companies. However, of the seven studies in which this result was found, only two were statistically significant. In addition to these studies Palmer (1973) has suggested that we should only expect ownership type to affect performance where a firm has a substantial degree of market power. Thus he looked at the effect of ownership within three groups of large corporations classified according to the height of their industry barriers to entry. He found that owner-controlled firms had significantly higher rates of profit than management-controlled firms only in the group with high entry barriers.

Thus it may appear that while the nature of control has some impact on corporate behaviour, this impact is neither very strong, nor conclusively proven. However, we would argue that these studies have not revealed the true impact of ownership on company behaviour.

One problem with previous empirical studies, already discussed, is that they have a very narrow conception of the nature of ownership, of how it should be measured and what its effects are likely to be. The standard methodology has been to look at the proportion of shares held by various categories and to classify a company simply as owner- or management-controlled on this basis. We have already suggested that a much deeper kind of study is required to reveal the proprietary interests in a firm.

A second problem is that several of the studies cited in the Appendix have looked at the impact of ownership within particular industries.[9] This is unfortunate, since as Table 3 shows, some industries are much more owner-controlled than others. Thus, for example, it probably does not make much sense to compare two management-controlled retailers with two who are owner-controlled. The latter dominate the industry, and to a large extent determine the constraints within which the former must work.

Another defect of these studies is that they are cross-sectional, and

---

[9] Especially Monsen *et al.* (1968) and Boudreaux (1973).

thus cannot distinguish between the ways in which managerial aims, as opposed to managerial efficiency, affect rates of profit and growth. The observed rate of profit and growth of any given company will depend on both the profitability/growth opportunities open to its management, and on the management's relative desires for profitability and growth. The first will depend—*inter alia*—on managerial efficiency, and the latter on managerial aims. Cross-sectional studies thus face an identification problem, which the use of longitudinal case-studies may be able to avoid. This identification problem is discussed in Wood (1971).

Moreover, it may be impossible to infer managerial motivation from statistics of controlling ownership. The percentage of a firm's shares which its management owns may be very small, but the absolute value of those shares may be high, and may well induce shareholder-oriented behaviour. Nyman (1974) has looked at the relationship between the absolute value of director's shareholdings in the top 100 U.K. companies and the rates of growth and profit of those companies. The higher this value, the higher are the rates of growth and profit. This result is statistically significant, although ownership still explains only a small proportion of the variance.

Current empirical studies, by concentrating on the supposed link between ownership and performance, are, therefore, deficient in a number of ways. That the measures of ownership may be inadequate is only one criticism. A more important defect is that the causal relationship between ownership and motivation is not explored, but simply taken for granted. Finally, the relationship between motivation and behaviour is not examined at all. To jump straight from 'ownership' to performance is therefore to ignore many of the most important aspects of the problem.

One of the most interesting things to have come out of our research is the great variety which ownership patterns can take. This was brought out by the consideration of stages of growth in the last section and also by Table 1. It is scarcely surprising, in the light of this, that differences in performance cannot be inferred from ownership statistics. Even when a firm is effectively family-owned, for example, motivation and behaviour may differ according to which generation is in control. The founder of the firm may himself have followed one of a number of different policies, and may not have been interested in profit maximization in any simple sense of the term. His successors may have taken a different line, either because circumstances had changed or because their motivation was different —possibly weaker, as authors since Alfred Marshall have argued.

Once control has passed beyond the stage of the family of the founder, it may pass to other families, possibly those linked with prominent chairmen or senior management whose ownership stake is not large. Such families may still exhibit an 'ownership' attitude, since they have become so closely identified with the good name of the firm. Beyond this stage, there may be no clear family or group in effective control of the firm, but the management may still be greatly influenced by the latent (or open) powers of those who own the firm. In our own research we have found examples both of the power exercised by other industrial firms and by financial institutions.

One simple differentiation of ownership which may affect behavior is that between

(a) Firms which are effectively owner-controlled by families, individuals, or the board, giving those firms a large degree of discretion;

(b) Firms controlled by outside shareholders such as other firms or financial institutions, severely limiting management discretion;

(c) Firms with no centre of control, where management has significant discretion, within the limits set by the product and capital markets.

A historical case-study approach brings out most clearly the wide variety of ways in which different types of owner may make their influence felt. We are carrying out such case-studies for all the firms included in our Growth of Firms project. This work is still in progress, and it is in any event impossible to report it here. One interesting feature already mentioned, however, is that financial institutions seem recently to have been exercising greater control than formerly when they have observed poor performance in firms in which they have a large measure of potential control. This has occurred most notably in two of our firms—Vickers and Debenhams (respectively ranked numbers 97 and 105 in the *Times* 1000).[10] It also occurred in G.E.C., another of our firms, but with less lasting effects.

In the case of Vickers, intervention by financial institutions occurred in 1970 as the culmination of a long series of events. After the Second World War Vickers had embarked on a programme of diversification into a very wide range of engineering products to take the place of much of its traditional armaments business. Most of these diversifications were not very profitable, and by 1970 pre-tax and interest profits were less than half their 1958 level, which itself had only provided a rate of return of 10 per cent. For the three years 1966-9 the dividend was uncovered, gearing was very high, liquidity low, and the company was kept going largely by the £16m. compensation it received early in 1968 for the nationalization of its steel interests.

Eventually in mid-1969 a group of institutions led by the merchant bank Hill Samuel, whose other members were the Prudential Assurance, Britannic Assurance, and Cable and Wireless Investment Trust, used their joint holdings of more than 10 per cent of Vickers' shares to initiate negotiations with Vickers' management.

---

[10] Information on Vickers and Debenhams comes from annual reports and newspaper articles.

The main effect of institutional intervention was to change Vickers' senior management, although while the negotiations were going on £12m. was raised by selling off trade investments in International Computers and Swan Hunter (shipbuilders). Early in 1970 a steelman, Niall Macdiarmid, was brought in as Deputy Chairman with the idea that he should replace the current Chairman in 1973. However, Macdiarmid left in 1971, for personal reasons, and in the same year Lord Robens, previously Chairman of the National Coal Board, was appointed as non-executive Chairman. The Vickers Board had reached an agreement with the institutions in early 1970 that a new chief executive should be appointed from outside the company, and in September Peter Matthews from the British Steel Corporation replaced an old Vickers' man as Managing Director. He immediately began to reorganize the company, getting rid of many senior executives, especially from the engineering divisions. He brought in a finance director from outside who introduced the strict financial controls whose absence had led to many of the previous difficulties. Capital spending was reduced and in 1971 and 1972 several businesses were closed, sold off, or rationalized. Between 1970 and 1973 total employment fell by 15 per cent. By 1973 profits had returned to their 1958 level, by 1974 the pre-tax return on capital reached 14 per cent, and the company had even begun to grow again. However, this had not prevented it from a relative decline from Britain's 15th largest company, by capital employed, in 1965 to 61st in 1974.[11]

At Debenhams, intervention by financial institutions also occurred in 1970. Established as a drapery business in 1813, Debenhams was built up by a series of take-overs to become the largest chain of department stores in the U.K. by 1965. The company had passed from family to career management control in 1928 and the most rapid phase of its expansion came under John Bedford, Chairman from 1956, who had risen to his position from being a sales assistant. By the early 1960s profitability had begun to fall and the company's operations were being financed externally, especially by long-term loans and bank overdrafts. By the end of the financial year 1969 (i.e. in early 1970) the rate of return for equity shareholders had fallen to 3 per cent, fixed interest payments were taking 40 per cent of profits after tax (but before interest), and the dividend was uncovered by operating profits for the three financial years 1967-9.

In this situation some of the institutional investors in Debenhams, with individually small holdings, forced Bedford to resign as Chief Executive in 1970 and as Chairman the following year. He was replaced by Sir Anthony Burney, a city accountant and director of an assurance company and several industrial firms, but with no experience of retailing. In the next three years Burney got rid of almost all the old board, and brought on to it a stockbroker and a financier. A property dealer joined the board of Debenhams Property

[11] *Times* 300, 1965; *Times* 1000, 1974.

Ltd. Finally in 1974 he appointed a new Chief Executive with outside retailing experience.

In terms of strategy, Burney's first move was to revalue the company's property and then to sell off a great many of the surplus stores, particularly in 1972. (By 1974 the number of stores had fallen from 115 to 72.) It is likely that even more would have been sold had the property boom not collapsed in 1973. His second move was to transfer the capital so raised into non-department store operations, especially the much more successful field of specialist retail multiples. This policy began in late 1972 and is still continuing, requiring a massive increase in borrowing. Thirdly the efficiency of the remaining department store operation has been improved, partly by a reduction of 30 per cent in staff during 1974. In the meantime Burney's connections with financial interests helped him to resist take-over attempts by at least two family-controlled retailers.

Thus the effect of finance capital's involvement in Debenhams, through the chairmanship of Sir Anthony Burney, has been to transform an unprofitable company, by raising money via the property market, by transferring resources from declining to expanding sectors, and by increasing the profitability of the main part of the business. It is very doubtful whether this would have happened had Debenhams' previous managers remained in control. It is also likely that the use of Debenhams' assets and its corporate strategy would have been very different if the company had been taken over by an established retailer, such as Tesco.

Fitch and Oppenheimer give a large number of examples of the power of financial institutions in American industry. They show that banks and other institutional investors have promoted mergers in some cases and blocked them in others. Such institutions were particularly active and influential in the conglomerate merger boom of the 1960s. One institution holding only 6 per cent of the shares of Polaroid pushed the company into expanding its sales goal, its advertising expenditure, and the number of its trained personnel. At times institutional holders have acted to curb executive salaries. Fitch and Oppenheimer provide many more examples of the power of financial interests, including the way in which they destroyed Howard Hughes' control over TWA. The authors' two most detailed case-studies show how financial interests built up one company in an expanding field (Union Oil) and destroyed another in a declining field (Penn Central).

Fitch and Oppenheimer document very fully their thesis that finance capital acts to transfer capital from declining to expanding industries more quickly than the market mechanism would allow. They also suggest further consequences. One is that there is a relationship between financial control and reciprocal purchases between companies. Another is that financial institutions, both as holders of stocks and shares and as lenders of money, are interested in the profits accruing to themselves rather than in the overall profits of the firms over which they exercise so much control.

8 Conclusion

We have tried to show in this paper that the assumptions about ownership and control on which managerialists have based their theories are, to a large extent, misconceived. Ownership interests control, in one way or another, the majority of large U.K. industrial companies, and the proportion of ownership control may well be increasing over time. At any event the picture of the large modern corporation painted by Galbraith, Marris, and others applies to only a minority of large U.K. firms, and probably of large U.S. firms also.

The growing importance of financial institutions has been one key development. These have always been important in European countries like Germany and France. Fitch and Oppenheimer, among others, have demonstrated their importance in the United States. Financial institutions, especially insurance companies and pension funds, have become increasingly large holders of industrial shares in a number of countries. These institutions are often closely linked, especially through interlocking directorships, with the commercial and merchant banks who wield additional power through their loan and new issue activity.

Table 1 shows that there are relatively few large British companies in which an individual financial institution holds more than 5 per cent of the voting shares. However, a more detailed study, which looked at all the major institutional investors in a company and the extent to which their directorates interlocked with each other and the company concerned, would, we believe, enable us to identify several other firms as being controlled by a cohesive group of financial institutions. Scott and Hughes claim to have found this for Burmah and Distillers Co. and we have suggested that it is the case at Vickers and Debenhams.

The tradition of financial institutions in Britain has been to be passive in the affairs of the companies in whom they hold shares. Their increasing stake has made this role an increasingly difficult one to play, especially in view of the falling profitability of British industry generally in the 1960s and 1970s. Financial institutions have begun to intervene in the affairs of companies like Vickers, G.E.C., Rank, and Debenhams. There is every reason to believe that the role of these institutions is likely to grow rather than to diminish.

If we are right about the strength of ownership interests in British industry, and especially the growing ownership by and through financial institutions, what are the consequences of this for managerial motivation and performance? The obvious answer seems to be that the forces making for greater profits have been much strengthened, although we would not claim that the firms concerned have been forced to 'maximize' their profits, whatever the term may be taken to mean. However, we would not argue that companies subject to potential pressure from financial institutions are always forced to act as if they were owner-controlled, since institutional intervention has occurred mainly in firms which have almost gone bankrupt after long periods of poor performance. The direction of capital accumulation in individual firms has been greatly changed in the course of this process. The Debenhams story, and that of Vickers, would seem to illustrate this. Fitch and Oppenheimer too present evidence that this is what has been happening. A further question raised by Fitch and Oppenheimer is how far policies are undertaken for the sake of profits for financial institutions rather than for the sake of industrial profits as a whole. There is no doubt that in the U.K. the activities of some take-over bidders and property speculators have been motivated by short-run profit prospects rather than by regard for the long-run interests of the firms involved. However, there is little evidence that intervention by the major British financial institutions has normally operated in this short-term manner.

There are a good many other things to be said about different aspects of the relationship between ownership and control and corporate behaviour. We have said little here, for example, about the implications of family ownership, or of control by other industrial companies: still far more important in aggregate in the U.K. than control by financial institutions. Nor have we said anything about the implications of different forms of ownership for the ways in which firms are organized, and how organizations change over time. We hope to discuss these, and other relevant questions, in the course of our further work.

Bibliography

1. Baumol, W. J. (1962), 'On the theory of the expansion of the firm', *American Economic Review*, lii. 1078–87.
2. Berle, A. A. (1959), *Power without Property*, New York: Harcourt Brace.
3. —— and Means, G. C. (1932), *The Modern Corporation and Private Property*, New York: Macmillan.
4. Boudreaux, K. J. (1973), 'Managerialism and risk-return performance', *Southern Economic Journal*, xxxix. 366–72.
5. Burch, Philip H. (1972), *The Managerial Revolution Reassessed*, Lexington, Mass.
6. Chevalier, J. M. (1969), 'The problem of control in large American corporations', *Anti-trust Bulletin*, 14, 163–180.
7. Elliott, J. W. (1972), 'Control, size, growth and financial performance in the firm', *Journal of Finance and Quantitative Economics*, Vol. 7, No. 1, 1972.
8. Fitch, R., and Oppenheimer, M. (1970), 'Who rules the corporation?', Parts 1, 2 and 3, *Socialist Revolution*, 4. 73–107; 5. 61–144; 6. 33–94.
9. Florence, P. S. (1962), *Ownership, Control and Success of Large Companies*, London: Sweet and Maxwell.
10. Francis, A. (1976), 'Families, firms and finance capital', Forthcoming. Unpublished working paper, Nuffield College.
11. Galbraith, J. K. (1967), *The New Industrial State*, London: Hamish Hamilton.
12. George, K. D. (1974), *Industrial Organisation: Competition, Growth and Structural Change in Britain*, London: Allen and Unwin.

APPENDIX

Emprical findings on the relationship between control type and corporate performance

Author	Country	Sample	Variable(s)	Effect of ownership control	Statistical significance
Florence (1961)	U.K.	223 firms, grouped in 8 industries	Retention ratio	Lower	..
Nichols (1969)	U.K.	Florence's 93 very large firms	Retention ratio	Lower	Worse than 5%
Kamerschen (1968)	U.S.	Top 200	Profit rate	Higher	None
Monsen et al. (1968)	U.S.	From top 500, 3 firms of each type in 12 industries	Profit rate	Higher	Significant for all industries
Hindley (1970)	U.S.	Steel and Oil firms in Top 200	(1) Growth of a dollar invested (2) Valuation ratio	(1) Less in oil, more in steel, (2) Higher in oil, lower in steel	(1) None (2) None
Larner (1970)	U.S.	184 of Top 200	(1) Profit rate (2) Variance of (1)	(1) Higher (2) Lower	(1) None (2) None
Radice (1971)	U.K.	89 firms in 3 industries	(1) Profit rate (2) Growth rate	(1) Higher (2) Higher	(1) Just worse than 5% when growth held constant
Elliott (1972)	U.S.	88 firms divided into below or above average growth for industry	Liquidity, leverage, growth, profit rate, etc.	Nothing significant except for liquidity—less	5%
Boudreaux (1973)	U.S.	Same as Monsen *et al.*	(1) Profit rate (2) Variance of (1)	(1) Higher (2) Higher	Significant Significant
Holl (1975)	U.K.	183 of Florence's firms	(1) Profit rate (2) Growth rate (3) Variance of (1) (4) Skewness of (1) (5) Distribution ratio	(1) Higher (2) Lower (3) Greater (4) Greater (5) Lower	None

13. Goldsmith, R. W. and Parmelee, R. C. (1940), 'The distribution of ownership in the 200 largest non-financial corporations. Investigations of concentration of economic power'. Monographs of the Temporary National Economic Committee, No. 29. Washington D.C.: Government Printing Office.
14. Gordon, R. A. (1961), *Business Leadership in the Large Corporation*, California, University of California Press.
15. Hindley, B. (1970), 'Separation of ownership and control in the modern corporation', *Journal of Law and Economics*, xiii. 185-222.
16. Holl, P. (1975), 'Effect of control type on the performance of the firm in the U.K.', *Journal of Industrial Economics*, xxiii. 257-71.
17. Kamerschen, D. R. (1968), 'The influence of ownership and control on profit rates', *American Economic Review*, lviii. 432-47.
18. Larner, R. J. (1970), *Management Control and the Large Corporation*, Cambridge, Mass.: Dunellan.
19. Lundberg, F. (1946), *America's Sixty Families*, New York: Citadel (originally published by Vanguard in 1937).
20. Marris, R. L. (1964), *The Economic Theory of Managerial Capitalism*, London: Macmillan.
21. —— and Wood, A. (ed.) (1971), *The Corporate Economy*, London: Macmillan.
22. Meeks, G., and Whittington, G. (1975), 'Giant companies in the United Kingdom, 1948-69', *Economic Journal*, 85. 824-43.
23. Monsen, R. J., Chiu, J. S., and Cooley, D.E. (1968), 'The effects of separation of ownership and control on the performance of the large firm', *Quarterly Journal of Economics*, 82. 435-51.
24. Moyle, J. (1971), *The Pattern of Ordinary Share Ownership, 1957-1970*, Cambridge: C.U.P.
25. National Resources Committee (NRC) (1939), *The Structure of the American Economy*, Washington, D.C.: Government Printing Office.
26. Nichols, W. A. T. (1969), *Ownership, Control and Ideology*, London: Allen and Unwin.
27. Nyman, S. (1974), 'Directors' shareholding and company performance—empirical evidence', Unpublished working paper.
28. Palmer, J. (1973), 'The profit-performance effects of the separation of ownership from control in large U.S. industrial corporations', *Bell Journal of Economics and Management Science*, Vol. 4, No. 1, Spring 1973, 293-303.
29. [Patman] Staff Report (1968), 'Commercial banks and their trust activities: emerging influence on the American economy', Washington D.C.: Government Printing Office.
30. Perlo, V. (1957), *The Empire of High Finance*, New York: International.
31. Radice, H. K. (1971), 'Control type, profitability and growth in large firms', *Economic Journal*, 81. 547-62.
32. Scherer, F. M.(1970), 'Industrial market structure and economic performance', Chicago: Rand McNally.
33. Scott, J. and Hughes, M. (1976), 'Ownership and control in a satellite economy: a discussion from Scottish data', *Sociology*, 10. 21-41.
34. Stanworth, P., and Giddens, A. (1975), 'The modern corporate economy: interlocking directorships in Britain, 1906-1970', *Sociological Review*, 23. 5-28.
35. Whitley, R. (1973), 'Commonalities and connections among directors of large financial institutions', *Sociological Review*, 21. 613-32.
36. Wood, A. (1971), 'Economic analysis of the corporate economy', in Marris and Wood (eds.), *The Corporate Economy*, London: Macmillan.
37. Zeitlin, M. (1974), 'Corporate ownership and control: the large corporation and the capitalist class', *American Journal of Sociology*, 73. 1073-1119.

13

Take-overs, Economic Natural Selection, and the Theory of the Firm: Evidence from the Postwar United Kingdom Experience[1]

by A. Singh

Introduction

Take-overs and mergers have become an extremely—and increasingly —important feature of advanced capitalist economies. Their main characteristics in the United Kingdom and the consequent economic implications were examined in detail for the years 1955–60 in Singh (1971).[2] This paper has two main aims: the first is to study the nature of the postwar take-over selection process in the United Kingdom over a sufficiently long time span to include considerable variety in underlying economic conditions. With this in mind, the take-over boom between 1967 and 1970 is examined in depth,[3] and is systematically compared with the results from the 1955–60 study, as well as with those from other studies which provide evidence for the intervening years. The second aim of the paper is to examine the implications of the results thus obtained for (i) the theory of the firm and the theory of economic 'natural selection', and (ii) the assessment of the efficiency of the take-over mechanism in reorganising resources in a capitalist economy, considering in turn the experience of the later 1960s take-over boom and that of the entire period (1955–70).

The paper is arranged as follows. Section 1 describes the magnitude of the international postwar take-over phenomenon, and, in particular, that of the 1960s boom. Section 2 initially analyses how the take-over mechanism has been integrated into the theory of the firm and, in particular, the role which it plays in the theory of competitive economic 'natural selection' among firms, and then discusses

From *Economic Journal*, vol. 85, No. 339 (Sept. 1975), pp. 497–515. Reprinted by permission of the author and Cambridge University Press.

[1] I should like to thank Mr P. Reeve of the Department of Trade and Industry, Professor G. Whittington, Mr G. Meeks and Miss A. Harris at Edinburgh University, and Professor W. B. Reddaway and Mr Alan Hughes at Cambridge, for their invaluable assistance either in data preparation or in providing helpful comments, or both. I am particularly grateful to Mrs S. Paine for constant criticisms and for her most constructive contribution. Of course, I alone am responsible for any errors which may remain.

[2] Subsequently referred to as *Take-overs*.

[3] The characteristics of take-overs during the later 1960s have not been comprehensively examined *per se*—the only comparable study covering these years (Kuehn, 1975) treats the whole period 1957–69 *together*, and so is unable to discover whether the nature of the take-over process changed during a period when its incidence virtually doubled (see Tables 1 and 2).

the theoretical issues raised by the actual take-overs themselves. Then in Sections 3–5 the nature of the take-over selection process in the United Kingdom between 1967 and 1970 is examined and compared with the situation between 1955 and 1960. In Section 6 the issues raised in Section 2 are broached directly in the light of the results of Sections 4 and 5 and of those from other relevant studies, followed in Section 7 by a summary.

1 Review of the Recent Take-over Phenomenon in Advanced Industrial Countries

1.1

The important role which take-overs and mergers have come to play in advanced industrial economies can be seen from the postwar United Kingdom experience. By the later 1950s, when most wartime restrictions had been removed and the stock market was functioning more normally, take-overs and mergers were occurring at a historically unprecedented rate: for a typical manufacturing firm (excluding steel) which was quoted at the beginning of 1954, the probability of 'dying' by the end of 1960 (i.e. disappearing from the list) was 1 in 4 and that of dying through acquisition was 1 in 5.[4] Then during the 1960s take-over activity increased still further: in 1964 a quoted U.K. manufacturing firm had a 1 in 3 chance of being taken over by 1970. Table 1, which shows death rates for quoted firms between 1885 and 1973, makes clear how high these have been from the mid-1950s onwards. Furthermore, the evidence shows that since then, *these deaths have been caused almost entirely by take-over or merger*, whereas before 1950 the main cause was liquidation.[5]

1.2

The increased scale of the take-over phenomenon has by no means been confined to the United Kingdom. For although the current U.K. merger wave appears to have started a few years earlier than those elsewhere, by the middle and later 1960s take-over and merger activity in virtually all leading industrial countries was exceptionally high. For example in the United States the take-over rate for large firms (with assets greater than $10m) rose from 0.5% p.a. in 1950 to 2.6% in 1960 and to 5.7% in 1968.[6] In terms of assets acquired,

---

[4] A take-over (acquisition) occurs when a firm A acquires more than 50% of the equity of firm B.

[5] Hart and Prais showed that between 1885 and 1950 liquidations appeared to be the main cause of deaths of quoted firms. In sharp contrast, from 1954 to 1960, 77% of deaths were caused by take-overs, 4% by mergers, 10% by liquidations and 9% by other causes. An analysis of the data for 1966–8 reveals a similar picture. For a discussion of the reasons for this important change in the mode of death, and for a complete survey of the magnitude of the take-over phenomenon during the 1950s, see *Take-overs*, chapter 2.

[6] Gort and Hogarty (1970).

Table 1

The Annual Death Rates of U.K. Quoted Companies, 1885–1973

(Percentage of the number of companies recorded at the beginning of each period.)

	1885–1896	1896–1907	1907–1924	1924–1939	1939–1950	1949–1953	1954–1960	1961–1964	1965–1968	1969–1973
Annual death rate	2.3	1.8	1.2	1.9	1.1	0.8	3.5	3.7	5.0	4.5*

Sources: For 1885–1960, Hart and Prais (1956), Ma (1960) and *Take-overs*; the figures for 1961–73 have been estimated from the data provided in D.T.I. (1970), *Business Monitors* for 1970–4, and from unpublished D.T.I. statistics. Note that for 1954–73 the figures cover only manufacturing industry, whereas those for earlier periods cover somewhat wider groups; also, quoted companies with assets under £½m are excluded for the last three time-periods. Thus the data are only *roughly* comparable over the long period.

*Provisional figure.

in both 1967 and 1968, acquired firms represented about 3% of the total assets of U.S. manufacturing industry. The comparable average annual figure during 1953–68 was a little over 1%, never exceeding 2%; the highest figure recorded during the merger wave of the 1920s was a little under 2.5% in 1929.[7] Similarly, in Sweden, employment in acquired industrial firms, which accounted for 0.58% of total industrial employment in 1950, rose to 0.75% in 1955, 1.56% in 1960, 2.35% in 1965, and 4.38% in1968.[8] Data from other countries (Canada, the Netherlands, Japan, etc.) also indicate a sharp increase in merger activity in the middle and late 1960s.[9]

These simultaneously high merger rates cannot be regarded as mere coincidence. In part they are a response to the liberalisation of world trade and to the increased international capital movements since the late 1950s. There is considerable evidence that in both Western Europe and Japan, large firms—as well as governments—have favoured bigger economic units in the belief that this would help them to face competition from larger U.S. firms.[10] These governments have thus permitted mergers to occur without much legal interference, if not with outright encouragement. United States companies in turn have tried to become larger still so as to face growing European competition, though whether this has been an important motive for U.S. mergers must remain for the moment a matter of speculation.

Inter alia, this world-wide merger movement has been a major factor in increasing the level both of aggregate and of individual industry concentration in industrial countries. This, however, is a large and important subject in its own right which, owing to space considerations, can only be touched on here. In the United Kingdom, for example, the assets of the 100 largest domestically owned manufacturing companies, as a percentage of the total assets of all quoted manufacturing companies, have increased from 55.9% in 1954 to 65.8% in 1964, and to 73.4% in 1968.[11] Furthermore, there is evidence that both in the United States and the United Kingdom aggregate concentration has increased relatively faster during the 1960s than during the previous half century.[12] However, this greater industrial concentration in advanced countries does not necessarily imply reduced competition. Indeed, the dramatic rise in international trade between industrial countries since the late 1950s may well have increased rather than reduced competition among producers, though this may have taken the form of oligopolistic competition between large international companies rather than of free competition of the textbook variety.[13]

[7] F. T. C. (1969); Ryden (1972).
[8] Ryden (1972), p. 51.
[9] *Ibid*. chapter 3.
[10] Hymer and Rowthorn (1970).
[11] Hughes (1973).
[12] Singh (1975).
[13] See, for instance, Parry (1973).

2 The Role of Take-overs in the Theory of the Firm and the Assessment of their Efficiency in a Capitalist Economy

Take-overs are not just a key feature of advanced industrial economies, they are also of central importance in the current controversy about the theory of the firm and that of economic natural selection. With the familiar, old, version of the latter, this was not so: the argument was that economic natural selection by means of competition in *product* markets would force firms to attempt to maximise profits, so that only firms pursuing this goal would survive.[14] This is, however, open to objections on both logical and empirical grounds. In an important theoretical paper, Winter (1964) showed that even if there were perfect competition in product markets, surviving firms need not necessarily be profit maximisers.[15] More importantly, the old description of the economic selection process is obviously inapplicable to modern corporations operating in imperfect product markets. Recognising this, neoclassical economists have recently argued that even despite the divorce between ownership and control in such companies, etc., managers would none the less be forced to pursue profit maximisation on account of competition in the *capital* market, i.e. the take-over threat, whether or not they preferred other goals; profit maximisation is thrust upon them by the sheer necessity of survival, for without it, non-maximisers will be taken over.[16] Other economists, however, argue that such non-maximisers can and do survive, either because the selection mechanism works in a rather loose and permissive way,[17] or because it selects on grounds other than profitability, such as growth maximisation.[18] Whether or not they are right is of crucial importance for neoclassical theory, as this depends on firms' maximising profits and so, in the usual way, bringing about optimal resource allocation.[19] Yet so far there has been comparatively little systematic empirical investigation into this subject.

In addition to its role in theoretical debates in the economic literature, the take-over mechanism is of great *practical* importance in advanced capitalist economies. First, the take-over *threat* is the only *market* constraint which could force managerially controlled firms to attempt to improve their profitability (or their stock market

[14] The best-known exposition is Friedman's (1953). For other references, see Winter (1964).

[15] In a subsequent paper (1971) he argued that, under such conditions, if profit maximisers only are to survive, a necessary—but by no means sufficient—condition is the existence of a selection process whereby profitable firms always expand, and unprofitable ones always contract.

[16] See, for instance, Alchian and Kessel (1962) and Meade (1968).

[17] This is common ground between the behavioural and other non-neoclassical theorists of the firm; see, for example, Williamson (1964), also Galbraith (1967).

[18] Marris (1968).

[19] See, for instance Hahn (1973), p. 327, where he points out the importance of the competitive selection process for neoclassical theory; also Johnson (1968), p. 9.

valuation).[20] Secondly, and more importantly, take-overs themselves
are one of the normal devices whereby a market economy reorganises
its capital resources as conditions change. *Ceteris paribus*, such
reorganisation will lead to an improvement in the profitability of an
amalgamated company if, for instance, a more skilled takes over a
less skilled management (even if both are attempting to maximise
profits), or if it permits the realisation of economies of scale, etc;
it may, however, also raise profitability by restricting competition.

Thus, given the theoretical and practical importance of the take-
over selection process, it is clearly necessary to investigate its precise
nature and characteristics. In the next three sections this is done for
the United Kingdom during the later 1960s, and the results obtained
are then systematically compared with (i) the situation during
1955-60 (as reported in *Take-overs*) and (ii) the results of other
recent studies, in order to discover what changes, if any, in the selection process took place over this time period. The basic question considered is how, if at all, did surviving ('living') companies differ from
taken-over ('dead') companies during the years 1967-70, or, to put it
more simply (and crudely), was it (say) the less efficient firms (as
measured by one or more of a number of economic and financial
variables) that were taken over? Then the other important question
about the nature of the selection mechanism is explored, i.e. how, if
at all, did acquiring companies differ from those acquired (taken-
over) during these years, or, in other words, were the acquiring firms
(say) more efficient than those which they acquired?[21]

3 Empirical Evidence—the Data and the Variables used in the 1967–70 Study

3.1 Data Used

The data used were obtained from the Department of Trade and
Industry's standardised accounting records of all quoted companies
in four U.K. manufacturing industries for the years 1963-70.[22]
The United Kingdom experience is particularly intresting not only
because the overall incidence of take-overs here has been very high,
but also because London has one of the most sophisticated and well-
organised stock markets in the world. During the last two decades
the take-over process here has been less subject to government
regulations and other restrictions than almost anywhere else (there
were, for instance, practically no equivalents to the U.S. Anti-Trust
Laws, etc.); it is therefore possible to observe the sort of selection

---

[20] For a detailed justification of this argument, see *Take-overs*, pp. 2–6.
[21] Evidence about the *actual outcome* of take-overs themselves is also presented and discussed in Section 6 below.
[22] More precisely, the population covered consists of all quoted companies
with net assets greater than £½m or gross income greater than £50,000 in 1964.
However, the D.T.I. records for these years do not include new companies, i.e.
those quoted for the first time after 1964.

process which emerges from the relatively free operation of market forces.

Furthermore, the period 1967–70 is itself of particular interest because of the unprecedentedly high incidence of take-overs which occurred. Indeed 112 of the 463 quoted companies in the four industries considered (food, drink, clothing and footwear, and non-electrical engineering) had been taken over by 1970 (Table 2): the overall annual incidence of take-overs was thus nearly double that observed in *Take-overs* for the period 1955–60, where the same four industries plus electrical engineering were considered. A typical quoted company in 1966 in the four industries examined had a greater chance of being acquired (24.2%) over the next *four years* than a comparable company in 1954 had over the next *six years* (20.5%). Furthermore, Table 2 also shows that the *relative* incidence of take-overs in the individual industries changed considerably. For instance, non-electrical engineering, which had the lowest incidence of take-overs in the earlier period, had almost the highest between 1967 and 1970; similarly, the ranking of the drink industry changed in the opposite direction. Of course, from the economic point of view, the latter is not particularly surprising as one would not expect a situation of take-over boom to occur simultaneously in different industries; nor would one expect industry rankings to be sustained over a long period.

3.2. Variables Used

In order to discover the precise character of the take-over selection process during the later 1960s, the records of both surviving and taken-over firms, and acquiring and taken-over firms were compared on both a univariate and multivariate basis. For each firm, the following variables were used, measured over different time intervals: profitability, change in profitability, growth, liquidity, gearing, retention ratio, and size (see Table 3 for the precise list). All these variables, either individually, or in combination with other variables, may influence a firm's probability of being acquired. The reasons for this, together with their relationship to the issues raised in Section 2, were discussed in full in *Take-overs*, and so need no repetition here.[23] The variables representing *changes* in profitability[24] were not included in that study, and were tried here to see if they performed any better than those representing levels of profitability. The valuation ratio,[25] which

---

[23] See *Take-overs*, pp. 46–51. Not only the exposition of the reasons for their inclusion, but also the definitions of the main variables used, and the discussion of the limitations of the basic data apply also to the 1967–70 study. For convenience, however, the accounting definitions of the variables are given here in the Appendix.

[24] A positive value indicates an improvement in, and a negative one a deterioration in profitability performance (see Appendix).

[25] The price–earnings ratio—the related more conventional stock market variable—was also considered in *Take-overs*—a point completely overlooked by Prais (1972), who also missed the report on its performance.

Table 2

Record of take-overs by industry, 1967–70, as compared with 1955–60

	Total no. of companies at end of 1966	Take-overs, 1967–70	Average probability of acquisition, 1967–70, for a typical company in 1966 (%)	Average probability of acquisition, 1955–60, for a typical, company in 1954 (%)
Food	62	16	25.8	26.5
Drink	76	18	23.7	28.4
Clothing and footwear	79	15	19.0	16.7
Non-electrical engineering	246	63	25.6	14.7
All 4 industries combined	463	112	24.2	20.5

Source: D.T.I. records of quoted companies.

was included in *Take-overs*, was not considered here; instead the results of other recent studies which did include it are reported below (section 4.5).

4 The Characteristics of Taken-over and Surviving Companies

4.1. The Results of the Univariate Analysis

The main results are summarised in Table 3, which shows for each variable the percentage of taken-over companies below the industry median.[26] During the later 1960s, it is clear that although (in most respects) taken-over companies have on average worse records than surviving ones (and are smaller in size), there is an *extremely* large degree of overlap between the characteristics of the two groups of firms. Ony two variables (one-year profitability and one-year change in profitability) showed a statistically significant difference at the 10% level, and only one (3-year profitability) at the 5% level,[27] but even for the latter, more than 41% of taken-over firms were above their industry median. The second major result is that, for the more important discriminators, the differences between taken-over and surviving firms were *in each case similar,*[28] but *markedly smaller* during 1967–70 than 1955–60 (see the last two columns).[29] In economic terms this is not surprising since the later period was one of take-over boom which would tend to increase variability *within* each group.

4.2. The Results of the Multivariate Analysis

If univariate analysis only is undertaken, it is impossible to know (i) whether greater discrimination between taken-over and surviving firms could be obtained by considering more than one variable simultaneously (e.g. the level as well as the change in profitability), or (ii) whether the relative discriminatory importance of individual variables when measured on a multivariate basis is changed when

[26] Since there are important inter-industry differences in firms' characteristics, particular care must be taken when aggregating data across industries. The method used above avoids this type of aggregation bias since the record of each taken-over company in the last accounting year before take-over is compared with the corresponding average record of all companies *in the same industry and in the same year.*

[27] The significance test is non-parametric; it assumes that the proportion of acquisitions falling below the industry median is a binomial variable.

[28] However, the significantly greater retention ratio for taken-over companies during the earlier period had disappeared by 1967–70.

[29] This is also confirmed by the comparison of the univariate distances ($|d/s|$) between the groups during the two periods, where d is the difference between the means of the groups, and s is their assumed common standard deviation. For instance, for two-year average profitability the univariate distance during 1955–60 was 0.38 and during 1967–70 only 0.11. The detailed results of the distance analysis (and of the conventional analysis of the differences between the means of the two groups) are not given here for reasons of space, but are available from the author on request.

Table 3

Percentage of taken-over companies below (or equal to) their industry median, 1967–70, with comparable data for 1955–60

	Non-elect. engineering	Drink	Food	Clothing and footwear	All indust. combined 1967–70	All indust. combined, 1955–60*
X_1 Size†	52.4	61.1	43.8	73.3	55.4	60.5[c]
X_3 1-year profitability	55.6	55.6	56.3	73.3	58.0[a]	62.2[c]
X_4 2-year average profitability	57.1	55.6	43.8	73.3	57.1	64.6[c]
X_5 3-year average profitability	60.3	55.6	50.0	66.7	58.9[b]	64.4[c]
X_6 growth ($t-3 = 100$)	58.7	52.9	62.5	46.7	56.8	63.3[c]
X_7 1-year change in profitability	55.6	61.1	50.0	73.3	58.0[a]	Not considered
X_8 2-year change in profitability	50.8	61.1	56.3	60.0	54.5	Not considered
X_9 1-year liquidity	55.6	50.0	50.0	46.7	52.7	54.6
X_{10} 2-year average liquidity	55.6	55.6	50.0	40.0	52.7	53.6
X_{11} 3-year average liquidity	50.8	55.6	62.5	33.3	50.9	52.8
X_{12} 1-year gearing	49.2	44.4	50.0	46.7	48.2	50.3
X_{13} 2-year average gearing	47.6	47.1	50.0	46.7	47.3	51.9
X_{14} 3-year average gearing	46.0	38.9	56.3	46.7	46.4	51.1
X_{15} 1-year retention ratio	46.0	61.1	62.5	40.0	50.0	42.2[b]
X_{16} 2-year average retention ratio	46.0	55.6	68.8	40.0	50.0	41.4[b]
X_{17} 3-year average retention ratio	52.4	44.4	68.8	33.3	50.9	41.4[b]
No. of companies taken over	63	18	16	15	112	181

Significance levels: [a]10%, [b]5%, [c]1%.

NOTE: a value of 50% indicates no difference between the characteristics of taken-over and surviving firms.

*Including electrical engineering.

†X_2 = log size, considered in subsequent analyses.

intercorrelation is taken into account; in other words, the univariate results are *necessarily* incomplete *per se*.[30] Consequently, multi-variate analyses (as used in *Take-overs*), i.e. discriminant analysis and Mahalanobis distance analysis, were carried out.

The results for the 105 different combinations of variables considered for various sets of data over the period 1967-70,[31] showed almost invariably that little greater discrimination between the groups was possible on a multivariate basis than had been achieved on the basis of the more important variables considered individually. For instance, for the matched samples of taken-over and randomly selected surviving firms for all four industries together, the expected probability of misclassifying a firm as taken-over or surviving was 46% on the basis of X_4 two-year profitability) alone, as compared with 43% in the 'best' multivariate case (consisting of X_2, X_4, X_6, X_7, X_{10}, X_{13} and X_{16} together), and with 50% on random allocation.[32] Altogether, however, the best discriminators on a multivariate basis were the two variables representing changes in profitability, followed usually by level of profitability, growth, and the retention ratio. This contrasts with 1955-60, when by far the most important one was profitability– though the variables representing changes in profitability were not considered.

4.3. Disaggregated Analysis: Size and Probability of Acquisition

The analysis of *Take-overs* indicated that in the 1950s there were important but complex non-linear relationships between certain

[30] For these reasons, Prais (1972) is completely mistaken in arguing that multivariate analyses are not required. He also mistakenly thought that the discriminant and distance analyses used in chapter 4-5 of *Take-overs* were undertaken 'to predict which firms *in particular* are to be taken over' (emphasis in original), and not to discover 'general regularities' concerning 'groups of firms'. It was, however, made clear (pp. 86-7, 94, 104) that the main aim of these multivariate analyses was to answer questions (i) and (ii) in the text above, i.e. questions precisely about 'laws' or 'general regularities' distinguishing 'groups of firms'. As discriminant and distance analyses are not often used in applied economics, their basic methodology was explained carefully in *Take-overs* (pp. 86-95, 117-120), with particular emphasis on their relationship with other multivariate methods (e.g. regression analysis) and their suitability for the specific empirical problems under consideration. The interested reader is referred to these passages for a full exposition of the applicability and the limitations of these techniques.

[31] In only five of these 105 cases were the multivariate 'distances' between the groups significant at the 5% level. The following sets of data were analysed: (*a*) matched samples of taken-over and randomly selected non-taken-over (surviving) companies for individual industries and for all industries combined, (*b*) a different set of samples in which each taken-over company was matched with a surviving company of a similar size within the same industry-year, and (*c*) all taken-over and surviving companies within individual industries.

[32] Compared with 1955-60, the multivariate results for the years 1967-70 showed even smaller additional discrimination between the two groups of firms. Corresponding to the figure of 43% for 1967-70 given above, the probability of misclassification in the 'best' multivariate case during the period 1955-60 was 32%.

variables (e.g. size and profitability) and a firm's probability of being taken over. To investigate this here, a more disaggregated approach was adopted. Table 4 reports the results for the relationship between *relative size within a firms' own industry* and its

Table 4

Average probability of a company being taken-over within a year for each size quintile (and for the top 10% and top 5%) on the basis of 1967–70 and 1955–60 experience:
all industries combined

Size category . . .	Q_1	Q_2	Q_3	Q_4	Top 20%	Top 10%	Top 5%	All cos.
Probability of acquisition 1967–70 (%)	3.0	10.1	9.7	6.5	4.5	2.6	1.4	6.7
Probability of acquisition 1955–60 (%)	3.6	4.2	3.5	3.1	2.5	1.6	0.8	3.4

Note: The figures for 1955–60 are on a somewhat different basis from those for 1967 and are therefore only roughly comparable.

probability of acquisition. Surprisingly, between 1967 and 1970, the probability of being taken-over within a year is *lowest* for firms ranked within the *smallest* size *quintile* within their own industry;[33] when all four industries are taken together[34] it is one-third lower than that for firms ranked in the highest 20% (3% as opposed to 4.5%). But from the third quintile upwards the relationship is more normal, i.e. probability of acquisition declines markedly with increases in firm size. This can be seen even more clearly when the top quintile is further subdivided into the top 10% and top 5%. In other words, there is an important curvilinear relationship between the two variables which was obscured by the aggregative and linear analyses of §§ 4.1–4.2, so that size seemed to be a statistically insignificant discriminator.

During 1955–60 the relationship between size and probability of acquisition was also inverse and non-linear, but of somewhat different kind. However, if it is compared with that observed for 1967–70 *when the smallest size quintile is ignored*, the two are remarkably similar, even though the probability of being taken over was higher in each size category for the later period, despite the shorter time interval.

The most likely explanation for the result showing the relatively

---

[33] Readers are reminded that only quoted firms are included in this study, so that 'small firms' means 'small *quoted* firms'.

[34] The pattern in each individual industry was much the same as that for all industries combined, but the complete data are not included here for reasons of space.

high immunity to take-over of small firms is that this group would contain many firms which are family controlled, and/or which do not have an active market in their shares. (In the four industries covered in this study, relatively small firms were mostly absolutely small.) The greater comparative immunity of this group during the later 1960s (as compared with 1955-60) can be explained by the higher take-over rates for the larger firms during the take-over boom.

4.4. Disaggregated Analysis: Profitability and Probability of Acquisition

The main results for 2-year average profitability are given in Table 5. First, during 1967-70, firms which fell within the three lowest profitability deciles (within their own industry) ran a risk of being acquired roughly one and a half times greater than those with higher profitability. Secondly, a firm's take-over prospects remained much the same from the fourth up to the highest profitability decile—thus a firm in the highest 10% in the profitability league had an appreciably high chance of being acquired, only slightly lower than that of the firm with average profitability (6.1% as compared with 6.9% respectively).[35] Thirdly, the overall pattern for 1955-60 is only slightly different from that for the later period.

Table 5
Average probability of a firm being taken over within a year for each two-year average profitability decile, on the basis of 1967-70 and 1955-60 experience: all industries combined

Profitability decile ...	Lowest 1	2	3	4	5	6	7	8	9	Highest 10	All cos.
Probability of take-over 1967-70 (%)	8.6	11.0	9.8	4.3	5.5	7.4	4.9	6.1	4.9	6.1	6.9
Probability of take-over 1955-60 (%)	7.4	5.3	2.9	4.4	4.0	3.4	3.4	2.7	2.9	1.7	3.8

The relationships between one-year and three-year average profitability and the probability of acquisition were also examined on a disaggregated basis, and were, not surprisingly, rather similar to those reported in Table 5.[36]

[35] The pattern for individual industries was, on the whole, remarkably similar, except for food, where the *most* profitable firms had a higher probability of acquisition than the remainder.

[36] Disaggregated analysis of the relationships between other important variables (such as growth, and changes in profitability) and the probability of acquisition were also carried out, but did not reveal any marked non-linearities. Nevertheless, the possibility of non-linear discrimination was also tried out for some combinations of variables, but the results did not seem to improve upon those based on linear discriminant functions.

4.5. Comparison with the Results from other Recent U.K. Studies[37]

Although most of the other recent (post- *Take-overs*) studies of take-overs in the United Kingdom have been primarily concerned with rather different issues (e.g. industrial concentration), some of their results are relevant here. First, most research covering the last two decades reports an inverse relationship, on the whole, between size and probability of acquisition, particularly for firms above a certain (fairly large) size. For instance, for a sample of 300 large companies (each with net assets of greater than £5m in 1957), Aaronovitch and Sawyer's study (1974) suggests that the average probability of acquisition over the subsequent 11 years (i.e. until 1968) was 1.6% p.a. for the 100 largest, 2.8% for the next 100, and 4.3% for the last 100.[38] However, no U.K. study has reported the kind of curvilinear relationship between the two variables described in section 4.3 above. This may have arisen because (as in Aaronovitch and Sawyer (1974) and Whittington (1972)) small firms were excluded, or because different time periods or different industries were covered; or because other studies have aggregated absolute size classes over all industries, whereas in the present study relative size classes were used in order to avoid any aggregation bias arising from the important inter-industry differences in the size structure of firms.

Two studies have dealt explicitly with the relationship between the valuation ratio and probability of acquisition—Newbould (1970) and Kuehn (1975). Newbould took a sample of 74 quoted firms which had been taken over in 1967 or 1968, and his results showed little relationship between the valuation ratio and probability of acquisition, although in *Take-overs*, for the period 1955–60, there was found to be a statistically significant but weak inverse relation-

---

[37] Although only U.K. studies are considered, some recent evidence from other countries supports the main results of sections 4 and 6 (e.g. Ryden, 1972).

[38] An inverse relationship between size and probability of acquisition also appears in the studies by Whittington (1972), who considers the 100 largest firms (in 1948) over the period 1948–68, and the D.T.I. (1970), which presents statistics on all quoted companies in manufacturing and distribution over the years 1957–68. However, Kuehn (1975) found little relationship between size and probability of take-over for U.K. quoted companies during 1957–69. But this conclusion does not seem to be supported by the data presented, which, in fact, indicate a statistically significant—albeit weak—inverse relationship between them. (In 56 out of 66 industries (pp. 64–70), the size variable had a negative coefficient, although it was rarely significant; the probability of obtaining such a high proportion of negative coefficients if there was actually no relationship between size and probability of acquisition is very small.) Furthermore, this relationship would have been stronger if Kuehn had not introduced major biases, the net effect of which most probably led to overestimation of the size of taken-over relative to surviving companies (*by comparing the former in the year before takeover with the 13- (or all available) year average for the latter*). Thus if one examines the results from Kuehn's *normalised* size variables (relative to their industry averages) the inverse relationship between size and probability of acquisition is considerably improved owing to the reduced bias (Table 3.3.).

ship between the two variables.[39] In contrast, Kuehn found a much stronger inverse relationship between the two variables, but this was based on a comparison of the valuation ratios of taken-over and surviving firms *which was not made over the corresponding time periods* (as in the case of size—see footnote 38 on page 254). In fact, when he normalised his variables (by dividing them by their appropriate industry averages), so making the two groups of companies more comparable, he found a very weak relationship between the valuation ratio and probability of acquisition. Thus, on the whole, the weight of the evidence for the later 1960s about the importance of the valuation ratio seems to be along the same lines as that for other variables reported in section 4.1, i.e. the degree of overlap between taken-over and surviving firms was probably greater in the later 1960s than in the earlier period.

5 The Characteristics of Acquiring and Acquired (Taken-over) Companies[40]

5.1. The Results of the Univariate Analysis

The main results, given in Table 6, show that acquiring companies during the years 1967–70 were, on average, bigger, more profitable, faster growing, more liquid, and more highly geared than those they acquired, and that they showed greater improvement in profits and retained more of them. The most important distinguishing characteristic between the two groups was, as expected, size, followed —perhaps surprisingly—by change in profitability: whereas there is only a small difference between the *average levels* of profitability of acquired and acquiring firms, the difference with respect to profitability *improvement* over the previous two years is clearly very marked—indeed, acquiring firms, on average, showed a small improvement in their profit records, while acquired ones showed a marked decline. For the remaining variables, the univariate distances between the two groups (given in column 5) were relatively small, indicating a considerable degree of overlap between them.[41] But as they were much larger in almost every case than those between taken-over and surviving firms (not reproduced here for reasons of space), this shows that the differences between the characteristics of *acquiring*

---

[39] Newbould found that 45% of the taken-over firms had a lower valuation ratio than their industry average, and that 55% had one above it. However, in *Take-overs*, for the 88 firms taken over between 1955 and 1960 in three major industries, the corresponding percentages were 63 and 37 respectively.

[40] Because of the importance of this topic in the characterisation of take-over selection process, parallel analyses to those in section 4 were carried out, even though the study could only be of a limited nature since the population was restricted to 82 firms (see notes to Table 6).

[41] When the standardised univariate distance (d/s) between two groups is equal to zero, they are literally indistinguishable; in general, the larger the value of (d/s), the greater the differences between the two groups.

Table 6

Univariate analysis of the differences between acquired and acquiring companies, 1967–70, with comparable results for 1955–60

	Acquired firms 1967–70		Acquiring firms 1967–70		1967–70		1955–60	
	Mean	S.D.	Mean	S.D.	d/s*	t	d/s*	t
Size (log)	3.60	0.44	4.37	0.67	−1.35	−6.21[c]	−1.50	−10.60[c]
2-year average profitability[†] (%)	12.07	6.69	13.83	5.34	−0.29	−1.33	−0.41	−2.93[c]
Growth ($t-3 = 100$)	127.93	42.60	142.92	43.17	−0.35	−1.60	−0.69	−4.91[c]
2-year change in profitability (%)	−4.20	7.64	0.23	4.70	−0.70	−3.20[c]	Not considered	
Liquidity (2-year av.) (%)	−13.42	17.82	−5.63	14.10	−0.48	−2.23[a]	0.17	1.18[b]
Gearing (2-year av.) (%)	17.72	13.18	22.78	13.27	−0.39	−1.77	−0.28	−1.96[b]
Retention ratio (2-year av.) (%)	37.83	29.57	44.17	29.27	−0.22	−0.99	−0.34	−2.43[b]

Significance levels: [a] = 10%, [b] 5%, [c] 1%.

Notes: For 1967–70, the number of firms in *each* group was 41, and for 1955–60, 100. In both time periods only acquisitions within the *same* industry were included so as to avoid problems raised by inter-industry differences in firm characteristics.

* d = difference between group means, s = (estimated) common standard deviation.

[†] Results for 1-year and 3-year (average) variables were similar but not as good.

and *taken-over* firms were greater than those between surviving and taken-over ones.

On the other hand, the comparable results for the years 1955–60 (see last two columns) show not just that the differences during 1967–70 are, on the whole, smaller than those found between taken-over and acquiring firms in the earlier period, but also that the profile of the typical acquiring company has changed: growth has become much less important a distinguishing characteristic, and liquidity more so, but in the *opposite* direction.

5.2. The Results of the Multivariate Analyses

In contrast to their results for taken-over and surviving firms, here the multivariate analyses definitely improved the discrimination between the two groups of firms (even when size was excluded). The computed discriminant function for 1967–70 on the basis of firm's two-year records (which yielded the best results) was:

$$z = 100 \log X_1 + 3X_4 + 0.5X_6 + 5X_8 - 0.5X_{10} - 0.5X_{13} + 0.5X_{16}.$$

This function is significant at the 1% level, and would be expected to classify 83% of the firms correctly if it were used to divide them into acquired and acquiring firms. This figure compares with 75% on the basis of (log) size alone, 80% on the basis of (log) size as well as change in profitability, and 50% on the basis of random allocation.[42]

It is also interesting that on a multivariate basis the differences between the acquired and acquiring companies during 1967–70 were *greater* than those during 1955–60, although on a univariate basis (as Table 6 shows) the reverse was the case. Furthermore, the multivariate analyses show that the most important discriminators on this basis during 1967–70 were size, followed by change in profitability and level of profitability. This differs from the results for 1955–60, when after size, growth was by far the main discriminator.

6 Implications of the Empirical Results

The empirical evidence about the nature of the take-over selection process will now be used to answer the two central questions raised in section 2: (i) can the take-over threat be expected to force firms to improve their profitability? and (ii) do take-overs themselves lead to a more profitable utilisation of available capital resources? To evaluate the present debate between the rival theories of the firm, it is the empirical results relevant to the first question which are required, and these are discussed in § 6.1 below; however, to assess

---

[42] Even without size, the differences between acquiring and taken-over firms were significant at the 1% level. For instance, the computed discriminant function on the basis of X_4, and X_6 and X_8 together was significant at this level, and yielded an expected probability of misclassification of approximately 30%.

the overall efficiency of the take-over process, the evidence reported in section 5 is of only indirect relevance as additional evidence about the characteristics of the *outcome* of the take-over process is required. This is introduced in section 6.2.

6.1. Implications for the Theory of the Firm[43]

Table 5 shows that during 1967–70, although the overall relationship between profitability and probability of acquisition is weak, and increased profitability would offer little, if any, additional protection to firms in the seven higher profitability deciles, those firms in the bottom three deciles can appreciably reduce their take-over danger (from about 10% p.a. to about 6% p.a.) through this strategy. In other words, there seems to be a significant degree of stock-market discipline for unprofitable firms. However, when this result is considered in the light of the relationship between size and probability of acquisition, and of the fact that size and profitability are unrelated,[44] it becomes clear that, as a survival strategy attempting to increase relative profitabilty may well be inferior to attempting to increase relative size, particularly so for larger unprofitable firms.[45]

[43] It should be emphasised that this study is not concerned with the many different motives there may be for take-overs, but rather with what *actually* happened (i.e. what kinds of firms survived and which did not, as a result of the operation of the 'market for corporate control' (i.e. take-overs)), and certain implications therefrom. Furthermore, given the impossibility of obtaining comprehensive evidence about what firms are *trying* to do (and the possible methodological objections to this), one cannot test if they are trying to maximise profits—or even just to improve profitability. Instead, one has to examine whether or not it has been, say, the *less profitable* firms in any given industry which have been taken over, and to calculate the *ex post* probability of acquisition on this basis. Obviously, a strong inverse relationship between profitability and probability of acquisition would provide strong evidence for the neo-classical model (though it would not be logically conclusive), just as a weak relationship (subject to the qualifications below) would provide strong evidence against it. In the subsequent interpretation of the empirical evidence, readers are reminded that the definition of 'industry' used is rather a broad one (as given in the SIC), and the profitability figures are based on accounting data—with the corresponding limitations (see further, *Take-overs*, § 3.1).

[44] The implications of the relationships of size and profitability with the probability of acquisition are discussed in detail because these variables have the most direct relevance to the theoretical issues considered; it was not felt necessary to discuss the results for the remaining variables in the same way because (*a*) their inclusion led to very little improvement in discrimination between taken-over and surviving firms, and (*b*) they did not on their own show any marked non-linearities with meaningful economic consequences. Level of rather than change in profitability is considered because in so far as a relatively unprofitable firm with an above average improvement in its profits does somewhat reduce its probability of acquisition, it only obtains short-term (i.e. one-year) protection—longer-term survival would require an increase in either two- or three-year average profitability, or relative size.

[45] For instance, as a firm moves from the top size quintile to the top decile and then to the top 5-percentile, its probability of acquisition is roughly halved at each step (see Table 4). In the individual industries, probability of acquisition fell more sharply with increases in size than is shown in Table 4 for all industries combined.

For, in theory, above a certain minimum size class (which varies between industries) all firms can reduce their probability of acquisition without increasing their rate of profit (even when this would actually fall) provided that they can achieve a *sufficient* increase in their relative size. However, in practice, owing to imperfections in capital markets, such an option is likely to be feasible only for larger and not smaller unprofitable firms; also, the results indicate that for any percentage increase in size, smaller firms would reduce their take-over probability somewhat less, even if they could do this.[46] In contrast, a large relatively unprofitable firm could increase its size through the take-over mechanism itself, e.g. by acquiring through share exchange even (relatively) profitable smaller firms whose price-earnings ratios may be less than its own simply because they are small and unknown.[47] Thus although the take-over mechanism may provide a measure of discipline for unprofitable small firms, it does so much less for large firms. In fact, rather than forcing them to improve profitability, the take-over process may well actually encourage salaried managers in large corporations to concentrate even more on size rather than profitability. Altogether, therefore, for larger firms the empirical evidence about the nature of the take-over mechanism supports the new managerial and behavioural theories of the firm, and gives very little support for the strict requirements of the neoclassical theory and of the associated doctrine of economic 'natural' selection in the sense discussed in section 2 above.[48]

The above conclusion with respect to the implications of the take-over selection process for the rival theories of the firm is essentially similar to that of *Take-overs* for the later 1950s. For although between 1967 and 1970, take-over discipline was probably equally strong for smaller unprofitable firms, it was, in general, weaker, especially for large firms, because the differences between taken-over and surviving firms were smaller. In addition, if the evidence

[46] On the face of it, the small–medium size class would benefit more by *reducing* their relative size (see Table 4); such an option is, however, unlikely to be of operational relevance for managerial firms operating in a dynamic environment. Furthermore, as argued above (p. 253), the main economic reason for small firms' comparatively high survival chances is that many are family controlled and not just small.

[47] See, for instance, the important work on this subject by Lynch (1971).

[48] Interesting further evidence is provided by Newbould's (1970) interview study, which suggests that one important reason why business managers take over other firms is to increase their own firm's size, and so reduce its probability of being taken over; it therefore confirms the implications of the *ex post* analysis above. However, it does not follow from the argument in the text that firms may not be maximising profits for other reasons (e.g. sociological ones). Indeed, increasing profitability is one obvious route to achieving an increase in size—even for large relatively unprofitable firms; the basic point is that since the take-over mechanism is highly imperfect, the doctrine of economic natural selection among firms provides a very weak empirical foundation for the neoclassical hypothesis of profit maximisation. (For discussion of the related issue concerning the relationship between firm growth and profitability, see Singh and Whittington (1968), pp. 143–90.)

of section 4.5 is also taken into account, so as to enable a review of
the take-over selection process during the entire period 1955–70,
there is clearly little empirical support for the neoclassical description of it.[49]

There are, *inter alia*, two very important economic reasons why
this description is inapplicable to the take-over selection process in
the real world. First, as mentioned above, the existence of an imperfect capital market means that for given rates of profit, it is much
easier for a large firm to take over a small one than vice versa.
Secondly, periods of exceptional take-over activity—and it could be
argued that by previous historical standards, not just 1967–70 but
the entire period 1955–70 was one of these—are characterised in
general by oligopolistic disequilibrium in product markets. Consequently, in an attempt to preserve their market share, larger firms
make defensive take-overs of many profitable small ones (and not
just less profitable ones), thus diluting the force of selection on the
basis of profitability.[50]

6.2. Impact of Take-Overs on Resource Utilisation

The evidence about acquired and acquiring firms in the later 1960s
presented in section 5 showed that although the profile of the typical
acquiring company had changed somewhat since the mid-1950s, it
was still the case that *on average*, larger more profitable firms took
over smaller less profitable ones.[51] This suggests that although the
take-over threat could not be relied upon to force firms to improve
profitability, take-overs themselves would be likely to bring about
more efficient resource utilisation, at least at the microeconomic
level (as measured by private profitability). Nevertheless, most of the
available evidence on this subject shows that this has not been so.
Most studies have been carried out for the United States, and Hogarty's
review (1970) of their results during the last 50 years shows over-
whelmingly that mergers and take-overs have had a neutral or negative effect on profitability. This seems to be confirmed by studies of
other countries (the United Kingdom and Sweden). For instance,

[49] This conclusion is of course subject to certain qualifications. Briefly, the
most important arises because take-overs can be voluntary: the owner may *wish*
to sell (e.g. because of impending retirement). This, it is argued, is what may
explain the appearance of profitable firms amongst take-over victims: if these
were excluded, the true efficiency of the take-over mechanism would be revealed.
However, this and other qualifications were examined in detail in *Take-overs*
(§ 6.3), and did not appear to weaken any of the main conclusions of the study.

[50] Of course, it could be argued that there is much more rigorous selection
on the basis of profitability during periods of normal take-over activity. However, this is not of much help to neoclassical theory if periods of exceptional
take-over activity can continue for a very long time (e.g. two decades) and
cannot be predicted in advance; in any case, there is no presumption that selection on the basis of size is any weaker during normal periods.

[51] However, 19 out of 41 take-overs in the 1967–70 sample, the acquired firm
was more profitable than the acquiring one, whereas in 36 out of the 41 cases
the acquiring firm was the larger of the two.

in *Take-overs* (for the United Kingdom during the period 1955–60), profitability of amalgamating firms relative to their industry average was considered for up to three years after take-over, and it was found that in more than half of the cases it declined. In a subsequent study covering the period 1961–70, Utton (1974) approached the question indirectly by comparing the profitability level of what he called 'merger-intensive' firms with that of similar 'non-merger-intensive' firms, and found that the latter performed better.[52] Thus in spite of the well-known limitations of such studies,[53] the results of this and other recent research strengthen the view that the take-over mechanism may well be doubly inefficient: first, it cannot be relied upon to force firms to maximise (or even improve) profitability, as it selects large rather than just profitable companies for survival, and secondly, it may well reduce post-amalgamation profitability.[54]

If one is to judge the efficiency of actual take-overs themselves from a *social* point of view and at the *macroeconomic* level, it is also necessary to consider the effects of increasing industrial concentration and of oligopolistic competition among multinational companies (discussed in section 1), as well as of other changes in the productive structure of industry (e.g. size distribution of plants, investment potential, etc.) which mergers may have brought about.[55] These important questions, which require careful research, must lie outside the scope of the present paper. There is, in addition, a further potentially important effect of the take-over phenomenon at the

[52] During 1961–5 the 'merger-intensive' group had profitability of 13.6% as compared with 15.4% for the control group; the figures for 1966–70 were 11% and 14.2% respectively. The sample consisted of 39 firms in each group.

[53] For example, it could be argued that the time periods which have been used in such studies have been insufficiently long to capture the full effect of economies of scale, etc., in merged companies. However, irrespective of the length of the time period selected, most studies, both in the United Kingdom and the United States have reached similar conclusions (see further Utton, 1974).

[54] Private profitability cannot of course be taken as an indicator of technical efficiency (in the sense of cost economies) at the microeconomic level, except under perfect competition. However, since in the real world of imperfect competition, merged firms are unlikely to charge lower prices than before (particularly in the case of horizontal mergers), it must be presumed, *ceteris paribus*, that unless there has been an increase in private profitability, there has probably been little improvement in the technical efficiency of the merged firms, although improved profitability is by no means a *sufficient* condition for improved technical efficiency. In other words, if there is no improvement in profitability, there is a presumption that there has been no increase in the efficiency of resource utilisation, even at the microeconomic level. On the other hand, in the case of conglomerate mergers, it could legitimately be argued that since mergers then lead to product diversification, even if profitability on combined assets does not increase, profit fluctuations will probably be reduced. (For a discussion of the empirical relationship between profitability, profit fluctuations, growth and size, see Singh & Whittington (1968) and (1975), and Whittington (1971).)

[55] All this of course required some agreed prior specification of the social criteria for assessment.

macroeconomic level which also requires careful scrutiny, particularly in a slow-growing economy like the United Kingdom. This arises because firms normally need to be of a minimum absolute size in order to invest abroad. So the merger movement could have created many firms of a sufficient size, that, rather than invest in the United Kingdom, they preferred—and were *able*—to invest abroad (say in the EEC), where they could obtain a higher rate of return. In other words, by investing abroad, such firms could free themselves from the shackles of a slow-growing economy, thus acting perversely from the social point of view in their home country.[56] If this has been a consequence of the recent U.K. merger movement, then the last Labour Government's policy of benign indifference toward the take-over market and of positive promotion of large-scale mergers (supposedly to meet international competition) may have produced results opposite to those intended.

7 Summary and Conclusion

Take-overs play a key role in the economic dynamics of advanced capitalist countries, where, during the last two decades, their incidence has risen substantially, particularly since 1960. A study of the take-over selection process during the later 1960s' take-over boom in the United Kingdom showed that although the characteristics of the group of taken-over firms differed substantially from those of the group of *acquiring* firms, there was a large amount of overlap between taken-over and *surviving* firms: indeed if profitability alone had been used to split the firms into these two latter groups, 46% would have been misclassified, as against 50% on random allocation; if all relevant characteristics are combined, the probability of misclassification is only reduced to 43%. As the corresponding probability for 1955–60 was 32%, there was clearly a very marked increase in the overlap between the characteristics of the two groups during the take-over boom. More disaggregated analyses for the later 1960s suggested that take-over discipline was in general rather weak, especially for large firms (and more so than it was during the 1950s): indeed, the take-over threat may well encourage comparatively unprofitable larger firms to increase their relative size still further rather than to improve their profitability.

The above conclusion is also supported by evidence presented in other post-war United Kingdom studies; yet, during the last two decades, important changes occurred in underlying economic conditions, in the incidence of take-overs, and in the precise character of the selection process. Altogether, a review of the United Kingdom evidence for this period shows that, in so far as the neoclassical postulate of profit maximisation relies on the doctrine of economic natural

---

[56] On the impact of foreign investment on the home economy, see Reddaway (1968).

selection in the capital market (via the take-over mechanism), the empirical base for it is very weak.

As for the actual effect of take-overs on improving profitability of assets of amalgamating firms, the evidence for the United Kingdom for the period 1955–70, and for the United States over 50 years, both suggest that the take-over mechanism is *at best* neutral in this respect. It was argued that in the real world of imperfect capital and product markets, far from being efficient (from either the private or the social point of view), the take-over mechanism might actually be perverse in a variety of ways which raise important issues of public policy for those governments in advanced industrial countries which have been encouraging mergers on the ground that this would improve organisation of resources. Given this policy goal, the results from this study suggest that such governments would find it advisable to scrutinise take-overs by large firms very much more carefully.

References

Aaronovitch, S. and Sawyer, M. C. (1974). 'Mergers, Growth and Concentration.' *Big Business: Concentration and Mergers in the U.K.* Macmillan.

Alchian, A. A. and Kessel, R. A. (1962), 'Competition, Monopoly, and the Pursuit of Pecuniary Gain.' In *Aspects of Labor Economics*. Princeton.

Department of Trade and Industry (1970). *A Survey of Mergers 1958–1968.* London: H.M.S.O.

Federal Trade Commission (1969). *Economic Report on Corporate Mergers.* Washington, D.C.

Friedman, M. (1953). *Essays in Positive Economics.* Chicago.

Galbraith, J. K. (1967). 'A Review of a Review.' *The Public Interest*, Fall.

Gort, M. and Hogarty, T. F. (1970). 'New Evidence on Mergers.' *Journal of Law and Economics*, April.

Hahn, F. H. (1973). 'The Winter of our Discontent.' *Economica*, August.

Hart, P. E. and Prais, S. J. (1956). 'The Analysis of Business Concentration: A Statistical Approach.' *Journal of the Royal Statistical Society*, series A (General), vol. 119, part 2.

Hindley, B. (1972). 'Recent Theory and Evidence on Corporate Mergers.' In *Market Structure and Corporate Behaviour* (ed. K. Cowling). London, Gray-Mills.

Hogarty, T. F. (1970). 'Profits from Merger: the Evidence of 50 Years.' *St John's Law Review.*

Hughes, A. (1973). 'Concentration and Merger Activity in the Quoted Company Sector of U.K. Manufacturing Industry 1954–69.' Mimeo, N.E.D.C.

Hymer, S. and Rowthorn, R. (1970). 'Multinational Corporations and International Oligopoly: the non-American Challenge.' *Yale University, Economic Growth Center Paper*, no. 149.

Johnson, H. G. (1968). 'The Economic Approach to Social Questions.' *Economica*, February.

Kuehn, D. (1975). *Takeovers and the Theory of the Firm.* Macmillan.

Lynch, H. H. (1971). *Financial Performance of Conglomerates.* Harvard.

Ma, R. (1960). 'Births and Deaths in the Quoted Public Company Sector in the United Kingdom 1949–1953' *Yorkshire Bulletin of Economic and Social Research*, November.

Marris, R. L. (1968), 'Review of J. K. Galbraith: The New Industrial State.' *American Economic Review.*

Meade, J. E. (1968). 'Is "The New Industrial State" Inevitable? *Economic Journal*, June.
Newbould, G. D. (1970). *Management and Merger Activity*. Liverpool.
Parry, T. G. (1973). 'The International Firm and National Economic Policy.' *Economic Journal*, December.
Prais, S. J. (1972). 'Review of A. Singh: Takeovers.' *Economic Journal*.
Reddaway, W. B. *et al.* (1968). *Effects of U.K. Direct Investment Overseas— Final Report*. Cambridge.
Ryden, B. (1972). *Mergers in Swedish Industry*. Stockholm.
Singh, A. (1971). *Takeovers: their Relevance to the Stock Market and the Theory of the Firm*. Cambridge.
—— (1975). 'Monopoly Capital Revisited: the Role of Centralization by Merger'. *mimeo*. Cambridge.
—— and Whittington, G. (1968). *Growth, Profitability and Valuation*. Cambridge.
—— (1975). 'The Size and Growth of Firms. *Review of Economic Studies*, January.
Utton, M. A. (1974). 'On Measuring the Effects of Industrial Mergers.' *Scottish Journal of Political Economy*. February.
Whittington, G. (1971). *Prediction of Profitability and Other Studies in Company Finance*. Cambridge.
—— (1972). 'Changes in the Top 100 Quoted Manufacturing Companies in the United Kingdom, 1948–68. *Journal of Industrial Economics*, November.
Williamson, O. E. (1964). *The Economics of Discretionary Behaviour: Managerial Objectives in the Theory of the Firm*. Prentice Hall.
Winter, S. G. Jr. (1964). 'Economic "Natural Selection" and the Theory of the Firm.' *Yale Economic Essays*, Spring.
—— (1971). 'Satisficing, Selection and the Innovating Remnant.' *Quarterly Journal of Economics*, May.

Appendix

Definitions of Variables

Size: indicated by the book value of 'net assets'. 'Net assets' are defined as total fixed assets, plus current assets net of current liabilities, where assets, as is normal in company accounts, are valued at historic cost net of depreciation.

Profitability: indicated by pre-tax rate of return on net assets and expressed as a percentage. In line with the definition of net assets, pre-tax profits include trading profits and investment and other income of the firm; they are net of depreciation and of charges for current liabilities (e.g. bank interest).

Change in profitability: indicated by the algebraic difference in the pretax rate of return on net assets over the last one/two years. Thus one-year change in profitability in year t is equal to profitability in year t minus profitability in year $t-1$; similarly two-year change in profitability in year t is equal to profitability in year t minus profitability in year $t-2$.

Growth: measured by the growth of 'net assets' over the last three years and expressed as an index, with $t-3 = 100$.

Liquidity: expresses net current assets as a percentage of the firm's total net assets, where net current assets are defined as cash, marketable securities and tax reserve certificates, *less* bank over-drafts and loans, dividend and interest liabilities, and current tax liabilities.

Gearing: expresses long-term liabilities plus preference capital, as a percentage of total capital and reserves, plus long-term liabilities.

Retention ratio: shows the percentage of the available disposable income (i.e.

earnings after tax and after fixed interest and dividend obligations have been met) retained within the firm.

Valuation ratio: expresses stock-market valuation of a firm's ordinary shares as a ratio of the book value of assets due to ordinary shareholders.

PART IV

SOCIAL AND PRIVATE ALLOCATION

Introduction to Part IV

A major criticism of the market system of allocation is that it only takes into account the private calculus of costs and benefits. Supply simply reflects the cost of any activity to the firm engaged upon it. Demand reflects the utility and satisfaction only to the individual consuming the product. The equilibrium price arrived at in the market thus measures the private costs and benefits to those involved in the transaction.

But are these the only costs and benefits? The pollution created by a factory is undoubtedly a cost of its activities to those living nearby. The benefits of a railway system may accrue not only to those who use it but also those using the less congested adjacent road. From the wider social viewpoint these costs and benefits should be taken into account. The resulting resource allocation might be significantly different from that created by the private market calculus.

Such an approach, however, faces a number of difficulties, not least that of influencing firms in a private property, profit-orientated market economy to allow for social costs and benefits. However, as was indicated in the introduction to Part I, a large proportion of total resource allocation is now under public ownership or control. The principle of social cost–benefit appraisal, it is argued, could at least be applied to activities in the public sector.

In a way social cost–benefit analysis is seen as a useful half-way house between the narrowness of an unreformed market approach and the subjectivity, lack of rigour, and non-evaluation of much public sector allocation. The market critic can point to an alternative, more socially conscientious yet still rational method of allocating resources. The public sector critic can advocate a market analogue for deciding the level of public sector activities.

The intellectual roots of the cost–benefit approach can be traced back to Dupuit, a nineteenth-century French engineer, and to Pigou, a later English economist. Whilst practical applications began to be developed in the 1930s, it was not until the 1960s that the technique attracted any substantial interest. Mishan's paper, which was published in 1971, starts with the statement that 'cost–benefit analyses are in high fashion'. Mishan explains in a clear and non-technical way the principles of cost–benefit analysis and some of the theoretical and practical problems that have to be overcome. He points out, for example, that the technique is not as objective or scientific as the uninitiated might think. It is usually impossible to cover *all* costs and benefits, or to measure them accurately. Thus the outcome of any study may vary, depending on what is included and how it is measured. Mishan also draws attention in his concluding section to the fact that cost–benefit analyses generally ignore equity calculations, the question of *who* is incurring the costs and receiving the benefits.

The next three papers cover a number of practical cost–benefit studies largely in the area of transport. The first, by Foster, evaluates the benefits of keeping open two loss-making suburban train services by estimating the costs or disbenefits that would accrue if the lines were closed. Foster claims that the study is 'one of the first which seeks to justify the retention of rail passenger services because of road congestion in urban areas'. The study is a good example of the manner in which a practical study deals with the problem mentioned by Mishan of what to include and how to measure it.

The costs of closure included were extra road congestion to existing road users, increased travelling time for existing road travellers, increased accident costs, and extra substitute bus and car journeys. The benefits were measured in terms of the costs of the railway services avoided by closure of the two lines. The calculations were undertaken for different assumptions about the service based on forecasts of likely future demand but all show a positive net benefit at a discount rate of 10 per cent. As Foster points out in his preface to the study (not included here), the people of the area 'would be worse off, if the services were not retained even in their present form. Therefore there is a case for using rate revenue to help meet the cost of the services over and above receipts from passengers and to provide some finance for improvements.' (Those working through the detailed figures will notice an error in the calculation of the increased travelling time for existing rail users where for 1973 education trips have been subtracted from rather than added to work trips. The effect on the over-all calculation is negligible.)

Whilst Foster's study provides an example of an actual cost–benefit analysis, the paper by Rees evaluates two studies carried out by others. In further contrast, while Foster's subject is the withdrawal of a service, Rees is concerned with new investments. The major part of Rees's paper is concerned with an appraisal of a cost-benefit analysis of the Channel Tunnel. Here too the problems of deciding what to include and how to measure it are highlighted. Rees, however, concerns himself with a number of other issues raised by Mishan such as price assumptions, investment criteria, and sensitivity analysis.

The price assumptions are an important component of the demand forecasts for the new tunnel. Rees argues that the charges assumed are arbitrary and do not sufficiently take into account economic principles for efficient resource allocation in the public sector. He deals with the criticism that the economists' marginal cost approach is naïve and concludes that following this approach more closely would 'increase the benefits to users, and reduce further the capital and operating costs of the alternative services, thus enhancing the attractiveness of the tunnel project'.

On investment appraisal Rees criticizes the assumptions under-lying the use of the Treasury's test discount rate approach. His strongest criticisms, however, are reserved for the sensitivity analysis used by the study to deal with uncertainty. He points out that the forecast of net present value for the project is highly sensitive to assumptions about the growth rate, the latter of course affecting traffic demand. He estimates that a reduction in assumed GNP growth from 2.8 per cent per annum to 2.0 per cent per annum transforms a positive net value of £147.9 million into a negative one of £16.9 million. Yet the study itself only showed the effect of a change from a 3.5 per cent per annum growth rate to a 2.8 per cent per annum rate. Thus he concludes that the sensitivity analysis is 'seriously inadequate for the purpose of presenting to the decision taker the information on which to base an evaluation of the riskiness of the project . . . . The Channel tunnel sensitivity analysis typifies the kind of incomplete and selective information about risk which often accompanies major investment projects. It is inconceiv-able that a sensible evaluation of a risky decision could be made on this basis.'

The Kirk & Sloyan paper takes us back to an actual cost–benefit study, this time of the new Covent Garden Market. It differs from the others in that it measures the costs and benefits of an investment that has already taken place rather than one that is proposed. This makes measurement easier although assumptions still have to be made. The study relates the net annual benefits estimated to arise from the move to the new market against its capital cost. The authors claim a neat 16 per cent rate of return, based on an annual net benefit of £5.7 million against a capital cost of £36.2 million.

Like all cost–benefit studies this one also is not immune from methodological criticisms. Perhaps the most important are the method of investment appraisal and the lack of sensitivity analysis. No time stream of benefits is used to relate net benefits over time to the original capital figure. Even if it is assumed that the benefits calculated for one year will be repeated in future years, the net present value of these future benefits will reduce each year. The major part of the net benefit of £5.7 million is taken up by the assumed net annual value of the property released at the old market (£3 million) and the reduction in wastage and pilferage (£1.4 million). Whilst the paper argues that the property valuation is an under-estimate, the effects of alternative assumptions on the rate of return would have been illuminating.

As can be seen from the studies, cost-benefit analysis is used to deal with investment or disinvestment decisions. But what of activities which are continuing and which are planned to continue? How can social cost–benefit considerations be inserted into an evaluation of these activities? The pollution of the environment is a good example of a continuing social cost resulting from a firm's production activity. Baumol & Oates in the reading selected here discuss the pros and cons of using the price system rather than direct controls to limit polluting activity.

Taxation and subsidy have traditionally been advocated by economists as the appropriate instruments for dealing with externalities. As the authors put it, 'by offering virtue its just (financial) reward we change the rules of the game to induce industry (and invididual consumers) to alter their behavior to promote an environmental objective.' Yet both polluters and environmentalists have rejected the tax-and-pricing approach in favour of direct legislative controls. Whilst the attitude of polluters might be dismissed as simply a reflection of the effectiveness of taxation as a control, the environmentalists' view is more difficult to understand.

Baumol & Oates argue that on a number of criteria such as dependability, permanence, equity, and economy the taxation approach is likely to prove more effective. They acknowledge that this approach poses a number of practical difficulties such as a judgement on the correct level of taxes or charges to achieve a given environmental target, but they argue that these problems can be overcome. Moreover, the practical difficulties are not in their view an adequate explanation of the reluctance of decision-makers to use a tax approach. The direct control approach also presents practical difficulties. In the end the explanation they hint at is the not very satisfactory one of the economic illiteracy of those involved.

Pearce, Edwards, & Harris in their study concentrate on the equity aspects of environmental control. In particular they set out to test the validity of the view perhaps associated most with Beckerman (1974) that environmental concern is an élitist pre-occupation, being, as they put it, 'a pastime of the more wealthy members of society rather than a concern of the lower paid.' If the costs of environmental control are spread equally in a society but the benefits accrue disproportionately to the higher income groups then that policy can be classed as inequitable. Even if costs were distributed proportionately to income but benefits disproportionately to income, the policy would have inequitable distributional effects.

The income elasticity of demand for environmental quality is therefore an important variable, and Pearce and his colleagues survey the methodologies and results of applied work in this area. They point out the problems of the hedonic technique which has traditionally been used and conclude that it 'cannot estimate valuations of the environment, and *certainly* cannot be used to determine the social incidence of environmental benefits'.

Nor are they happy about alternative methods used in applied work. They focus particularly on studies undertaken in the USA to study the social incidence of the costs and benefits of the 1970 Clean Air Act. Once again methodological difficulties inhibit any generalized conclusion, and in their view existing studies cannot be used to support the argument that the net benefits of environmental programmes favour the rich.

The authors are more optimistic about the social survey approach in which respondents are asked to value the benefit to them in terms of what they would be willing to pay for a specified element of pollution control such as noise abatement. This might at least give some notion of income elasticity of demand for the benefit of environmental control to be measured against an assessment of the income distribution of its costs. The overwhelming feeling from reading the study of Pearce *et al* is that empirical work to date has not really taken us very far and that the discussion of the social incidence of environmental control is still in the realms of conjecture.

The final reading in this section and in the book appeared in the first edition. It is retained because it seems appropriate at the end of a book of readings which are based on the traditional assumptions of microeconomics to consider some evidence which seems to contradict the usual predictions of economic behaviour. Douty's concern is the resource-allocation effects of a sudden change in the external environment. He takes as his example natural or other externally originated disasters where the evidence of a number of studies is that firms do not seek to maximize their profits or consumers their individual utilities. Firms do not set market-clearing prices and consumers do not use their purchasing power to increase their own consumption at the expense of others. Charitable rather than selfish behaviour seems to be the norm in such situations.

Douty applies the tools of conventional analysis to explain this behaviour. Thus firms may be acting in their own long-run profit-maximization interests in not seeking to exploit short-term shortages through price increases. Memories are long and, when normality returns, anti-social behaviour may be remembered. From the consumer's point of view it is argued that the individual's utility function includes a charitable element which is 'disaster elastic'. Thus it may be consistent for an individual to maximize his individual utility by increasing his charitable acts during disasters. The paper is a fascinating example of how neoclassical thought can provide insights into economic behaviour even if there is more than a slight suspicion of stretching definitions and concepts to make them compatible with the evidence.

Reference

W. Beckerman (1974), *In Defence of Economic Growth* (London: Cape).

14

The A B C of Cost-Benefit

by E. J. Mishan

Cost-benefit analyses are in high fashion. Scarcely a week goes by without an authoritative voice asserting that, in connection with some project or other, a thorough cost-benefit study is needed. No matter how heated a controversy, a government spokesman can still the protests of the critics and be assured of a respectful silence simply by announcing that a cost-benefit analysis is in progress. The popular belief is that this novel technique provides a 'scientific' assessment of the social value of a project or at least an 'objective' assessment. True, if every benefit and every cost associated with a proposed project or investment is properly evaluated and brought into the calculus in a systematic way, the resulting sum—whether an excess of benefits over cost or the other way round—can hardly be challenged. Yet such a statement is not much more than a tautology. The fact is that evaluating 'properly' all relevant economic data is a guiding ideal, not a current practice. For, although the procedure used in cost-benefit analysis follows certain conventions, the outcome may vary according to the economist in charge of the study, because of differences in judgement with respect both to *what* is to be included and *how* it is to be evaluated. With the passage of time, one can hope that such differences of judgement will narrow but, in the meantime, and in the absence of a consensus, the individual judgement of whoever is in charge is an important factor in the outcome.

One question that a cost-benefit study sets out to answer is whether or not a particular investment project, say project A, should be started. More generally, the question is whether a number of projects, A, B, C, D, etc. should be introduced and, if the investible funds are limited, which one, or which two or more, should be selected. Another question to which cost-benefit analysis addresses itself is that of determining the level at which a plant should operate, or the combination of outputs it should produce. I follow custom, however, in confining my attention largely to the former questions concerning the choice of investment projects.

Costs and Benefits

In order to appreciate some of the issues raised in the technique of

From *Lloyds Bank Review*, July 1971, pp. 12-25. Reprinted by permission of the editor of the journal and Lloyds Bank Ltd.

cost–benefit analysis, we can ask the question: Why cost–benefit analysis? Why not plain honest-to-goodness profit and loss accounting? The simple answer is that what counts as a benefit or a loss to one part of the economy—to one or more persons or groups—does not necessarily count as a benefit or loss to the economy as a whole. And in cost–benefit analysis we are concerned with the economy as a whole; with the welfare of a defined society, and not any smaller part of it. A private enterprise, or even a public enterprise, comprises only a part of the economy, often a very small part. More important, whatever the means it employs in pursuing its objectives, the private enterprise, at least, is guided by ordinary commercial criteria that require revenues to exceed costs. The fact that its activities are guided by the profit motive, however, is not to deny that a large number of people other than its shareholders benefit from it. It confers benefits on its employees, on consumers and—through the taxes it pays—on the general public. Yet, the benefits enjoyed by these others continue to exist only so long as they coincide with profits to the enterprise. Without a public subsidy the enterprise will not survive if it continues to make losses. If it is to survive as a private concern and to expand, it must, then, over a period of time, produce large enough either to attract investors or to finance its own expansion.

There is, of course, the metaphor of the invisible hand; the *deus ex machina* discovered by Adam Smith which directs the forces of private greed so as ultimately to confer benefits on society. And one can, indeed, lay down simple and sufficient conditions under which the uncompromising pursuit of profit acts always to serve the public interest. These conditions can be boiled down to two: that all effects relevant to the welfare of individuals be priced through the market, and that perfect competition prevail in all economic activities. Once we depart from this ideal economic setting, however, the set of outputs and prices to which the economy tends may not serve the public so well as some other set of outputs and prices. In addition to this possible misallocation of resources among the goods being produced, it is possible also that certain goods which can be economically justified do not get produced at all, whilst others which cannot be economically justified continue to be produced. Again, certain goods having beneficial, though unpriced, 'spill-over effects' qualify for production on economic grounds, notwithstanding which they cannot be produced at a profit. The reverse is also true, and more significant: profitable commercial activities sometimes produce noxious spill-over effects to such an extent that on a more comprehensive pricing scheme they would be unable to continue.

The economist engaged in the cost–benefit appraisal of a project is not, in essence, then, asking a different sort of question from the accountant of a private firm. Rather, the same sort of question is asked about a wider group, society as a whole, and is asked more searchingly. Instead of asking whether the owners of an enterprise will be made better off by the firm's engaging in one activity rather than another, the economist asks whether *society* as a whole will be made better off by undertaking this project rather than not undertaking it, or by undertaking, instead, any of a number of other projects.

Broadly speaking, for the more precise concept of revenue to the private firm, the economist substitutes the less precise, yet meaningful, concept of *social benefit*. For the costs of the private firm, the economist will substitute the concept of *opportunity cost*—or the social value forgone when resources are moved away from other economic activities and into the construction and running of the project in question. For the profit of the firm, the economist will substitute the concept of *excess social benefit over cost*, or some related concept used in an investment criterion.

However, it cannot be stressed too strongly that the result even of an ideally conducted cost–benefit analysis does not of itself constitute a prescription for society. Since it simulates the effects of an ideal price system, an ideal cost–benefit analysis is subject also to its limitations. This means that any adopted criterion of a cost–benefit analysis requiring, as all such criteria do, that benefits exceed cost, can be vindicated only by a social judgement that an economic arrangement which *can* make everyone better off is an improvement. Such a judgement does *not* require that everyone actually be made better off, or even that nobody be made worse off. The likelihood—which, in practice, is a virtual certainty—that some people, occasionally most people, will be made worse off by introducing the investment project in question is tacitly acknowledged. A project that is adjudged feasible by reference to a cost–benefit analysis is, therefore, quite consistent with an economic arrangement which makes the rich richer and the poor poorer. It is consistent also with manifest inequity. For an enterprise that is an attractive proposition by the lights of a cost–benefit calculation may be one that offers increased profits and pleasures to one group, in the pursuit of which substantial injury may be suffered by other groups.

In order, then, for a mooted enterprise to be socially approved, it is not enough simply to show that the outcome of an ideal cost–benefit analysis is positive. It must also be shown that the resulting distributional changes are not regressive, and that no gross inequities are perpetrated.

Sophisticated cost–benefit analysis clearly requires a high order of skill in the application of quantitative techniques. More important still, it requires thorough familiarity with the economics of resource allocation. For it is more important to be measuring the right thing in a crude sort of way than to be measuring the wrong thing with impressive refinement. This dictum will be more readily appreciated after we have touched upon some of the problems that arise in the application of cost–benefit methods, problems which fall conveniently into three categories. In the largest group are the problems of designating the relevant magnitudes and evaluating them. Having evaluated the benefits and costs over time there is, secondly, the problem of choosing an investment criterion to enable us to select and rank alternative investment projects. There is, however, always some uncertainty about the expected values of future benefits and costs. This leads to the third problem: that of making allowance for uncertainty.

What and How to Measure?

We can divide this group into four sub-groups, beginning, first, with the question of relevance.

Relevance

The treatment of direct taxation offers a simple instance. Whether a domestic enterprise is private or public, the net benefit in any year is taken to be equal *not* to net profit or net benefit, less tax, but to net social profit or benefit *before* tax. For the tax payments are simply that portion of the net benefit that is transferred, through the government machine, to the rest of the community. If, however, the enterprise is established in a foreign country the taxes paid to the foreign government *do* represent a transfer of net benefits to foreigners. Consequently, such taxes have to be deducted from the net profits or net benefits available to the home country. Moreover, if new investments in a particular foreign country have the incidental effect of lowering the rate of return there on previous investments from the home country, the losses suffered on all these older investments have to be deducted from the net profit or net benefit on the prospective new investments.

Other instances will illuminate the nature of this kind of problem. Consider investment in a railway. The rise in the rents of sites near the railway station might, on first thoughts, be regarded as one of the benefits. But the rise in such rents is nothing more than the capitalized value of the annual worth of the extra convenience provided by sites that are close to the new railway station. If the cost–benefit analysis has calculated future benefits year by year, as it ought, this increase in annual worth has already been included. Adding the rise in capital values would, therefore, amount to counting the same benefit twice, once as an annual flow and then, again, as the capital value of that flow.

Again, suppose an increase in the retail sales of a small town, the result of the movement of staff associated with the establishment of a new airport in the vicinity. The increase in profits cannot be counted as benefits of the new airport. Most, or all of it, is simply a transfer of purchasing power from one part of the country to another; in so far as sales and profits rise in the new town they fall off in other parts of the country.

Shadow or Accounting Prices

In the absence of spill-over effects (which I discuss presently) and excise taxes, a highly competitive full-employment economy would, it is believed, provide an ideal background to a cost–benefit analysis, inasmuch as the 'true', or *opportunity*, cost of all productive services would be equal to their market prices. This is valid, however, only if the owner of such services, a skilled workman, say, is indifferent as between one occupation and another. But such an assumption is too restrictive. In general, therefore, the economist will conceive of the true cost of a man's labour as equal to the value it produces in the occupation from which it is to be transferred *plus* any additional sum above his existing wage that is required to induce a worker to transfer his labour into the new project.[1] This direct method of calculation provides a guiding rule for estimating the 'shadow prices' of all productive services needed in any investment project.

It follows, therefore, that it is wrong to value productive services at their *market* prices, if they are transferred from the production of goods subject to excise taxes. If, say, tax added 50 per cent to the price of a competitively produced good, the value associated with the labour of a worker to be withdrawn from the production of this good would be 50 per cent more than his wage-rate there—at least, if we assume the labourer to be indifferent as between his present occupation and that of the investment project in question. If he is not indifferent, but prefers his existing occupation, then the premium necessary to induce him to move into the new enterprise has (as indicated above) to be added.

Again, if a man is unemployed, his labour is not to be valued at his unemployment pay, say £10 a week, since this is not the value of his current work, but simply a transfer payment to him from the rest of the community.[2] It may be that his apparent contribution to national income is zero. However, he himself may place some value on his 'non-market activities' or, if entirely idle, he may enjoy his idleness to the extent that some minimum sum, say £12 a week, has to be paid to induce him to accept work in a new enterprise. The true cost to the economy of his work in the enterprise is this minimum sum of £12 less the £10 transfer payment, or £2. For, in agreeing to work for £12, he no longer receives his unemployment pay of £10, which now reverts to the rest of the community. Since the cost to the community of engaging his labour is only £2 a week, there is a gain if his weekly labour adds a value in excess of £2.

In general, however, new investment in one sector of the economy has repercussions in all sectors. The total numbers brought into

---

[1] If, instead, he prefers to work in the *new* project, we have to subtract from his value in the old occupation a sum equal to the difference between his old wage and the minimum wage he would accept to work in the new project.

[2] In a popular sense, he may have 'earned' his unemployment insurance money by paying regularly his unemployment insurance premiums. But such insurance transactions are wholly 'transfer payments' within the economy.

employment as a result of this initial investment, and their costs to the economy, can be estimated, provided that the average unemployment rate for each sector and/or region is available. For there is a known relationship between the unemployment rate in a sector, and/or area, and the probability that any newly employed labour there will come from the unemployment pool. (In the United States, for example, this probability approaches 100 per cent when the percentage unemployment in a sector or area is about 25 per cent.) Investment projects which would not be economically feasible in conditions of virtually full employment may, of course, become so in conditions of low employment.

For a final example of shadow prices, consider the imports of goods by countries that are chronically short of foreign exchange. If the additional imports of some material, say copper, can be afforded *only* by relinquishing other imports to an equal value in terms of the scarce currency, the shadow price of these additional copper imports has to be taken as equal to the domestic value of the particular goods that are no longer imported. For this is the value that has to be forgone in order to obtain the additional copper. If, on the other hand, the additional copper imports are paid for by additional exports, their shadow price is the domestic value of the particular goods exported to raise the needed foreign currency.

Spill-over Effects

The pricing of 'intangibles' or 'spill-over effects' can be thought of as the limiting case of a shadow price. For the market prices of spill-over effects are generally zero. In the manufacture and use of certain goods, incidental by-products are generated such as smoke, pollution, noise and so on[3] which are not recorded by the market. However, those people who have to put up with these noxious effects are not compensated in any way. It is the task of the economist, therefore, to bring them, as Pigou would have said, 'into relation with the measuring rod of money'.

The principle used is the straightforward one of accepting the scale of values of the people directly concerned. The loss of any good—including such 'free' goods as quiet, clean air, pleasant scenery, etc.—is to be valued, therefore, at the minimum sum people would be willing to accept as just compensation for their loss. These spill-over costs, together with resource costs, have to be less than the value of the total benefits if an investment is to be accepted as economically feasible.

Although the principle is straightforward enough, difficulties are encountered in obtaining reliable approximations to the value of spill-over effects. In attempting to evaluate aircraft noise, for example, the Roskill Commission made use (among other information)

---

[3] Though spill-over effects can also be beneficial, their treatment is symmetric with that of adverse spill-over effects.

of replies to a questionnaire by a sample of those householders who would have to move if their neighbourhood were to be taken over for the third airport site. The key question was framed as follows:

Suppose that your house was wanted to form part of a large development scheme and the developer offered to buy it from you, what price would be just high enough to compensate you for leaving this house (flat) and moving to another area?

A number of weaknesses are apparent in the Commission's procedure.[4] First, although 8 per cent of the householders interviewed asserted that they would not move at any price, the compensatory sum attributed to them was an arbitrary £5,000. One suspects that a good interviewer might well have elicited a finite sum from them, though one probably well in excess of £5,000. If, however, it were true only of a single case that nothing money could buy would suffice to compensate for the losses suffered in moving from the neighbourhood, then, strictly speaking, no cost–benefit analysis would admit a third London airport.

Secondly, no allowance was made for the disturbance suffered by people subjected to aerial disturbance below 35 NNI (NNI is an abbreviation for noise and number index and was developed as an index of aircraft annoyance by the Committee on the Problem of Noise). Symmetry of treatment would require that no benefits be entered for people whose enjoyment of an air journey fell below a particular point on some arbitrary index. No physical measure of pleasure is available, however, so that no matter how impulsive the decision, and no matter how marginal the benefit, each trip was valued at its full fare. Finally, the framing of the question gave the impression to householders that only a limited move was contemplated—a question of making land available for some new development. The disruption involved in parting from old friends, in changing jobs, in moving children to new schools, may not have occurred to them. What is more, even if the purpose of the questionnaire had been made perfectly explicit, the compensatory sum required by the family would vary with circumstances about which it could not hope to have accurate information. The sum would be smallest if as quiet a neighbourhood could be found only a short distance away. It would be larger if the number of such neighbourhoods within commuting distance of work and schooling were limited. And it would be largest if no comparable neighbourhoods could be found anywhere. Again, the compensatory sum would vary according to the spread and intensity of traffic noise expected elsewhere over the future, being lower for expectations of a gradual abatement than for the reverse, and more likely, expectations. If,

[4] For a highly critical appraisal of the Roskill Commission's Report, the reader is referred to my paper, 'What is Wrong with Roskill?', first published in the *Journal of Transport Economics and Policy* (Sept. 1970).

however, the spread of noise were expected to engulf the original neighbourhood in any case, then, with respect to the noise factor, it would not matter where the family moved, and the sum would be nil—notwithstanding which the family's welfare would decline over time, though not as a result alone of the establishment of a third London airport.

The Problem of Constraints

In any cost–benefit analysis there will be a number of political or institutional conditions, more or less restrictive, which the economist has to accept. The issues they raise can be illustrated by the unlikely example of a man lawfully installing a steam hammer in his back yard. In response to the outcry, the enterprising town council hires an economist to undertake a cost–benefit study to determine whether all the houses in the neighbourhood should be sound-proofed. The total costs of the sound-proofing of all the houses affected is reckoned at £85,000. But, since the benefits over the future of the sound-proofing are reckoned to exceed £100,000, the scheme is approved.

If the economist were able to move away from his terms of reference, however, he would propose a court order preventing the operation of the steam hammer. The loss by the would-be entrepreneur might be of the order of, say, £1,000 a year or a capital value of £15,000, but the savings to the rest of the community would be £85,000. Indeed, in the absence of the court order, the council should be willing to pay the £15,000 to bribe the man not to operate his steam hammer—provided the law is able to uphold such contracts. The trouble about bribing a potential offender where the law is permissive of noise and smoke pollution is that it lends itself inadvertently to blackmail.

Consider now a more topical example: a proposal to widen a road so as to allow for three lanes of traffic each way, instead of the existing two. As before, the economist, keeping strictly to his terms of reference, may come up with a positive figure for the benefit 'enjoyed'. Allowed more latitude, however, he might point out that the traffic is already so heavy on the two-lane highway that a sizeable net gain can be achieved by a system of tolls, or taxes, calculated to reduce the traffic to an 'optimal flow'. Once the traffic approaches this level, it may transpire that an efficient public transport service is profitable and, in these new circumstances, a cost–benefit calculation can no longer justify the road-widening scheme. Moreover, the economist might wish to point out that the improvement of an existing rail service would cost much less, and yield at least as much benefit, as the road-widening scheme.

Such alternatives, however, will not emerge if the economist has to work strictly within his terms of reference or if, for political reasons, the alternatives are to be regarded as 'impractical'. Indeed, it is not too often that the economist is asked to consider all alternatives relevant to a broad problem before choosing that which offers the greatest net benefit to the community. It is more common to enlist his expertise in order to reach a decision about a particular kind of investment. Yet no matter how uneconomic they are, if political or administrative constraints are expected to remain operative during the period of time covered by the cost–benefit calculation, the economist has no choice but to accept them as part of the data.

Criteria for Investment Projects

The benefits from an investment project by the government come to fruition over the future, and some of the costs may also be incurred over the future. In general, then, there is a distinct 'time-profile' of benefits and costs corresponding to each of the investment projects under consideration. Thus, the time-profile for one project may have large net benefits during, say, the first three years and small net benefits thereafter. For another project, the time-profile may be the reverse of this. Yet a third project may have more modest net benefits spread evenly over a longer period than the other two. For an unambiguous comparison of the value of such projects it is clearly necessary to reduce all these time profiles to a single figure.

Of the two usual methods used, the more popular is the discounted present value (DPV) method, which consists of discounting all future benefits and outlays to a present value by means of some appropriate rate of interest. If that rate of interest were, say, 10 per cent per annum, a certain benefit valued at £1,100 next year, or one valued at £1,210 in two years' time, would have a discounted value of £1,000. The alternative method is that of calculating the internal rate of return (IRR) of the stream of future benefits and costs. The resulting figure purports to be an average rate of growth of (the present value of) the sum invested. An IRR of 15 per cent calculated for a twelve-year investment stream indicates an average annual growth rate of 15 per cent per annum of the present value of the total outlay.

An investment criterion can base itself on either of these two methods. If the DPV method is adopted, it might be thought that any public project is economically advantageous if the DPV of its benefits exceeds that of its outlays. Alternatively if the IRR method is adopted it might be thought that any project having an IRR greater than the market rate of return should be undertaken. But it is not so simple as that. In fact, the investment criterion to be adopted depends on three related factors: on political and administrative constraint (on which I have touched earlier); on the uncertainty surrounding the size of expected future benefits and outlays (which I discuss in the following section); and on the alternative opportunities open to the investible funds which the government raises either by borrowing, by taxation or by a combination of the two.

If, say, it is doubled to raise £10 millions through taxes that fall wholly on current consumption, and to spend this sum among several public projects from a list of approved investment projects, provided it is 'economically justifiable', the task of the economist is straightforward. Suppose he elects to use a DPV criterion. If there is agreement that society as a whole regards the consumption of £105 worth of goods next year as equivalent to the consumption of £100 today, he can use 5 per cent as the appropriate discount rate. Any of the approved projects is then eligible for the short list if, using this 5 per cent rate, the DPV of its benefits exceeds that of its costs. Should it happen that the total cost of the number of public projects that are eligible on this criterion exceeds the £10 millions available, the economist simply ranks the projects in descending order and goes down the list until the total outlay required does not exceed £10 millions.

If, to take another example, it were decided instead to raise the whole of the £10 millions by borrowing (the effect being supposed to reduce private investment by £10 millions) the economist may not regard any public investment as justifiable unless it can earn at least as much as is being earned by private investment. An expected yield of, say, 12 per cent in private investment then justifies his choice of 12 per cent as the appropriate discount rate. Clearly, if only a part of the £10 millions is to be raised by reducing current consumption and the remainder by reducing current private investment, the criterion has to be adapted accordingly. Finally, if there is no constraint whatever placed on the use of the £10 millions then, *no matter how the sum is raised*, the economist is justified in using a discount rate of 12 per cent. For now all, or any part of, the £10 millions made available for public projects may be invested instead in the private sector at a 12 per cent yield.

In practice, DPV is the more popular of these two methods, for two reasons: first the use of IRR criteria occasionally produces a ranking of investment projects contrary to that produced by DPV criteria, and the logic of the DPV method appears unassailable. Secondly, a DPV criterion invariably produces a single benefit–cost ratio whereas, for some investment streams, there can apparently be more than one internal rate of return.

Uncertainty

In the evaluation of any project there is sure to be some guesswork about the size of future costs and future benefits, arising in the main from technological innovations, shifts in demand and political changes. The problem of how to reach decisions in situations where knowledge of the past affords little guidance for the future is one that continues to attract attention.

The more familiar methods of allowing for future uncertainty may be grouped into two categories: those operating through a choice of the rate of interest in a DPV criterion; and those operating through revisions of expected future prices.

The Rate of Interest

Since the risk of loss is not compensated by an equal chance of gain, one method is to add a percentage point or two on to a pure, or riskless, rate of interest. This was the method, for instance, that was used in evaluating the Channel tunnel project. The benefits were projected up to a 50-year period, and a 7 per cent rate of discount was adopted as being the conventional rate for long-term planning in France and Britain. There is, of course, the practical problem of discovering this riskless rate of interest, to allow for future uncertainty. Although the concept of a riskless rate of interest—one reflecting society's preference of present over future consumption—is clear, the difficulties of measuring it in an existing dynamic economy are formidable. In the event, the riskless rate of interest on long-term government bonds has been proposed as a tolerable proxy (riskless, that is, in respect of default only: obviously, government bonds may fall in value over time, either in money or real terms without any fear of default on the nominal interest payments). This bond rate, it is acknowledged, is likely to be much lower than the current rates of return on commercial investments. But, then, a private firm is more likely to default than a central government.

Whilst this is undoubtedly true, it may not always be relevant, which brings me to the second method of choosing the rate of interest in a DPV calculation: to adopt the rate of return in private industry as the appropriate rate of discount. As those favouring this method point out, any funds raised by the government for public projects can, in principle, at least, always be invested in private industry. Now, the riskier the type of private investment the higher, in general, is the actuarial rate of return—a result arising both from risk-aversion and tax disadvantages under the existing fiscal system. But, whatever the reasons for this higher actuarial return on risky private investment, they do not of themselves weaken the argument. If the placing of government funds in the riskier types of private investment can, in fact, realize over time these higher returns, then no public investment should be undertaken that yields rates of return below them. To the extent, however, that political constraints are imposed on the use of investible public funds, the appropriate rate of discount is below the private investment yield.[5]

Future prices

We can also allow for risk by estimating or guessing (in addition

[5] If, as is common, estimated future benefits and costs are calculated in terms of current prices, the market rate of return on private investment has to be deflated for the annual expected price rise. Expectations of a rise in prices of, say, 6 per cent per annum entail a reduction of a nominal yield of, say, 25 per cent per annum to a real yield of approximately 19 per cent per annum.

to the most likely future price, and quantity, of each input and output over the future) upper limits and lower limits. In this way three cost–benefit estimates are produced: a most likely, a most optimistic and a most pessimistic net benefit for each project. Although this is better than a single most likely estimate, it has the distinct disadvantage that the chance of the most likely cost–benefit occurring can turn out to be very small. One can go some way to remedy this by consulting with experts on the likelihood of each uncertain future price or quantity having different values. From such information a 'probability' table can be constructed.

This resulting 'probability' table cannot, of course, be any more accurate than the subjective estimates of the experts on which it is based. But it does bring out the full implications of these estimates, and enables us to say much more than before. In some hypothetical project, we should be able to say, for example, that there is a 90 per cent chance of the net benefit falling between £150,000 and £210,000; that there is only a 2½ per cent chance of the net benefit being zero or negative, and so on.

If public investment in the economy is large enough to be spread over a great many projects to be undertaken within a year, then it is not unreasonable to decide each project on the basis of a single most likely cost–benefit outcome, using as discount rate the highest average rate of return accruing to risky commercial investment. Such a procedure will tend to produce for public sector investments an average rate of return above that which the same total amount of investment would have obtained if, instead, it had been invested in the private investment sector of the economy.

If, on the other hand, only a few large public investments are undertaken from time to time, it would be advisable to be guided in any decision by the sort of subjective probability table briefly described above.

Conclusion

I conclude by summarizing the phases in a cost–benefit study in which judgements may differ. Following the order in which we have treated the subject they are to be found in the choice of which items are to be valued at market prices and which are to be valued at shadow prices; in the methods used to evaluate the shadow prices; in the range of 'intangibles' to be included in the study; in the methods used to evaluate these 'intangibles'; in the choice of an investment criterion; and in the devices used to make allowance for future uncertainty.

It must not, however, be supposed that all such sources of potential discrepancy are of equal importance, or that judgement in the above respects is evenly diffused among all economists. It is probably true to say that it is easier, at present, to secure agreement among economists on the first five of the above phases than on the last.

Moreover, for many projects, the differences remaining may have little effect on the final recommendation. Nevertheless, there can be occasions where, as between one economist (or one group of economists) and another, differences in the evaluation of large public projects are critical and arise largely from differences in skill and care.

It is well to bear in mind that, in the present stage of its development, cost–benefit analysis—and, for that matter, all systems analysis —is an imperfect calculus, as much an art as a science or, more precisely, as much a matter of judgement as a technique. In many a large project it is quite possible for an economist to be swayed by prevailing fashions or the public mood or by political biases, conscious or otherwise, in favour of or against the scheme—especially in the choice of prices to be attributed to spill-over effects and in the method used to allow for uncertainty. For this reason, the interests of society are better served by making public not merely the findings of a cost–benefit study, but also the methods employed and the sources of data. Thus, although there may be good reasons for dissatisfaction with the findings of the Roskill commission, it had the great merit of making its methods explicit.

It remains only to remind the reader that, even if repeated scrutiny by fastidious and disinterested economists confirms the positive findings of cost–benefit study, the question of equity remains to be debated by the public. But there is nothing in the literature of economics to support the current prejudice that considerations of equity should defer to those of allocation.

15

Social Cost-Benefit Study of the Two Suburban Surface Rail Passenger Services

by C. D. Foster

1 Nature of the Problem

Sevices selected for study

The Study team was asked to consider the social case for keeping open the commuter services on the lines between Manchester (Piccadilly) and (1) Hadfield/Glossop; (2) Marple/New Mills. Both lose money. Hadfield/Glossop lost £304,000 in 1972; Marple/New Mills lost £445,000 in the same year. If the only considerations were commercial, both services would have been discontinued several years ago.

Effect of 1968 Transport Act

Under the 1968 Transport Act, British Rail receive grants from the Department of the Environment to cover losses incurred on passenger services which are considered to be socially desirable. The size of the grant is at present determined by what is known as the Cooper Brothers' formula. The grant payable includes provision for depreciation and in some cases replacement of assets and for interest charges on the assets used in providing such services, plus the appropriate share of the joint costs of track, signalling, etc.

Role of SELNEC P.T.A.

Because the two lines are within the area of the South East Lancashire and North East Cheshire Passenger Transport Authority, the obligation to pay this grant now belongs to the P.T.A. The D.O.E., however, still make a substantial contribution.[1] Both must decide whether they are gaining enough value for money in keeping these services open. To cover any losses incurred in operating public transport (bus and rail) the P.T.A. can make a precept on the rates of the local authorities participating in the P.T.A. The question it must ask in each case is whether the ratepayers' interest is better served by precepting and keeping the services open, or by withdrawing the services and being able to reduce the rate call.

From 'Social Cost Benefit Study of Two Suburban Surface Rail Passenger Services' (British Rail, London, 1973). Reprinted by permission of the Press Officer, British Railways Board.

[1] In 1972 the D.O.E. paid   90%
In 1973 the D.O.E. will pay 80%
In 1974 the D.O.E. will pay 70%

The two services studied are only two among many such rail commuter services in the Greater Manchester area. Table 1 lists the rail services with considerable commuter traffic in the Manchester area which are in receipt of grant and shows (for 1972) the estimated passenger miles generated in the SELNEC P.T.A. area for each service as a rough indicator of their relative importance to the Manchester area.

Table 1

Grant Aided services in SELNEC P.T.A. area carrying commuter traffic to Central Manchester in a Summer week in 1972

	Services to Manchester	Passengers miles for the SELNEC P.T.A. section of the service (000's)
1	Blackpool–Preston–Bolton	408
2	Altrincham–Sale	380
3	Crewe–Stockport	358
4	Bury–Prestwich	308
5	Stafford–Macclesfield–Stockport	307
6	Buxton–Stockport	279
7	Southport–Wigan	278
8	Liverpool (L. St.)–Warrington (C)	267
9	New Mills–Marple	239
10	Bradford–Rochdale	211
11	Crewe–Styal	196
12	Blackburn–Bolton	194
13	Hadfield–Glossop	161
14	Chester–Northwich	122
15	Oldham–Failsworth	119
16	Huddersfield–Stalybridge	45
17	Liverpool–Wigan	20

From the table it can be seen that neither the Hadfield/Glossop nor the Marple/New Mills lines are among the most important unremunerative commuter services in the P.T.A. area. They were chosen for this analysis because they were judged to be 'marginal'—after consultation with the P.T.E.[2] it was felt there was a reasonable doubt whether the social value of retaining them was worth the cost to the ratepayer. This does not mean there was any intention to withdraw them; but that it was felt that the case for retaining them was not so overwhelming that there would have been no point in a study.

Social Cost/Benefit Studies

Several studies have been done to estimate the social worth of retaining railway passenger services that are financially unprofitable.

---

[2] Passenger Transport Executive which operates the public transport services for the Passenger Transport Authority.

What distinguishes this study is that it is one of the first which seeks to justify the retention of rail passenger services because of road congestion in urban areas. The essential case, if proven, must be that the traffic they divert from the roads reduces congestion by an amount sufficient to justify the rail subsidies required. Underlying this is the proposition that users of city roads pay less through taxation for using them than covers the real costs of that use.

Highway Congestion

Road users pay large sums in highway taxation and the most recent official opinion[3] is that in total, and on average, they probably pay more than enough to meet all the costs of building, maintaining and operating the road system. If this judgment needs modification, it is almost certainly because not enough weight was given to environmental costs; but this does not affect the point at issue here. Whatever may be true on average, road users in cities pay substantially less than the costs they occasion. The greater the congestion, the truer this is. Every motorist, added to the traffic flow on a congested road will slow down all the other traffic on the road. Their vehicle operating costs will rise. The slower the traffic the greater the fuel consumption, the more wear and tear on tyres, brakes, and clutch linings etc. All the traffic on the road will take more time to reach their destination. The extra cost or, as economists would call it, the marginal social cost, of an extra vehicle coming on to a road is quantifiable. It depends on the traffic speed and flow already on the road in question. The lower traffic speeds already are, the progressively greater the congestion—and, therefore, the higher the marginal social cost—caused by additional vehicles. Wherever there is congestion, the marginal social cost will be greater than the actual cost to the individual road user (often called the marginal road user) since the costs to him of using the road are his vehicle costs and his time. He does not have to take into account the costs he imposes on other road users—and on pedestrians.

Pricing Policy

On the other hand, if rail transport in cities is required to cover costs, it will then be over-priced relative to users of urban roads, since rail users will be required to cover all the real costs they give rise to, while road users will not. There may be peak over-crowding on well-used urban rail services but this does not normally slow down journeys appreciably, neither does it increase significantly the costs of railway operation per person carried. Rather, in general, the greater the density of traffic on a rail line, the lower the unit cost of carrying a passenger (though if the railways' capacity is stretched in the peak, adding to capacity may itself have a very high marginal cost to the railways). Therefore, if an urban rail service sets out to cover its costs without subsidy, the marginal social cost, so defined,

[3] *Road Track Costs*, Ministry of Transport, H.M.S.O. 1968.

will not normally exceed the fare paid by the passenger.

The effect of this difference in pricing policy is an inefficient distribution of traffic between road and rail. Less traffic travels by rail, especially in the peak, than is efficient. This will be truer where there is excess capacity on the railway even in the peak. In such circumstances shifting traffic from a congested road system to uncongested rail lines will lead to a more efficient use of the urban transport system. There will be a benefit to road users that remain on roads—through higher speeds and lower vehicle operating costs, which is a social benefit, not captured by the ordinary processes of the market (and there will be other benefits and costs to be discussed later in this section).

One way of getting prices right would be to raise the price of urban road use until both public and private road transport covered its real costs. Fuel duty cannot be used for this purpose. Although fuel consumption and, therefore, fuel duty paid rises per mile in congested areas, it rises less than the marginal social cost. If road users were to pay the real cost of using roads,some new method of pricing would have to be introduced which could be made to vary with the degree of congestion. Since 1962 there have been many discussions on the possibility of introducing road pricing.[4] To do this one would have to introduce car meters, special congested area licences or other devices to make it possible to charge road users in a way which varied with congestion. While the Transport and Road Research Laboratory has shown that such a system would be feasible technically as well as relatively cheap to install and operate, there are administrative problems which seem to make it unlikely that any city would adopt such a system for at least 10 years. Meanwhile, what is happening in Manchester, as in other cities, is that parking restrictions and charges plus traffic management are used to reduce peak traffic volumes and raise road speeds. But while better than nothing, it seems improbable that this will raise the price of road use to a level where it can be said that road users are meeting the real costs of road use.

If we accept that it is politically imprudent or undesirable to raise the cost of using roads to a level where marginal social costs are covered, one can attempt to get the correct relationship between road and rail by the opposite course of action, that is by keeping rail fares lower than they would be if the railways charged what the market would bear rather than raising road prices. This is the essence of the case for rail subsidies; and it is the main reason why the 1968 Transport Act made it possible for P.T.A's. to subsidise rail services within their areas.

---

[4] See for example *Road Pricing: the Economic and Technical Possibilities*, H.M.S.O., 1964; *The Better Use of Town Roads*, H.M.S.O., 1967; G. J. Roth, *Paying for Roads*, Penguin, 1967; and A. A. Walters, *The Economics of Road User Charges*, World Bank, 1968.

Value of Rail Services to the Community

The amount of congestion varies between roads and accordingly so does the effect of a subsidy on influencing passengers to give up using their cars for commuting. The effect also varies depending on many factors including the length of their journey, their out-of-pocket costs, and their incomes. If one were exceptionally thorough one might note that to get the best results in terms of reducing road congestion, the amount of fare subsidy would also vary from route to route and possibly person to person. But any such system would be impracticable.

The question asked in this study is how much extra road congest-tion there would be if these rail services were discontinued. As we have seen, an extra carload or busload of commuters in the peak will slow down all other road users by a measurable amount, depending on the levels of congestion on that road and the volume of ex-rail traffic that is assumed to divert to a particular road. Later in the report it will be explained what assumptions were made to determine the alternative routes ex-rail passengers would use, as well as the proportions of them that would use bus and those that would commute by car.

SELNEC Area Land Use Transportation Study (SALTS)

The needs of the greater Manchester area were analysed by the SALTS study, a large scale comprehensive transport and land use study of the area.[5] Many earlier studies of other cities focussed too much attention on road planning and neglected public transport. The Ministry of Transport, as it then was, helped design the SALTS study to correct this pro-highway bias. The alternative transport strategies designed and evaluated for the Greater Manchester area were genuine mixes of road and public transport proposals in varying proportions. In the event many of the public transport proposal schemes showed up very well—including several investments to improve rail services. Not only was this demonstration important for Greater Manchester but the study is an example of how it is possible to have a land use transport study which gives due weight to public transport.

Wherever possible the information and the assumptions used in this study are those of the SALTS study itself. As will be clear from the footnotes, the forecasts of population, employment, car-ownership and traffic generation are those of the SALTS study. The methods used to predict what rail passengers would do if the services were closed down, the assumptions about vehicle operating costs and the value of time are comparable with those used in the SALTS study to predict the effects of various new transport investments. Before too long there will be another breakthrough in the methodology of

[5] *SELNEC Area Land Use and Transportation Study, Report of the Technical Control Team*, March 1972.

transport planning and it will be comparatively easy for us to take any proposal for a new investment or for a rail closure, feed it into a computer and receive an analysis of its impact. Unfortunately, techniques are too time-consuming and expensive for this to be possible at present. Besides, the SALTS methodology did not get down to the level of detail where it could isolate and identify the effects of withdrawing or retaining these two services. Therefore, the study team had to engage in laborious calculations of their own.

Social Cost/Benefit Study of the Effect of Withdrawing the Manchester (Piccadilly)–Hadfield/Glossop and Marple/New Mills Suburban Railway Services

This cost/benefit study concentrates on estimating the social cost of increased road congestion from closure. This in itself was a major task, but there are other motives for retaining a rail passenger service. Like all cost/benefit analyses this does not pretend to have measured every relevant factor. The remainder must be left to the judgment of the reader.

What may be said, however, is that virtually all the other factors that could be judged relevant would strengthen the already strong case for retaining the service. They are:

(1) Reducing the volume of road traffic—or restraining its rate of increase—will mean that those adjacent to main roads will experience less noise than they otherwise would. While a reduction in rail traffic could diminish the noise experienced by those near the track—depending on how it affects train frequency —it is usually argued that this will be less noticed. Because these railways have existed for so long, there will have been a self-selection process by which households and other activities will have located there which are less sensitive to noise and pollution. Indeed, the former steam trains were much noisier and dirtier than the present multiple units.

(2) Because air pollution per passenger by rail is much less than by road, there will also be less air pollution than there would be otherwise. This environmental effect, like the last, may be small for these two lines, considered on their own. It would, of course, be less true for the Manchester rail system as a whole. The nuisance value of air pollution depends on particular climatic factors as well as on volume. In San Francisco the new rapid transit lines will only remove a few per cent of cars from the roads by attracting people to trains, but the climatic conditions are such that even this will reduce air pollution by a valuable amount. Nuisance from air pollution is less likely to be so affected in Greater Manchester because the climatic conditions are different. No one has estimated the effect on the citizen's exposure to pollution if there were a dramatic increase in cars on the roads. Pollution might increase substantially if everyone were to

consider large-scale rail closure or if the bus system were to collapse in the face of rapidly rising car use. It was found in the course of the study that the increases in car miles due to withdrawal of the two rail services were in 1973—10,854 car miles, rising to 23,289 car miles in 1984 per a.m. peak period.

(3) In principle, the effect of withdrawing rail passenger services may simply be to increase road congestion somewhat; or it may lead indirectly to increased or accelerated road-building. There are many reasons for thinking that all the environmental and other social costs of road-building are not taken into account when these projects are authorised. There are not only noise and air pollution but also vibration, visual intrusion and what is often called severance or the ability of a motorway or main road to divide a neighbourhood and so damage its efficiency and its sense of being a neighbourhood.

(4) Increased road traffic means greater difficulties and impediments to pedestrians.

(5) There is also the problem of those unable to use cars. They may be too old, too young, too sick or too disabled. They may also be too poor. If public transport is cut back, there will always be many who cannot use a car and who will be seriously disadvantaged. This is not a problem growing affluence will solve. As American experience shows there will always be a very large minority for whom a car is not an alternative. There may not be a case for keeping open a particular rail line if there may be an alternative bus route which could serve these social purposes as efficiently. But along the routes there are many without access to cars who would be substantially worse off if the rail service were ended even though they had an improved bus service.

While some of these unmeasured factors reinforced the case for retaining the services—to an unknown extent—it is difficult to see what valid argument could be advanced to suggest that by omission the social benefit of keeping the lines open had been overstated. The case that has been demonstrated is sufficient in the present state of knowledge, without being complete. It also sets out a method which could be used elsewhere to evaluate the case for retaining urban rail services. Broadly, the case is that the people of Manchester would be worse off if these rail services were discontinued. They would lose more from road congestion in aggregate than they would gain from saving the subsidy;[6] and that this would be true even if one were to imagine the people of Greater Manchester in their capacity as taxpayers meeting the D.O.E. contribution as well as that which they make directly as ratepayers.

[6] Because the subsidies are met by precept on the rates one cannot estimate what will be the distribution of the benefits and costs of closure. Some may lose, some gain. But overall the benefit to the Greater Manchester area from closure will be negative even if we were to suppose the area met the cost of the D.O.E. subsidy.

Table 2

General Information about Rail Services for a Typical Weekday in 1972

| | No. of trains to Manchester Piccadilly Station on Weekday | No. of trains to Manchester (P) Station in peak 07.05–09.01 incl. | No. of daily journeys to Manchester (P) on typical weekday | No. of daily journeys other than to Manchester (P) Station | Peak journey time to Manchester (P) Station by quickest route (Mins). | Typical peak journey time to Central Manchester by road | |
						Car (Mins) 1966	Bus (Mins) 1969
New Mills (Central)	16	4	126	107	32	50+	64
Strines	16	4	24	25	29	50+	55
Marple	33	6	380	294	24	46–50	49
Rose Hill	17	3	162	162	24	46–50	47
Romiley	50	9	509	489	19	41–45	44
Woodley	15	4	86	79	23	36–40	45
Hyde (Central)	15	4	50	71	20	31–35	26
Hyde (North)	15	4	57	52	17	31–35	26
Guide Bridge	40	8	330	558	11	26–30	28
Fairfield	31	7	33	27	9	21–25	22
Gorton	38	8	351	278	7	21–25	15
Bredbury	34	4	323	384	17	36–40	40
Reddish (North)	34	4	253	311	12	21–25	19
Belle Vue	34	4	187	195	9	21–25	12
Ashburys	73	12	241	372	4	16–20	11
Ardwick	14	5	0	85	2	11–15	8

Hadfield	25	4	150	270	36	45 +	50
Glossop	25	4	332	397	28	45 +	50
Dinting	25	4	155	156	25	45 +	46
Broadbottom	25	4	126	233	20	41–45	44
Godley Junction	25	4	106	156	17	41–45	32
Newton for Hyde	25	4	155	145	15	31–45	28
			4,136	4,846 in both directions		Data taken from SEL-NEC Transportation study report P. 26	Data based on Manchester Corporation Bus timetables

N.B. No. of passengers using lines
= 4,136 + 4,846/2 = 6,559 in one direction.

Journey Times
Car times are overall times.
Bus and rail times only include in vehicle times.

2 Description of the Routes Served by the Two Services

Area served by the two Services

The Manchester (Piccadilly)–Glossop/Hadfield and Manchester (Piccadilly)–Marple (R.H.)/New Mills services serve the area to the South-East of Manchester lying between Stalybridge and Stockport. [. . .]

Frequency of Service and Type of Trains

The Glossop/Hadfield service is electrically operated and has a half-hourly frequency in the peak period with an hourly frequency in the off-peak period and on Saturdays; there is no Sunday service.

The Marple/New Mills service is operated, as two sub-services, by diesel multiple unit trains. One service runs direct to Marple via Reddish (North), the other service runs via Guide Bridge and Hyde (Central) to New Mills. There is roughly a quarter-hourly frequency in the peak period and a thirty minutes frequency off-peak and on Saturdays. There is an hourly Sunday service on the route via Reddish (North).

[. . .] General information about numbers of passengers etc. is contained in Table 2. [. . .]

3 Traffic Diversion

Basis of Diversion

This study is based on assessing the disbenefits of increased travelling time, road congestion costs, etc., which would arise if the passengers estimated by SALTS to be using the two services in the 1966 base year and the 1984 design year were diverted into the alternative bus services and highway networks.

SALTS information was used to base all the selection of alternative routes used by former rail travellers and the modal split for car owners between Public Transport (P.T.) and car. For 1984 the data used was taken from P.T. network R.30. (P.T.N.) and Highway network (H.N.) H3/2 model run 26. Detailed description of these networks are contained in the SALTS report of the Technical Control Team 'A Broad Transportation Plan for 1984.'

Peak Period Traffic

If the two lines are worth keeping open, it is because of the traffic carried during the morning (07.00–09.00) and evening peaks. Almost all such journeys are to work or to school.

Peak journeys on the two lines are found to be approximately 70% of weekday journeys. But this understates their importance in a social cost/benefit anaysis. Off-peak, the alternative road routes are less congested and, therefore, the social cost of diversion to them is likely to be smaller. It is the peak journeys that would increase road congestion substantially if diverted from rail. No attempt is made in this study to estimate the congestion benefits of retaining off-peak traffic on rail. This means some under-estimation of social benefits of retention, but not to an extent to justify the considerable additional calculations that would have been required.

In the whole SALTS area 95% of all peak journeys are either to work or to school. It was also easy to predict the alternative routes commuters and schoolchildren would use. Other peak rail users may be more likely to change their destination rather than their route. For example, if a housewife now uses the train in the peak hour for a weekly shopping expedition, her reaction to closure of the line might be to travel to the same shops by bus or car, but at a different time, or to go to different shops that are more accessible to her. Even so, she will be worse off through closure of the line, but to a lesser extent. Because these other peak journeys are omitted from the calculations social benefit is again under-estimated. It was decided to do this rather than run into the opposite error of possibly attributing too much social benefit to them.

Non-peak Period Trips

Weekday off-peak, Saturday, and Sunday trips are approximately 40% of all trips in a week and were omitted. Though, these are mostly made when the road system is not so congested, there is still a substantial Saturday mid-day peak on the rail system, but it was felt that it was too difficult to attempt to forecast whether this peak would disappear over the planning period. This would depend on what view was taken of changes in working and shopping habits. Yet again, if one assumes that there is less social benefit in retaining these services on rail, this must understate congestion benefits but probably not to any great extent.

Existing and Alternative Routes for Rail Passengers

To estimate the effects of diversion, it is necessary to map the present route a passenger takes from origin to destination, using rail for part of the journey and then map his best alternative route by bus and car, if the railway closed. This was a laborious task which had to be undertaken manually. For the purposes of analysis, the SALTS study divided the Greater Manchester area into 322 traffic zones, and the surrounding area was divided into some 40 'external' zones. 29 of the 362 zones were selected as most likely to contain the origin of traffic using the two lines. In 1966, the base year, 86% of traffics using the lines were found to originate in these 29 zones. In principle, it would have been possible to inspect journeys originating in the other 293 zones in order to account for 100% of the traffic. But the process was lengthy and it was decided to exclude the remainder. Of course, this will also tend to under-estimate the social costs of closure.

Reconciliation of B.R. and SALTS Traffic Flows

At this stage the study ran into a major difficulty. In its analysis of public transport flows—using 1966 data—the SALTS used techniques which had notionally assigned some 9,200 trips on to the Glossop and New Mills lines. Of these 1,200 correspond to trips omitted in this study as described in the last paragraph because they began outside the 29 zones analysed. Even with these excluded, SALTS assigned some 8,000 morning peak trips, whereas in 1971 British Rail found that only 4,600 comparable trips were made. The discrepancy cannot be explained by a decline in rail carryings since 1966. Though there are no detailed figures for B.R. carryings on the two lines before 1968, it is known that, overall, there has not been much change since then. One should not be too surprised by this since SALTS and the D.O.E. have said, on reflection, that the techniques they used assigned too much traffic to rail by comparison with bus because they failed to reflect sufficiently several specific characteristics of bus and rail travel. The techniques used were based on the average characteristics of routes and modes in the Greater Manchester area. One should, therefore, not be surprised to find that on a given rail route the traffic is above or—as in this case—below the average they hoped to predict. What this means is that there are various characteristics of these two lines (by comparison with the alternative road routes) which make rail relatively less attractive to travellers.

Table 3 relates actual B.R. trips in 1971 to SALTS predictions, station by station. It seems that the ratio of SALTS trips to B.R. trips varies considerably from station to station. If one traces the line from New Mills inwards as far as Belle Vue there are differences between trips made in 1971 and the 1966 estimates but they largely average out along the line. Indeed, on these sections as a whole the SALTS predictions exceed B.R. trips made by little more than 5%. The same is true of the line from Hadfield and Glossop as far in as Newton. The station totals vary but over the section taken as a whole there is little difference between the 1966 prediction and trips made in 1971. It is from Guide Bridge inwards that the predictons using the SALTS method were substantially higher than the amount of traffic actually carried. The same is also true of the Woodley-Hyde North loop. The most likely explanation of this is: (1) changes in the comparative quality of the bus and road systems along the route; as column 5 shows, bus frequencies tend to be far higher on the section where rail carryings are most below SALTS predictions; (2) it is possible that the longer the rail journey, the greater the relative preference people have for rail, other things being equal. The divergence between SALTS forecasts and actual carryings appears sensitive not only to bus and rail frequencies, but also to differences in bus and rail times and possibly facilities available for car parking at stations. While this detail is important to the transport planner, there is not a great difficulty in evaluating the withdrawal of the two services, provided forecasts are based on actual travellers using the services in 1971 and not on the SALTS forecasts. This has been

Table 3

Comparison Between the Number of Trips Forecast by SALTS Techniques in 1966 and Actual Number of Trips Carried by B.R. during an A.M. Peak Period (07.00–09.00) in October 1971

Station	B.R. Trips October/71		Total SALTS work and education trips from 29 zones analysed		Trips from SALTS zones not analysed	Total SALTS	Ratio of total SALTS trips to B.R. trips	Bus Freq/ hr.	Rail Freq/ hr.
		Sub-Total		Sub-Total					
New Mills, Strines	162		189		11	200	1.2	2	2
Marple and Rose Hill	906		1,341		31	1,372	1.5	2	5
Romiley	656		485		85	570	0.9	2	5
Bredbury	412		390		—	390	0.9	2	2
Reddish North	213		—		—			2	2
Belle Vue	112	2,461	203	2,608	—	203	1.8	26	2
Woodley	120		470		2	472	3.9	15	2
Hyde Central	58		614		36	650	11.2	25	2
Hyde North	81	259	115	1,199	108	223	2.8	12	2
Hadfield, Glossop & Dinting	500		461		2	463	0.9	7	2
Broadbottom	249		44			44	0.2	2	2
Godley Junction	60		195			195	3.3	12	2
Newton	125	934	246	946		246	2.0	12	2
Guide Bridge	211		773		245	1,018	4.8	8	4
Fairfield	53		605		—	605	11.4	24	3
Gorton	329		1,257		70	1,327	4.0	24	4
Ashburys	127		561		73	634	5.0	24	6
Ardwick	7	727	87	3,283	58	145	20.7	24	3
Manchester (Piccadilly)	235	235	—		476	476	2.0		
	4,616	4,616	8,036	8,036	1,197	9,233			

done. Because the total benefits are scaled down in proportion to trips, no allowance has been made for removal of excess trips on rail at any particular station, that is to say, trips from Marple have been factored down by the same amout as from Belle Vue. Since the social costs caused by trips from stations further out, such as Marple, are greater than those from stations further in, because the distance travelled by road is greater, though the roads may be less congested, this is another reason for thinking that social costs of withdrawal have been under-estimated.

Effect of Withdrawal of the two Rail Services

The next stage was to calculate what would have happened in 1966 if the two services had been withdrawn. The routes now taken by passengers were analysed to estimate for each flow the best alternative route by public transport. For most it was bus, but for some e.g. in the Marple area it was to take a bus to Stockport and travel by train. Selection of the best alternative route was on the basis of relative time and costs and was based on Department of the Environment methods using Generalised Costs. [. . .] Experience has shown that the most important factors affecting the choice of route are differences in passenger fares, differences in journey time, with extra weight given to waiting and walking time and a factor to represent the inconvenience of changing buses en route. To make this operational, values have to be assumed for time spent travelling. The values used were those recommended by the Department of the Environment for analysis of the modes of travelling. [. . .] The result of this re-assignment of traffic to buses was a need for a substantial increase in bus frequencies on some routes. Since this reduced waiting time and so increased the attractiveness of the service, this was allowed to affect the volume of traffic predicted to divert to such a bus route. Withdrawal would also have meant a decline in traffic on some bus routes passing rail stations. The exercise was repeated for 1984 and some bus feeder services were assumed to be withdrawn. [. . .]

It might have been thought that an alternative which should have been considered was the running of express buses which would provide a quality and speed of service of a far higher standard than the ordinary bus. However, given traffic and road conditions it was felt this could not be achieved without substantial investment in the road network. To be able to estimate the amount of investment required, a comprehensive exercise would have to be undertaken to ascertain what improvements would need to be made in the road network. It would also be necessary to take account of the social and environmental aspects of the road widening and interaction improvements that would be required.

If rail services had been withdrawn, all traffic would not have diverted to bus. Many passengers would have used their cars. The SALTS modal split procedure was used to decide what proportion of journeys would be by car for each flow. This prediction is also based on relative costs and journey times by the two modes for those owning cars. It was predicted that 21% of former rail trips would have used a car in 1966. A car occupancy ratio of 1.27 was assumed (also based on SALTS data).[7] Some people from non-car-owning households might be expected to join a car pool if the services were withdrawn. These have not been allowed for in the study.

Withdrawing services may have reduced the trips made. The additional costs and times of the best alternative routes would have persuaded some to change their workplace, school or home, or even to retire from active employment. These effects are difficult to predict because of the absence of relevant experience elsewhere. As few passengers experienced substantial increases in costs and losses, it was assumed that few journeys would not be made, and that they could be neglected. Therefore, the same number of trips, approximately 4,600 (see Table 3) per morning peak, were assumed made between the same origins and destinations, before and after the hypothetical 1966 withdrawal of the services.

At this stage it is worth looking at a few examples. Let us consider someone who was taking an average train journey in 1966. As it happened there were a number of people starting their journeys in zone 311 (Bredbury) who joined the train at Bredbury where they travelled into Central Manchester with a final destination in zone 002.

On average, using SALTS information and 1966 values of money, their journey time, per person, would have been as follows:

Journey between zones 311 and 002

	Before withdrawal by rail from Bredbury to Manchester (P)	After withdrawal by bus to Stockport thence by rail to Manchester (P)	Increase in values following withdrawal
1. *Per Peak*			
a) *Journey Time (mins)*			
waiting time	17.6	18.0	0.4
in-vehicle time	18.0	16.0	/2.0/
interchange penalty	—	4.0	4.0
walking time	18.0	28.0	10.0
TOTAL (mins)	53.6	66.0	12.4
b) *Fare (p)*	8.7	10.2	1.5
c) *Cost (p)*			
Time + Fare	23.4	29.3	5.9
SALTS value of time in 1966 was 16.5p per hour.			
2. *Total per Year*			
a) Journey Time (hrs)	446.7	550.0	103.3
b) Fare (£)	43.5	51.0	7.5
c) Cost (£)	117.2	141.8	24.6

[7] SALTS, Technical Working Paper Number 4, Page 31.

Now let us consider a motorist using a link on the route to which this passenger is diverted. The link is only 0.1 miles long, a small part of his journey. Travelling along it used to take him 0.584 minutes and cost him £0.0016. If the train service is discontinued, his operating costs will rise by £0.00004 and his journey time by 0.014 minutes. On this short part of his journey he is over the year worse off by 0.12 hours and £0.04 in terms of money and time. This is very small relative to his average income but when one sums up all the effects on all the people who are affected in this way by the closure, the result will be large.

One should remember that it is rare that anyone's journey-time improves or deteriorates as a result of a single event. It is an accumulation of small deteriorations which lengthens journey-time and an accumulation of small improvements which make a road-user better off. One cannot afford to neglect something because it is relatively small. All the factors that affect journey-times in urban areas tend to be relatively small, but the cumulative effect of several small changes on a large number of people can sum to large amounts of money.

At the other extreme let us suppose someone whose journey starts in zone 106 and who travels from Gorton into Central Manchester, his journey ending in zone 012. The time and money he spends on the train is much less. The effect on him of closure will be a daily increase of fare (a) £0.009, time (b) 0.8 minutes and cost (c) £0.011 for a single journey or (a) £4.45, (b) 6.66 hours and (c) £5.5 per annum. Again one must remember that people's journeys are affected by a great many factors which tend to speed them up or slow them down. While each in itself may be small, the cumulative effect, which is the sum of a large number of small factors, may be important.

More important than the losses to those who diverted from rail would have been the effects upon those already using the road system. Because only journeys originating from the 29 zones were analysed, not all diverted journeys were assigned to the road system. It is probable that the 471 links to which diverted traffic was assigned in 1966 and the 1,547 to which they were assigned in 1984 were those where it was most important to estimate the effects of diversion. In most cases the number of trips diverted to other links were small, absolutely and relatively to the number of trips already on these road-links. For each of the links to which diverted traffic was assigned, the peak speeds were estimated, using methods recommended by the D.O.E. [. . .] Given an estimate of the numbers of vehicles of different types on the road-link, their speed and their operating costs, their link costs and journey times were calculated. Using the same values of time, 'generalised' costs in terms of money and time were calculated. The cost per mile calculated varied depending on the volume of traffic in relation to the capacity of the road, that is, congestion. For example, bus operating costs were 7.9p per mile at speeds of 15 m.p.h. When speeds fell to 8 m.p.h., operating costs rose to 11p per mile. The effect of the diverted traffic in reducing link speeds and increasing link time and operating costs had to be estimated. The greater the pre-existing level of congestion, the more the impact of additional vehicles. There was also great variation between the links in the speed reduction affected.

As an example, we may imagine someone using a particularly heavily congested link to which rail traffic is diverted on withdrawal. The effect on him will be increases in vehicle operating costs of (a) £0.0006, his time by (b) 1.96 minutes and (c) £0.006 combined time and vehicle operating costs for each day; similarly, (a) £0.3, (b) 16.33 hours and (c) £3.00 per annum.

It was assumed that each passenger made 250 round trip journeys in peak periods in a year. What information there is suggests little variation in peak hour travel throughout the year. There is some decline in the holiday period but not sufficient to make it worthwhile to alter the figures used here which were based on average costs. An exactly similar exercise was performed to calculate the social costs of closure in 1984.

4 Forecasts

SALTS Estimates

After the calculations just described were carried out for the SALTS base year 1966, they were then repeated for 1984, the SALTS design year. This study, therefore, relied on the SALTS estimates of the volume and distribution of trips that would be made by 1984, though as in 1966, similar adjustments and assumptions were made to estimate the trips that would be relevant for this study—in particular:

(1) morning and evening peak journeys to work and to school on the Glossop and Marple lines;
(2) traffic flows on competing and feeder roads and bus routes.

The SALTS trip forecasts—and, therefore, those of this study—were based on forecasts including population, the size of household, mean household income, employment and car ownership.

Population

This will affect the level of trip-making. Separate population forecasts were not made for each zone but for twelve districts into which the zones were grouped; their population was 670,000 in 1966 and is expected to be 620,000 by 1984. [. . .]

Household Formation

The size of household does affect the number of trips forecast. The SALTS forecast is that average household size will rise from just over 2.8 persons to just over 2.9 persons, between 1966 and 1984. Therefore, the number of households will fall slightly faster than population.

Mean Household Income affects car ownership levels and trip-making. [. . .] There was great variation, the mean level of the highest (£1,543 p.a.) being 175% of the lowest (£868 p.a.). SALTS assumed 3% growth in mean income per annum for the whole Manchester area—the relative differences between districts remaining the same. This study was in no position to do better. (If mean incomes rise faster fewer people will use the railway but, other things being equal, there will be more cars and, therefore, both more congestion and more social costs from closure.)

Employment

These estimates were also needed to predict where people would be journeying to. [. . .] The totals for the 13 districts were (including Central Manchester), predicted to be:

1966	439,000
1972	423,000
1984	408,000

Car Ownership

[. . .] The method used was based on that developed for London Traffic Survey. A separate calculation was made to estimate the number of households likely to own two cars. [. . .]

Social Costs of withdrawal of the two rail services

As will be described in the next section this study proceeded to calculate the social costs of service withdrawal for 1966 and 1984. However, this seems the point at which to explain how another problem of forecasting was overcome. It was decided to consider the effects of withdrawal for the purposes of this study—not in 1966 and 1984, but assuming closure on 31.12.72 and 31.12.83, the first years that social costs would arise being 1973 and 1984 respectively, 1972 was chosen as representing the option of closing the lines 'now'. Although it is now 1973, it can be taken as roughly representing the consequences if it were decided to close the line in the near future, 1983 was chosen as the year in which SALTS assumed that the planned new roads, rail improvements and revised bus services would be completed.

[. . .] There was a choice between either drawing straight lines between 1966 and 1984 values on a graph and 'reading off' the values for intermediate years, or trying to estimate more carefully what values between 1966 and 1984, the relevant factors (household income, population, employment) would have taken. Both methods were examined and for every year the benefits of retaining the rail service were greater by using the straight line method. It was, therefore, thought appropriate to adopt the second course which, though it produced lower benefits, appeared to be more satisfactory in that it took more account of changing conditions between 1966 and 1984.

As will be clear this was especially important for levels of road congestion. Congestion on every road in the Manchester area cannot be assumed to deteriorate uniformly over the period. Allowance had to be made for changes in highways and vehicle mix.

One important problem was to decide how to reflect improvements in the quality of rail services planned from 1973 onwards. To a large extent these could be treated as reducing rail times.

Evaluation

Basis of Study

For the purposes of the study it was assumed that the two rail services would be withdrawn at the end of 1972 and the disbenefits caused to the former rail users were then estimated year by year from 1973 to 1997 inclusive. These disbenefits were then treated as the benefits of retaining the services.

Two levels of service were assumed. Firstly an improved railway service with higher frequencies and the introduction of new bus feeder services together with new stations at Hattersley, Gamealy and Brinnington. Secondly a service of the same frequency as in April 1972 without new bus feeder services or new stations. In both levels of service it was assumed that Hyde North, Hyde Central, Woodley and Rose Hill would be closed.

Elements Quantified

Six main elements in the cost/benefit analysis were quantified as follows:

(1) Disbenefits to road-users through additional congestion.
(2) Disbenefits to former users of rail services.
(3) Changes in accident costs.
(4) Resource costs of substitute bus services.
(5) Resource costs of substitute car journeys.
(6) Avoidable cost of railway services.

Disbenefits to road users through additional congestion

Changes in vehicle speeds were calculated using D.O.E. formulae and changes in vehicle operating costs using the Transport and Road Research Laboratory formula. The increase in vehicle time was valued by using vehicle occupancy figures and D.O.E. values of time. Basically the values of time are calculated for working time and leisure time. In relation to road congestion calculations working time has been applied to bus crews and C.V. drivers and all other road users i.e. car occupants and bus passengers are assumed to be travelling in their leisure time.

For 1973 and 1984, withdrawal of improved rail services would have had the following consequences (for one year of 500 peak periods[8]):

	1973 (000)	1984 (000)
Annual person hours lost		
Leisure time	1476	4287
working time	203	493
Total	1679	4780
Value of this time	*(£000)*	*(£000)*
Leisure time	282	1132
working time	151	519
Total	433	1651
Increase in vehicle operating costs	113	325

Disbenefits to former users of rail services

As long as the rail services continue, prospective passengers have a choice of train, bus and, in some cases, car. Between any pair of zones relevant for this study, each of these three modes may be characterised by an average cost and by an average expected journey-time. The cost of using a train or bus is the fare. The only relevant car costs are those which vary with use, plus parking costs in Manchester. If the rail services stop, some of those who went by rail will find their out-of-pocket expenses by car or bus less than their old rail fares. Most will find their journey-times longer. (If it were not for parking costs, many more would find it cheaper to go by car than by rail.) Someone who goes by rail now when it is quicker but dearer than using the bus or his car, must be assumed to believe that the savings are worth the extra expense. Someone who goes by rail even though it would be both cheaper and quicker to go by car or bus, must be assumed to have other reasons for using rail.

So far as the switch to buses is concerned, the gain a rail-user experiences when he pays a bus fare lower than his previous train fare, is exactly matched by the corresponding loss to the P.T.E. since it subsidises both services, and therefore can be ignored as an income transfer. Inspection of study data suggested withdrawal of rail services would as often lead to increase in money costs as reductions for those transferring to cars. Therefore it was decided to value changes in journey time only.

---

[8] It is usual in studies of this kind to assume that morning and evening peak periods have identical characteristics.

For 1973 and 1984, withdrawal of improved rail services would have had the following effects:

	1973	1984
Annual person hours lost		
Work trips	27,600	381,700
education trips	33,500	277,500
Value of this time	£	£
Work trips	5,272	100,769
education trips	2,134	24,143
Total	3,138	124,912

Work trips are commuting journeys and education trips are journeys to school college etc. for the purpose of studying. Both types of trips are valued as leisure time.

Whilst in 1973 rail passengers would gain overall, the situation changes in 1974 whereby rail passengers would be worse off in terms of journey time after withdrawal of the rail services.

Changes in Accident Costs

SALTS have estimated accident experience by type of road and volume of traffic. Using accident values provided by the D.O.E. it is possible to estimate the cost of withdrawal through increasing the volume of traffic on the roads.

For withdrawal of improved rail services the effect is as follows:

	1973	1984
Increase in number of road accidents (rounded)	14	28
Cost of these accidents	19,875	41,180

Resource costs of substitute bus services

The method used to estimate the resource costs of the alternative bus services is described in part II of the study [...]

The operating costs for 1973 and 1984 and the number of extra buses needed were estimated as follows:

	1973	1984
Operating Costs	£135,330	£34,700
Number of buses	39	10

Resource costs of substitute car journeys

The former rail passengers who now travel by road incur resource

costs in the form of higher expenditure on petrol, oil, and maintenance costs. [. . .]

The additional costs for 1973 and 1984 were estimated as follows:

	1973	*1984*
Car Resource costs	£112,900	£250,400

Avoidable cost of railway services

[. . .] The costs that B.R. would 'avoid' having to pay out if the
services were withdrawn at the end of 1972 were estimated for each
year from 1973 to 1997 and treated as the avoidable costs of running
the two rail services. It was assumed that there would be an increase
in value of real wages at 3% p.a.; pensions and N.H.I. contributions
were excluded. Allowance was made for sale of scrap, land, buildings,
etc. and where necessary the gradual reabsorption of displaced staff
into productive work.

It must be pointed out here that the avoidable costs of running
the railway services after 1977 are based on the assumption that the
'Picc.-Vic.' tunnel will open in 1977. It is not possible to amend
these costs to take into account the delay in opening the tunnel until
a new completion date for the project is known. The avoidable costs
of running the services are therefore slightly understated in the four
alternatives examined by very roughly £30,000 p.a. discounted (due
to higher maintenance costs for old rolling stock) for each year's
delay in the completion of the tunnel. [. . .]

The costs that B.R. cannot 'avoid' e.g. the share of the costs of
track and signalling which the services now bear, would in the event
of withdrawal have to be reallocated amongst the other services
using the route.

It is sometimes argued that this understates the costs of withdrawal as follows: if the services are withdrawn then any costs that
are joint between those services and others that are retained will
have to be covered by revenue from the retained services, thus increasing their costs. Thus avoiding those costs increases is a benefit
of keeping the services open. But this is double-counting. What is
relevant are the marginal or avoidable costs and benefits related
to a service that is up for withdrawal: do the benefits forgone or
avoided by withdrawal exceed the costs avoided? The unavoidable
costs by definition are not affected by whether the service is withdrawn or in operation. Therefore they are irrelevant to the decision.

The avoidable costs of operating improved railway services were
estimated as follows: (at 1971 price levels)

1973	£443,000
1984	£1,767,000

The higher figure for 1984 reflects heavy expenditure on rolling
stock renewals.

6 Results of Study

Costs and Benefits of the Improved Railway Services—Alternative (a)

The results of the study showed a substantial benefit to the comminuty in favour of retaining the rail services.

The costs and benefits of retention of the services were estimated year by year from 1973 to 1997 and discounted at 10% back to 1973 to give the following net benefit:

		£m
Net Benefit = £13.0m	Road Congestion Cost	12.4
	Additional journey time	0.7
	Additional vehicle operating costs	2.4
	Operating costs of extra buses	0.9
	Bus capital cost	0.4
	Cost of substitute car journeys	1.9
	Accident cost	0.3
		19.0
	Less avoidable costs	6.0
		13.0

This very favourable result is largely due to the considerable increase in the number of passengers using the services between 1966 and 1984 due to the improvement of the rail services and the introduction of feeder bus services.

The changes caused to these figures by varying the discount rate and the value of time were also explored. Changing the discount rate from 10% to 5% had the following effect:

	£m
Total benefits discounted at 5%	32.9
Less total avoidable costs discounted at 5%	9.3
Net benefit	23.6

The effect of keeping the discount rate at 10% but halving the value of time was as follows:

	£m
Total discounted benefits	11.2
Total discounted avoidable costs	6.0
Net Benefit	5.2

In 1966 the a.m. peak period trips were estimated to be 4,414 rising to 12,531 in 1984.

Costs and Benefits if the Services were not Improved—Alternative (b)

If the services were not improved it is estimated that the a.m. peak trips in 1984 would be 4,855.

The costs and benefits of retaining the two rail services but not improving them from 1973 to 1997 and discounted at 10% to 1973 yield the following estimated net benefit:

		£m
Net Benefit = £4.5m	Road congestion Cost	5.9
	Additional journey time	/0.4/
	Additional vehicle operating costs	1.2
	Operating cost of extra buses	1.1
	Bus capital cost	0.5
	Cost of substitute car journeys	0.9
	Accident cost	0.2
		9.4
	Less avoidable costs	4.9
		4.5

The effect of reducing the discount rate from 10% to 5% was as follows:

	£m
Total benefits discounted at 5%	15.5
Less total avoidable costs discounted at 5%	7.7
Net Benefit	7.8

The effect of keeping the discount rate at 10% but halving the value of time was as follows:

	£m
Total discounted benefits	6.7
Less total discounted avoidable costs	4.9
Net Benefit	1.8

Avoidable costs and social benefits of continuing to operate a non-improved service until the end of 1983 and the subsequent cash savings and social disbenefits due to the withdrawal of the services during the years 1984 to 1997 inclusive—Alternative (c).

The costs and benefits were again discounted at 10% to 1973.

1973–1983   £m

Net Benefit = £2.5m   Road Congestion Cost   3.0
                      Additional journey time   /0.2/
                      Additional vehicle operating costs 0.7
                      Operating costs of extra buses 0.9
                      Bus capital costs   0.4
                      Cost of substitute car journeys 0.6
                      Accident costs   0.1
                                                      ───
                                                      5.5

                      Less avoidable costs   3.0
                      Net Benefit   2.5

   A withdrawal date at the end of 1983 was chosen because 1984 is
the first year of full operation of the SALTS transportation plan. We
also calculated the net benefit of retention until 1997 rather than
withdrawal in 1983.

1984–1997   £m

Net Benefit = £2.4m   Road Congestion Cost   2.9
                      Additional journey time   /0.1/
                      Additional vehicle operating costs 0.5
                      Operating costs of extra buses 0.3
                      Bus capital costs   0.2
                      Cost of substitute car journeys 0.3
                      Accident costs   0.1
                                                      ───
                                                      4.2

                      Less avoidable costs   1.8
                      Net Benefit   2.4

*Avoidable costs saved and social disbenefits caused by withdrawing
the existing services at the end of 1972—Alternative (d)*

The savings in expenditure and the disbenefits caused by withdrawing the services at the end of 1972, discounted at the rate of 10%
from 1973 to 1997 were estimated as follows:

                                                      £m

Net Disbenefit = £4.5 Road Congestion   5.9
                       Additional journey time   /0.4/
                       Additional vehicle operating costs 1.2
                       Operating cost of extra buses 1.1
                       Bus capital costs   0.5
                       Cost of substitute car journeys 0.9
                       Accident cost   0.2
                                                     ───
                                                     9.4

                       Less avoidable costs saved   4.9
                                                     ───
                                                     4.5

The effect of reducing the discount rate from 10% to 5% was as follows:

	£m
Total benefits discounted at 5%	15.5
Less total avoidable costs saved discounted at 5%	7.7
Net Disbenefit	7.8

The effect of keeping the discount rate at 10% but halving the value of time was as follows:

	£m
Total discounted disbenefits	6.7
Less total discounted costs saved	4.9
Net Disbenefit	1.8

It will be noted that this alternative is the reverse of that described [. . .] on page 310.

16

Cost-benefit Analysis in Transport

by R. Rees

Introduction

This paper is concerned with describing and appraising two applications of cost-benefit analysis in the transport sector. Choice of the
two simply reflects interest subject to constraints, rather than an
obvious logical connection. The only apparent relation they have is
their dissimilarity. The first, the cost-benefit analysis of the Channel
Tunnel,[1] concerned a single, very large, probably controversial
project, which would have supplied a marketed output in competition with existing services; although in 1975 the Government for the
time being rejected this proposal, its analysis is nevertheless of
continuing interest. The second is an attempt to introduce cost-
benefit principles at the grass roots of road investment planning,
related to a large number of small projects, and though published,[2]
is primarily an internal exercise within the Department of the Environment. Discussion of the two proceeds by taking them separately,
but an attempt will be made to draw implications common to both
of them at the end.

The Channel Tunnel cost-benefit analysis

In broad outline, the analysis was concerned with estimating the
social costs and benefits which would arise from the introduction
into an existing system, of a new type of cross-channel facility. This
involved forecasting the likely demand for tunnel transport services,
and the consequent cost and time benefits to travellers; reductions
in resources which would otherwise be required to meet the demand
by the existing system; and the revenue losses to existing operators
arising from the traffic diversion. The analysis was greatly helped by
the existence of a large body of detailed and sophisticated work,
which has been carried out in evaluating the financial profitability
of the tunnel.[3] In addition to the usual kinds of divergences between
private profit and social net benefit, there was in this case the further
difference that benefits and costs accruing only to UK households
and firms were to be considered.[4]

The outcome of the evaluation can be briefly characterised as
follows: from the UK point of view the tunnel would have involved
an investment[5] of £261 m., which would have resulted in a saving of

From *Public Expenditure*, ed. M. V. Posner (Cambridge University Press,
1979), pp. 179-203. Reprinted by permission of the author and Cambridge
University Press.

£156 m. in capital expenditure, and £347 m. in operating costs, on the alternative sea and air services required to meet the demand. The tunnel represents a transport facility which is rather more capital intensive, but with much lower operating costs, than alternative sea and air transport. Thus, simply on the grounds of minimising cost of an overall transport network, construction of the tunnel would appear justified. In addition, there would have been a net gain in consumers' surplus[6] of £49 m., thus increasing the attractiveness of the tunnel.

The remainder of this part of the paper is concerned with examination of the basis for these conclusions. It is convenient to describe and appraise the analysis under five main headings:

  (i) demand forecasts
 (ii) calculation of user benefits
(iii) calculation of capital and operating-cost savings
(iv) procedure for calculating a net present value
 (v) sensitivity analysis of results to changes in assumptions.

Demand forecasts

Two approaches to the forecasting problem are possible. The more general is to regard the decisions on whether to make a trip, the destination, means of transport, and specific route, simultaneously. Thus the choice of destination depends on the time, cost, and other characteristics of the routes by which one gets there, and these, with other characteristics of the possible destinations, influence the decision on whether or not to make a trip. Alternatively, the decisions can be ordered sequentially, with the decision at each stage independent of those which succeed it. First would come the decision on whether or not to make a trip; next the precise destination and holiday type (car tour, package etc.); next the choice of transport; and finally the specific route (where routes may differ only in relation to a particular segment of the journey, e.g. the channel crossing). Thus the decision at each stage constrains the choices at the next. This second approach implies a hierarchy of forecasting models, with the forecast at each stage providing an aggregate to be decomposed among the alternatives at the succeeding one.

The forecasts[7] underlying the cost–benefit analysis essentially adopt the second approach. A justification is attempted by citing the evidence of an in-depth questionnaire inquiry on the household decision process. It appears that people actually make decisions in this sequence. This is hardly conclusive evidence, however, and runs the risk of confusing the apparent process by which decisions are taken with the nature of the decision itself. It is probable that people have information on the possibilities at later stages when they begin the sequence, and it is also likely that they would revise decisions earlier in the sequence if they acquire new information when they consider a decision at a particular stage.

The forecasts take some account of this, as described below. However, the main assumption of their approach is that the total demand for trips abroad is independent of the cross-Channel route decisions, and so will be unaffected by introduction of the tunnel route. The real justification of the assumption must be on grounds of its feasibility. The analysts were confronted with the problem of predicting, on the basis of past data, the effects of a significant change in costs, duration, frequency, and convenience of the Channel crossing. In the past, however, the latter have varied relatively little compared to the variations in demand for foreign travel, and so past data provide no firm basis for prediction. The conservative assumption of no overall 'generation effect' of the tunnel on demand for trips abroad is perhaps, therefore, the most acceptable one. The implications of this are further discussed below.

Given the basic methodology, forecasts were obtained in the following way: forecasts of total trips abroad, disaggregated into holiday and business trips, were made for each of the years 1980 and 1990; a distinction was also made between long holidays, lasting five days or more, and short holidays. The holiday markets were then further disaggregated in each of two ways: first into type of holiday, e.g. package, or car-accompanied; second into country or zone of destination. Finally, given holiday types and destinations, forecasts were made of demand for the various cross-Channel routes.

The forecasts for total holiday demand were based on a cross-sectional analysis of holiday travel data for the year 1971. A large amount of data was collected by questionnaire methods, and the propensity to take a holiday abroad was then related to socioeconomic variables such as income, age, sex, marital status, number of children, occupational category, and so on. Linear regression models were used to quantify the relationships, and then forecasts were made using the resulting equations. In order to do this, it was necessary to forecast the independent variables for 1980 and 1990. For example, the income variable was forecast by assuming a rate of growth of GNP and a constant distribution of income by household. The resulting total forecasts were checked by comparison with an extrapolation of the time-trend of past growth in demand, and were found to be not unreasonable.

It is rarely difficult to find criticisms of any set of forecasts. The following are perhaps the most important in this case:

(a) There are well-known objections to using cross-section relationships for making forecasts over time, of which the analysts showed themselves to be somewhat aware, hence the time-trend extrapolation.

(b) The various socioeconomic characteristics can be expected to be highly collinear. Indeed, because not all respondents to the questionnaire gave their incomes, income was regressed on the other characteristics and assigned to them in this way. An implication of collinearity is that the regression estimates of the separate coefficients may not reflect accurately the real influence of each variable taken separately. Hence, if the variables change differentially over time, there may be distortion in the forecasts. The existence and implications of this problem were not considered in the Report.

(c) As well as the issue raised in (a) there could be some doubt about the stability of coefficients estimated on only one year's data.

(d) Finally, no attempt was made to estimate the variance of the forecast errors, even though, as is discussed below, these are important in determining the overall probability distribution of net benefits of the tunnel.

In breaking down the total demand for long and short holidays into holiday type—long holidays into car-accompanied, package, and independent; short into package and others—a similar procedure to that described above was used. The propensity to take a particular holiday type was regressed on socioeconomic characteristics, the resulting relationships then being used, in conjunction with forecasts of the characteristics to provide breakdowns of the holiday markets in 1980 and 1990. These forecasts are therefore subject again to criticisms (a)-(d).

Analysis of holiday demand by destination was carried out rather differently. The fraction of total holiday traffic going to each country was related to: the number of friends and relatives of holiday-makers in that country (found from questionnaire surveys to be a highly significant variable); length of coastline; climatic conditions; population; and a 'generalised travel cost'. This last variable, appearing for the first time in the analysis, consists of the amount of money spent on average in getting to the holiday destination, plus a money allowance for the travelling time taken. As a result of the analysis of past decisions, it was possible to impute a value of 5p per hour to the latter, implying that travel time was not, on average, of prime importance in choice of holiday country.[8]

At this point it is worth noting that influence of a fall in time and cost of the Channel crossing is, as a result of the specification of the forecasting models, restricted to the choice of holiday destination, and will in any case be very weak. The time-saving will be given very little weight, and the scope for switching from destinations which do not require a Channel crossing, to those which do, is very limited by the nature of the holiday market. This, together with the fact that there is no increased total demand for holidays, and no change in type of holiday, accounts for the very small 'generation effect' of the tunnel, and in turn the rather low value of user benefit in the final table of the cost–benefit analysis.

The forecasts of holidays by type and destination permitted a forecast of total demand for Channel crossings, which then had to be allocated among the various routes: ferries, hovercraft, and tunnel.

The basis for this allocation was a regression analysis which related cross-Channel route-choice probability to money cost, service frequency, and time. In the course of this analysis it was found that 'rational' factors of time, service frequency, and cost explain route choice in the past only with a large residual error, which was held to be due to 'imperfect information, route loyalty-cum-inertia, or qualitative preferences'. In other words, because they could not or did not do the sums correctly, or because they have preferences over routes, travellers chose particular routes even when they were not the best on time and cost grounds. This, the analysts called an 'error structure', and incorporated it into the models explaining past route choice.

In forecasting the future route distribution, the tunnel was given specified values for its toll, journey time, and service frequency. Then, given corresponding values for all other possible routes, forecasts of traffic on each route were obtained from the regression equations. However, given the importance of the 'error structure' in explaining past route choices, there is the problem of attributing one to the tunnel. The report is a little inexplicit on this point, but since it states that in all respects other than time, cost, and frequency, the tunnel was treated as an additional Dover–Calais *sea route*, the safest conclusion seems to be that the same error structure was attributed to the tunnel as to the Dover–Calais sea ferry. That is, in terms of 'imperfect information, loyalty-cum-inertia, and qualitative preference', there will be the same propensity to choose the tunnel when it is not best on time, cost, and frequency grounds, and the same propensity not to choose it when it is the best, as for the existing Dover–Calais ferry service.

If this indeed is the assumption of the study, it is a very heroic, and not very plausible, one. It is surely difficult to identify the 'route loyalty-cum-inertia' of a completely new service with that of a long-established route. Moreover, in terms of qualitative preference, the reliability, comfort, and claustrophobia of a train journey through a tunnel would seem to be rather different to the experience of a sea crossing. The problem facing the analysts is clear: given the importance of the 'error structure' in explaining route choice, how does one evaluate this for a facility which doesn't yet exist? It is not difficult to take exception to the solution adopted. Unfortunately, there is insufficient information in the report to allow an estimate of the importance of this factor to the tunnel traffic forecasts.

To conclude the discussion of demand forecasts, we move from the forecasting procedures to the forecasting assumptions. It was necessary to assume future values of:

(i) national income and its distribution by household (required for forecasts of total holiday demand and holiday type)
(ii) population size and socioeconomic structure (forecasts of total holiday demand and type)

(iii) holiday costs, number of friends and relatives abroad, car ownership levels (holiday location)
(iv) the prices, travel times, and frequencies, of tunnel facilities and
competing services (holiday location, cross-Channel route choice).

This in itself would be a major forecasting exercise. I do not propose to discuss (ii) and (iii) in this paper. (i) is discussed below. At
this point, the problems associated with (iv) can usefully be looked
at in some depth.

The analysts viewed the market for cross-Channel transport
essentially as a duopoly, with the tunnel on one hand and the ferry
operators on the other.[9] In order to predict the final market shares
resulting from a given toll, trip duration, and service frequency for
the tunnel, it seemed necessary to predict the reactions of the ferry
operators. However, the analysts chose a fairly simple duopoly model,
since they assumed that the tunnel policies are held completely fixed
throughout.[10] Then, fleet operators choose, for any given fleet size,
the levels of fares and frequencies which maximise profit; and finally
that fleet size is chosen which yields an 11 per cent d.c.f. rate of
return. This gives the values of fares and frequency which are used, in
conjunction with the values assumed for the tunnel, to predict the
final cross-Channel market allocation.

There are two main criticisms of this exercise:

(i) the tunnel toll was set at the level of the 1971 Dover–Calais ferry
fare, incorporating various off-peak concessions, adjustments for
car size, etc. The basis for this choice is never made clear, and
bears no discernible relationship to the economics of the tunnel.
Yet it has important consequences. First is that, in the model just
discussed, it is an important determinant of the overall allocation
of traffic by routes, and therefore has an important influence on
the outcome of the cost–benefit analysis. Second, it means that
virtually the only type of benefit received by the majority of
travellers who divert to the tunnel is a time saving: they will in
general not save money. Paradoxically, the travellers who do save
money, but not time, are those who continue to travel on existing
ferry routes, since they gain from the competitive fare reductions.
In the absence of information to the contrary the choice of this
toll assumption seems, to the writer, at least, due to the fact that
no agreed policy on the tunnel toll yet exists, and so the analysts
have had to choose the least contentious guideline they can find.
(ii) The second criticism is that the analysts have carried out the
wrong kind of exercise. The particular toll assumption underlines
the fact that there is no awareness in the study of the possibility
of choosing allocatively efficient prices. There are strong reasons
for suspecting that existing ferry fares incorporate insufficient
peak/off-peak differentiation, and generate excessive profits
overall.[11] To incorporate these features into the tunnel toll

assumptions therefore begs a lot of questions. Given the fact that a large part of the ferry capacity is owned by nationalised industries, while there will be a substantial public interest in the tunnel, a subject which should be explored is the question of an allocatively efficient set of prices for the entire network of cross-Channel facilities, and its implications, *via* its effect on demands, for the overall results of the cost–benefit analysis. In other words, there *is* a relationship between pricing and investment.

There are several possible objections to this second criticism. The first would be to call it naive. The fact that existing ferry capacity is largely state-owned has not precluded policies which look very much like straightforward exploitation of monopoly power. There is nothing therefore to suggest that a policy of social-welfare maximisation would be adopted in the future, Monopolies Commission not-withstanding. This is reinforced by the probable presence of a strong private financial interest in any tunnel. This point, however, raises an issue common to all public-enterprise economics: there is still an almost complete separation between practical decision taking in public enterprises, and the rules and criteria developed in the area of economics concerned with optimality of public-sector resource allocation. The defence of the latter also applies here: allocative efficiency matters, and it is important to examine its consequences for any particular area of decision, in order to appraise existing pro-cedures, and identify potential improvements.

A second objection is that although a large part of the cross-Channel facilities are state owned, there would also be sizeable private sector participation. However, this does not so much pre-clude social-welfare maximisation as change the definition of the problem.[12] There are two possibilities: first, it could simply be assumed that the private sector would be required to observe the optimal pricing policies, either by direct control, or by appropriate tax-subsidy policies; alternatively, the optimum for the public sector of the industry could be sought, taking into account the effect *via* the consequential decisions of the private sector, on the social welfare of consumers of the private-sector service. In either case, we would expect the pricing system to differ from that assumed by the analysts.

Finally, we have the objection that since the profits on cross-Channel operations accrue to the state, they can be regarded as indirect taxes, and there seems to be no reason for not levying indirect taxes on services which are, in total, fairly price inelastic, and consumed by relatively high-income groups and foreigners. Again, however, this point simply changes the nature of the problem,[13] rather than ruling out social-welfare optimisation. If a specific amount of revenue is required by the Exchequer, then this can be levied by an optimal set of mark-ups on prices, where the characteristic of these mark-ups is that they are inversely proportional to the price elasticities of demand of the services on which they are levied.

It therefore seems to be worthwhile to consider the kind of pricing systems which would be optimal for the entire system of cross-Channel facilities. First there would be differentiation of prices according to peak characteristics. Something which the Reports stress, but then do not incorporate into their pricing assumptions, is the extreme peakedness of the annual demand pattern; 60 per cent of the annual flow takes place in July, August, and September, and two-thirds of the flow in any week takes place at the weekend. This suggests at least four demand periods. Then, in the absence of indirect taxation and assuming that the private sector is regulated, the optimal pricing system can be taken to be marginal cost based. It is, therefore, likely that midweek and weekend prices in the July/August/September period will cover running costs and capital charges, while the off-season prices will involve running costs only. Given the high degree of capital intensity of the facilities, this is likely to imply large price differentials. Moreover, because of the much lower operating costs, we would expect that off-peak tunnel charges would be well below those of other routes. It should, perhaps, be mentioned that this marginal cost pricing system need not result in financial losses. The total revenue from peak and off-peak tolls for the tunnel will cover total costs, including depreciation and the required rate of return on capital, provided that the capacity of the tunnel is not larger than the rate of peak demand at the appropriate price. Moreover, even if this were so initially, over time peak tolls would have to be raised to restrict demand to capacity and avoid congestion, thus generating net profits over and above the required rate of return, in a way quite consistent with allocative efficiency. Likewise, since long-run marginal costs of ferry services are likely to be constant or rising no losses will result here.

The effect of imposing an overall profit requirement would be to lead to larger rises in prices of less price elastic services, and therefore, assuming that off-peak demand would be more elastic than on-peak, there would be an even greater peak/off-peak differential. Finally, if the private sector were to be left unregulated, and influenced only through prices of the public-sector services, there would optimally be relatively lower prices of those services which have close private sector substitutes. To summarise: the tunnel toll assumption adopted in the study is arbitrary, and ignores the possibility of establishing an allocatively efficient set of prices for cross-Channel services. These prices are likely to be lower in general than those currently prevailing, with a much greater degree of peak/off-peak differentiation. The result of changing the toll assumption in this way would be to increase the benefits to users, and reduce further the capital and operating costs of the alternative services, thus enhancing the attractiveness of the tunnel project.

User benefits

In calculating user benefits resulting from the tunnel, total traffic was divided into holiday, business, and freight. The benefit to each category consisted of a fall in its 'generalised travel cost', the sum of money and time costs.
Table 1 gives the sums involved.

Table 1
User benefits

	1980	1990	Present value[a]
	(£m.)	(£m.)	(£m.)
UK holiday passengers	12.4	18.8	108.7
UK business passengers	2.6	7.9	40.9
Freight	3.3	6.6	36.1
Total	18.3	33.3	185.7

Source: Table 7.1, page 42 of [1].
[a]in 1973 at 1973 prices, for years 1973–2030.

The time valuations and motoring costs used in deriving these were provided by the DOE; it is not proposed to go into the basis of those valuations here. The following points are worth noting, however:

(i) the cost (both money and time) of 1 mile travelled on the Continent by a British motorist was taken as exactly half that of a mile in the UK. This was based on the view that the Continental journey was 'part of the holiday', and so was less onerous. It was also said to 'reflect' the findings of the consultants in the demand forecasts. The latter study did not, however, produce this particular figure, but only the conclusion that 'travel time (on the Continent) is not of prime importance in the choice of holiday, country or region'. This particular value is therefore, likely to be even more arbitrary than most values of time.

(ii) On the other hand time spent crossing the Channel, of direct relevance to the cost–benefit analysis, is valued at the full DOE leisure rate of 23p per hour, thus assuming that travellers do not regard this as 'part of the holiday', or indeed something to be positively enjoyed.

(iii) A problem arose in this study which is common to many transport cost–benefit analyses. In making predictions of route choices, the travel costs which are used are those actually *perceived* by travellers. However, in evaluating the consequent benefits, the values which are used are the estimates of the 'true' travel costs, which in general differ from those which are perceived, due possibly to incomplete information or the inadequate computational ability of travellers. It follows that some travellers will be predicted as switching to the tunnel when they 'shouldn't' have, and some will be predicted as not switching when they should. In the former case, there is actually a disbenefit from the tunnel, and, in the latter case, a loss of potential benefit. The issue here is essentially one of misinformation. Indeed, by computing the sum of disbenefits to erring switchers and potential benefits to erring non-switchers, we obtain a measure of the benefit from providing *correct* information to travellers, which can be compared to the costs of doing so. The case for providing the information can then be evaluated. Indeed, an interesting case could arise in which a project would have a negative net benefit if this information were not provided and a positive net benefit if it were. However, assuming the information not to be provided, it surely has to be accepted, if one accepts as valid the analysis underlying the forecasting, that the loss of benefit predicted for travellers who switch 'wrongly' is a consequence of the project, and should logically be included as a cost. The present study, however, sets these disbenefits at zero, arguing that it is impossible to accept that someone would voluntarily make himself worse off. This is completely at odds with the logic of the forecasting and evaluation procedures on which the study relies quite crucially: the analysts cannot disregard the implications of the procedures when it suits them to do so, without bringing into question the validity of all the results based upon them.

(iv) As described above, the fare used in calculating the generalised travel cost of the tunnel was the Dover–Calais ferry rate, and so the user benefits arising from money savings to tunnel users will be very small.

(v) There is no weight given in the study to other possible sources of benefits to users, particularly greater reliability[14] and comfort from tunnel services across all weather conditions.

The study (in 1973) noted that if the tunnel were certain to be constructed, ferry operators would, from 1975 onwards, reduce their investment in a new capacity, in anticipation of lower demand. This in turn would have created shortages and peak congestion on ferry services until the tunnel came into operation. This would have represented a disbenefit to travellers of £15 m., discounted to 1973. The extent of the under-capacity was estimated from the fleet-scheduling model described earlier. The valuation of the loss of benefit was a matter of some difficulty, involving as it did assumptions on the way in which capacity would be rationed. The Report acknowledged the arbitrary nature of the final estimate.

Net capital and operating cost savings

These cost savings represent the difference in capital and operating costs of the ferry and aircraft services with and without the tunnel. Their magnitude therefore depends, first, on the extent of traffic diversion to the tunnel, and second, on the projected capital and operating costs of ships and aircraft. The latter were estimated by projecting information on current costs obtained from operators, on the basis of assumptions on rates of change of prices and wages, and future technology. These costs then played an important part in the fleet-scheduling model, which in turn helped produce the traffic diversion forecasts, as discussed earlier. Hence, errors in the estimates of future costs are not independent of errors in the tunnel traffic forecasts, but rather accentuate them. For example, if the estimate of ferry operating costs were 'too low', this would imply, through the fleet-scheduling model, an underestimate of traffic diversion to the tunnel (ferry fares are lower, given the 11 per cent target return, due to lower costs), and will also under-value the resources which would be saved by this diversion. Thus, the overall results are likely to be particularly sensitive to the cost estimates.

The calculation of a net present value

The various forecasting exercises and analyses, most of which have been described above, result in six time streams of costs or benefits:

(i) The UK share of the tunnel construction costs, and capital costs of a new rail link
(ii) capital and operating cost savings from slower growth of sea and air transport capacity
(iii) tunnel operating costs
(iv) benefits to UK users, consisting essentially of time savings to those who use sea and air routes
(v) revenue losses to existing operators, representing the extent of the pure transfer from producers to consumers
(vi) disbenefits to UK users arising out of smaller ferry capacity in the period 1975–80.

Each of these streams is discounted at the Treasury test discount rate (t.d.r.) of 10 per cent, and the resulting present values summed to give the net present value of benefits.

To criticise this procedure is essentially to criticise the Treasury doctrine on investment appraisal, a subject on which there is quite an extensive literature. The analysts were bound to follow this doctrine, and so they are guilty only by association. In this context, use of the procedure assumes:

(i) the present value of UK consumption which will be foregone, as a result of the tunnel, is equal to the present value of capital expenditure;
(ii) likewise the present value of UK consumption generated by the

capital and operating cost savings is equal to the present value of the expenditure savings.

(iii) the discount rate(s) which would be applied by all travellers to the future stream of benefits projected for them is a uniform 10 per cent.

(iv) the discount rate applied by all transport operators to the revenue losses is a uniform 10 per cent, and these losses correctly measure the future loss in producers' surplus arising from the tunnel.

(v) the discount rate applied by all travellers confronted with reduced quality of service in years 1975–80, to the disbenefits they will incur, is a uniform 10 per cent.

(vi) the distributional implications of the precise incidence of costs and benefits among UK households can be ignored.

The general arguments which could be levelled against these propositions—that household time-preference rates differ from the social opportunity cost of capital, and that market prices in which costs and benefits are measured may not reflect social opportunity costs, are well known and will not be rehearsed here.[15] One particular aspect of the project can, however, be mentioned, which has special bearing on assumption (i). This is that a significant proportion of the funds required for the project (the Report on the financial aspects of the Tunnel says 25 per cent) are expected to be raised abroad. The consequences of this could be quite significant.

To fix ideas, let us consider two extreme cases:

(*a*) Only financial flows are involved: the inflow of funds simply goes to expand UK foreign currency reserves or replace other foreign borrowing. The future repayments of the loan likewise are made out of reserves or replace other loan repayments. There are therefore no real resource effects.

(*b*) The inflow of funds represents a net addition to foreign borrowing, which results in the finance of a flow of imports of real goods and services. Thus, there is no corresponding loss of UK consumption or investment as a result of capital expenditure on the project in the years in which finance is provided. Thus, other things being equal, the social opportunity cost of the project is below its capital expenditure. However, it is then consistent to assume that future payment of the debt is made at the expense of future real consumption and investment. If, then, the UK time-preference rate on consumption is greater than the interest rate at which it has borrowed from abroad, the present value of foregone future consumption is less than the initial gain in consumption, and so the net opportunity cost of the project is less than the capital expenditure.

In practice, of course, the actual effect may be a combination of these two cases, and this poses considerable difficulties of estimation. Moreover, there could be an objection on conceptual grounds: it is reasonable to assume an increase in aggregate UK foreign borrowing because of the undertaking of a specific project, since an excess of the UK rate of time preference over the interest rate on borrowing abroad indicates that we would gain by expanding our foreign borrowing anyway. Indeed, the logical conclusion of this point is that foreign borrowing should be conducted up to the point at which the rate of time preference equals the interest rate, in which case the latter could be taken as the basis for public-sector discounting. This argument would certainly be true if we could imagine the UK public sector as an agent in a perfectly-competitive international capital market, able to borrow in a generalised way by issuing bonds. However, the international capital market is likely to be too imperfect to enable such a neat solution, and in particular the possibility of loans may be linked with the undertaking of specific projects. In that case, it is preferable to adopt a project-oriented approach, with an attempt to calculate the precise opportunity cost of a project given the extent of its foreign financing, the interest rate on this, and the time-preference rate.

Sensitivity analysis

All the estimates which have been described so far correspond to what the study calls the 'central case'. Tests of the sensitivity of the results for this case to changes in assumptions take two forms:

(i) the consequences for all benefit and cost streams of a lower GNP-growth assumption are set out in the so-called 'low case'. Thus, the central case assumes a UK GNP growth rate of 3.5 per cent p.a. from 1973–90, while the low case assumes a growth rate 20 per cent lower, at 2.8 per cent p.a. The differences in some of the main magnitudes are shown in Table 2. The table indicates a high degree of sensitivity of the final result to the growth-rate assumption, essentially reflecting the effect on total holiday demand of variations in the rate of growth. The tunnel project is highly 'geared' in the sense that benefits, particularly the most important single category, operating cost savings, are very sensitive to growth-rate variations whereas costs are not so.

(ii) The second kind of sensitivity analysis took the form of a series of *ceteris paribus* changes in individual assumptions, with a statement of the effect on the internal rate of return (i.r.r.) of the project in both central and low cases:

(*a*) the assumption of a high-speed rail link could be replaced by a 'low rail-investment strategy', which reduces capital expenditure but so increases journey time that there is no 'material effect' on the i.r.r.

(*b*) if fleet operators were to replace existing policies by greater use of peak-load pricing and consequent reduction in existing capacity there is less scope for capital cost savings resulting from the tunnel, and the i.r.r. is marginally reduced.

(c) the present Monopolies Commission inquiry could result in fare reductions on existing services before introduction of the tunnel. This reduces user benefit from the tunnel, since there is less

Table 2
Sensitivity to GNP growth assumptions

	Central case	Low case	Unit effect[a]
	£m.	£m.	£m.
Capital cost savings	156.1	129.9	3.7
User benefits	170.9	128.2	6.1
Operating cost savings	347.1	246.6	14.4
Decrease in revenues	121.5	99.9	3.1
Net present value[b]	291.8	147.9	20.6

Source: Tables 8.1 and 8.2, pp. 43, 44 of [1].
[a]Reduction in sum per 0.1 reduction in growth rate.
[b]Not the sum of previous items in this table.

possibility of competitive price reaction, and there is a loss of one point on the i.r.r. for each 30 per cent price reduction.

(d) An escalation in capital costs of the tunnel of 20 per cent, in real terms, accompanied by a two-year delay in completion, reduces the i.r.r. by 2–3 points.

(c) A 20 per cent reduction in future operating costs of ships and aircraft below the levels assumed in the study would reduce the i.r.r. by 2–3 points.

(f) Halving user benefits, equivalent to assuming zero values for time savings of UK holiday and business passengers, reduces the i.r.r. by 1½–2 points.

Before going on to more basic criticisms of both aspects of the sensitivity analysis, it could be said that choice of the i.r.r. in which to express sensitivities is curious. For well-known reasons the appropriate criterion for decision is the net present value of the project, and the change in the i.r.r. between assumptions may not be a reliable guide to the change in net present value at 10 per cent. If the elasticity of net present value with respect to the discount rate changes between cases, then a small change in the i.r.r need not imply a small change in the n.p.v. at 10 per cent. Thus, suppose in Figure 1 curve *A* corresponds to a 'favourable' and curve *B* to an 'unfavourable' assumption. Then, because of the change in slope of the curve, the sensitivity of the n.p.v. at 10 per cent is much greater than that of the i.r.r. If further illustration is required, note that when the income growth assumption is changed, the i.r.r. falls by three points from 17.6 per cent to 14.6 per cent, or by about 17 per cent, while the net present

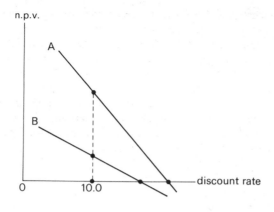

Figure 1

value falls from £291.8m. to £147.9 m., or by about 50 per cent.

A more important point is that the analysis of the effect of vary-ing the GNP growth rate is incomplete. On its own admission, the 'low case' in the Report is more important than the 'central case', because a growth rate of 2.8 per cent per annum is much more con-sistent with the past performance of the UK than one of 3.5 per cent. However, even the 2.8 per cent rate is no worse than a good average of past UK performance, and even if it is regarded as the central value in the distribution of future UK growth rates, there is a significant probability that the actual growth rate could lie below this. The outcome of the investment in such a situation is, however, left unexplored. Some idea of the consequences may be gained, in a rough and ready way, from the calculations of the 'unit effect' in Table 2. If we assume that there is a simple linear relation between growth rate and net present value of the project, then the unit effect gives the reduction in n.p.v. for each 0.1 point reduction in the growth rate. On this basis, the out-turns would be as in the table below

GNP growth (% per annum)	2.8	2.6	2.4	2.2	2.0
Net present value (£m.)	147.9	106.7	65.5	24.3	−16.9

Little more is intended by these calculations than to show what *could* be true. Given that whatever may be our hopes, our expecta-tions of future growth must include rates in the range 2.2–2.8 per cent with non-zero probabilities, the Report fails to provide informa-tion which would allow the sensitivity of the results to these pos-sibilities to be assessed.[16] This leads to the central criticism of the entire sensitivity analysis, which is that it is seriously inadequate for the purpose of presenting to the decision taker the information on which to base an evaluation of the riskiness of the project. The procedure of *ceteris paribus* relaxation of one assumption at a time, with vague information on likelihoods, allows only an impressionistic, and quite possibly wrong, view of the risks associated with the project to be formed. Suppose, for example, there was to be a 2.6 per cent growth rate, a 20 per cent escalation in tunnel construction costs, and a 20 per cent reduction in operating costs of ships and aircraft. From the results as presented, it is not possible to say what the outcome would be, nor how likely this outcome is relative to the more favourable outcomes. A more general approach to the measurement of risks should be taken, rather than that which selects a single 'central case' and then considers piecemeal adjustments to it.

There are three main sources of risk in this kind of cost–benefit analysis:

(i) that arising from the possibility that the hypothesised relationships, for example, those underlying the demand forecasts, may not continue to hold
(ii) that arising from the error variance of the forecasts made from regression relationships
(iii) that arising from the fact that values of independent variables in forecasting relationships, and of crucial valuation parameters, for example operating costs of ship and aircraft, value of time, and prices of competing services, cannot be known with certainty.

In some respects, it could be argued that given choice of the basic forecasting model, we simply have to accept the uncertainties arising from the possibilities (a) that it may not be the 'true' model for explaining the past, and (b) even if it is so, it may cease to be so in the future. An alternative approach would be to attempt to attach some prior probability of the 'truth' of the model, which could then be used to attach probabilities to the outcomes predicted by it. Where several models are regarded as possibly true, this approach could be extended by postulating a prior probability distribution of models. Such a 'Bayesian' approach to the problem is still relatively undeveloped, however, and most analysts would prefer simply to assume that the model will continue to be true. Given the choice of model, and assuming it is estimated by standard regression methods (as in the present study), it is in general possible to use the estimate of the variance of the distribution of error terms in the equation to obtain the variance of forecasting errors, conditional upon fixed future values of the independent variables. It is then possible to make statements about the interval within which the future value will be, around the forecast value, with a given probability. Increased emphasis on the provision and interpretation of interval forecasts, rather than point forecasts, would greatly increase the general understanding and credibility of forecasting exercises, and of the economists engaged in them.

The interval forecasts just described are themselves conditional on the assumed values of the independent variables. In general, these can only be predicted in terms of a probability distribution rather than a single, certain number. To assume otherwise is to leave out of account a significant aspect of the riskiness of a project. Given these distributions, it is then possible to combine them with the conditional interval forecasts to obtain a revised interval forecast which will incorporate the greater risk inherent in the stochastic nature of the independent variables.[17] Finally, by postulating, where appropriate, particular distributions of valuation parameters, e.g. ships' operating costs, interval estimates can be made of the final net present values of projects.

My basic contention is as follows: adopting this approach to the risks inherent in an investment project will certainly increase the scale and complexity of the analytical work; there will also be 'subjective' elements, such as the derivation of probability distributions of independent variables and valuation parameters. These are, however, differences of degree, and not kind, to existing appraisals. The information on the outcome of an appraisal should be presented to a decision taker in the form of a gamble, which is what the decision is. One should be able to state the odds on whether the net benefits of a project will turn out to be positive or negative, or greater than some alternative. It is both arrogant and wrong to suppose that civil servants and politicians would not 'understand' results so presented. The Channel tunnel sensitivity analysis typifies the kind of incomplete and selective information about risk which often accompanies major investment projects. It is inconceivable that a sensible evaluation of a risky decision could be made on this basis.

Conclusion

This paper has concentrated on the forecasting procedures and assumptions, and problems of cost-benefit analysis specific to this project, rather than general issues such as the appropriateness of considering only UK costs and benefits, the doctrine underlying the discount rate, and measurement of the value of time. It has also ignored what many may regard as the major sin of omission in the Report, namely the question of the amenity and environmental effects of the tunnel. The main points of principle which have been raised concern the price assumptions and treatment of risk in the study. The assumption on the level of the tunnel toll is extremely arbitrary, particularly when contrasted with the sophistication which went into estimation of the ferry operators' competitive responses; and the question of allocatively efficient prices should be pursued. In my view, the sensitivity analysis in no way presents a decision taker with the type and quality of information which is required to evaluate what is essentially a risky decision, and is *unnecessarily* inadequate. These are two areas in which more work should be done before a final decision on the tunnel is made.

The COBA Manual

A point which was mentioned in the previous section, and which forcibly strikes an economist working in the theory of public-sector resource allocation when he comes into contact with the operational realities, is the relatively small area of intersection of theory with practice. The COBA Manual is an attempt to introduce methods of cost–benefit analysis into perhaps the most basic level of road-investment decision taking, that concerned with small-scale projects for road improvement and realignment; improvements and capacity increases of junctions; and small-town by-passes. Such projects would typically have capital costs of between £¼ m. and £10 m. COBA consists of a standard computer programme, for which the planning engineer concerned provides certain input information on the road network before and after the investment, such as traffic flows, congestion, accident levels, etc. The programme simulates the operation of the network, pre- and post-investment, for each of thirty years. It then calculates time and vehicle cost savings, and accident reductions, as between the two situations, evaluates them using standard DOE valuation parameters, and produces a time-stream of net user benefits. These are then discounted to a present value, reduced by the amount of present value of capital expenditure, and the resulting n.p.v. is expressed in a ratio to the latter. The programme permits assessment of different project designs and timings, and also of the effects on a given project of the introduction, up to ten years later, of related schemes. It is also straightforward to test the sensitivity of results to changes in parameters—both input data and valuation parameters.

The COBA procedure is therefore almost the ultimate in routinisation of cost–benefit analysis. It is also a highly decentralised system with the analysis being conducted by those directly concerned with the project, who will often be non-economists, unindoctrinated in the rationale for the procedures they are using (the brief account of the concepts of consumers' surplus and discounting given in the manual perhaps allays doubts but hardly educates). The central control is provided by the choice of the key valuation parameters, as well as of the cut-off ratio of net present value to capital expenditure. Some measure of the scale of the innovation is obtained if COBA is compared to the system it replaces, under which projects were ranked on the basis of the ratio of user benefits in the first year of operation only, to the capital expenditure!

The main technical limitation of COBA is that it can handle neither trip redistribution, i.e. change of destination nor trip generation, i.e. increased demand for journeys, arising from the investment. It assumes that the number of trips between all origins and destinations is the same in the two situations, and so can only take into account diversion of traffic to different routes between given destinations. This means that it cannot handle two important classes of projects:

road construction and improvement schemes in urban or largely urban areas; and major, long-range inter-urban routes, where trip redistribution and generation are important consequences. Presumably this limitation is a matter of time and research effort.

Given the class of projects which it can handle, there are five main comments, some of them critical, which can be made about the COBA procedure. First is the omission from the present value of costs of the project, of the time delays and accident increases which are often experienced in the construction phase of projects such as these. The logic of the consumers' surplus approach requires that they be measured and included; they are unlikely to be a trivial element in the final n.p.v. of many projects, not least because they occur early in time and will be less heavily discounted.

It is interesting to note that because there will be a relatively large number of independent projects of this kind, the averaging which is involved in calculating valuation parameters, traffic flow relationships, etc., is unlikely to involve distortion for the outcome of the programme taken as a whole, because of a law-of-large-numbers effect. It could, on the other hand, matter in the choice between two mutually exclusive localised projects, in areas where the overall average value of, say, the value of time, was untypical. Likewise, some element of redistribution is involved, in that the benefits of projects in areas of high incomes and therefore high time values will be understated, and conversely those in low-income areas will be overstated. Given that workability of the procedure depends on its acceptance by planning engineers, the extent to which its results meet their *a priori* notions of what seems right and sensible may determine its success. The coincidence between results and expectations in turn depends on the extent of local deviations from the overall average, i.e., on the variances of the distributions of the parameters. It could turn out, in fact, that the procedure is over-centralised, and that greater leeway would have to be allowed to local planners to find the valuation parameters appropriate for their areas.

This point also relates to the riskiness of the projects. Since there is a large number of small independent projects, it would seem that risk could be ignored; the operation of the law of large numbers would imply that the variance of benefits of the entire programme would be very small, and so expected value maximisation would be appropriate. However, if the distribution of benefits of a project is not normal, the expected value of benefits is not the same as the most likely value of benefits, and it is far from clear that it is the former and not the latter which is calculated under the procedure.

The main doubts about the COBA procedure, however, arise in relation to the discounting and project-ranking procedures. The procedure has to confront a capital-rationing problem, in which the total budgets are set for some years ahead. Moreover, these budgets are such that projects whose n.p.v.'s are positive when discounted at

the t.d.r. of 10 per cent are rejected. The solution adopted is to calculate present values of benefits and costs at 10 per cent, rank projects on the ratio of n.p.v. to capital expenditure, and then apply
a cut-off point at a value of the ratio greater than zero.

No justification of this procedure is attempted in the COBA
Manual and indeed none is possible: it has no optimality properties
whatsoever.[18] First, consider the choice of discount rate. The rationale
of the t.d.r. is that it reflects the marginal rate of return on low-risk
private-sector investment. But since the capital expenditure of the
programme is fixed, this is no longer the relevant opportunity cost
of any investment within the programme. Thus, use of the discount
rate is inconsistent with the rationale of the t.d.r. Moreover, the fact
that projects with positive n.p.v.'s at 10 per cent are rejected means
that the shadow prices of the budget constraints in each period
exceed 10 per cent. Hence it is inappropriate to evaluate costs and
benefits accruing at different points in time at the 10 per cent rate.
In the most general case, a specified utility function defined on net
benefits at each point in time would be required before the problem
of optimal choice could be solved. If, however, the special form of
function:

$$U = \sum_{t=0}^{\infty} \rho^t B_t \quad 0 < \rho < 1$$

could be assumed, where B_t is total net annual benefit in year t,
then net present values of benefits could be directly computed using
the value ρ. The problem is that no one seems prepared to specify
a value of ρ.

Secondly, even given the appropriate values of n.p.v.'s, the use of
the ratio of n.p.v. to capital expenditure in ranking projects is inappropriate whenever capital expenditures are incurred in more than
one period. The use of the present value of capital expenditure in
the denominator of the ratio solves the problem of transforming a
vector into a scalar, but does so in a way which need not reflect the
relative scarcities of capital in each period and the relative demands
which projects place on them. It is, in fact, quite easy to construct
numerical examples which show that the fact that project A has a
higher n.p.v./capital-expenditure ratio than project B is neither
necessary nor sufficient for an optimal choice of A.

It is of interest to consider the question of deriving a fairly simple
rule for solving these problems,[19] and this can be done by examining explicitly the programming problem underlying them. Suppose
that we have some value for ρ in the above equation (Professor
Williams suggested basing it upon 10 per cent), together with a
specification of projects' capital expenditures, and the total
budget, over the planning horizon. Solving the primal programming
problem would provide an optimal investment plan; solving the
dual programming problem, which has the same information

requirement as the primal, would provide a set of shadow prices of capital for each time period, say λ_t, where these have the property that:

$$\frac{\delta \ \Sigma_t \rho^t B^*_t}{\delta C_t} \leqslant \lambda_t$$

where B^*_t is the value of benefits in year t arising from the optimal solution, and C_t is the capital ration in year t. Now if capital expenditures of projects are very small relative to the budget, then a close approximation to λ_t, the shadow price of capital in year t, is the present value of benefits of the 'best excluded project', which could be undertaken if the constraint in year t were relaxed. Now, from the so-called 'complementary slackness conditions' of linear programming, it can be shown that the property of any project which should be rejected is that:

$$\Sigma_t \rho^t B^j_t - \Sigma_t \lambda_t C^j_t < 0 \quad j = 1,2,\ldots,n$$

where B^j_t is the benefit in year t per unit of project j, and C^j_t is its per unit capital cost in year t. For practical purposes it could be considered worthwhile to try to obtain some kind of set of estimates of the λ_t, *without* having to go through the procedure of solving the entire problem. The solution suggested by Professor Williams is to assume the λ_t are all equal, and given by an estimate of the present value of benefits of the best excluded project, say, last year. This obviously involves a very strong assumption about the time patterns of benefits, capital expenditures, and budgets over the planning horizon. Nevertheless, the empirical research which could be carried out on past programmes would throw some light on this, and would be a significant step towards improvement in the existing procedures. Note, however, that it would not suffice to base estimates of the λ_t on the returns to the 'best excluded projects' under the existing COBA procedure since, as already pointed out, this has none of the optimality properties of the programming procedure suggested above: we would not be able to say that the 'best excluded project' under COBA is the one which would result from the programming analysis.

Conclusions

The COBA procedure is a significant contribution to solution of the problem of relating apparently optimal decision criteria to actual decision taking in the public sector. Its basic weaknesses relate to the procedures for evaluating and ranking projects, but these are not really of its own making. The attempt to operationalise the criteria set out in the 1967 White Paper [7] serves to bring out very clearly the ambiguities and contradictions inherent in the policy set out there. These weaknesses would, therefore, exist in any set of investment or pricing rules which attempted to do the same thing. That this is not more often brought to our attention is due to the fact that so few attempts are made.

General conclusion

The fact that the main criticisms of the studies do not overlap reflects the basic dissimilarity of the two. The issues of the pricing assumptions and treatment of risk do not arise in the case of COBA, while, because it will presumably not be counted as part of the general transport budget, the question of capital rationing and its effect on the appraisal does not impinge upon the Channel tunnel. However, it is possible to draw some general conclusions on the practice of transport cost–benefit analysis from the two studies. Each is a detailed study carried out within a common framework, consisting of certain centrally-determined valuation parameters and procedures. The defects in these studies relate primarily to this framework, rather than to the detailed attempts to provide the raw material of the evaluations.[20]

The appropriate form of presentation of a project's risks, the consistency of discounts rates with capital budgets, the correct calculation of opportunity costs of a project, the allocatively efficient pricing policies of a publicly-owned cross-Channel transport network, are all problems whose correct solutions need to be found centrally. I think it is fair to say that the guidance that project analysts have had on these subjects, when it exists, is either ambiguous and vague, or wrong. And yet the scale and sophistication of the research effort required to improve the evaluation framework common to all projects, is probably no greater than that invested in any one of the larger of them.

Notes

1. Described in the Report by Cooper and Lybrand Ltd., entitled 'The Channel Tunnel: a United Kingdom transport cost benefit study'. HMSO, 1973, and subsequently generally called the Report.
2. The discussion in this paper is based on the 'COBA Manual' which is an internal DOE memorandum. A summary of the procedure has, however, been published and is available from HMSO.
3. This work is described in a series of reports by the consultants. This paper draws particularly heavily on part 2, section 1, Passenger Studies, and the report on the Fleet Scheduling Model.
4. Strictly speaking the study would only justify the 'UK half' of the project, therefore, and overall acceptance of the project would still require it to be acceptable to the French.
   An interesting situation would arise if the desirability of the project altered with the side of the Channel from which it was approached (a possibility which I previously found unlikely, but persuasive arguments from Professor Williams have made me reconsider). Might there then be a case for side-payments?
5. This represents half the tunnel construction costs, plus the cost of a new

rail link, respectively £160 m. and £101 m. All figures presented in this paragraph are *present values* at 1973 in January 1973 prices.

6. Arising from time savings plus fare reductions, less revenue losses by ferry operators, this latter being the amount of pure transfer from operators to travellers. The relatively low value for consumers' surplus is commented on later in this paper.
7. A detailed description of these is found in the Report on Passenger Studies.
8. Note that this relates to choice of holiday location primarily within Western Europe where differences in travel time are relatively small.
9. A description of this part of the analysis is found in the report on the Fleet Scheduling Model.
10. Thus, a toll is assumed for the tunnel which is held unchanged throughout the analysis. There is a single sentence at the end of the analysis to the effect that it would not be worthwhile for the tunnel to enter into a 'price war'. This is a rather puzzling statement, in the light of the high cross-elasticities of demand between the cross-Channel services, given in the report. Did the analysts baulk at the problem of finding a solution to a full-scale duopoly problem? There are further reasons, discussed below, for regarding the toll assumption as unsatisfactory.
11. Thus the report itself tells us that there is over-provision of capacity because of an unwillingness to restrict peak demand sufficiently; and cross-Channel services are currently the subject of a Monopolies Commission inquiry.
12. For a theoretical treatment of this kind of problem, see Rees [5].
13. Again, for a treatment of this problem, see Rees [5].
14. This is measured in terms of the degree of dispersion of actual journey duration about its average value: the greater the dispersion, the less the reliability. At a guess, the tunnel would be more reliable, in this sense, than ferry services, particularly in winter.
15. My views on the correct approach to public sector investment appraisals can be found in Rees [6].
16. Mr D. Barrell, in his very helpful discussion of this paper, made the important point that the Report does not show the extreme sensitivity of the 'high railway investment strategy' to the growth rate assumption. It appears that even on the 'low case' assumption of 2.8 per cent p.a. growth, the n.p.v. on this investment, *considered separately from the tunnel*, is almost zero. This reinforces the point made here of the uninformative nature of the Report in presenting the risks inherent in the investment to a decision taker.
17. See, for example, Rees and Rees [4], where a procedure is set out for calculating the probability distribution of forecasts from a linear regression model with random independent variables.
18. See, for example, Rees [6], page 38.
19. This paragraph has been added to the paper since the Conference, and was stimulated by some comments from Professor Alan Williams; it is indeed an elaboration of some suggestions he made.
20. In relation to the tunnel-demand forecasts, although I criticised them and pointed out several areas in which they could be questioned, I regard the basic defect as the failure to translate the possible errors and uncertainties, which no forecasting exercise, however good, is without, into a description of the risks associated with the project.

References

[1] 'The Channel Tunnel: A United Kingdom transport cost–benefit study', a report by Cooper and Lybrand Associated Ltd., HMSO, London, 1973.
[2] Reports by the Joint Consultants to the Channel Tunnel Company, unpublished. Available on request at the library of the Department of the Environment, 2 Marsham Street, London, SW1.
[3] The 'COBA Manual', Internal Department of Environment document.

[4] J. A. Rees and R. Rees, 'Demand Forecasts and Planning Margins for Water in S.E. England', *Journal of Regional Studies*, 1972.
[5] R. Rees, 'Second Best Rules for Public Enterprise Pricing', *Economica*, 1968.
[6] R. Rees, 'The Economics of Investment Analysis', Civil Service College Occasional Paper 17, HMSO, 1973.
[7] 'Nationalised Industries: A review of financial and economic objectives', Cmnd 3437, HMSO, 1967.

17

Cost–Benefit Study of the New Covent Garden Market*

by J. H. Kirk and M. J. Sloyan

Introduction

This cost–benefit study, commissioned by the Covent Garden Market Authority, has tried to ascertain whether the relocation and rebuilding at Nine Elms, Vauxhall, of the horticultural wholesale market formerly at Covent Garden has proved worthwhile. It had then been in operation at the new site for nearly two years, an opportune time for making an appraisal with most of the benefits of hindsight. The study has covered all traceable costs and benefits attributable to the move, whether they have accrued to the Authority, its tenants (mainly wholesalers), growers, importers, retailers or the community at large. As we have been concerned only with the effects of changes from one site and one set of buildings to another, a complete accounting was unnecessary. For example, the number of market porters employed in 1976 was immaterial, but the reduction in number since 1974 had to be counted and valued. Although the new market is officially known as the New Covent Garden, we refer to it as Nine Elms. Repeated comparisons between New Covent Garden and 'old' Covent Garden would soon become tiresome.[1]

Both the relevant costs and relevant benefits cover a wide range. Some are large, others small; some immediate, others deferred; some relate wholly or mainly to Nine Elms, others to Covent Garden. For our purpose both costs and benefits have been grouped into two broad categories:

(a) Differences of operational costs (and benefits) at Nine Elms compared with Covent Garden (i.e. does the new market work more economically and effectively than the old?), and
(b) Benefit of released land and buildings at Covent Garden.

Both (a) and (b) have been considered on an annual basis, and the net effect (to anticipate, this will be a plus value for benefit less cost) has been considered as a rate of return on capital outlay at Nine Elms.

From *Public Administration*, Spring 1978, pp. 35–49. Reprinted by permission of the authors and the Royal Institute of Public Administration.

*This study was undertaken during the summer of 1976 and completed in September 1976. The figures given for wage rates, property values, etc. relate to that time.

There has been a complication in stating the amount of this since the Authority has erected at Nine Elms a twenty-one storied office block (Market Towers). A small part of this is used by the Authority, rather more is used for other purposes connected with market trading (banks, restaurants, etc.) and some of the rest by firms and organizations concerned with horticultural trading. We subtracted the non-market share of the capital costs of Market Towers from total capital costs, and consequently the rents received from non-market interests have been ignored.

NINE ELMS, CAPITAL COSTS

	£m.	£m.
Land*, ex Market Towers		6.7
Buildings, ex Market Towers		20.3
Market Towers	7.8	
Less: Non-market use	5.2	2.6
Authority's contribution to cost of improving Nine Elms Lane		0.4
Fees and interim finance, ex Market Towers		6.2
Total:		36.2

*Land=cost of acquisition and clearance (68 acres in all)

Most cost–benefit studies concerned with social costs and benefits necessarily include items difficult to quantify. If all costs and benefits not exactly measurable had to be ignored or excluded, few public investment projects would ever get started, since in the public sector as a rule more of the costs than of the benefits are measurable, the latter being widely dispersed and perhaps having no pecuniary value. The rule we adopted was to make our best estimates of the not fully measurable items, provided, and the proviso is important, that we were confident that our estimate was at least of the right order of magnitude. We left the remainder without any numerical values attached, however important they may be.

Operational Costs and Benefits

(a) *Labour and Machinery*

At Covent Garden there was a wasteful use of labour and one of the explicit objects of the move was to eliminate this. It was due in part to the fragmented and highly inconvenient layout of the market which impeded the deployment of labour and prevented the introduction of machinery on any scale.

Labour—We were able to obtain an exact account of the number of market porters saved since November 1974 from two sources: the Secretary of the Tenants' Association and the records of the severance scheme (severance payments to Covent Garden staff becoming redundant). We could feel fairly confident that this saving was due to the move, over and above the slow contraction in the manual labour force that had been occurring at Covent Garden over the years. Information on basic rates of pay and holiday pay was supplied by the local representative of the Transport and General Workers' Union, and we made our own estimates of national insurance contributions and workers' perquisites. In addition, we interviewed a sample of wholesalers and asked them detailed questions, on labour and machinery usage.

The number of porters saved by the move of the fruit and vegetable section of the market was 193, and in the flower section 4 (11 saved by private employers less 7 extra employed by the Authority). The estimated wage cost per man (including basic pay, holiday pay, porterage payments, perquisites and national insurance) was reckoned at £4,069 in the fruit and vegetable market, and multiplication by 193 gave £785,000 approximately. In the flower market the 11 men saved by private employers has economized £42,000 offset by an extra expense to the Authority of £23,000. The net saving in the flower market was therefore £19,000 and in the market as a whole, £804,000.[2]

Machinery—The principal classes of machinery and equipment used at Nine Elms were:

(i)   189 forklift trucks, for loading, unloading, stacking and internal movement over the storage or trading space;
(ii) racking: metal racks on which pallets holding produce can be stacked, one layer above the other, thus saving both space and labour in handling;
(iii) 8 electric pallet trucks used in the flower market;
(iv) 97 second-hand milk floats used in the fruit and vegatable market.

We were able to obtain exact information on the two largest items, forklift trucks and racking, from the supplers of these, and this information covered number, cost and length of life. Information on fuel and maintenance costs of vehicles was supplied by the Authority from their own records. Of the 189 forklift trucks, 81 remained the property of the supplier, and the traders paid a rent, which was of course ascertainable.

The following were the main annual costs:

	£
Forklift truck rentals	218,700
Forklift trucks, depreciation and interest on purchase	124,200
Pallet trucks, depreciation and interest on purchase	7,500
Milk floats	4,800
Battery replacement (mainly for forklift trucks)	68,900
Fuel for batteries	88,100

Pallet racking, depreciation and interest on purchase   23,200
Other equipment   2,600
                                                           ───────
                                                           599,900*

*of which £20,000 was in respect of the flower market

Labour and Machinery—The cost of mechanization, £600,000, therefore fell short of the saving on labour, £804,000, but only by a margin of about £200,000. On the other hand, part of the mechanization has had no close connection with labour saving but was introduced for the sake of speed and convenience. In that case signs of a beneficial effect would be seen elsewhere in this study.

(b) *Waiting Time of Delivery Vehicles*

These are the lorries which deliver produce from farms, country depots, ports, British Rail depots (principally Hither Green) and various points of departure on the continent. A majority of the vehicles belong to haulage contractors. We conducted a survey, which entailed interviewing 168 drivers, and counted the numbers of lorries entering and leaving Nine Elms on five nights between 22.30 hours and 08.00 hours. From these observations we estimated that during the year something like 110,000 trips are made by delivery vehicles to the fruit and vegetable market, and about 20,000 to the flower market.

Nearly all the drivers had previously delivered to Covent Garden and could be quite precise about the difference in waiting time at Nine Elms. The average time per trip saved in the fruit and vegetable market was given by the drivers as 2 hours 12 minutes, and at the flower market 1 hour 5 minutes. The weighted average was just about 2 hours.

This may seem very large. Nevertheless a main reason for leaving Covent Garden was to put to an end the extreme congestion in the streets up to a quarter of a mile from the centre of the old market. Vehicles had to fight for or queue up for parking space—there being virtually no authorized parking areas in the neighbourhood—and the wait could be very long, not only because of the number of vehicles, but because each had in the end to draw up more or less outside the place of business of a particular wholesaler (or perhaps several of these in succession). Matters were made worse by the great size of some of the lorries, particularly the articulated ones, together with the narrowness of most of the streets and abundance of sharp right-angled turns. When the lorry had finally drawn up, it had a long wait while being unloaded, often by hand, since the general Covent Garden layout permitted little use of pallets.

At Nine Elms, by contrast, there is an abundance of parking space, all of it off the public street; each of 400–500 lorries per day draws up at the rear entrance of the wholesaler's stand, and goes in a loading bay designed for that purpose just as soon as it becomes free. Because the market layout facilitates palletization, a large part of the produce arrives on pallet, which enormously speeds up unloading.

We next had to consider what use is made of the waiting time saved, totalling about 250,000 hours per annum. First of all, in most cases the vehicle is owned by a haulage contractor. What does he do with driver and vehicle arriving back two hours earlier than in Covent Garden days? Obviously no one can know in detail, but it is the business of a haulage contractor to find profitable loads so as to keep his drivers employed up to near the legal maximum of hours and keep the vehicle on the move almost all the time. We felt it reasonable to assume that most contractors have been able to replan their routes and loads so as to absorb at least some of the time saved at Nine Elms.

Another class of case is the short haul, e.g. from the London docks, Tilbury or Sheerness, where the saving of two hours may be just sufficient to allow driver and vehicle to make two trips in the working day instead of one. Next, there is the long haul within Great Britain where, except for the saving of time at Nine Elms, it would have been necessary for the driver to make a long stop-off, or seek a night's lodging, so as to comply with the maximum spread-over of hours (11) allowed by the Road Traffic Act, 1968. We saw least scope for profitable use of time saved in the middle distance routes (well within the Traffic Act limits but too long for two journeys a day) and on journeys from Poland, Bulgaria, etc., where a two hours saving at destination is neither here nor there.

The theoretical maximum saving is 250,000 hours, but we have assumed that the actual saving is half that, i.e. 125,000 hours. The value we placed on each hour was the driver's wage (night time rate), insurance contribution, etc., plus some small saving per hour on the vehicle, which even if not profitably used, should be incurring less wear and tear in its own garage than in the streets around Covent Garden, as used to be the case. We have taken the combined saving to be £4 per hour yielding an aggregate saving of £500,000 per annum.

(c) *Saving of Waiting Time: Wholesalers' Collection Vehicles*

Although most produce is collected from the market by retailers in their vans and cars, a substantial proportion (about one-third) has always left Covent Garden/Nine Elms in lorries owned by secondary and travelling wholesalers. Secondary wholesalers have their main place of business in provincial markets, and it is largely their use of Covent Garden/Nine Elms as a source of supply which gives this the character of a national market. Travelling wholesalers buy in the market (and elsewhere) and deliver to a round of retail shops, often via one of their depots.

We can estimate the number of trips per annum made by 'wholesalers' collection vehicles since the number of lorries at the market at collection time (deliberately made later than delivery time) was counted, and apart from a few belonging to chain retailers, these should be secondary and travelling wholesalers' lorries. An average saving of two hours per trip (the same as for delivery lorries) seemed a reasonable assumption, and the total hours saved per annum came out at 50,000. At £3 per hour this would be worth £150,000, of which we have assumed £100,000 to be productive saving.

This has left out of account, and we have not attempted to value, some further consequences of time saving at the market. If the secondary wholesalers can get back to their bases two hours earlier, they should be more competitive there, and be able to offer produce earlier and fresher. For the same reason the radius of travel to London from provincial markets has increased or should do so. The travelling wholesalers will also have the benefit of delivering earlier and with fresher produce, and should therefore be able to extend the distance they travel.

(d) *Retailers*

We found this the least satisfactory part of our enquiry. Of the retailers known to us through possessing authorized entry permits, a surprisingly large proportion could not, for one reason or another, be tracked down at their shops, or had had no previous experience of old Covent Garden, or spoke in a fashion which seemed confused or even contradictory. The sample we ended up with was only seventy-six independent greengrocers, apart from chains and stallholders.

Many retailers denied that they had saved any time. Either the distance from their shops to Nine Elms was greater than to Covent Garden, or they were taking longer at Nine Elms to contact those particular wholesalers with whom they were accustomed to deal. Unless remarks of this kind were being made for effect, the average time saved by independent retailers cannot have amounted to more than half an hour or so per trip. There was also a good deal of reluctance to admit that time saved—time acknowledged to have been saved—was being put to any useful purpose. Some retailers simply said that they used the saving to drink a coffee or to read the paper. A few said that they spent the time saved on extra dressing of the shop. None would go further than that though in eight cases where the retailers were buying at Nine Elms but had not bought at Covent Garden, we suspected they had changed their practice because Nine Elms was quicker. Our enquiries from two particular branches of the retail trade—the stallholders and the chains of specialist green-grocers—did not add very much.

Clearly one cannot begin to put a precise value on all this. The pluses evidently outweighed the minuses, perhaps by a large margin if one attached more weight to the probabilities than to what retailers have said. Since senders to the market and wholesale buyers were clearly profiting handsomely from the saving in waiting time (our estimate was £6,000 per annum) it would seen inconsistent if retail buyers were not also benefiting—and to a similar extent from a rather smaller saving in waiting time per vehicle but one applying to as many as 1,500 retailers (compared with 300 wholesalers). In the upshot we decided to credit Nine Elms with a benefit of £500,000 per annum by way of a token. For comparison, the retail value of produce coming from Nine Elms must have been at least £150 million per annum. The token sum took into account one or two secondary consequences of the saving of time such as the retailer being able to start serious business earlier in the day and with fresher produce, and finding it worthwhile to attend market in person from a greater distance than hitherto, hence buying to better advantage.

(e) *Wastage and Pilferage*

Wastage—Covent Garden was notorious for the waste occurring there. It was common for the streets and alleyways to be littered with it— not a few scraps here and there, but quite often drifts and mounds. In part this was due to the congestion and fragmentation of the site, resulting in much backing, sharp turning and manoeuvring of vehicles, so that fruit and vegetable containers could be jerked off the lorries or crushed against some obstruction. In part it was due to mainly manual loading and unloading of vehicles, with much rough handling, particularly the throwing of boxes or cartons, or setting them down with a bump. Where wastage took the form of spillage or destruction it could be seen to be something that took place in the market. But wastage of that kind might well have been surpassed, in terms of lost value, by bruising, which would show its effects later in shops or in the home, and hence not necessarily be attributed to the market.

A further cause of wastage, particularly affecting flowers, was that most of the premises were more or less open to the weather. Delicate produce suffered severely in hot, dry weather during the summer, or in very wet, cold or windy weather in winter. For all the more delicate types of produce, fruit and vegetables as well as flowers, waste can also occur if it fails to sell on the day of arrival because of irregularities of supply and demand and will not keep until the next day.

At Nine Elms, vehicle movement and manoeuvring take place at specially constructed bays, and a high proportion of produce is moved on pallet, both from the delivery vehicle and within the trader's premises. There is better protection from the weather throughout, and the covered unloading bays contrast strongly with unloading from the open street at Covent Garden. Produce awaiting sale is much better ventilated than at Covent Garden because of the better layout, and this is reducing deterioration during the summer months. The new flower market is a special case in that 24 hours a day air-conditioning is provided throughout the year, with great benefit to the life of flowers and shrubs during the summer. At Covent Garden only a small proportion of flowers unsold at the end of one-day's trading would be worth bringing forward for sale the next day. At Nine Elms there is little not worth holding over.

The fairest estimate we could make of former wastage at Covent Garden was 1½% in the fruit and vegetable sector and 5% for flowers. Probably these estimates were on the low side. It would not, we reckoned, be unreasonable to assume that since the move to Nine Elms, wastage of fruit and vegetables had been halved, and of flowers reduced from 5 to 2%. Applying these reductions to £84.1 m. of fruit and vegetables and £18 m. of flowers, both at wholesale values—though retail values might be more appropriate for much of the damage—the benefit of the move came out at £1.17 m. per annum. Insofar as the reduced wastage of flowers—say £540,000 out of the total of £1.17 m.—had been brought about by the air-conditioning system, we treated the cost of operating that system as an offset.

We could roughly cross-check this estimate. At the time of the study wastage at Nine Elms equalled 6,600 tons per annum—this is weighed as it is removed. It seemed to be a common opinion in the market that wastage had been reduced by two thirds since Covent Garden days, so that 13,200 tons of wastage had been saved. The best, though admittedly rough, estimate we could make of the total tonnage handled at Nine Elms was 600–700 thousand tons per annum, and as the aggregate value was about £120 m. a year, this gave an average per ton of £170–£200 (about 8 p per lb.). Applying £170 per ton to 13,000 tons gave a saving of just about £2 m. Our own estimate of £1.17 m. (previous paragraph) was related to a saving of just over one-half rather than two-thirds of the former waste, and we preferred the lower figure, even if it was a bit too modest.

Pilferage—For obvious reasons we could do little more than speculate about the extent of pilferage in the old market, though this was known to be considerable. The whole site, being intersected by public streets, was open to the public, and many drivers were obliged to draw up their vehicles at positions where they were out of sight while the driver was reporting arrival of his load—or in the case of retailers, doing business in the market. Unattended loads were of course highly vulnerable, even to the extent that whole cartons, crates and sacks could disappear. Many traders were driven to use the services of so-called 'cart minders' and the fees charged by these people were also a form of loss even if their services were effective, which was not always the case. A second source of loss was stealing, as a rule on a smaller scale and not involving a whole package, on the part of people employed in or in connection with the market, amounting to a great deal in aggregate.

At Nine Elms all the vehicles pass through gateways manned by the Authority's staff, and must halt at these to give their particulars. Vehicles of unfamiliar types which look out of place are challenged, and so are persons with no obvious business in the market. This system cannot of course keep out all unauthorized strangers and their vehicles, but they are open to challenge in a way that was not previously possible. Backing this up, the Authority employ security officers who are at all times on the look out for organized gangs.

But not much has been done, or could be done, to prevent small scale pilferage by persons who have the right to be in the market.

Pilferage was probably on the border line of items just worth trying to quantify, bearing in mind our criterion that we must be fairly confident of the order of magnitude. After due deliberation we estimated losses in the fruit and vegetable section of old Covent Garden as having been 1%, or £900,000 a year at recent values, and ½% in the flower market, or £100,000. We further assumed that pilferage of fruit and vegetables has been reduced by one quarter and of flowers by one eighth. The combined saving was worth approximately £250,000 per annum.

(f) *Adminstration and Maintenance*

Our starting point here was the Authority's annual accounts, which on the face of things showed that the move to Nine Elms had been accompanied by a rise in expenses of the order of £750,000 a year. Some of this represented inflation, some an improvement in the level of service, and part of the remainder was explained by the fact that the Authority are now rendering services centrally which formerly were shared by them, the traders and the local authorities. What we were primarily concerned with was any increase in administration and maintenance costs to which none of these explanations satisfactorily applied.

Salaries and pensions contributions—The increase of about £150,000 was partly attributable to inflation, partly to a higher level of service (e.g. increased security services) and partly to the centralization in the Authority's hands of services previously carried out by other parties. No doubt there was a valid explanation for the whole of the increase, but we felt that for the purposes of the study £50,000 per annum could be considered as a new social cost.

Rates—The difference in rate burden is in principle a social net cost (or benefit, depending on where the difference lies), but little further can be said since the rate liability at Nine Elms had not yet been determined, and the payments actually made had been provisional. The Nine Elms market area is about four times greater than Covent Garden, but the intensity of use is much lower and the site is away from Central London.

Maintenance repairs and renewals—The increase of about £150,000 a year was explained mainly by the fact that the Authority are now responsible for repairs of all buildings and not, as at Covent Garden, only for buildings on 6½ out of 15 acres. How much private landowners at Covent Garden previously spent on repairs is anyone's guess. In general we could not see how the cost of maintenance of a few large modern concrete buildings could exceed the cost of maintenance, if properly carried out, of an equivalent trading area occupied by 400–500 separate buildings, all old-fashioned and showing the effects of age. If anything, we felt it reasonable to surmise that the new market deserved a credit of about £50,000 per annum.

Repair bills have also to be incurred on machinery, and there is more of this in use at Nine Elms than at Covent Garden, even apart from forklift trucks and the like—for example, the air-conditioning plant, the central boiler system, and much electrical switchgear. The cost of maintaining this equipment could not be judged from less than two years experience of using it, but we suspected that the saving of cost on structural maintenance was roughly offset by the costs of maintaining more equipment. The benefits of the extra equipment were taken into account elsewhere in the study.

Cleaning—The increase of about £125,000 in the Authority's accounts seemed astonishingly large until one remembered that at Covent Garden much of the litter and dirt was deposited on public roads and other public spaces, so that responsibility fell on the local authorities for gathering it up and removing it, and swilling down. Traders were of course responsible for litter in their own premises, so that to the extent that the Authority now act as their agent, performing a cleaning service reflected in the rents charged, there was an increase in apparent cost.

In general we did not see how there could have been a real increase in cleaning costs in and around new and properly designed buildings, which are relatively easy to clean, and form part of a layout calculated to minimize spillage and wastage. On the other hand, Nine Elms may have a greater total floor area to be swept. We decided to credit the new market with £50,000 per annum on the ground that the true costs of cleaning have probably been reduced by at least that much, though we recognized that in practice this benefit might be taking the form of a cleaner market rather than a lower cost.

Heating and Lighting—The increased cost in the Authority's accounts was about £170,000 a year, made up of higher rates of charges for electricity, centralization of service in the hands of the Authority, and a higher level of service (e.g. an estimated £85,000 per annum for air-conditioning of the flower market). We could but speculate whether it cost more or less to heat and light, probably to lower standards, some 15 acres of old fragmented properties at Covent Garden. Our conclusion was that it was justifiable to debit the new market with £85,000 a year, the estimated cost of the air-conditioning service, on the grounds that we had already taken credit for a smaller wastage of flowers. The remaining factors relating to heating and lighting appeared too uncertain to pursue.

Depreciation—Comparison with Covent Garden was impossible. Probably many of the private landowners were not in practice making any depreciation charge in their accounts on the ground (probably specious) that after 200 years the buildings could be considered as written down to nil. In the circumstances we felt that this subject could not be further pursued.

The costs and benefits considered in this section appeared to have roughly cancelled out. This conclusion could be little more than a guess but we had no hesitation in dismissing as of no real significance nearly all the apparent big increase in administration and maintenance expenses following the move to Nine Elms.

(g) *Traffic Flow*

Messrs. Freeman Fox (the Authority's advisers in 1966) gave a lot of attention to this aspect, and made two estimates, both of the order of £200,000 per annum at 1966 values, of the social benefit of certain major road improvements in the vicinity of Nine Elms, if the move there was in fact accompanied by the improvements. No allowance was made, however, for interest or other annual costs of these works on the ground that they were due to be carried out anyway and that market traffic would be only a small proportion of the whole.

The improvements have in fact been made—by the Greater London Council. We understood that although the work would have been done anyway, it was brought forward because of the impending relocation of the market. Hence we should, strictly speaking, have charged the market move with the interest cost over the period between when the work was done and when it would otherwise have been done. We doubted, however, whether enquiries of the Greater London Council on this point would be fruitful.

On the benefit side there was now obviously much less congestion around Covent Garden, benefiting both the main thoroughfares and the lesser streets. The relief which the move to Nine Elms has afforded has become visible even to the casual observer in Long Acre, and is appreciable in the Strand and Wellington Street. Messrs. Freeman Fox gave a figure of £550,000 (1966 values) for the social cost of traffic congestion at Covent Garden and in Central London, due to market traffic. For our part we have thought that quantitative estimates in this area are altogether too speculative. We have, however, observed that the traffic flow in the vicinity of Nine Elms appears to be at an acceptable level, and that the presence of the market there has proved to be no disadvantage to non-market traffic. This was partly due to the road improvements, and partly due to the speeding up of operations in the market so that the peak of market traffic is over before the ordinary morning peak has begun. For the rest we have supposed that the relief of congestion at Covent Garden, considered as a benefit to non-market traffic, must amount to much more than the interest charge attributable to bringing forward the date of the road improvements at Nine Elms, and we regret having been unable to measure the former (relief at Covent Garden) since it must be very substantial indeed.

Values of Released Property at Covent Garden

If the cost of the land acquired at Nine Elms and the buildings erected on it is an absorption of national resources, the same logic requires that the land and buildings released at Covent Garden shall be valued and set against costs at Nine Elms. The area is about 15 areas—6½ arces formerly owned by the Authority and 8½ owned by a variety of persons and firms who either were or had let premises to market traders.[3] The value of the released land has been considered on an annual basis and treated as a current benefit to be set against current costs at Nine Elms. The alternative method of deducting the capital value of the Covent Garden land from the capital expenditure at Nine Elms, and then dividing the remainder into the net cost or benefit resulting from the other items, so arriving at a rate of return (positive or negative) has seemed to us open to the risk of exaggeration.[4]

Most rebuilding and relocation projects involve the valuation of released land and other resources, and doing this is seldom easy. Before and shortly after the transfer there will not have been enough transactions to establish average values. At the time of the study about 7½ acres had changed hands out of 15—6½ formerly belonging to the Authority and one acre of privately owned miscellaneous properties—but neither group was fully representative.

Planning Restrictions

Secondly, one has had to consider the uses to which the released land is or may be put. In theory perhaps the Covent Garden land should be valued at what it would fetch on the open market, taking the highest valued use, which in this case would be as offices, and disregarding the eventual actual use. There is, however, no commercial need for 15 acres of new office blocks in the Covent Garden neighbourhood[5] and even if there were, such a monolithic type of development would be a negation of planning. The planning authorities, mainly the Greater London Council, had not yet decided in a positive and affirmative way what uses they would allow and promote over the Covent Garden area as a whole. They had, however, made certain negative decisions which were almost as important. They were, for instance, opposed to any new office development—even in some cases to the continued use of premises as offices—and were not much better disposed to development in the form of shops, eating places, etc. Apart from that part of the area in the vicinity of the Opera House which has been reserved for public purposes, it seemed that the remaining permitted uses would, for the most part, be either residential (flats) or low grade commercial, e.g. warehouses, both types of uses being rather unremunerative.

Listing

Moreover, these existing and prospective restrictions are being accompanied by the listing of many buildings as of outstanding architectural or historical importance. There are many such buildings in the Covent Garden area since much of it was built over in its present form in the architectural style of the eighteenth century. The Greater London Council had already listed 120 buildings on its own initiative when the Secretary of State for the Environment added 130. Most of the 250 are buildings formerly used by market traders, and something like half the premises formerly so used are now listed.

Listing, however well justified it may be, has various effects on capital values. First a listed building cannot be used by its present owner or any purchaser for purposes incompatible with preservation in its present state: the range of possible uses is restricted and some remunerative uses will be excluded. Secondly, the owner is deprived of the opportunity of modernizing or enlarging and is saddled with an eighteenth century type of structure for an indefinite period. Thirdly, if the building cannot be pulled down it must be kept up, an and this will require heavier expenditure on painting, roofing and other repairs than most of these buildings have had hitherto. On the other hand all this listing might attract a new class of purchaser, i.e. the residential owner with artistic tastes, as has happened elsewhere, but our judgement was that the net effect of listing could be substantially prejudicial to capital values, whether the land was held for use or as an investment.[6]

Capital Values

It was useful, and perhaps necessary, to consider the 15 acres under three different heads:

(a) 1.9 acres at the southern extremity (the 'core' of the old market) almost all of which was occupied by a massive market hall (the 'dedicated market'). This was transferred from the Authority to the GLC at a price in the region of £400,000 negotiated between the parties under the eye of the Department of the Environment.
(b) 4.6 acres adjacent to the dedicated market, mostly publicly owned, having changed hands since the move to Nine Elms in November 1974. The sale price was £8.7 m., i.e. £1,900,000 per acre on average.
(c) 8.5 acres to the north and north-west of blocks (a) and (b).

(a) and (b) both changed hands at the end of 1974 or beginning of 1975, when property values in Central London were somewhat higher. The subsequent relapse was an annoying complication, somewhat arbitrary in its effects, but we needed to consider property values at Covent Garden at the same dates as those applying to the evaluation of costs and benefits at Nine Elms, so that like could be compared with like. Our best guess was that in August 1976 the £200,000 per acre actually realized for block (a) would have been £180,000 and that £1.9 m. for block (b) would have been £1.7 m.

Virtually all of block (c) is in private ownership. We had to ask ourselves whether it is likely to fetch more or less per acre than block (b) to which it is fairly similar. For three reasons we thought that on average it would fetch more:

(i) most of the properties are of a general purpose type, capable of a fair range of uses, and through their location they merge into the mixed commercial area of St. Giles (north of Covent Garden proper and south of the British Museum);

(ii) they should be rather less subjected to planning restrictions than the properties lying nearer to the Strand and the Covent Garden Opera House;

(iii) the owners can take their own time about selling, which was not altogether true of the disposals that have already taken place in block (b).

On the other hand block (c) can be regarded as lacking in character compared with block (b), and some business firms might find addresses within it to be lacking in prestige.

We decided to take £1.9 m. per acre as the fairest estimate we could make for the average of block (c).

Averaging blocks (a), (b) and (c) we got—

(a) 1.9 acres at £180,000	= £ 340,000
(b) 4.6 acres at £1,700,000	= £ 7,820,000
(c) 8.5 acres at £1,900,000	= £16,150,000
Total: 15 acres at £1,620,000	£24,310,000

We had now, for the reasons already given, to convert this into annual values. These were even more difficult to ascertain by observation than were capital values since not many properties had been let since the move to Nine Elms, and those that had been, did not seem to be representative. Fortunately, we could use the concept of number of years' purchase, which is an established convention. If the net annual rental value of a property is known, multiplication by the appropriate YP will give the maximum sum worth paying as a capital outlay: conversely if the capital value is known, division by the YP will give the minimum net annual rental necessary to justify purchase at that price. If the Covent Garden properties were just ordinary commercial properties in Central London, subject to no particular planning restrictions, we understood that the appropriate number of years' purchase would be 10–12. The various restrictions already in operation at Covent Garden or likely to be, made this figure much too high. We had in mind both listing and, perhaps more important, the restriction of most of the development to housing and warehousing, less remunerative uses than prevail over most of Central London. We believed the appropriate YP to be 8 in this case. In other words, although the restrictions diminish the freedom of occupiers and interfere with their operations, they bite even harder on owners and thus alter the relativity between capital value (the owner's equity) and annual value (what the property is worth to its occupier).

A division of £1.62 m. by 8, and multiplication by 15 (acres) resulted in an aggregate annual value of just over £3 m. We took this as a form of revenue to be set against cost at Nine Elms.

Summary and Conclusions

The various possible benefits we considered can be arranged thus:

	Net Benefits £'000 per annum
Operational Costs and Benefits	
Labour and machinery use	200
Saving of waiting time: delivery vehicles	500
Saving of waiting time: wholesalers' collection vehicles	100
Retailers (various aspects)	500
Reduction of Wastage and Pilferage	1,420
Administration and Maintenance	Nil
Traffic Flow	No estimate
Value of released land at Covent Garden	3,000
TOTAL:	5,720[7]

We saw that the capital investment at Nine Elms was £36.2 m., and some £5.7 m. of net benefit represents a return of almost 16%. As this rate exceeds that commonly expected of and received from public enterprises generally, little further comment seems called for. But one point is worth repeating. If the land and buildings at Covent Garden could have been sold subject to no severer planning restrictions than apply in Central London generally, the annual value would have been greater, and the rate of return on the move to Nine Elms likewise.

Finally can it be said not only that operations at Nine Elms are more efficient and economical than at Covent Garden, but that these benefits have been receiving recognition in the form of a larger volume of trade? Statistics of turnover are collected by the Authority, but are necessarily out of date and need careful consideration and interpretation. To venture on a summary statement, however, it appeared to us that the first year of operations at Nine Elms had resulted in a volume increase not far short of 10%.

Notes

1. Following are previous appraisals, both made before the move: (i) an unpublished report (1966) by the consulting engineers, Messrs. Freeman, Fox, Wilbur Smith and Associates, on the basis of which the decision to make the move was reached; and (ii) an article (*Journal of Agricultural Economics*, Vol. XXIII, No. 1) by A. J. Le Fevre and J. F. Pickering (1972).
2. In making these calculations a tricky point arose in connection with porterage payments worth £1,150 per man in the fruit and vegetable market and £780

in the flower market. Porterage payments are a form of piece work pay additional to the basic time rate. As the number of 'pieces', i.e. packages, had not fallen, but probably risen, the same or a larger sum of money was being shared by 200 fewer men. At first sight the saving in labour cost ought not to include the saving on porterage payments formerly paid to 200 men, since these had been absorbed by the remaining men: but the proper way to look at this was that the total labour saving included the porterage payments of the men no longer there, but that this part of the benefit had been pre-empted by the remaining labour force. In a *social* cost–benefit study society includes market porters, and anything which raised their earnings was their share of the benefit.

3. Precision about the area is not possible. Firms on the fringe of market trading may or may not have been included in the 1971 GLC survey, and some traders had sublet the upper floors of their buildings to non-market interests.

4. For instance, if the capital value of land released at Covent Garden nearly equalled the outlay at Nine Elms, even a trifling net operational gain from the move would show up as an enormous percentage.

5. For convenience 15 acres of land is thought of as affording 15 acres of office space, but the ratio, not necessarily 1.1 would depend on the layout and design.

6. Much of the discussion in this sub-section has been based on information supplied by Messrs. Knight, Frank and Rutley who act for the Authority in respect of their remaining interests at Covent Garden. They have supplied useful information on the disposal possibilities of many of the Covent Garden properties and on the values realized so far, i.e. the Arts Council property, the GLC purchase of nearly two acres and the Poupart building.

7. A subsidiary calculation, not worth spelling out in detail, has attributed at least £3 millions of this gain to 'market users', i.e. all those directly or indirectly connected with the market by way of trade.

18

Pollution Control—Direct Controls Versus the Pricing System

by W. J. Baumol and W. E. Oates

---

1 A Pluralistic Approch to Environmental Policy

While economists and other interested groups have agreed upon the desirability of environmental protection, they have taken quite contradictory positions on the best way to do the job. Economists have, with few exceptions, rejected both direct controls and calls for voluntary compliance, the methods preferred by many others concerned with the environment. Instead, economists advocate the use of pricing measures—monetary rewards and penalties—which they believe to be more efficient, more permanent, and more desirable for a number of other reasons. Other groups have often shown little interest in such pricing approaches and have instead turned to appeals to conscience or, more commonly, to the instruments of the law: the regulatory agencies, the police powers, and the courts.

Our own position is that the outlook of both groups is too narrow; neither view has taken adequate account of the merits of the other. In fact, we will argue that each of the available policy instruments has its particular virtues (and shortcomings), and that each is best adapted to deal with particular circumstances. [. . .] In our view, effective policy requires a wide array of tools and a willingness to use each of them as it is needed.

We begin our study of policy instruments in this chapter with an examination of the role of price incentives; we shall explore the virtues of the fiscal approach in relation to those of direct controls. Let us stress that we do not do so because we believe price incentives are the only effective instruments for environmental protection. Rather, we want to show that the policy maker who is not prepared to consider their role in environmental programs embarks on a difficult task with one hand tied behind his or her back. This assumes a special importance in view of the demonstrated reluctance of environmentalists to make use of pricing incentives for protection of the environment.

2 The Economic Rationale of the Pricing Approach

The fundamental logic of pricing incentives is straightforward. Put very briefly and a bit superficially, the basic source of our

From *Economics, Environmental Policy and the Quality of Life* © 1979, pp. 230-245 (Prentice Hall, Englewood Cliffs, NJ, 1979). Reprinted by permission of the publishers.

environmental problems is the fact that the price system simply is not applied to many of society's resources. [. . .] The air and our other environmental resources can be used by anyone who chooses to do so, without payment for the privilege.

The proposal that the economist makes is, consequently, an obvious one: our scarce and valuable natural resources should be provided at an appropriate price. More specifically, the economist calls for a reorientation of the tax system—not necessarily increasing the overall level of taxes, but changing *relative* prices to provide incentives for the conservation of environmental resources. Once again, an example will help to clarify the issue.

Suppose we decide that the oil industry is currently paying the right total amount in taxes, but that it is also desirable to encourage the removal of lead from fuels. For this purpose one could *reduce* the tax on unleaded gasoline, and *increase* it on leaded gasolines. This would give the industry the opportunity to behave in a manner consistent with social goals with no loss to itself. Nor need this procedure constitute either a drain on the public budget or a subsidy to industry. Given the efficiency with which private enterprise pursues its profits, the speed of the resulting changeover to lead-free fuels would, no doubt, be impressive. Similarly, much could be done to reduce airplane noise by the imposition of substantial differentials in landing fees based on the noise level and pollution emissions of the airplane.[1] As another example, we can reduce the flow of trash by imposing a significant tax on no-deposit, no-return containers, perhaps accompanied by a reduction in sales taxes on returnable containers [. . .]. In each of these cases the basic notion is the same: by offering virtue its just (financial) reward, we change the rules of the game to induce industry (and individual consumers) to alter their behavior to promote an environmental objective.

3 Criteria for Evaluating Environmental Policies

Before examining in detail the advantages and disadvantages of the pricing approach to environmental protection, we want to consider the criteria on which to base the evaluation. The following list seems to us to encompass the most pertinent considerations for the appraisal of environmental policies:

a. *Dependability*. How reliable is the approach in achieving its

---

[1] There have been a number of discussions of the use of fees in inducing reductions in aircraft noise. See, for example, J. P. Barde, 'Aircraft Noise Charges', *Noise Control Engineering* 3 (No. 2, September–October 1974): 54–58, and David Pearce, 'Charging for Noise', OECD (Paris, 1976). The Japanese have actually instituted 'noise charges' for aircraft; in September 1975, they adopted a set of landing charges where the fee per aircraft landing is based on the noise category of the airplane.

objective? Are its workings fairly certain and automatic or does it depend on a number of unpredictable elements?

b. *Permanence*. Is the program likely to be effective only so long as it captures public interest, or can it be expected to endure even when other issues have seized the attention of the media and the public?

c. *Adaptability to Economic Growth*. Is the program flexible enough to adapt to normal expansion in economic activities and population growth, both of which tend to accentuate problems of environmental damage?

d. *Equity*. Does the program divide its financial burdens among individuals and enterprises fairly?

e. *Incentives for Maximum Effort*. Does the program offer inducements to individuals or enterprises to minimize environmental damage, or does it encourage no more than barely acceptable behavior?

f. *Economy*. Does the program achieve its results at relatively low cost to society, or does it waste resources?

g. *Political Attractiveness*. Is the method likely to recommend itself to legislators and to voters?

h. *Minimal Interference with Private Decisions*. Does the method tell the individual or the businessman exactly what to do, or does it offer the broadest scope of choices consistent with protection of the environment?

Let us now see how the pricing approach performs in terms of each of these criteria.

4 Dependability: Tax Measures vs. the Criminal Justice System

One of the fundamental differences between pricing techniques and the direct-controls approach to environmental protection is that the latter characteristically treats environmentally damaging activities as illegal acts, while the former considers them normal consequences of economic activity which should certainly be curtailed, but without the use of the police powers of the state. Economists maintain that, where a phenomenon such as waste emission is an inherent, regular, and continual part of human activity, it must be controlled by continuous methods that are correspondingly routine and regular. The fiscal approach typically uses the meter rather than the police inspector for enforcement. For example, the proposed tax on leaded gasoline requires no more than a record of how much of that type of gasoline has been sold. The emissions of pollutants by a factory can also, in principle, be metered, billed, and paid for like electricity, gas, and water. There are no crimes to be discovered, no legal battles over the level of fines. Enforcement is not sporadic: it is routine, continuous, predictable, and, consequently, effective.

In this respect, the use of pricing incentives, at least in principle, differs markedly from the reality of outright prohibition. The effectiveness of prohibition clearly depends on the vigor and clout of the enforcement mechanism. Violators of a regulation must first be caught in the act. They must then be prosecuted, found guilty, and given a substantial penalty. If any of these steps fails, the violators get away (virtually) free despite their disregard for the law. No such problem arises in a system of fees under which polluters simply receive their monthly bills as a matter of course.

A typical example of the workings of direct controls is the de facto erosion of the laws forbidding the use of garbage incinerators in apartment houses. Landlords, who are occasionally subjected to token fines on a rather random basis, find it far cheaper to pay the fines than to close down their incinerators. So the incinerators continue to pour forth noxious fumes, even though their use has been prohibited absolutely and categorically.[2] There are, in fact, many instances of fines so low as to render regulation ineffectual.[3] Enforcement by inspectors, moreover, offers a temptation for evasion, and often for bribery and outright corruption. Tax collectors are probably no more law-abiding than inspectors, but the operation of the tax system is characteristically too businesslike and the record-keeping too systematic and routine to provide the widespread opportunities for evasion offered by periodic personal surveillance.

5 Permanence and Adaptability to Growth

A major problem that besets most regulatory efforts is that the effectiveness of the regulation is dependent on a high level of public

---

[2] Another interesting case of the failure of a policy of outright prohibition is the ban on the sale of the skins of certain endangered animals in the United States. The result has been the creation of a lucrative black market, with an incentive for poachers to kill as many of these animals as they can. Alligators are one example.

[3] The following examples indicate the sorts of fines to which polluters have been subject: '2 Companies Admit Polluting Harbor: Each is Fined $750' (*New York Times*, January 31, 1970, p. 25); 'Consolidated Edison admitted that it was guilty of having discharged oil into the East River . . . [it is] liable to a maximum fine of $2.500 . . . ' (*New York Times*, January 31, 1970, p. 22); 'Ten Philadelphia firms were fined a total of $2900 Friday in the seventh week of the City's accelerated drive for violation of the air-pollution code' (*Philadelphia Inquirer*, October 30, 1970); 'The Justice Department filed charges today against seven companies, including two steel concerns, accusing them of polluting waterways in the Chicago area . . . . The maximum penalty is a $2.500 fine for each offense' (*New York Times*, September 21, 1971, p. 74); '[New York City] has collected $800,000 in fines against air and noise polluters over the last three years . . . ' (*New York Times*, June 25, 1974, p. 37). However, it should be noted that very recently financial penalties upon polluters have, in a number of cases, risen significantly. An example is the case of the discharge of the extremely toxic chemical, Kepone, into the Virginia-Maryland coastal region by an Allied Chemical plant. Allied was originally fined $13.2 million for damages to the James River and surrounding area (the fine has recently been reduced to $5 million because of Allied's cooperation in mitigating the damages).

concern. The effects of regulation are often transitory. In the first blush of public enthusiasm, an agency may uphold the severity of standards by relatively effective enforcement. However, some years later, when public attention has focused on other issues, the strength of the enforcement mechanism ebbs. The regulatory agency then takes on the characteristic bureaucratic lassitude that is compatible with self-preservation and the avoidance of trouble.

On the other hand, fiscal incentives, *once instituted*, need no reinforcement. 'Nothing is certain,' says the homily, 'but death and taxes.' It is this assurance of the arrival of the periodic tax bill that gives a fiscal program its reliability. A tax on smoke emissions that is billed monthly will continue to exert its influence on managerial decisions indefinitely. Unlike a program dependent on the vigor of a regulatory agency, the tax incentive does not require continued enthusiasm for the cause.[4]

There are, however, two possible sources of erosion of the effectiveness of a fiscal program: inflation and economic growth. A tax bill of a fixed number of dollars per unit, which might have been rather substantial twenty years ago, may have become relatively modest with a decline in the purchasing power of the currency. Moreover, if there is growth in population and industrial activity, pollutant emissions will rise unless the tax rate is increased steadily.

One way to get around the inflationary effect is to base tax payments on the price that polluters charge for their final output, which should increase with the general price level. Or [. . .] a fiscal alternative to effluent charges, the auctioning of pollution permits, can deal quite effectively with both the problems of inflation and growth. But tax measures themselves can be responsive to inflation. If they become an important source of revenue to state and local governments, rising budgetary pressures will generate inducements for increases in tax rates. In any event, it seems clear that, despite the problems of rising prices and economic growth, we can expect the effectiveness of fiscal programs to be far more durable than that of direct controls.

[4] It should be emphasized, however, that this conclusion holds only after an effective system of charges has gone into full operation. It would be naive to expect that those who seek to escape effective environmental measures will not find ways to combat a system of charges. One can be sure that, if such a program becomes a serious possibility, lobbyists will set themselves the task of inducing legislators to reduce the fees to a minimum—to a point where they become ineffective. One can also expect that such legislation, once passed, will be tied up in the courts for years by a variety of legal challenges. But there is still a difference here from the case of direct controls. In the latter, enforcement can require continual court battles—battles against the erosion of enforcement and penalty levels. In the case of a system of charges, once an adequate level of charges has been set by the legislature, and once the courts have confirmed its legality, its enforcement becomes largely automatic and requires little governmental vigilance except in billing for and collecting the fees. [. . .]

6 Equity

The regulatory approach is often thought to be superior to the use of pricing incentives in terms of fairness. Consider, for example, the case where an environmental authority determines that BOD* emissions into a particular waterway should be cut in half. The most fair or equitable method of realizing this objective would appear to require all polluters to reduce their BOD discharges by 50 percent.[5] This would seem to allocate the necessary reduction in BOD emissions in a nondiscriminatory way.

Unfortunately, the appearance of fairness is largely illusory. We reemphasize the wide variations among industries and plants in the cost of pollution abatement. Some industries can easily recycle and make other adjustments in production processes, but for others, reductions in pollution are much more expensive. An order to reduce BOD emissions by 50 percent is likely to prove far more expensive for some firms than for others. If our objective were to distribute emission quotas fairly, perhaps we might do better to require reduction quotas such that the unit *cost* of the cutbacks were the same for all polluters. From this perspective, effluent fees may arguably be more equitable than a uniform percentage reduction in wastes.[6]

But even this is only half the story. If there remains any fairness in the uniform quotas among polluters, it will largely disappear in the chaotic process of issuing permits and administering the program. A recent study of the allocation of emission quotas among polluters along the Delaware Estuary provides some instructive insights into this issue.[7] The Delaware River Basin Commission (DRBC) selected a set of targets for levels of dissolved oxygen. Deciding against the use of fees, the Commission set a requirement for an essentially uniform percentage cutback (between 85 and 90 percent) in BOD discharges for all polluters.

This might seem simple enough, but the implementation proved far from easy. From what was the uniform percentage reduction

---

*Biochemical oxygen demand. A measure of the organic waste load of an emission. Used as an index of the quality of effluents [Ed. Note].

[5] In fact, this is not how regulators have acted in practice. In part this is because they have responded to special problems of different polluters. The Clean Air Act, the Water Pollution Control Act, and the Noise Control Act all direct the regulator to take into account the individual polluter's cost of abatement and ability to reduce polluting activities.

[6] However, this is only part and, indeed, the less important part of the equity issue. Ultimately, a substantial part of the costs will be borne by buyers of the polluters' products, and the heart of the equity question is whether these customers will be predominantly rich or poor. [. . .] It must nevertheless be recognized that there is justice, in one sense, if costs are borne predominantly by consumers choosing to buy products whose manufacture generates a great deal of pollution.

[7] Bruce A. Ackerman, Susan Rose Ackerman, James W. Sawyer, Jr., and Dale W. Henderson, *The Uncertain Search for Environmental Quality* (New York: The Free Press, 1974).

to be made? Surely, a refinery that has already instituted extensive and costly treatment procedures should not be required to reduce its emissions by the same proportion as a neighboring factory that has been emitting untreated wastes into the river. To deal with this issue, the DRBC staff had to undertake the enormously complex task of determining the hypothetical 'raw waste load' for *each* major polluter to serve as a benchmark for determining its pollution quota. The result was a case-by-case process specifying a quota, typically followed by a protest from the polluter, with some sort of compromise eventually emerging from a series of bargaining sessions. The anomalies in the final set of permits are quite striking: for example, the final pollution quotas for petroleum refineries on the estuary ranged from 692 pounds to 14,400 pounds of BOD per day! This experience suggests that neither in principle nor in practice are direct controls fairer than a system of fees that require the polluters to pay for the damage they do to the resources of the community.

7 Inducement for Maximum Effort

Since no manufacturing activity can be expected to reduce its wastes to zero, it becomes necessary, under direct controls, to assign some sort of quota or other behavioral rule to *each* polluter (i.e., to establish a clear definition of what constitutes violation of the law). If, for example, the environmental authority requires a polluting firm to reduce its emissions to 50 percent of the amount it discharged in the previous year, then a discharge equal to 49.7 percent of that base level is legal and presumably virtuous, while if the emissions equal 51 percent of that figure, they suddenly become illegal and reprehensible.

Aside from the inherent absurdity of such a thin separation between virtue and vice, this approach has an extremely questionable practical consequence. Consider a plant that can reduce its emissions to 50 percent of the base level by an investment of $1 million, while by an outlay of $1.1 million (i.e., for an additional outlay of $100,000) it can cut its discharges to a mere 20 percent of the base figure. The fine line between reward and punishment inherent in the regulatory quota offers absolutely no incentive for this relatively inexpensive additional contribution to the welfare of society. Once it reaches the 50 percent reduction required by law, the firm has no inducement whatever to cut further its emissions one iota, no matter how low the cost.

The fiscal approach, however, need not be subject to such an anomaly; it can provide a continuum of rewards or penalties, defined according to a fixed schedule that is known by the polluting firm. The less it emits the less its tax bill, and that is all there is to the matter. If by reducing its emissions from 50 to 20 percent, it can decrease its tax payments by $450,000 over the lifetime of its plant, it will obviously pay the firm to invest an additional $100,000 required for the purpose. There is no inducement to stop reducing emissions once the standard is reached.

Thus, one of the attractive features of the fiscal approach lies in its use of a more or less continuous schedule of financial inducements. The better the performance of the decision makers in reducing their pollutant emissions, the better off they will be financially.[8]

8 Economy

In choosing among instruments for environmental protection, economists place heavy emphasis on the efficiency with which they can be expected to do the job. We will argue that efficiency is one of the major advantages of fiscal methods.

It is all too tempting to decry the economist's preoccupation with 'mere' dollars and cents, when the issues at stake for environmental policy are so important for the health and welfare of the community. Yet efficiency and economy in environmental protection measures are obviously important, if for no other reason that that, if the cost is unnecessarily high, it becomes that much more difficult to push environmental legislation through Congress

But concern over social costs is not simply money grubbing. It represents a matter of profound importance for the interests of society. The community is constantly beset by many pressing claims upon its limited resources—health, education, sanitation, street maintenance, welfare programs—and there are never enough resources to do everything. No easy solutions have been proposed for the problems of poverty, decaying cities, crime and disease, but it is clear that each of them is going to require massive outlays of labor and other resources. Each time we institute a wasteful measure for the protection of the environment where a more efficient alternative is available, we effectively undercut some other valuable service. The problems of society are surely too urgent to permit that sort of casual misuse of critical resources.

The possible savings in resources that the use of effluent fees can effect is readily illustrated. Suppose that we have a world of two polluters, each initially emitting the same quantity of effluent, but in which the first can reduce waste emissions at a cost of five cents per pound, and the second at fifteen cents per pound. In addition, assume that our environmental objective requires a 50 percent cutback in total effluents. If under a direct-controls approach, we require each of the polluters to halve its emissions, this would

---

[8] There is, of course, the danger that in practice a legislature will produce a system of charges that is far from this ideal. If, for example, it is decided to assess charges only for 'excessive' emissions, then even under a program of charges the polluter will lose any incentive to reduce emissions by any significant amount below the borderline between 'acceptable' and 'excessive' discharges. Obviously, a poorly designed system of fiscal incentives can perform just as poorly as any other instrument of control, and it is never safe to assume that in reality a system of charges will be well designed.

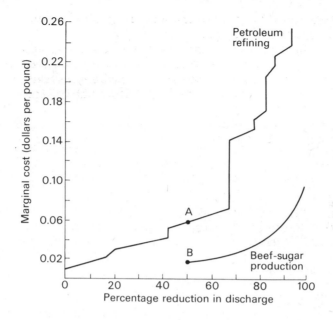

Fig. 1. Comparison ofMarginal Costs of BOD-Discharge Reduction in Petroleum Refining and Beet-Sugar Processing [. . .]

entail an average cost of waste reductions of ten cents per pound. However, we could obviously achieve our objective more inexpensively by placing the whole of the cutback on polluter number one (perhaps with some compensation paid to it by the other polluter); in this instance, the cost of the reduction would be only five cents per pound, and we would have cut the social cost of our environmental program in half.

The central point is that the second outcome is precisely the one that results from the pricing approach. Suppose that the environmental authority were to levy a tax on emissions of six cents per pound. All the reductions would then come from the first polluter which would find it profitable to avoid the tax altogether by stopping all its emissions; the second polluter would find it cheaper to pay the fee of six cents per pound and would maintain its level of waste discharges. The pricing method, in this instance, achieves the environmental goal at the least cost to society.

As a second and more realistic illustration, let us return to the case of the petroleum refinery and the beet-sugar plant that we examined in Chapter 14. In Figure 1, we display both of these cost curves for reducing BOD discharges on the same diagram. Suppose that, in an effort to cut down emissions, a regulation were passed which ignored this cost differential and required that each plant cut its discharges by 50 percent. Figure 1 indicates that the marginal cost of a one-pound reduction in BOD emissions would then be six cents in the petroleum refinery (see point *A*) but only about one cent in the beet-sugar plant (point *B*). This would be grossly inefficient, for society would effectively be paying six times the necessary cost for each additional pound of BOD reduction. By simply shifting a pound of the cutback from the petroleum refinery to the beet-sugar plant, we could reduce the cost of the marginal pound of emissions reduction from six cents to only a penny.

As in our preceding illustration, the use of effluent fees will lead automatically to the least-cost pattern of pollution reductions. In particular, if the environmental authority were to set an effluent charge of four cents per pound of BOD emissions, we can see from Figure 1 that the petroleum refinery would find it profitable to cut its discharges by about 25 percent, while the beet-sugar plant would reduce its emissions by roughly 75 percent. If the volume of initial emissions were the same in the two plants, this fee of four cents per pound would generate the targeted 50 percent reduction in aggregate emissions. Note that the cost of reducing emissions by an additional pound would never, in this instance, exceed four cents.

The pricing approach to pollution control thus promises significant cost savings in comparison with a set of quotas, because fees implicitly take full advantage of the difference in the costs of pollution abatement.[9] And [. . .], in terms of some actual cost estimates the potential savings from the use of fees instead of direct controls is a sizeable sum, often of an order of 30 to 50 percent of the total costs of pollution abatement.

9 Political Acceptability

Effluent charges certainly have met with very little success in the political arena. Both in the United States and in most other capitalist countries, they have so far proved uniformly unattractive to those in political power.[10] Yet the use of pollution taxes (or alternatively, the sale of effluent permits) does have one great political virtue. Unlike most other measures for pollution control, it need not add to the financial burdens of the public sector.[11] In view of the tremendous and growing fiscal pressures, particularly on state and local governments, the resistance of public officials to new programs making heavy demands on the public purse is understandable. For this reason alone, politicians should be far more receptive to a fiscal program that promises to bring in, rather than disburse, revenues.

[9] It is possible to show that for a regulatory agency to select emissions quotas that are as effective in keeping down the total costs of the pollution program, it would have to have access to an enormous quantity of information of a sort which it could normally not obtain in practice.
[10] It is somewhat ironic that the Soviet economies seem far more willing to use the price mechanism and financial incentives to carry out their environmental programs! [. . .]
[11] This obviously does not apply to the use of public subsidies.

The potential revenue contribution of these taxes is by no means negligible. Some recent, and admittedly rough, calculations for the state of New Jersey suggested that charges of twenty cents per pound on sulfur-dioxide emissions from fixed-point sources, ten cents per pound on BOD emissions into the water, and five dollars per ton for landfill disposal of solid wastes could together generate annual revenues on the order of $225 million. For New Jersey this is roughly equivalent to the revenues from an increase in the state's sales tax of 1½ percent.

When new tax programs are under consideration, there are good grounds for the inclusion of a program of charges upon environmental damage in the tax package. For such charges can achieve two goals for the price of one: an augmentation of the flow of revenues into the public treasury and the introduction of powerful incentives for improvements in the quality of life. Most taxes carry with them an incidental set of economic incentives leading to decisions *not* in the interests of the community; they may, for example, discourage saving or the rehabilitation of slum properties. Economists say such taxes impose an 'excess burden' on the community (i.e., a burden of undesirable incentives above and beyond their direct dollar cost to the taxpayer). However, taxes on environmental damage, rather than imposing an excess burden, offer an offsetting benefit; they provide economic incentives for decisions that serve the public interest by, for example, inducing reductions in emissions of various pollutants.

10 Minimal Interference with Private Decisions

Before concluding our discussion of the virtues of pricing for environmental protection, we mention one noneconomic advantage of the fiscal approach: the fact that it keeps to a minimum governmental interference in the individual decision. By relying on price incentives, the regulatory agency need not tell individuals or business managers what type of fuel they must use or what sorts of technology they must employ; the fiscal technique assigns no quotas, nor tells people how to run their life or their business. Instead, it merely modifies the structure of market prices by, for example, changing the relative prices of leaded and unleaded gasolines or of fuels with differing sulfur content, and leaves it to private decision makers to adjust to such price information as they see fit.

This, incidentally, can also result in an important additional benefit: it leaves greater scope for innovation. A regulation forbidding a certain process that creates a great deal of smoke, even if it contributes to a cleaner atmosphere, may not be the most efficient way of carrying out the task *for all polluters*. Suppose the addition of a system of filters to the old process is a cheaper way for some plants to achieve the same reduction in smoke. The business that is taxed for its emissions will seek the least expensive way of reducing them; in our example, it will compare the costs of an entirely new process to that of the system of filters and may select the latter. Even the best-intentioned bureaucrat cannot, in general, possess the detailed information needed to determine the least-cost method of compliance for each polluter. The fiscal approach, in an important sense, makes much less in the way of informational demands on the environmental authority.

If governmental interference is undesirable in itself, then the fiscal approach certainly comes out ahead on this score. It would seem that under these circumstances the business community would be unified in its support of fiscal methods as against direct controls. However, the reverse seems to be true. Our encounters with business managers have revealed a determined, and sometimes bitter, opposition to fiscal methods of environmental control. Two reasons for their opposition have been suggested. The first is that taxes on environmental damage, when once enacted, are not easily escaped or repealed; in short, they work. The enforcement of direct controls, on the other hand, typically allows a certain amount of leeway; the polluter may be able to negotiate with the regulatory agency or take its case to the courts, where for a variety of reasons, it may find an easy escape. Certainly, the low fines for violations of prohibitions that were cited earlier lend some support to their view. The assertion is that prohibition, for all its uncompromising aura, very often turns out to be a lamb in the guise of a lion.

James Buchanan and Gordon Tullock have recently proposed a second explanation.[12] They argue that, paradoxically, while emissions taxes will normally cause some reduction in the profits earned by a firm, direct controls can conceivably even increase profitability. If those controls effectively limit outputs and the entry of new firms into polluting industries, environmental measures may succeed in restricting production. The result is, in effect, a legal cartel which, by enforcing scarcity, increases both prices and profits. The applicabilty of these hypotheses certainly requires further evidence. However, they do offer a somewhat plausible explanation of what otherwise seems a puzzling phenomenon: the business community's determined opposition to the policy approach which best preserves its freedom of decision making.

11 Some Limitations of Pollution Charges

We have built what seems to us a strong case for a widespread use of effluent charges to achieve our environmental objectives. However, it is also important to recognize several difficulties in their use. Though we are convinced of the great promise of pricing instruments in pollution control, we must not exaggerate the scope of their effective use.

[12] 'Polluters' Profits and Political Response: Direct Controls versus Taxes,' *American Economic Review* 65 (March 1975): 139-47.

One significant weakness of the tax method, which may account for much of its unpopularity among environmental protection agencies, is uncertainty about the magnitude of its effects. Suppose we enact a tax of five cents per pound on effluents. Just how large will the response of polluters be? Will it be enough to permit the community to achieve its environmental goals? If the response proves inadequate, one can try to return to the legislature to get approval for an increase in tax rates. But that certainly takes time, and the legislature may simply reject the proposal. We should not, however, exaggerate our inability to predict, at least roughly, the response of the level of waste discharges to fees. [. . .] Considerable research has been devoted to the study of the costs of pollution abatement on an industry-by-industry basis. Consequently, we have a pretty good idea of how high a charge will make it profitable, for example, for a petroleum refinery to curtail its BOD emissions by 50 percent (recall Figure 1). [. . .] This is not to say that such projections are highly reliable; there is surely a nonnegligible margin of error. But we do have a basis for reasonable estimates. Moreover, with more actual experience and research, we should become increasingly able to make reliable predictions of the response of pollution levels to varying schedules of tax rates.

A second, and perhaps more serious, difficulty besetting effluent charges is their relative inflexibility. For political and other reasons, it is typically a long and difficult process to change tax rates once a tax schedule has been established. The process often involves months of hearings, legislative wrangling, and other time-consuming steps. Moreover, it is expensive for business enterprises to have to adjust production to frequent changes in the level of fees; stable tax rates reduce uncertainty and lower costs of production.

A third problem of the tax approach is that the environmental authority may encounter troublesome political obstacles to levying different tax rates according to the *location* of polluters. In many cases such variations in tax rates are essential for the efficiency of a program. As we stressed in Chapter 15, a given level of emissions is frequently far more harmful in one location than in another; smoke spewn forth in a sparsely populated area will produce far less damage than in a residential neighborhood. Wind factors can also be important; the smoky factory will do significantly more damage to the community if it is located to the windward, rather than the leeward, side of the municipality. The problem is that identical tax rates in the two locations will provide equal incentives for the curtailment of emissions in areas in which it is highly beneficial and in those in which the advantages it confers are small.

Inflexibility of tax rates *over time* can also be highly disadvantageous. The reasons are essentially the same as for geographic uniformity: a given emission may cause more damage at some times than at others. A period of drought can reduce substantially the ability of a river to absorb and disperse pollutants; this obviously increases the potential damage from waste discharges. Similarly, in periods when low wind velocity and other atmospheric conditions combine to produce an atmospheric 'inversion,' emissions into the air can become much more dangerous than usual.

The dilemma here is that a tax rate sufficiently high to deal with such a pollution emergency will be far too restrictive and impose too high a level of pollution-control costs during normal periods. On the other hand, a tax rate low enough for ordinary purposes may be critically inadequate in times of adverse environmental conditions. Since we cannot predict such environmental crises very far in advance, we cannot expect to be able to adapt tax rates to them with sufficient speed. In addition, as already noted, the immediate effect of changes in tax rates on pollution is likely to be quite uncertain; this can obviously be of overwhelming importance in time of emergency.

We can reduce somewhat the inflexibility resulting from uniform charges by building variations into the schedule of fees itself. *Peak-load pricing* is widely used in a number of activities. Telephone rates, for example, are lower during periods of relatively unused capacity (the night hours and weekends) to induce a shift of calls away from the busy weekday hours. Likewise, a number of bus companies and railroads regularly charge reduced fares for off-peak travel. There is no reason in principle why an environmental authority cannot employ such pricing techniques. As one example, the authority may adopt two schedules of effluent charges for BOD emissions into a river, one for the winter months and a second with higher rates for the summer months, to encourage lower emissions when the river's absorptive capacity is at its lowest levels. As long as these schedules of charges are published well in advance, polluters will be able to plan their operations accordingly, thereby increasing the effectiveness of the measure as a protector of water quality.

As mentioned earlier, inflation and growth also constitute problems for the tax approach. A continuing rise in the price level will eat away at the real value of an effluent charge and will thereby reduce over time its effectiveness in the curtailment of effluents. Similarly, the growth of population and of industrial activity will generate increases in emission discharges at a given tax level. To hold the line on polluting activities, we shall probably find that periodic increases in fees are necessary; this is a distinct disadvantage, for it places the burden of maintaining environmental standards on the environmental authority, not on polluters.

Finally, we must mention one crucially important practical matter for the implementation of the pricing approach (as well as for at least some forms of direct controls); the monitoring and measurement of levels of polluting activities. In order to charge individual polluters for their waste emissions, the environmental agency must be able to measure the discharges. This may not be a simple matter. For example, in taxing discharges into waterways, the authority may want to base the charge on the BOD content of the effluent, the concentrations of various nondegradable chemical substances and suspended solids, and, perhaps, even the temperature. All this involves some fairly sophisticated problems in monitoring. The standard techniques for measuring the BOD content of effluents, for example, are still rather primitive, time-consuming, and not completely reliable. [. . .] They require that samples of the waste emissions be put to laboratory tests that reveal, some days later, a measure of BOD concentration.

The acceptability of metering procedures is often a matter of degree. In many cases, costlier metering techniques may provide more detailed and reliable data, but the additional information simply may not be worth the cost. An annual automobile inspection does not give as much information about car emissions as a weekly or even a monthly examination of the vehicle. However, the nuisance and administrative costs of the more frequent inspections are almost certainly not justified by the improved information they would provide.[13]

It must be admitted that taken overall the art of monitoring is in a relatively primitive state. There is often no way one can place a meter on the discharger's outflow pipe and expect the meter to keep a record of the quantities of the varying damaging emissions it spews forth. There may, however, exist some acceptable shortcuts. [. . .] Moreover, with increasing use and demand for metering, we can expect the development of less expensive and more effective methods of measuring polluting activities.

12 A 'License to Pollute'?

One of the most persistent arguments against fiscal incentives is the assertion that pollution taxes (or the auctioning of pollution permits) are basically immoral. Many environmentalists contend that a pollution tax is, in effect, 'a license to pollute'—that whoever is willing to pay a price can abuse the environment. Economists have, of course, not been surprised at the united opposition to fiscal methods from those who have the most to lose—the polluters. More astonishing is this resistance by dedicated environmentalists. Two recent incidents will illustrate the fervor of the opposition. When a bill imposing effluent charges for the protection of our rivers was introduced into the Senate, an indignant editorial in a leading liberal newspaper asserted that this immoral piece of legislation *sold* the right to pollute our rivers. At about the same time, a group of public-spirited, liberal businessmen asked several economists to address them on environmental issues. The businessmen were shocked at the idea of a tax approach to environmental control; they asserted that business should cooperate *voluntarily* to protect the environment, simply because it is the just and virtuous thing to do. One of them asked,

[13] This point and the example were suggested to us by Professor William S. Vickrey.

'Would you really tax General Motors for selling unsafe cars? Isn't that selling the right to destroy human life?' The economist thought for a moment and replied, 'Surely, it is better than giving that right free of charge.'

That is precisely the heart of the issue. Society has been giving away free too many of its precious resources far too long. It is *not* scandalous to decide that everything has its price; the real scandal lies in setting that price at zero or at some token level that invites us all to destroy these resources. By imposing essentially no cost on the individual for polluting activities, we have instead shifted the very heavy costs upon society. Unless we recognize the legitimate role of price incentives for the control of pollution, we may end up with our sense of morality intact but our environment the worse for continued abuse.

19

The Social Incidence of Environmental Costs and Benefits

by David Pearce, Ron Edwards, and Tony Harris

Introduction

In recent times there has been a general acceptance that the enjoyment of an unpolluted environment is in some sense an elitist pursuit, being a pastime of the more wealthy members of society rather than a concern of the lower paid. The aim of this study is to test the validity of this piece of casual empiricism by examining some quantitative indicators of the social incidence of environmental benefits.

Apart from the obvious academic value of such information, there are certain policy implications. If resources are to be used optimally, then the benefits of any environmental improvement (or conservation) programme should be weighed against the costs of its implementation. This is true, not only at the national, or regional level, but also at the micro or individual level where certain distributional questions arise. For instance, if the costs of an environmental programme are spread equally over all members of society, and the benefits of the programme accrue only (or mainly) to a certain section of that society, then the policy may be regarded as being in some sense inequitable, i.e. if the environment is indeed valued more highly by the more wealthy, then any policy which does not involve the latter in a greater share of the cost will result in a redistribution of benefits away from the poor, and towards the rich.

There are two basic, interrelated problems in a study of this nature. First, it is necessary to establish some method of determining the socially differentiated benefits (if they are in fact differentiated) of environmental amenity. One answer (albeit fairly crude in the light of arguments about an income based definition of social class) is to examine the way in which valuations of the environment differ between individuals receiving different levels of income. If it is found that this valuation increases as income rises, then it can indeed be argued that the environment is a kind of luxury commodity.

A simple way in which this can be done is to study the *income elasticity of demand* for environmental quality. The income elasticity of demand is a measure of the sensitivity of demand for a commodity to changes in income, and is defined as the *proportional* change in demand divided by the *proportional* change in income. For most goods, this will be greater than zero, i.e. demand will increase as income increases. For some commodities it is greater than unity, implying that as income increases, a *greater proportion of income is spent on the commodity*. This would for instance be the case with fur coats, or diamonds. An income elasticity of demand greater than unity is quite simply a reflection of the increasing value (or importance) of the good in question *vis-à-vis* other commodities to the individual as income rises.

Consequently, if an income elasticity of demand for environmental quality can be established, we immediately have an indicator of the social incidence of environmental benefits. If it turns out to be greater than unity, then the view that the environment is an elitist, or pro-rich concern is vindicated, and the appropriate policy conclusions and prescriptions drawn.

Having solved the first of our problems, we have in fact posed the second. The calculation of an income elasticity requires that the benefits of environmental amenity, or the demand for environmental quality should somehow be quantitatively measured. It may be possible to measure the physical benefits of environmental improvements by say calculating the cost of repairing pollution damaged buildings, and recognising that such costs will not be incurred if pollution is abated.

This, however, misses the essential point, which is the subjective value which individuals place on an unpolluted (or less polluted) environment. The difficulty is of course, that there is no *market* for environmental amenity, and hence no explicit revelation of the demand for environmental quality, or the price which people would be willing to pay for improvements in their surroundings. If, of course, there were such a market, it would be possible to observe how much any individual was willing to pay for improvement (i.e. his valuation), and to see how this varied with income level, i.e. it would be possible to calculate an income elasticity.

In the absence of such a direct method of assessing the value which people place on the environment, we must fall back on other approaches, and it is in fact to this valuation question that the major part of this study is devoted. There are two distinct approaches which have been of particular interest in the recent literature on environmental matters. These are examined in what follows, together with some of their results and difficulties.

The Hedonic Approach to Estimating Environmental Benefits

The basis of the so-called hedonic approach is that, although there is no market for environmental quality, there are marketed commodities (i.e. goods which are actually bought and sold, and which consequently command a price) whose *market value* is affected by the environment. Although there are many such goods, an obvious example, and the one on which most applications of the hedonic approach have been concentrated, is housing.

In an ideal situation, if two *identical* houses were sold, one in an unpolluted area, the other in a heavily polluted area, we would expect the former to command a higher price than the latter, because of the subjective valuation placed on the environment by the purchaser. Consequently, *if all else were equal*, it could be inferred that the difference in price between the two houses is a measure in monetary terms of the benefit to the individual of the extra environmental amenity around the 'clean' house. It is in fact the 'price' he is willing to pay for the environmental quality *vis-à-vis* that surrounding the other house, and consequently reflects his *demand* for that environmental quality.

If we could observe many situations of this sort, it should be possible to determine how this demand changes as individual incomes vary, and thus establish the desired income elasticity discussed earlier.

It is, of course, virtually impossible in practice to find such an ideal case, i.e. a set of houses which are identical in *all* respects (including location etc.) other than in some narrowly defined environmental respect, so that we are forced to consider houses which differ in many respects. The market value of a house will naturally be affected by a very large number of factors such as number of rooms, age, proximity to shops and schools, etc., as well as any environmental factors, such as noise, air pollution and so on. The argument for the hedonic approach suggests, however, that it is possible to *standardise* for all other factors except the particular environmental characteristic in question, and consequently to proceed as before.

The way this is done is to identify those housing characteristics which are likely to affect the house price, and to carry out a regression of the house price on the quantities of each of these characteristics, including any environmental factors. The straightforward interpretation of the regression coefficient on a pollution variable suggests that it is the partial effect of a change in that pollutant on the house price, i.e. that it is the value which is placed on the removal of a unit of that pollution. For instance, if noise pollution were our concern, and a regression of this type were carried out, we would expect a negative coefficient on the noise variable (increasing amounts of noise should have a negative effect on house prices). The interpretation of the regression is such that if the noise level were decreased by one unit, the house price should increase to the extent of the absolute value of the coefficient. This coefficient can then be interpreted as the price which (on average) individuals are willing to pay per unit noise reduction, and as such obviously reflects the demand for noise reduction.

Although most studies which have used this technique have been confined to the measurement of environmental benefits, several have actually attempted to trace the demand for certain types of environmental amenity. These include studies by Nelson,[1] and Harrison and Rubinfeld.[2] Both of these reported income elasticities of unity.

The implication of this finding is that, while the demand for environmental quality increases with increasing levels of income, the environment cannot quite be regarded as a pro-rich commodity in the sense that the rich demand more *proportionately* than the poor. For example, an income elasticity of unity implies that one individual with double the income of another will demand twice as much environmental amenity (perhaps half as much ambient noise for instance) than the other. He does not however demand more *in proportion to his income level* than the poorer individual.

In terms of a single individual, an income elasticity of unity can be interpreted to mean that he would be willing to spend a constant proportion of his income on environmental quality, as his income changes, i.e. if his income doubled, he would be willing to spend twice as much on his environment. This simply means that his *valuation* of the environment is constant relative to the other commodities he purchases. This point is discussed in greater detail in Pearce.[3]

The curious conclusion of these studies is, then, that the benefits of an environmental improvement programme are completely neutral in a distributional sense, being worth no more (as a proportion of income) to the rich than to the poor. Thus, any inequity in an environmental programme can only arise as a result of an unequal distribution of its costs.

A Critique of the Hedonic Approach

This rather surprising result stimulated a thorough appraisal of the validity of the hedonic approach to the monetary valuation of environmental amenity. From the point of view of this study it was essential to answer two basically interrelated questions. First, can the hedonic technique produce meaningful estimates of the monetary value of (i.e. individuals' willingness to pay for) environmental quality? Second, if it can do this, can this measure be used to estimate the income elasticity of demand for environmental amenity?

The attempt to answer these questions necessitated an examination of the economic theory underlying the whole approach. If the numbers generated by the technique are to be interpreted as anything other than an empirical association between property values and ambient environmental attributes, we must hypothesise some sort of mechanism whereby the environment affects the welfare of an individual and thus (in conjunction with his economic circumstances) is translated into the monetary transaction which we can observe.* It is in the nature of this mechanism that most of the difficulties of the hedonic approach lie.

The topic is discussed at considerable length both in terms of its theoretical context and its policy relevance in Pearce,[4] Pearce and Edwards,[5] Harris,[6] and Edwards.[7] Though involving many technical considerations, it is possible to give an intuitive summary of the major objections to the hedonic approach.

It transpires that there is a range of alternative circumstances under which the answer to the first of the questions posed above is in the affirmative. The unfortunate fact is that the conditions which are most theoretically plausible require empirical information which is simply not available. Conversely, in order to utilise the sort of data which is available (or indeed which can possibly be made available), assumptions have to be made about human nature which are unacceptable.

As noted above, the hedonic technique relies on the appropriate interpretation of a regression coefficient. For this to represent a willingness to pay, it is necessary to assume that each individual in the sample values the environment *independently* of all of the other commodities he consumes.† If this is not the case, then the value that he will place on the environment will depend on the amounts of other goods he consumes. An example would be an individual who enjoys listening to quiet music. He will presumably place more value *ceteris paribus* on a quiet environment than someone who enjoys rock music, which is relatively unaffected by ambient sound levels'. Although the technicalities are far more complex than this simple instance suggests, it is relatively easy to see that this independence (or '*separability*') assumption is difficult to justify empirically.

The problem is that if the valuation is not independent, then it is difficult to define a generally applicable willingness to pay for environmental amenity. It is no use attempting to interpret the regression coefficient in this light, since it will consist of a confused mixture of environmental valuation *and* the satisfaction obtained by the individuals in question from all sorts of combinations of other goods.

To identify the 'pure' value of the environment *per se* in the absence of separability, it would be necessary to choose individuals for our regression sample who were consuming the same amount of all commodities other than the environmental attribute we are

---

*This may be referred to as a utility function, whereby the amounts of goods and services (including perhaps the environment) which an individual consumes are translated into some measure of satisfaction. It is normally assumed that an individual will maximise this utility subject to the constraint of the resources available to him. This process can then predict *either* the amounts of the various goods he will buy at a certain set of prices, *or* (more relevant to this study) the price he is willing to pay for a given amount of commodity.

†This means that the utility function must be separable between the environment and other commodities.

trying to value, so that this dependence on other commodities is, in a sense, standardised for. This process should then be repeated for all groups consuming different 'bundles' of commodities, to obtain their respective valuations. In practice, of course, it is very rare to find even two individuals consuming exactly the same goods as each other, let alone the same amount of each good. This renders it an empirically, if not a logically impossible task to round up sufficient people for such a regression sample.

The only way we can empirically use the technique is to make the unrealistic independence assumption mentioned, and the only way we could work with a relatively realistic idea about the way individuals value the environment would be to have data which does not and possibly cannot exist!

A second, and essentially related problem is that for the technique to generate numbers which can be interpreted as independent valuations of the environment, people must maintain the same valuation regardless of their overall level of welfare. If this is not the case then the average 'value' will once again be a mixture of that which is placed on the environment, and that placed on other commodities.

The way out here is to attempt to identify groups of people whose welfare levels are identical, and carry out separate regressions for each of the groups. The practical problems of this are of course tremendous, and perhaps insuperable. It is once again a problem of impracticability on the one hand, and irrelevance on the other.

This sort of problem must lead to the conclusion that it is not possible to interpret the results of hedonic analyses as valuations of the environment. The adherents of the approach (e.g. Freeman[8]) have, however, argued that the necessary assumptions about the way in which they value the environment are not bad *approximations*, and since it is impossible to determine any systematic bias in the way they might affect the results of a hedonic analysis, the techniques can at least give us a rough idea, which is arguably better than none at all.

If we accept this for the moment, the question remains as to whether or not the estimates can be used to give us our indicator of the social incidence of environmental amenity, i.e. the income elasticity. The particular restrictions (or assumptions) required for the hedonic 'valuations' to have the correct interpretation conspire to form a very special hypothesis about the way in which people value commodities.* It turns out (see Edwards[7]) that if these restrictions were met in practice, the income elasticity of demand for environmental attributes (and indeed for all commodities) would of necessity be unity! The restrictions themselves imply this.

*In fact, the combination of separability and independence from utility level implies a *homogeneous* utility function, which, in the absence of a survivor set (which must be the case in long run equilibrium) implies a straight line income-consumption curve through the origin, and consequently an income elasticity of unity.

It is consequently impossible to *estimate* an income elasticity from a hedonic value. It is only possible to *estimate* something if it is not predetermined by the assumptions. Yet if these restrictions do not hold, the numbers on which the estimate would be based cannot be interpreted as valuations of the environment! The answer to our second question is negative almost by definition.

Difficulties of this sort are supplemented by perhaps more fundamental questions about the applicability of this sort of 'traditional' economic methodology to a market as complex, and as imperfect as that for housing. Indeed other writers (see Mäler[9]) have posed some very serious questions for the hedonic technique along these lines. A fairly detailed analysis of this and related topics is to be found in Harris.[6]

The failure of the hedonic method in this instance lies in its very conception, i.e. in its indirectness. The main conclusion is that it is impossible to standardise for all of the factors which might vary, in a way which maintains a useful result for the present purposes. It is difficult to see how the necessary assumptions can be justified, or how the necessary information can be obtained in the absence of these assumptions. As a consequence, the suggestion of this study is that the hedonic technique *almost* certainly cannot estimate valuations of the environment, and *certainly* cannot be used to determine the social incidence of environmental benefits.

National Incidence Studies

In the light of the serious difficulties of the hedonic approach, it is worthwhile considering the alternative methods used by other researchers in estimating the distributional aspects of environmental programmes. This work relates mainly to environmental programmes on a national scale in the USA. Most of it, in turn, is concerned with the social incidence of the costs and benefits of the 1970 Clean Air Act, and its subsequent amendments. These studies are critically surveyed in Pearce.[3]

The basic methodologies are understandably crude, particularly on the benefits side. For instance, in Dorfman,[10] estimates of the benefits of all anti-pollution policy in the USA were obtained from replies to a National Wildlife Survey questionnaire which had asked respondents for their willingness to pay for the environment to be 'cleaned up'. No quantification of the degree of pollution abatement was mentioned. Nonetheless, the responses were compared to the incomes of the individuals who had made them. Similarly, estimates of the social incidence of the costs of the abatement programme were made by an examination of the way in which the tax burden was distributed between different income classes. The result was that low income groups were shown to be net losers *vis-à-vis* high income groups, in the sense that the former appeared to be paying more in tax than their expressed evaluation of the benefits of the programme, whilst the latter seemed to be gaining more benefit from pollution abatement than they were actually paying for. That is, environmental quality was overprovided to the first group, and underprovided to the second.

This result does seem to support the hypothesis of a 'pro-rich' distribution of environmental quality. It also fits an economic 'theorem' due to Baumol,[11] to the effect that because a clean environment can be enjoyed by everyone to the same extent, there will be a conflict between rich and poor which will lead to a compromise whereby the rich will not get as much abatement as they desire (at the going 'price' or tax), whilst the poor will get too much.

It must, however, be admitted that the bringing together of the estimates of costs and benefits in this way is very suspect, since the former relate to specifically defined quality objectives, whilst the latter specifies no consistent quality (i.e. different individuals may have had different ideas of how much pollution abatement would be involved in expressing their willingness to pay). This caveat is not made in Dorfman's paper, though it is only fair to say that many other methodoligical weaknesses are pointed out.

Another example of this type of national incidence study is a substantial piece of work by Gianessi *et al.*,[12] which concluded that the benefit distribution of the Clean Air Act was in fact 'pro-poor'! There is, however, a major problem in this study in that the estimates of the benefits of the Act were taken from work done by the US Environmental Protection Agency in 1974. Inspection of these estimates shows that they were the result of adding the valuations produced by early house price studies (i.e. the hedonic method discussed above) to other estimates of pollution damage. Even if one believed in hedonic studies, it is almost certain that some of these 'other' damages would already be reflected in the way house prices changed, so that the resulting estimates will almost inevitably involve some 'double counting' of the benefits and will be overestimates by an uncertain degree. In short, however sophisticated the mechanism is for allocating a national benefit estimate between income groups, the figures mean very little if the national benefit estimate is itself highly questionable.

In the Gianessi study the costs of environmental programmes were found to be regressive, i.e. they accounted for a larger proportion of the income of the poor than of the rich. Similar results are found in all other national cost studies for the USA although the conclusion does not appear to hold so generally for regional studies.

Unfortunately, the information available for countries other than the USA is very limited. Indeed for most other countries it appears to be the case that we do not even know the actual magnitude of total expenditure on anti-pollution policies. There is therefore an immediate difficulty in suggesting that a cost incidence study should be carried out in the UK, though if such magnitudes did exist it would be worthwhile attempting to discover how the cost was distributed across income groups.

On the benefits side, however, the conclusion is much more pessimistic. Owing to the entirely unconvincing methodoligies used elsewhere it seems likely that the estimation of a national benefit figure is not within the capacity of economic methodology as it relates to environmental damage. This is not seen as being due to an underdeveloped 'state of the art' but more as a reflection of the inappropriateness of the fundamental 'economic' way of looking at the potential benefit of environmental programmes.

Social Survey Approaches

The overwhelming difficulty of all of the approaches examined so far, particularly to the estimation of the benefits of environmental programmes, is their inherent indirectness. Since it is necessary to follow very roundabout routes to obtain the final estimates, the problem is one of not really knowing the characteristics of the resulting data. It seems impossible to take into account and standardise for all of the influences along the route, so that the result is almost inevitably a confusion of the desired evaluation, and totally irrelevant factors. If the latter do not systematically *bias* the results (as suggested by Freeman[8]), they do introduce so much undesired variability that the potential inaccuracy of any estimates renders them totally unacceptable.

In the light of this it would seem desirable to adopt as direct a method as possible of estimating the benefits of environmental programmes. In fact, one answer appears to be to actually go out, and simply ask people how much a particular policy has been (or would be) worth to them, i.e. to mount social surveys on the issue.

The practicalities are obviously not as trivial as this suggests, and the inherent difficulties of obtaining the sort of information are fully recognised (see Harris[13]). There are, however, very few examples of surveys in this area, and it is strongly felt that there is much room for improvement with practice, and at least some hope *vis-à-vis* the other methodologies of actually obtaining some useful results. The basic advantage of a survey is that any researcher can almost define the characteristics of the resulting data, in that with judicious choice of questions and validation he should at least be aware of whether responses will be over-estimates or under-estimates etc. Even this limited degree of certainty is unachievable through hedonic studies, where the magnitude *and* direction of inaccuracy is completely indeterminate.

Owing to resource and time constraints, it was clearly beyond the scope of the present study to mount and process its own survey. It was possible, however, to take advantage of a survey carried out by Dr John Langdon of the Building Research Establishment into the effects of traffic noise. This was undertaken in 1972, and covered some 2945 residents at 55 sites in the Greater London area.[14]

Along with certain validation questions, the main query from the point of view of this study was: 'How much do you think it would be worth per week to you to keep the traffic noise down to a reasonable level?' The potential advantages and disadvantages of this approach are analysed in some detail by Harris,[13] as indeed are the results of the survey.

The main purpose of this part of the study was to regress the responses to the above question (i.e. the monetary evaluation of a quiet environment) on a variety of characteristics of the respondent and his ambient noise level. In particular, it was the relationship between the responses and income levels of the individuals surveyed which was of interest, since from this (as Harris shows) it is possible to derive an income elasticity of the demand for noise abatement (or for 'peace and quiet') which is our chosen indicator of the social incidence of environmental benefits.

Although he carried out many fairly detailed regressions on the responses to the survey, it is possible to summarise his work by an examination of one regression which included all of the relevant information. Table 1 gives the coefficients and associated statistics obtained from a double-log regression of the monetary value placed on 'peace and quiet', and a range of independent variables including income.

Table 1

Dependent Variable	Income	Noise Measure	Length of Residence	Education	Size of Household	Constant
Coefficient	0.30	0.92	−0.06	0.21	0.14	−3.64
t-statistic	9.68	3.19	1.94	5.5	2.92	2.96

$\overline{R}^2 = 0.135$ $F(5,) = 53.56.$

Although the adjusted coefficient of determination ($\overline{R}^{-2}$) is quite low, this is only to be expected in a cross section study involving a very large sample. It is easy to see that income is a very important factor in determining the size of the monetary evaluation.

Using a suitable transformation, (see Harris[13], pp. 10–11) it is possible to derive the income elasticity of demand. This turns out to be 0.3 in this case, i.e. well below unity. Indeed, in his more detailed (i.e. disaggregated) regressions, Harris finds implied income elasticities ranging between 0.24 and 0.43, all well below unity.

Since this implies that the demand for noise abatement falls as a proportion to income, as income rises, it must be conluded that this particular environmental attribute is *not* pro-rich. In fact, if anything it is *pro-poor*! Alternatively, it can be regarded as a basic *necessity*, like bread!

The particular survey in question does, however, have many weaknesses, and it is not ideal for studying this question. However, the result is interesting, and, is quite sufficient to justify more work along these lines.

Conclusions

The results of this study can be summarised as follows.

i) It was argued that house price depreciation studies (the hedonic approach) are not valuable for the purposes of estimating either the monetary value of pollution abatement or (consequently) the social incidence of its benefits.

ii) By implication, money estimates of damage based on house price studies should not have policy relevance. This includes any cost-benefit study aimed at deciding on the acceptability of pollution generating or pollution reducing projects, or aimed at determining some pollution tax or standards.

iii) No conclusion can be reached from *existing* literature about the incidence of benefits from pollution reduction.

iv) The balance of argument seems to be in favour of the supposition that the costs of abatement are regressive (i.e. borne less heavily by the rich), but it should be emphasised that this requires acceptance of the general applicability of results referring only to one programme in the USA. Since, in particular, the UK has no nationally agreed estimate of pollution abatement costs, it is difficult to see how any cost incidence study can be carried out for this country without first addressing this question.

v) It is impossible to argue on the basis of existing studies that the social incidence of net benefits of pollution programmes is pro-rich, since national benefit figures produced so far seem to be highly dubious figures. At the more popular level, it is suggested that those who wish to argue that the environment is an 'elitist' concern have no case to present. Accordingly, presumption about biases in the benefits of environmental programmes should not at this stage be allowed to interfere with policy.

vi) It is suggested that social surveys could *possibly* produce the information that other studies fail to do. In particular, the analysis undertaken on this study of the Building Research Establishment survey on traffic noise has indicated that one environmental good—quiet—has an income elasticity less than unity, and is not therefore pro-rich in its distributional impact.

vii) Future research in this field could usefully follow up the suggestion about the use of surveys. In particular, it would seem sensible for interested researchers to be informed of social surveys taking place, which would perhaps be amended slightly to incorporate questions aimed at discovering a relationship between the monetary valuation of environmental amenity, and income.

References

1. Nelson, J. P., 'Residential Choice, Hedonic Prices and the Demand for Urban Air Quality' in *Journal of Urban Economics* Vol. 5, No. 3, July 1978.
2. Harrison, D; Rubinfeld, D., 'Hedonic Prices and the Demand for Clean Air' in *Journal of Environmental Economics and Management* Vol. 5, 1978.
3. Pearce, D. W., 'The Social Incidence of Environmental Costs and Benefits' in *Progress in Environmental Planning and Resource Management* Vol. 2, No. 1, 1979.
4. Pearce, D. W., 'The Valuation of Pollution Damage: Noise Nuisance' in *University of Aberdeen, Department of Political Economy. Occasional Paper 77-12* 1977.
5. Pearce, D. W.; Edwards, R., 'The Monetary Evaluation of Noise Nuisance: The Implications for Policy' in *Progress in Environmental Planning and Resource Management* Vol. 1, No. 1, 1978.
6. Harris, A., 'Valuing Environmental Amenity—A Critique of the House Price Approach' in *University of Aberdeen, Department of Political Economy. Occasional Paper 78-01* 1978.
7. Edwards, R., 'On the Impossibility of Estimating the Social Incidence of Environmental Disamenity through the Use of House Price Depreciation Models' in *University of Aberdeen, Department of Political Economy. Occasional Paper 78-02* 1978.
8. Freeman, A. M., 'Hedonic Prices, Property Values, and Measuring Environmental Benefits: A Survey of the Issues' in *Resources for the Future, Discussion Paper D-37* 1978.
9. Mäler, K. G., 'A Note on the Use of Property Values in Estimating Marginal Willingness to Pay for Environmental Quality' in *Journal of Environmental Economics and Management* Vol. 4, 1977.
10. Dorfman, R., 'Incidence of Benefits and Costs of Environmental Programs' in *American Economic Review* Papers and Proceedings, Vol. 67, No. 1, February 1977.
11. Baumol, W., 'Environmental Protection and Income Distribution' in Hochman, H. and Peterson, G. (eds.), *Redistribution through Public Choice* Columbia University Press, 1974.
12. Gianessi, L., Peskin, H., Wolff, E., 'The Distributional Impact of the Uniform Air Pollution Policy in the United States' in *Resources for the Future, Discussion Paper D-5* 1977.
13. Harris, A., 'Is Quiet a Luxury Good?—A Survey Approach' in *International Journal of Social Economics* Vol. 6, No. 3, 1979.
14. Langdon, F. J., 'Monetary Evaluation of Nuisance from Road-Traffic Noise: An Exploratory Study' in *Environment and Planning A* Vol. 10, 1978.

20

Disasters and Charity: Some Aspects of Co-operative Economic Behaviour

by Christopher M. Douty

Recent investigations by economists and other social scientists into events pursuant to natural disasters have revealed an unexpected pattern of behaviour. Economic theory suggests that the sudden, largely unanticipated destruction of wealth by an external force—the characteristics which define a disaster—will lead to a higher price level for necessities. It may also be expected that the cloak of the ensuing mass confusion and uncertainty will result in an increase in all forms of antisocial behaviour. Yet, empirical research has repeatedly shown that prices rarely rise enough to clear markets, that natural disasters are typically followed by an increase in charity by residents of the disaster zone, and that there is an increase in 'community feeling' generally. The fact of post-disaster charity, and of generally heightened concern for the well-being of others, is of greater theoretical interest than its quantitative importance. Apparently, for some time after disaster, resources are typically used differently and with more generosity towards others.[1] This fact presents an anomaly for economic theory to explain. It is the task of this paper to offer such an explanation. It is hoped that the theory advanced also serves to shed light on the 'social cement' that normally exists within a community.

The behaviour pattern to be discussed has been observed not only after natural disasters, but after virtually all disasters of external origin.[2] Systematic empirical studies of the effects of the 1917 munitions ship explosion in Halifax harbour, of the social effects of World War II bombing, of the events following the 1953 tornadoes at Worcester, Massachusetts and at Waco and San Angelo, Texas, and a study of the 1961 disaster caused by Hurricane Carla have all revealed similar post-disaster behaviour.[3] More recently, the economic

From *American Economic Review*, Sept. 1972, pp. 580-9. Reprinted by permission of the American Economic Association and H. M. Douty.
[1] However, an intellectually dissatisfied economist may still derive much emotional satisfaction from these unexpected benevolent actions of human beings under trying circumstances.
[2] Internally generated disasters, such as civil disorders, apparently result in a different behaviour pattern.
[3] See D. C. Dacy and H. Kunreuther, *The Economics of Natural Disasters: Implications for Federal Policy* (New York, 1969); H. E. Moore, *Tornadoes over Texas* (Austin, Tex., 1958), and *. . . and the Winds Blew* (Austin, Tex., 1964); and S. H. Prince, *Catastrophe and Social Change* (New York, 1920).

investigations by Dacy and Kunreuther into the 1964 Alaskan earthquake and a study by Douty[4] of the effects of the 1906 earthquake and fire in San Francisco have turned up essentially the same sequence of events.

This sequence, which Hirshleifer[5] calls the 'disaster syndrome', has been described in terms of sociological theory by Thompson and Hawkes.[6] The community is seen in 'normal' periods as a multipurpose system that is organized to enable it to utilize its resources for the achievement of many simultaneous objectives. A disaster is seen as an event that destroys not only wealth but also the allocative and 'integrative' (organizational) mechanisms. Initially, a disaster sharply reduces the interaction—exchange and otherwise—among primary units (i.e. families); this is soon followed by a resurgence of interaction among primary units in relief and rescue operations, but with much greater dependence upon non-market co-ordination than normal. Despite plentiful opportunities, there is virtually no looting or other antisocial behaviour; instead the community appears as a 'super-organisation' with allocative decisions made by a centrally controlled bureaucracy often headed by the pre-disaster civic leaders. Co-operation and generally selfless behaviour by the victims and others near the disaster zone is strikingly evident. However, with the beginning of long-run recovery, individuals resume their normal degree of egocentredness, with the centralized allocative mechanism either breaking down or withering away.

Discussions of the disaster syndrome have suffered from *ad hoc* theorizing and the difficulty of disentangling reports of events from theories about human behaviour under the specified conditions. Several writers anxious to improve on this state of affairs and convinced that economic theory ought to be able to say something about disaster phenomena, have produced the theoretical work that is critically summarized in Section I. Section II develops an alternative theory and its implications are examined.

1 Some Economic Interpretations of Post-Disaster Behaviour

An obvious peculiarity of observed post-disaster economic behaviour is the failure of prices to rise as rapidly as would be suggested by simple supply and demand analysis. The destruction of the stocks of 'necessity goods', of which food, clothing, and shelter are prime examples, might normally be expected to lead to sharply rising prices during the Marshallian market period (which lasts at least until

[4] C. M. Douty, 'The Economics of Localized Disasters: An Empirical Analysis of the 1906 Earthquake and Fire in San Francisco', unpublished doctoral dissertation, Stanford University, 1969.

[5] J. Hirshleifer, *Disaster and Recovery: An Historical Survey*, Rand Corporation RM–3079–PR (Santa Monica, Calif., 1963).

[6] J. D. Thompson and R. W. Hawkes, 'Disaster, Community Organization and Administrative Processes' in G. W. Baker and D. W. Chapman (eds.), *Man and Society in Disaster* (New York, 1962).

outside aid is received), as competition for the remaining supplies of necessity goods intensifies.[7] However, social scientists who have studied disasters assert that prices rise less than would be predicted on the basis of pre-disaster economic relationships and the magnitude of the disaster involved.[8] Apparently, a disaster motivates persons within the disaster zone who have retained undestroyed stocks of necessities to increase their charity. Dacy and Kunreuther and Louis De Alessi have offered theoretical explanations for these phenomena which we shall discuss.

The empirical evidence on post-disaster price behaviour is sketchy and impressionistic. Breakdown of communications and transportation obviously fragment markets and increase the expected price dispersion for a commodity within a given geographical area. Records of transactions are few and of certain representativeness. Consequently, we shall not attempt to argue that after a disaster prices go up 'much' or 'little'. What is clear is that transactions typically occur at prices that would seem far below what the market would bear. Collateral evidence that this is so, is the prevalence of queues for all sorts of goods with no appreciable tendency for supplies to disappear (to black markets) and queues to rapidly shorten.

In analysing the behaviour of suppliers (donors) in disaster zones, it is useful to divide them into the following groups: (1) households within the disaster zone with accessible undestroyed stocks of necessity goods; (2) large business firms operating wholly or substantially within the disaster zone; (3) private economic units located in 'support' zones; (4) the central and state (or provincial) governments having sovereignty over the stricken area. With the probable exception of category (1) above, the donor is unacquainted with the recipients of his charity; therefore most charity is given to a generalized group called 'victims'. The analysis of this section applies only to donor categories (1) and (2); in Section II all four categories are considered.

The observed failure of post-disaster prices to rise as sharply as might be expected, indicates to Dacy and Kunreuther, pp. 63–70, that there has been a structural shift in the utility functions of the stricken population. Their analysis assumes, conventionally, that (1) individuals maximize their utility; (2) that the utility enjoyed by each individual depends only on his own consumption of goods and services; (3) business firms seek maximum profits in order to maximize the consumption possibilities of their owners, and (4) philanthropic behaviour is inconsistent with profit maximization. These assumptions, commonplace in economic textbooks, imply that a

[7]This statement implicitly assumes a high survival rate of the population relative to that of non-human wealth and that the victims retain some means of making their offers of exchange for goods and services effective. The former assumption is empirically correct; the latter often is not.

[8]This should not be interpreted as meaning that there are never any price increases or that 'extortionate' prices are never observed. See the next section.

disaster-caused leftward shift of market-period supply curves coupled with unchanged demand curves, should result in higher short-period equilibrium prices for necessity goods.[9] Though the extent of these price increases may be mitigated by expectation of outside aid, the failure of prices to rise at all following the disasters considered by Dacy and Kunreuther is seen (by them) as due to 'emergent altruism' among those disaster zone residents whose circumstances permit them to offer charity.[10] Thus their explanation of upward price stickiness is that tastes have changed to include more altruism. They allege that at some later date the taste for altruism disappears, thereby 'explaining' the fact that the observed increase in community feeling is only temporary.

De Alessi[11] points out that the explanation offered by Dacy and Kunreuther cannot be empirically refuted because no one has yet learned how to directly observe shifts in utility functions. However, he notes that if 'interdependence of utility functions' is admitted, then it is possible to retain the customary assumption that utility functions are unchanged, and yet to develop hypotheses that are, in principle, empirically testable. Interdependence is assumed to imply that individuals feel compassion for those who are less well off materially than themselves. This compassion manifests itself normally in a steady flow of charity from relatively wealthy to less wealthy individuals, with the utility of the donors being maximized when the marginal dollar used for the 'purchase' of charity yields an increment of utility equal to that yielded by the marginal dollar spent on any other commodity.

A disaster changes the relative asset positions of the donor and the recipient. Assuming that the pre-disaster recipient is so unfortunate as to be a disaster victim, the relative deterioration of his position will increase the marginal utility to the donor of a given amount of charity, subject only to the condition that the donor's indifference curves be convex. Therefore the donor will increase his flow of charity until he is again maximizing his utility.

The alleged interdependence of utility functions also provides a basis for an explanation of the post-disaster charity given by business firms (see De Alessi, 'The Utility of Disaster', *Kyklos*,

---

[9] The decrease in community wealth occasioned by a disaster could also lead to a leftward shift of demand curves, assuming that wealth (or income) elasticities of demand are positive. However, Dacy and Kunreuther believe, pp. 65–6, that in the wake of disaster, purely egoistic concerns would lead to an increase in hoarding, causing the demand curves to shift to the right thereby accentuating upward pressure upon prices.

[10] Chapter 5 of their book contains a fairly extensive presentation of relevant data on the 1964 Alaskan experience and briefer descriptions of observed price behaviour following other disasters. However, evidence presented by Douty, ch. 4, on San Francisco's 1906 earthquake and fire indicates that completely stable post-disaster prices are not universal. Although some of the data are unreliable, it is unquestionable that room rents rose substantially.

[11] L. De Alessi, 'A Utility Analysis of Post-Disaster Cooperation', in Virginia University, *Papers in Non-Market Decision Making*, 3 (Fall 1967), 85–90.

vol. 21 (1968), pp. 525–32). If the utility functions of individuals who are managers contain non-pecuniary elements, business conduct inconsistent with the presumed goal of the maximization of the present value of the owners' equity will be generated. The tendency for such conduct to exist will be stronger if the owners and managers are different sets of people, than if there is owner management.[12]

The fact that many firms give some charity during non-disaster periods is taken by De Alessi to be evidence that firms may increase their philanthropic activity in post-disaster situations. Furthermore, if the firm counts goodwill among its assets, managerial utility maximization through post-disaster donations of some of the firms's wealth may be consistent with the wealth-maximizing interest of the stock-holders. The existence of goodwill implies that the market in which the firm sells its products is imperfect. Charity may be offered to help the firm maintain its goodwill. Therefore De Alessi concludes, '. . . other things being the same, the smaller the degree of competition, the more post-disaster charity a firm will give' (1968, p. 531).

This argument has considerable appeal because of its simplicity, its ingenious use of conventional economic theory and because it provides testable implications. However, it also has some disturbing implications and leaves unanswered a number of important questions. De Alessi's analysis says little about the characteristics of the donors and the recipients. Perhaps it can be reasonably assumed that all 'needy' victims receive aid, from a 'spontaneously generated' post-disaster relief organization. Such organizations do in fact often arise, but what causes their emergence? Is it possible to predict who will lead these organizations? Is post-disaster charity given only by individuals who have been benefactors of the relatively poor prior to the disaster?

Let us see what can be said on these matters. In regard to business firms, is the degree of imperfection of competition a relevant factor in determining their post-disaster behaviour? Can anything be said about external aid, including that of governments?

---

[12] This statement is true if the income of managers is only loosely correlated with their success at maximizing profits. Non-employee stockholders have the option of selling their stock in firms which from their point of view are managed poorly, a fact that enlarges the potential scope for 'non-economic' managerial behaviour still more. (It is presumed here that existing managements can be dislodged only with difficulty.) The managers of a regulated public utility have especially great scope for discretionary behaviour; the guaranteed profit rate that their firms typically enjoy means that non-economic managerial behaviour has relatively little adverse effect on the owners' equity position. Therefore the scope of such behaviour is limited only by the ability of the regulatory commission to enforce standards of managerial competence. However, any degree of monopoly in the seller's market permits some non-economic behaviour (see A. A. Alchian and R. Kessel, 'Competition, Monopoly and the Pursuit of Pecuniary Gain, in *Aspects of Labor Economics*, Universities-Nat. Bur. Econ. Res. Conference Series (Princeton, N.J., 1962)).

II A Theory of Post-Disaster Co-operation

The proposition that an individual makes those decisions that best serve his own interest, narrowly conceived, has been found to be highly useful in economic analysis. Therefore, it is incumbent upon us to develop a theory of post-disaster charity that shows that 'altruistic' behaviour may under some circumstances be consistent with enlightened self-interest.

At the risk of belabouring the obvious, we note that interdependence of economic units constitutes much of the subject matter of economic analysis, with market interdependence receiving the greatest emphasis. Theorizing about market behaviour has most often proceeded as though the institutional environment were a constant.[13] The institutional environment includes the network of rules and regulations by which a society lives. Some of these are formalized into law; others are self-enforcing customers. The institutional environment is a sort of collective good that can be regarded as the result of a consensual agreement.[14] The agreement need not be universally accepted in all particulars, but it must be generally adhered to if the environment is to be viable. This agreement provides a set of guidelines that specifies the allowable scope of actions that an individual may take in his own interest. Such guidelines are required if there is to be substantial market interdependence and a high degree of specialization according to comparative advantage. The benefits of a stable institutional environment are shared in some degree by all members of the community. A major task of government is to see that these benefits are in fact widely diffused and are not captured entirely by a small minority of individuals within the community who undertake illegal or unethical actions.[15]

[13] Neoclassical economists generally only enumerated the functions of government which they saw as consistent with a *laissez-faire* economic framework. The choice of an actual institutional framework was seen as something apart from economic analysis. In recent years theoretical work on the nature of social choice and collective goods and the related work by Alchian, Harold Demsetz and others on the theory of property rights has introduced a degree of integration of institutional choice and market behaviour into the mainstream of economics. Needless to say, the 'Institutionalists' (e.g. John R. Commons) did not take the institutional environment as a constant. The same applies for economic historians and economists working in many applied areas, especially in economic development.

[14] Hirshleifer, whose paper 'Disaster Behavior: Altruism or Alliance' (1967; unpublished) has been very helpful in the formulation of these ideas, calls the consensual agreement an 'alliance'. This term, in turn, has been borrowed from Mancur Olson, *The Logic of Collective Action* (Cambridge, Mass., 1965).

[15] One of the characteristics of a viable institutional environment is that it must provide for an 'equitable distribution of the benefits of the consensual agreement. If the distribution of benefits is seen by a substantial number of the members of a community (not necessarily a majority) as inequitable, the agreement is no longer sufficiently consensual and will be much more difficult to maintain.

This discussion is relevant in this context because the rapid change in the physical environment that an unexpected disaster imposes causes the pre-disaster institutional arrangements to become largely inoperative. The degree of the breakdown of institutional arrangements is in large measure a reflection of the magnitude of the disaster and of the uncertainty that it creates. The existence of uncertainty causes individual behaviour to be governed by indefinite expectations concerning the future. Among the major factors that determine these expectations are the memory of the pre-disaster institutional environment and the individual's perception of his current situation in relation to that of the rest of the community. The former includes the individual's pre-disaster web of social and economic relationships. The latter, of course, will change as the individual gains a clearer perception of his and the over-all post-disaster situation. The analysis that follows emphasizes the effects of the continuing reassessment of the post-disaster situation by all of the affected individuals, showing in particular that the widely noted increase in community feeling is the expected outcome of individualistic rational behaviour.

However, the increase in community feeling is usually not the first collective post-disaster reaction. The initial reaction is the fragmentation of the stricken community into very small units that have been called 'kinship groups'.[16] At this point the victims probably observe that a large part—perhaps most—of the pre-disaster population seems to have survived, although much of the capital stock has been destroyed.[17] However, the individual ignores the larger community until the survival and well-being of persons with whom he had maintained his closest personal ties has been determined. The determination of the survival status of family members can be regarded as the first step in the reduction of post-disaster uncertainty, without which rational decision-making is impossible. During this interim period of community fragmentation, market transactions, if any are consummated, are often at elevated prices.[18] However, when the survival status of close relatives is determined, usually through a reunion with them, the period of fragmentation ends. The problem as seen by the individual then becomes the survival of the larger community and the restoration of a viable institutional framework.

Assuming that a supply of 'necessity goods' survives the disaster in usable form, these must be distributed in such a manner as to allow the victims to subsist without being forced to evacuate the

[16] On fragmentation, see Thompson and Hawkes and the references therein. On the concept of kinship groups, see the references in Olson, pp. 17–18.

[17] The behaviour of victims who become totally disoriented by the disaster is not considered here. Most disaster studies indicate that disoriented victims are the exception, rather than the rule.

[18] There were many dramatic reports of prices being increased to anywhere from ten to fifty times their pre-disaster levels following the 1906 San Francisco earthquake and fire. See Douty, ch. 4, for references. Recent disasters have produced few such reports, however. The generally smaller magnitude of recent disasters may be responsible.

disaster zone. The charging of elevated prices, or even positive prices, for these goods is inconsistent with the maintenance of the population unless these prices are within the means of all of the victims.[19] A means of non-price rationing is probably required since many of the victims are likely to be without accessible liquid assets.[20] The desire to see a continuance of the community leads to the development of such a rationing system and causes social pressure to be brought to bear on possessors of 'necessity goods' who are attempting to 'extort' high prices from the victims. These phenomena deserve further attention.

Consider the social pressures that a small grocer with an undestroyed inventory stock faces. He has tomorrow as well as today to think about. His regular customers will be aware of his elevation of prices. The grocer will know that if other grocers are not raising prices, his short-sighted behaviour could cost him his clientele—if not immediately, then in the near future. This implies that the desire to maintain continuing economic, as well as personal, relationships will moderate any tendencies to attempt to extract all of the consumers' surplus from buyers. Furthermore, if many of the victims are unable to buy food and if none is donated to them, the grocer could soon find that he is unable to prevent the removal of his merchandise without the formality of payment. Hunger pangs are not to be denied. Therefore, if the grocer perceives that he will receive little revenue is realized by this act of charity, but it may be that there is then decide that the rational thing to do is to offer his merchandise free to the victims, on a first come, first served basis. No current revene is realized by this act of charity, but it may be that there is no long-run sacrifice as the grocer's charity may gain him goodwill in the future. Thus it may be possible to rationalize behaviour that appears altruistic as reflecting a long-run view of self-interest. A similar rationale may apply to many other acts of kindness commonly observed after a disaster; for example, families taking in homeless

[19] In an article on non-price rationing ('The Political Economy of Consumer's Rationing', *Rev. Econ. Statist.*, vol. 24 (Aug. 1942), pp. 114–24), Tibor Scitovsky defined a shortage as existing when the rise of the price of a commodity would cause it not to be distributed on an 'egalitarian basis', or if the charge of any commercially viable price would cause a great inequality of distribution of that commodity. Obviously, this definition can be reasonably applied only to necessities, such as staple foods and shelter. However, these are the types of commodities for which sharp advances in prices would be expected following a disaster if economic individualism was carried to an extreme. A disaster creates shortages in Scitovsky's sense of the term; since these shortages exist, there is a case for non-price rationing.

[20] It is conceivable that individuals in the disaster zone who possess accessible liquid assets could lend money to those in need of it. However, in this context, such loans are unlikely to be forthcoming even at very high interest rates because the overwhelming environmental uncertainty would create doubt as to the borrower's earning capacity and hence his ability to repay the loan. Finally there is the possibility that the banks will be closed, causing most of the liquid assets of *all* persons within the disaster zone to be inaccessible.

friends and relatives (sharing housing) without compensation; donating or lending clothing without reward.

Reconciling this type of behaviour with the hypothesis of individual utility maximization—which is maintained—presents an interesting theoretical challenge with several different, though not mutually exclusive answers. First, families, both primary and extended, and networks of friends are linked together in an unwritten mutual insurance plan against economic adversity. The implicit obligation to help others in need is especially strong when the utility loss is great and is manifestly unrelated to any failure on the part of the victim. Natural disasters clearly qualify as situations where 'insurance benefits' may be claimed. The obligation to render assistance, upon those able to do so, is enforced *de facto* by the (implied) threat of thereafter being denied insurance protection. As implicit contracts of this sort cannot be enforced through the courts they tend to arise among people who can exert social pressure upon one another to honour commitments; for example, such implicit contracts are likely to arise among members of an ethnic, racial or religious group. Much altruism is this sort of honouring obligations to members of one's 'mutual insurance club.'[21]

But it is also necessary to account for charity towards total strangers, which is frequently observed in the aftermath of a disaster. Part of the explanation lies in the breakdown of communications and transportation so that the normal sources of aid from mutual insurers are temporarily cut off; also a clustering of members of an insurance network (not uncommon) may put great strain upon or overwhelm those located elsewhere; this increases the importance of aid from 'outsiders'. That is, a natural disaster tends to put pressure upon all members of a community to act as though there were an informal reinsurance society to backstop the informal (primary) insurance networks.

To specify the channels through which this pressure is exerted requires identifying a second spring of altruism: community leadership. Community leaders all have an important stake in maintaining a sense of community values. A sense of community values is manifested by participating in the production or purchase of public goods without being overtly covered; i.e., by not attempting to act as a free rider. Religious leaders benefit from a wide diffusion of a sense of community values in that it facilitates money raising and the contribution of free time. Military leaders benefit by getting more willing soldiers; political leaders by making it easier to collect taxes,enforce laws, get public support for costly public goods, etc. Business leaders obviously have an interest in promoting respect for law and order.

---

[21] Of course this is not an attempt to describe the psychic states of charity givers in a post-disaster situation. The argument contends only that the donors act 'as if' they were optimizing individual utility in the circumstances in which they find themselves.

Failure to provide for needy members of the community in time of need engenders cynicism towards community values and resistance to demands made in their name. Conversely, manifestation of community values by provision of disaster insurance promotes belief in an unwritten social (insurance) contract respect for which enhances the utility of community leaders. The ability of leaders to reward those who co-operate with them and punish those who do not is obvious.

Yet a third rationale for post-disaster benevolence is the need for immediate community approval. Normally, the sanctity of life and property are protected by the courts and the armed force they can muster to enforce their decisions. In the aftermath of a disaster, courts cannot function and soldiers cannot be mobilized. An individual more fortunate or foresighted than others cannot expect safely to hold his property for what he thinks the market will bear, secure in the knowledge that his property is sacrosanct, regardless of the needs of those around him. On the contrary, his property may be seized and his person severely punished as an engrosser. Security of life and property may depend upon close conformity to community norms of behaviour, particularly as regards prices charged. A stricken community has little tolerance for entrepreneurial deviance.

In the terse language of the theory of choice, most individuals own one or more (unwritten) insurance policies which 'pay off' when their income falls below a certain minimum level for a socially acceptable cause (e.g. a natural disaster). Conversely, they have a contingent obligation to aid others in danger of falling below the implied minimum for an unacceptable reason. The enforcement of this obligation is by social pressure, subordination to which is necessary to avoid unacceptable risks to life, property and reputation (implicitly related to ability to buy and sell on the same terms as others). Nothing further need be said about the characteristics of anyone's utility function, though, 'true altruism' may be present in post-disaster situations.

It may be recalled that De Alessi (1968) concluded that any firm in the stricken area may give charity if its managers have a positive taste for charity. Firms in imperfect competition give more charity than atomistically competitive firms in order to protect their goodwill, as indicated above. However, the postulated taste for altruism is not required if the argument is reframed in terms of the degree of involvement of the firm with the stricken community and the firm's size. Our primary concern here is with large firms, as small firms (i.e. small grocers, etc.) have already been considered. However, it is a fact that the largest private benefactors of a stricken community are large firms that had enjoyed extensive operations in the disaster, with many of their assets intact.[22] The location of the surviving assets,

---

[22] Two examples will suffice. The Southern Pacific Company was San Francisco's largest benefactor following the 1906 disaster (Douty, ch. 4). In Alaska

whether inside or outside the disaster zone, is not relevant. Size is relevant, however, because it connotes identifiability (particularly if the firm deals with the general public rather than with a specialized group of customers), a significant financial capacity and a degree of goodwill in the markets in which it sells. The firm has an incentive to protect its goodwill if possible. This goodwill is threatened if the firm engages in behaviour that the disaster victims regard as unfair. Local executives, whether or not these be the firm's top management, sense this intuitively and therefore extend charity to the victims. Furthermore, they might press for charity from branches of the firm located outside the stricken area. Franchised monopolies are the most vulnerable if they fail to be charitable; 'profiteering' at the expense of the victims could cause the firm's franchise to be revoked. The executives can be regarded as part of a 'privileged group' whose welfare is tied in a very intimate way to that of the community as a whole. As a result we often observe post-disaster charity not only by large firms, but the executives are frequently prominent in leading the relief bureaucracy. Only if a firm had been suffering chronic losses and planned to go out of business would it have no self-interest in appearing charitable. In this case, the disaster, by causing an 'instant amortization' of the firm's local assets only hastens its departure from the stricken region. However, in most cases, large firms will give more charity than small because of their probable greater financial capacity, their greater identifiability and because they possess more goodwill, than smaller firms.[23] But in cases of both large and small firms, business philanthropy can be explained entirely without reference to altruistic motivations.

Firms that do not have a major commercial interest in the survival of the stricken area are not, in general, important post-disaster donors. Again, this proposition could be tested empirically. Also, the *typical* individual located outside the disaster zone cannot be expected to give charity. Yet disasters do frequently result in a flood of uncoordinated contributions of cash and goods in kinds from outside individuals. Some of this charity is undoubtedly given

in 1964, the Safeway supermarket chain did not increase the prices charged for staple food items, and in a few cases lowered some of them, despite the existence of shortages (Dacy and Kunreuther, pp. 113–18).

[23] It might even be conjectured that large firms will give relatively more charity than small firms (as a percentage of their tangible assets); however, this is far from certain. In the absence of perfect knowledge, 'unreasonable' demands could be made on relatively weak firms that happened to be readily identifiable to a large segment of the victims. The determination of the optimal amount of charity (defined here as the equating at the margin the benefit to the firm in the form of a higher level of goodwill than would otherwise be realized in the post-disaster period with the cost of the goods or revenue donated) is not totally within the donor's range of discretion. Under conditions of uncertainty, the optimal amount of charity could vary for firms of equal financial capacity, raising the possibility that small firms could be called on to give relatively more charity than large firms.

by persons who have relatives or good friends living within the disaster zone.[24] But it cannot be assumed that this accounts for all outside private charity. Some post-disaster philanthropy can be regarded as evidence of pure altruism, motivated by a vague feeling of cultural identification with the victims, and perhaps by the knowledge that their gifts will be put to a use that the donors believe is appropriate.[25] However, only a small portion of the persons residing outside the disaster area do give charity and the size of their individual gifts is usually quite small relative to the donor's assets. It is quite possible that individuals who give post-disaster charity give less than they otherwise would have to other eleemosynary institutions during the relevant time period; i.e. a disaster may have the effect of shaping the timing and form of philanthropy by non-residents, but not its total amount. Regardless of the empirical validity of this last statement (which would be very difficult to test), the existence of outside charity is extremely important in enabling the stricken community to hold together during an emergency period. Whilst individual outside donations are uually very small, in the aggregate they often bulk very large relative to the immediate needs of the victims.

Despite the regularity of the outpouring of private outside post-disaster charity, federal aid has become increasingly important in more recent disasters. Much of this aid is intended to facilitate private reconstruction, but some emergency aid is extended through the Office of Civil Defense and other agencies. Most of the emergency aid is designed to help maintain order, to assist in the administration of private charity, and in population evacuation if it is required. But the fundamental purpose appears to be improvement of the post-disaster environment. These efforts apparently have the approval and support of the federal government's constituency. There is no effective way that a private individual living outside the disaster zone can organize an order-keeping force; nor is there any incentive for him to try to do so, as he would share the 'benefits' of the order-keeping machinery whether or not he bears any of its costs. The federal government has order-keeping machinery at its disposal and can effectively carry out the wishes of its constituents in this regard.

Delayed federal aid which is aimed at facilitating private reconstruction is offered because the stricken community has suffered a net loss of wealth for which it is not fully compensated by private charity and insurance payments. If the loss of wealth exceeds the magnitude of private transfer payments (including insurance) from

[24] Evidence that there are personal ties between outside residents and the victims is the existence of the 'convergence' problem, where communications and other links to the outside world become overloaded. This problem has been noted frequently in sociological investigations. See Charles Fritz and J. H. Mathewson, *Convergence Behavior* (Washington, D.C., 1957).

[25] The bulk of outside charity to victims comes from individuals sharing the same nationality, implying the importance of cultural identification.

external sources, there may be conern that the pre-disaster institutional environment cannot be restored. Compassionate feelings for the victims may also have been stirred. As with emergency aid, the incentive for a private individual to extend reconstruction aid is very weak because of an absence of a connection between the cost outlays of the donor and the benefits received. Hence there is a rationale for federal aid.[26]

The argument of this paper refers only to disasters from 'external' causes. It does not directly apply to disasters such as civil disorders. In principle, our analysis could be developed so as to apply to post-riot behaviour as well as post-earthquake. However, this development would require more conceptual apparatus than we have presented here.

III A Concluding Note

It perhaps is not too surprising that societies that experience a severe externally derived source of stress should exhibit an intensified degree of community feeling. Mere threats of destruction by an external agent, such as a threat of aggression by a foreign power, often appear to draw societies more closely together. The conditions for increased community or national solidarity as a result of a threat are that the threat be credible to the populace and that there be an effective consensual agreement concerning the preservation of pre-existing law and custom. If or when such a threat materializes, consensual agreement operates to generate superficially selfless actions. The interests of the community and the individual's own self interests are both served by individual philanthropy.

Further Reading

Demsetz, H., 'Toward a Theory of Property Rights', *Amer. Econ. Rev. Proc.*, vol. 57 (May 1967), pp. 347–59.
Ikle, F. C., *The Social Impact of Bomb Destruction* (Norman, Okla., 1958).
Kunreuther, H., 'The Case for Comprehensive Disaster Insurance', *J. Law Econ.*, vol. 11 (Apr. 1968), pp. 133–68.
Leibenstein, H., 'Bandwagon, Snob and Veblen Effects in the Theory of Consumer's Demand', *Quart. J. Econ.*, vol. 64 (May 1950), pp. 183–207.
Wallace, A. F. C., *Tornado in Worcester* (Washington, D.C., 1954).

[26] Current [U.S.] federal policy towards disasters has been devastatingly criticized by Dacy and Kunreuther, ch. 9–12; also Kunreuther. The critique is restricted to the method of providing reconstruction aid, which is seen as leading to inequitable treatment of the victims. His point is only to show that some federal aid will be offered following any well-publicized disaster, regardless of the institutional framework for providing that aid. Admittedly, the offer of emergency aid is more certain than of reconstruction aid.

Author Index

Italic type indicates bibliographical reference

Index of Subjects